I Ask for Justice

Book Thirty-Three
Louann Atkins Temple Women & Culture Series
Books about women and families, and their changing role in society

For the bright, industrious, and resourceful women and girls closest to my heart: Mom, Sarah, Ava, and Kate

In memory of Mary, Bob, and Jay, who all passed away while I was writing this book

Contents

Illustrations, Maps, and Tables

Illustrations

Maps

Tables

Foreword

PABLO PICCATO

Prologues like this can be rhetorical obstacles to reach the substance of the book they intend to open. Brevity, therefore, is the greatest virtue of such exercises. The reader may skip these pages and come back to them after reading the book or read them now before plunging into the fascinating history that follows. My goals are simply to suggest some general conclusions around the themes of silence, justice, and the truth and to point to connections with other histories beyond Guatemala.

I Ask for Justice uses judicial and administrative sources to document legal conflicts and their resolution. With the use of these sources, the book establishes the positions of the various social actors who, voluntarily or not, had to present their points of view in front of the representatives of the law who dutifully recorded their testimonies. While relations of power were not fundamentally altered in this judicial realm, they were negotiated and transformed. The law itself, its text and its interpretation, changed in the course of these transactions. Carey argues that citizens' decisions to seek legal recourse transformed their relationships with the state, even in places and among people who had remained marginal to the project of that state.

This insight requires a critical look at the received explanations it complicates, for it affects the very ways we learn about social relations. Historians of Guatemala and other Latin American countries have assumed that the hegemony of one sector of the population over another was merely an exercise of power at the expense of the truth. Social domination subordinated the rights of the less powerful members of society and undermined their words by denying them credibility and even rationality. Since Spanish arrived as the language of colonial rulers, words have had different value depending on who utters them and in what tongue. Translation, then, was not an innocent displacement of meaning from one language to another but

further confirmation, for those who already held such notions, of the inferiority and dissembling manners of indigenous speakers and of the need
to counsel them against their voluntary ignorance of the law. Racism later
reinforced these attitudes by arguing that those descending from the pre-
contact populations had lesser intellectual abilities than those of European
inheritance. The Guatemalan history of the second half of the twentieth
century emerges from this narrative of power as the continuation of a series of overlapping processes of silencing the voices and claims of the majority, now most notably through the U.S.-aided repression of any attempts
to assert autonomy or democracy. Exploitation of indigenous labor and the
suppression of dissent, whether through colonial hierarchies or postcolonial
violence, were undeniably at play in the history of the country; yet the findings in this book suggest that it is not enough to think that inequality of
power effectively silenced all possibility of speaking the truth or claiming
rights.

When suspects or victims faced the state in court or in other situations
prescribed by the law they did not willingly accept the lesser value imposed
on their words. As many examples in the following pages illustrate, these
men and women presented facts about their lives and deeds that their interlocutors had to accept as valid because they fit their own knowledge about
reality. Testimonies and complaints were part of narratives about domestic relations, economic activity, and reputation that the representatives of
the state could not just brush aside if their decisions were to have any authority. As Carey shows, the place of those representatives in the communities where they worked depended on their ability to acknowledge voices
to which the national state's ideology was not willing to grant much weight.
Judicial venues, by definition, required the confrontation of multiple perspectives to build the factual or moral certainties that *letrados* then situated
in the coordinates of the law to resolve each case. *Letrados* did not write a
monologue: clerks, judges, and other actors with access to literacy certainly
gave "political order [a] rigorously elaborated cultural expression," yet they
were constantly grappling with the need to register dissonant voices.[1] The
judicial operation of recording and interpreting examined by Carey had to
be repeated every time order was challenged, and it could not be completed
in the absence of the subjects of that law.

If not silence, it could instead be claimed, hegemony produced truth; by
dictating the rules to generate valid statements about reality, "power," vari-
ously embodied by state officials or by its subjects, made sure that any claim
about rights or facts would emerge within a system that ultimately preserved inequality. This book engages Michel Foucault's ideas about the dis-

ciplining effects of punishment, but it also proposes that, before authorities decided and executed penalties, the rules governing opposing statements in court had the effect of empowering precisely those actors who seemed to be the least powerful. When indigenous women claimed that they were involved in bootlegging because of need or that their husbands had failed to fulfill their parental duties, their words educated judges and officials about the failure of the national state to guarantee a sustenance to all its citizens and to extend the benevolent effects of patriarchy to all households. Carey notes that while arguments like these could eventually reinforce gender and class hierarchies, the women who testified cared less about that somewhat abstract effect of their testimonies than about their own pragmatic goals in front of municipal administrators seeking to punish them for tax evasion or husbands using violence to assert control. We can even argue that these women spoke the truth in a way that implicitly contradicted political and familial hierarchies. Suspect María Coroy, for example, went so far as to argue that being accused of selling alcohol, which she did not consider a crime, unfairly damaged her reputation (p. 124). Reconstructing the precise institutional and social contexts in which they made such claims is a central empirical contribution of this book. In doing so, it alters the ultimate meaning of their words by placing them against the grain of a history of Guatemala that equated power with silence or with the artificial production of truth.

There is an aspect of this tension between power and truth that has permeated our reading of other moments of Guatemalan history. The debates about the facts and intentions behind the massive attacks against indigenous communities and leftist opposition in Guatemala in the second half of the twentieth century revolved largely around the production and definition of the historical truth: Can it be found in official documents such as the recently and accidentally found archives of the National Police in Guatemala City? Or in the testimonies from people who endured that violence and hoped their words could eventually lead to justice? Understanding exchanges in local courts before the onslaught that began with the coup against Jacobo Arbenz in 1954 may help us better read the troubling legacy of human rights abuses in the second half of the twentieth century. Too often, and mistakenly, political actors from various ideological positions present as irreconcilable the opposition between factual, juridical truth and narratives of personal experience during those decades of violence. This faulty distinction often leads to value judgments that, as Greg Grandin has pointed out, accept subjective experience from educated authors but discount it when coming from those on the receiving end of prejudice.[2]

While the dichotomy is misleading in highly public and dramatic cases like that of Rigoberta Menchú, the same simplification can also tarnish our understanding of more mundane documents about routine conflicts. There are different ways to attack the problem. In the case of the repression to which Menchú bore witness, a large, international effort to establish the truth has accomplished what Grandin terms "a victory"—discerning responsibility and intent in general terms, allowing for the cathartic work of memory. The debate about Rigoberta Menchú's *testimonio*, its factual truth and its broader historical significance, can be settled, argues Grandin, thanks to the findings of the Guatemalan Truth Commission. Similar efforts, such as the *Nunca más* report on disappearances, continue to shape the disputes about the juridical and historical truth in Argentina.[3] There is no equivalent authority for the cases examined in this book. To answer questions about facts and responsibilities it seems necessary instead to build a historical perspective that will give words their proper context and identify their possible meanings. Carey has summoned the tools of his craft to carefully lay the foundations for that perspective. In the stories he presents in this book there is a more modest but potentially as enlightening effort to reveal what happened. The right to speak the truth was claimed there on a smaller scale but with comparable significance if our goal is to understand the historical construction of other rights such as due process, equality, and petition. The small-scale victories and defeats of Maya actors in this book revolved around the empirical value of their words and the interpretations those words supported. The routine of courts and the vagaries of local archives (state officials' compulsion to write down everything and then misplace the papers, in sum) made it possible for these smaller voices to escape anonymity and oblivion, and to tell stories that force us to transcend epistemological simplifications.

That reconstruction of contexts and meanings results in another thesis that might seem surprising if we assume coercion as the ultimate guarantee of rule: by presenting their points of view and demands in front of judicial authorities, argues Carey, the least powerful Guatemalans contributed to strengthening the legitimacy of the national state. One could doubt the importance of judicial venues in a society where informal mechanisms of coercion and deference cemented a long tradition of tribute and forced labor; if power neatly divided society, then legitimacy was the product of a formalistic republican structure written into the law but rarely observed. Democracy being a rather short chapter in the longer narrative of Guatemalan nationhood, one could also argue that the rule of law was not essential to understand politics. Carey, however, explains that the law and courts had enough discretion built into them—mainly through the agency of judges, prosecutors, and other representatives of the state—to make it strategically feasible for women, indigenous people, and other actors to seek its protection. Bringing to court conflicts derived from offenses against honor, for example, was useful because it provided a public venue in which to counter attacks that were equally public. Carey proves those actors had considerably more knowledge about the legal system than has usually been presumed of them. They did not expect the impartiality and rigor of the law but instead the flexibility of its agents to adapt the outcomes of cases to the views and needs of local actors. For citizens, speaking in court meant that the rules of the judicial game were valid, and by extension, so was the legal system—even if other parts of it, like vagrancy laws or the tax system, were instruments of exploitation and discrimination. Placed in the broader context of economic and social relations, the evidence from these cases suggests that those who usually suffered that exploitation did not conceptualize the legal system as a coherent unit but rather assumed that parts of it were more receptive and others less permeable to their words.

Considering the intervention of subjects defined by their indigeneity makes such a realization all the more surprising. Long experience had taught them that the playing field was always inclined against them. Yet, in specific contexts, indigenous people could use the law to solve problems involving family relations, violence in deeds and words, and perceived abuses against their autonomy as economic agents—producers and sellers of alcohol or traders in the local market.[4] Being an Indian during the years discussed in this book could also be used rhetorically as an argument to seek—yet not demand, as would have been the case under the colonial regime—the protection of the state to uphold their corporative rights and original pact with the sovereign. During these decades, the seemingly traditionalist use of law and custom was part of strategies that also involved engagement with the market and the national state. Moonshining could thus be justified both as an old practice and as involuntary ignorance of contemporary regulations.

So much for the historiographical straw man of a polarized Guatemala. The opposition of indigenous society and ladino state does not seem so neat under the sharp light of the documents that form the basis of this book. *I Ask for Justice* is part of a rich literature that challenges dichotomous views and increasingly gives depth to the multiple ways in which diverse actors participated in forging their own fates during the national period.[5] There is always something incomplete and tentative, however, about efforts to claim autonomy through institutions—a feeling that they are futile attempts to ignore the implicit coercion that weighs over the words of actors. Yet we do not need to surmise from that possibility that morality and dignity do not have a history too, as do the law or violence, or that their study is less valuable because it is fraught with ambiguity.[6] This book documents not just the hidden or public transcripts of power but also interactions around justice and truth in which power was not assumed to be exclusively on one side, thus making the game useless to play.

A specific kind of reading is necessary to make those nuances epistemologically fruitful. Carlo Ginzburg compares the inquisitor with the anthropologist to illustrate the importance of an innovative and systematic inquiry on judicial sources. As they built their archives, through statements or field diaries, both worked in contraposition to defendants and "natives," respectively—categories often collapsed in this book. The result was not an archive of repression, claims Ginzburg, but productive interactions of great empirical value beyond their intended uses. Judicial archives, as much as field notes, are "intrinsically dialogic" documents.[7] They do not express a single mind but multiple voices engaging each other. As can be glimpsed from some of the cases cited in this book, this creates a polyphonic effect that, in history as much as in novels, can be useful to build a strong narrative, firmly anchored to reality even if not always conclusive regarding facts or the moral of the story. The historian, to continue with the parallelisms proposed by Ginzburg, shares the judge's attention to proof yet is less concerned with normative goals than with the reconstruction of events and practices.[8]

We can go even further and say that these dialogic sources make possible a better reading of other historical documents that represent a single author in a position of power. Even if the voices registered by judicial institutions reflect interests and biases, the historian can still use them—as long as her goal is not objective certainty about subjective intentions or the factual truth but an understanding of practices and interactions in their public, disputed, daily texture. The truth, in other words, is not an intrinsic quality attributable to a statement in relation to objective reality but the product of a dialogue in which the speaker and his or her interlocutor establish the validity of statements in relation to a reality that both constitute through their dialogue and their interactions with other actors and material forces. For any statement to be valid it has to be subject to critical, that is, open and rational, scrutiny.[9] Thus, even the voice of a dictator can only be heard and acquire political value against the background murmur of negotiations and contradictions produced by regular citizens.

Two examples of that constructed reality should help us appreciate the value of dialogic sources to illuminate social life beyond the traditional arenas of crime and conflict usually associated with judicial sources. One is the system of exchanges built around local markets examined in Chapter 3. Conflict, and even violence, were not foreign to the everyday lives of vendors and customers. Yet acrimony did not undermine the value of the economic activity taking place in markets; it was evidence of the constant effort to agree on the terms of exchanges, on the rights of different actors to converge in a space, to enforce regulations that were as much legal as they were customary. The state, already exposed in Chapter 2 in its feeble attempts to control *aguardiente* production, became even less coherent in its enforcement as municipal and higher-level representatives behaved according to different logics in front of market vendors. Even patriarchy has to be scaled down as the autonomy of women (expressed in very "masculine" ways through haggling, shouting, and fighting) became evident in documents that by necessity recover the dialogues of female vendors, customers, and bureaucrats. If we compare the polyphonic soundscape emerging from local markets with the majestic landscape that would come from an administrative report (a hypothetical one in this case) on the functioning of local markets, the main difference would be that the latter would emphasize the essential coherence of economic activity, capitalist profit seeking, and the need to merely tinker on the edges to reconcile that small place of trade with the national and international market that made possible statebuilding. The harmony of political economy would certainly contrast with the dynamic interactions among actors of diverse status and interests recorded in the cases examined by Carey.

Part of the acrimony of market life, a central part I would argue, were the disputes about honor that brought actors to court and are examined in Chapter 6. When the reputation of a woman who traded in public was challenged, she had to respond because the very viability of her place in the economy of the local market was at stake. Trust has a history and incarnates in specific names and faces; part of that history, the best documented perhaps, involves the defense of honor. This is not honor in the colonial sense of inherited status or even the gender-specific attribute examined by anthropologists of Mediterranean societies during the twentieth century but a republican sentiment linked to public perception. Honor, at the intersection of self-esteem and reputation, mobilized resources among a diverse spectrum of the population in terms of class, age, and gender. From our contemporary perspective, honor seems anachronistic, but examined historically it shows that we cannot simply define actors by their position in a continuum of domination and subordination. Disputes about honor started with words or actions that challenged somebody's reputation. The response was immediate for two reasons: the offense hurt the feelings of self-regard of the target of those words, thus requiring a prompt correction, and it undermined the public's opinion about the victim, particularly in social interactions where trust had material value, such as in the market or the family. Violence could be one way to redress the damage, but seeking public vindication through a court hearing and a sentence was effective, if possibly costlier, because its outcome was more permanent and more easily translatable into words. The premise of this reasoning is that there was one shared space of publicity where all the actors converged, where the law had legitimacy, and where only the conclusions of a debate in which multiple voices participated could give the validity of truth to any statement—however difficult it was to reach an agreement and however biased were the representatives of the state who documented the conversation.

For us, readers and historians, the emphasis on dialogic sources and the messy texture of everyday arguments might seem to be a burden. It would mean that single archives, documents, or top-down perspectives cannot convey reality. How many of these other cacophonous, often mutually contradictory sources do we need to read and analyze in order to achieve the same level of certainty that unified perspectives purport to offer? It is not only a matter of counting (although counting can help) but of reconstructing the rules of the debate so we can predict the results of some of those cases, not only in their sentences but also in their impacts on the lives of the actors involved. It is a burden to read these dialogic sources, then, because it is harder to synthesize the realities they document, and we are never certain about the results. But that also makes them fascinating and worth the effort: they lead to stronger proof and deeper learning, as long as we read them with the systematic rigor and engaging clarity of this book.

Notes

1. Ángel Rama, *The Lettered City* (Durham, NC: Duke University Press, 1996), 7.

2. Greg Grandin, *Who Is Rigoberta Menchú?* (London: Verso, 2011).

3. An exemplary contextualization in Emilio A. Crenzel, *La historia política del Nunca más: La memoria de las desapariciones en la Argentina* (Buenos Aires: Siglo Veintiuno Editores, 2008).

4. Our knowledge about the mobilization of legal resources is probably more developed for the colonial period. See Annick Lempérière, *Entre Dieu et le roi, la république: Mexico, XVIe–XIXe siècle* (Paris: Belles lettres, 2004); Bianca Premo, *Children of the Father King: Youth, Authority, and Legal Minority in Colonial Lima* (Chapel Hill: University of North Carolina Press, 2005); Woodrow Wilson Borah,

Justice by Insurance: The General Indian Court of Colonial Mexico and the Legal Aides of the Half-Real (Berkeley: University of California Press, 1983).

5. Useful comparison in David McCreery, "'This Life of Misery and Shame': Female Prostitution in Guatemala City, 1880–1920," *Journal of Latin American Studies* 18, no. 2 (November 1986): 349–350. For Mexico see Peter F. Guardino, *Peasants, Politics, and the Formation of Mexico's National State: Guerrero, 1800–1857* (Stanford, CA: Stanford University Press, 1996).

6. Osvaldo Barreneche, *Dentro de la ley, todo: La justicia criminal de Buenos Aires en la etapa formativa del sistema penal moderno de la Argentina* (Buenos Aires: Ediciones al Margen, 2001); Pablo Piccato, "The Hidden Story—Violence and the Law in Guatemala," *Law and History Review* 24, no. 2 (2006): 427–433.

7. Carlo Ginzburg, "The Inquisitor as Anthropologist," in *Clues, Myths, and the Historical Method*, translated by John Tedeschi and Anne C. Tedeschi (Baltimore, MD: Johns Hopkins University Press, 1992), 158, 156.

8. Carlo Ginzburg, *The Judge and the Historian: Marginal Notes on a Late-Twentieth-Century Miscarriage of Justice* (London: Verso, 1999).

9. Jürgen Habermas, *The Theory of Communicative Action*, vol. 1: *Reason and the Rationalization of Society* (Boston: Beacon Press, 1984), especially 8–26.

Acknowledgments

As I was researching and writing this book, my daughters, Ava and Kate, were born. I want to thank them first and foremost. Although they undoubtedly slowed my progress on this project by enriching my life with their antics, laughter, and questions, they constantly, if unwittingly, reminded me that the historical actors about whom I was writing had far fuller lives than the archival records betrayed.

While I was conducting research in Guatemala, a number of Kaqchikel families in the highlands and Guatemala City generously opened their homes to me: Herlinda Roquel, Gregorio and Gregoria Simon, Edgar and Alberto Esquit Choy, and Teri Perén and Victor Apén. Mardoqueo de León and his extended family (especially Lisette and Ana) were always welcoming when I stayed in Antigua. Ixey and Ixk'at from Comalapa and Ixkawoq from Patzicía conducted invaluable interviews. The Kaqchikel elders from whom they and I learned gave generously of their time and knowledge. Guatemala's endemic violence cautions against revealing their identities. Memories of the time, conversations, and life I shared with these friends (many of whom I have come to think of as family) often provided the inspiration I needed to keep writing when I was thousands of miles away from Guatemala.

At the Archivo General de Centro América in Guatemala City, Anna Carla Ericastilla first pointed me in the direction of the judicial records that inform this book. Thereafter the AGCA staff was ever patient and kind as they located the materials I wished to consult. At a point when I was unable to return to Guatemala, Héctor Concohá took digital images of documents for me at the AGCA. At the Hemeroteca Nacional de Guatemala, Director María Eugenia Gordillo facilitated my research and permissions. Tomás Chitic did the same at the Centro de Investigaciones Regionales de Mesoamérica (CIRMA). I especially want to thank Edgar Esquit Choy for introducing and orienting me to the Archivo Municipal de Patzicía and the municipal employees there who facilitated my use of it. Similarly, in San Juan Comalapa, the municipal secretary and his staff afforded me access to early twentieth-century municipal meeting minutes. In Sololá, I had all but given up hope of locating archival materials when Lesly Araceli Celada de León showed me the few surviving municipal records there.

My research in the United States took me to the Bancroft Library at the University of California, Berkeley; the Nettie Lee Benson Latin American Collection at the University of Texas, Austin; the Latin American Library at Tulane University; Boston Athenaeum; and the Osher Map Library at the University of Southern Maine (USM). The staff members at these libraries were always friendly and helpful.

At USM, I have been fortunate to work with many outstanding students, three of whom—Shaun Haines, Lucas Desmond, and Chriss Sutherland—made exceptional contributions to this project by helping to organize my copies of archival materials. The insights and reflections they shared in our conversations about these documents influenced my thinking about how crime shaped Guatemala's past. Chriss also helped to create the appendix tables. Ron Levere, Sam Shupe, and David Neikirk sharpened and formatted the *Gaceta* images. USM librarian extraordinaire Crystal Wilder frequently tracked down obscure books and articles for me. Also at USM, Laura Nadeau lent her technical expertise by formatting the final manuscript and tables for submission.

USM, the John Anson Kittridge Educational Fund, and the American Historical Association generously funded my research in Guatemala. A USM Trustee Professorship afforded me the funds to conduct research at the Bancroft and Benson Libraries and time to finish the first draft of the manuscript. A USM sabbatical thereafter allowed me the time to revise the manuscript and to prepare it for publication.

The number of colleagues who so generously offered to read my work in its various stages humbles me. John Watanabe, Bill Taylor, and David McCreery all read the manuscript in its entirety and graciously offered critiques and suggestions that greatly improved it. I am also indebted to the following scholars whose comments on earlier versions of parts of the manuscript strengthened the book: Allen Wells, Avi Chomsky, Jim Handy, Ginny Garrard-Burnett, Ann Twinam, Matthew Restall, Pablo Piccato, Ann Blum, Jolie Olcott, Brianna Leavitt-Alcántara, Todd Little-Siebold, Judie Maxwell, Patti Harms, Wendy Chapkis, Adam Tuchinsky, Rayne Carroll, and Janice Jaffee. Feedback from audiences where I gave public presentations based on parts of this work also pointed me in fruitful directions. These venues included the Latin American Studies Association International Conference, the American Historical Association Annual Conference, the New England Council on Latin American Studies Annual Conference, the University of Texas, Austin, Pennsylvania State University, and Tulane University.

It has been a profound pleasure to work with Theresa May at the University of Texas Press. She believed in this manuscript from the beginning and seamlessly shepherded it through the review, editorial, and production processes. Lynne Chapman, too, was wonderful to work with at UT Press. As the copy editor, Tana Silva vastly improved the book with her eye for detail and style.

The book draws on materials that appeared in published articles or essays in *The Americas, Ethnohistory, Latin American Research Review*, the *Journal of Women's History*, and the edited volume *Distilling the Influence of Alcohol*. I thank these journals and the University Press of Florida for their permission to republish those materials here.

During the course of this project, my wife, Sarah, offered sage advice about both writing and content; more importantly, she continues to inspire me to be a better scholar, activist, and person. My parents and brother Bob encourage my scholarship with their interest and insights. I accept full responsibility for any errors of omission or commission in my attempt to portray the complexity of twentieth-century highland Guatemalans' lives.

I Ask for Justice

Justice, Ethnicity, and Gender in Twentieth-Century Guatemala

When ladinos pray, they ask for miracles. When Indians pray, they ask for justice.
CALIXTA GUITERAS HOLMES

When Pedro Coroy shot his wife, Lorenza Pata, in their Santa Cruz Balanya home in 1913, local authorities quickly investigated the incident and prosecuted Coroy. Although the couple would have preferred the episode be forgotten, the thirty-three-year-old, illiterate *jornalero* (day or wage laborer) Lorenzo Chonay insisted it not be. Convinced the mayor had failed "in his role as *juez de paz*" (justice of the peace) by "leaving the crime in impunity," Chonay hired a scribe to write a letter to the Chimaltenango department judge some eight months later, on February 5, 1914. (A Guatemalan department is comparable to a U.S. state.) As we will see, accounts of violence against women abound in Guatemala's judicial record; what stands out in this petition is the progenitor's determination not to allow "a public crime in which society was interested . . . [to] remain unpunished."[1]

Shortly after the department judge ordered Balanya's new *juez de paz* to investigate Chonay's claim, Pata testified in municipal court that while she "was grinding corn for their daily sustenance," her husband was cleaning his pistol and it accidentally went off, shooting her in the buttocks. Certain her husband meant her no harm, the indigenous *molendera* (female corn grinder) pleaded with the authorities not to punish him. She also rejected their attempt to send her to the hospital; insisting she was in no pain and had no trouble walking, she opted to cure the wound herself. Her husband suggested another reason for her recalcitrance: the wound was "in an embarrassing place for a woman."[2] Pata's ability to keep authorities' and doctors' hands off her body stands in stark contrast to her counterparts who were forced to undergo state-sanctioned gynecological examinations because they were victims of rape, were accused of reproductive crimes, or cross-dressed.

Despite Pata's pleas, the *alcalde segundo* (subordinate, literally "second" mayor) Carlos Marten, who like Pata was "illiterate and of indigenous race," sentenced Coroy to ten days in prison commutable by five pesos a day.[3] After spending a night in jail, Coroy paid the fine and commuted his sentence. Not noteworthy in other regions, *indígenas* (indigenous people) rarely presided over municipal litigation in central Guatemala, where upper- and middle-class ladinos (non-indigenous Guatemalans) dominated state-sanctioned municipal posts. The forty-two-year-old *jornalero* Marten noted in Balanya municipal court a few months after he stepped down from his post as *alcalde segundo* that he had this opportunity because the *alcalde primero* (first mayor) was otherwise occupied when the shooting occurred. Explaining that he had imprisoned Lorenzo Chonay numerous times over the previous year for his "many crimes," including fleeing a *finca* (large landed estate) before working off his debt, Marten suggested that the enmity between him and Chonay inspired the "fugitive . . . and debtor" to petition the Chimaltenango judge.

As this case demonstrates, Guatemala's judicial system was put to many uses by a broad spectrum of people. The same system that helped wealthy landowners corral their indebted workforce offered a fugitive *jornalero* the opportunity to exact retribution against an official who had punished him. "The law may serve those who contest authority as well as those who wield it," observes anthropologist John Comaroff.[4] Although many like Coroy and Pata would have preferred to settle their affairs privately and avoid the state's gaze, others invited its intervention. At once fleeing from and appealing to the law, Chonay embodied these contradictions.

In courts and the broader legal system that included petitions like Chonay's, subalterns and agents of the state literally spoke not necessarily to each other but about their interests (and self-interests) in power-laden situations with real, tangible outcomes. This interface of power reveals on the one hand the limits of state rule, particularly over *indígenas*, poor ladinos, and women, and on the other hand the state's ability to co-opt Guatemalans, especially the poor and disenfranchised, into its state-building project by hearing their voices and dispensing "justice," however ineffectually.

Adjudicating disputes helped the state to foster compliance, which, as such theoreticians as Max Weber and Antonio Gramsci have suggested, served the state better than coercion.[5] Although historians have argued that the Guatemalan courts, particularly those under General Jorge Ubico Castañeda and his predecessors in the 1920s, lacked legitimacy,[6] the extent to which indigenous people used the legal system indicates that they considered it a legitimate arbiter of their grievances and an important tool for advancing their agendas, even if it was not always just.

To understand why so many indigenous people availed themselves of the courts, anthropologist Sally Engle Merry's conceptualization of legal legitimacy is helpful. In her study of race and class in Boston she found that subalterns "do not go to court with illusions about its equality, fairness, or justice."[7] Rather, they approach the courts as a resource to help them achieve their goals and mitigate their hardships. Even legal systems that seldom meted out justice provided forums to air disputes.[8]

Highland plaintiffs conveyed a sense of urgency and importance by signing off with some variant of the formulaic phrase *Pido justicia*, "I ask for justice." Rather than appeal to abstract notions of justice, petitioners underscored their hopes—and at times expectations—that judicial officials would help them achieve their practical and pressing goals: cessation of violence, however temporary; restoration of one's good name; restitution for damaged or stolen property; the return of a child. Some petitioners proposed how injustices inherent in Guatemala's social structures and relations might be righted, while few acted as if they would be. Indigenous people knew that racism influenced the Guatemalan judicial system. As one female Kaqchikel elder, Ixki'ch, lamented, "Ladinos . . . made bad laws."[9] To borrow Donald Black's concept, Ixki'ch recognized that ladinos (and elites) enjoyed "more law," while *indígenas* had to get by with less law.[10] In light of the poverty and discrimination they faced in their lives, when indigenous litigants asked for *justicia* their objective for its application tended to be more immediate and personal than long-term and national. Most people turned to the courts to protect themselves, demand retribution, air their grievances, or recover their losses.

Instead of conceptualizing courts as simply state institutions that meted out punishment and inculcated social norms, *indígenas* approached them as venues where their social values could be professed and acknowledged. By formally identifying themselves as *guatemaltecas* (female Guatemalans) before judicial authorities and publicly shaming men for acts that ranged from insults and neglect to domestic and sexual violence, indigenous women encouraged more inclusive notions of citizenship and less exploitive gender relations. Like their counterparts elsewhere in Latin America, women often played authorities against local patriarchs and at times pitted different representatives of the state (mayors, judges, governors, police, and even dictators) against each other.[11] Because it was one of the few institutions that held ladinos, elites, and men accountable, indigenous women used a legal

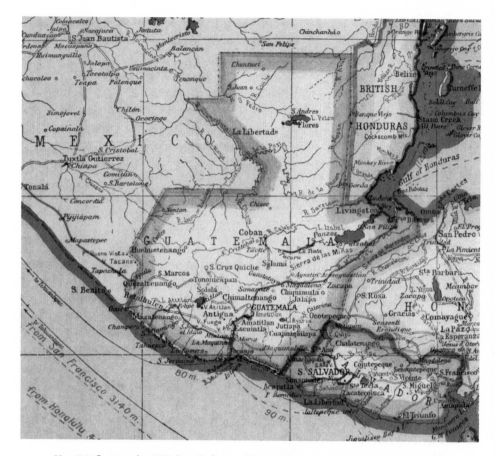

Map 0.1. Guatemala, 1922. Detail of map of Central America in *Harmworth's Atlas of the World*. Courtesy of the Osher Map Library, University of Southern Maine.

system that often restricted their rights as a mechanism for gaining leverage against their opponents and advancing their positions within their families, communities, and nation. Their litigation demonstrates how constraints could be used as tools for empowerment.

As indigenous people who lived in a nation that defined *indios* (Indians) as a problem,[12] Mayas faced significant obstacles to their economic well-being, social mobility, and political freedoms. As disenfranchised laborers who were viewed as little more than commodities and as rural residents who were discriminated against by urban elites, the highland poor had few opportunities for advancement. As females who lived in a patriarchal nation, women not only faced discrimination but oftentimes had to compensate for their male kin whose power was limited by their ethnic and class status. Saddled with all four of these identities, rural, poor, indigenous women were among the most marginalized of Guatemalans.

Questions of citizenship, belonging, and their related privileges and responsibilities provide one entrée into the disingenuous discourse, conditional participation, and exclusion that marked Guatemala's state-formation process in the nineteenth and early twentieth centuries. Following independence from Spain in 1821, Creole (descendant of American-born Spaniards) and ladino elites tried to create a nation that would identify with its European influences and circumscribe its indigenous heritage. Armed with positivism, a French social doctrine that emphasized scientific method over metaphysical thinking to achieve civic order, Liberals espoused the principle of individual equality before the law even as they treated indigenous people as subjects, not citizens. When they came to power in 1871, Liberal leaders never intended to advance full citizenship to *indígenas*; for that indigenous people would have to acculturate to ladino norms since, according to many elites, *indios* were poor, dirty, ignorant, and susceptible to disease and crime by their very nature.[13] Dependent on their labor for the agricultural export economy, Liberals were in no hurry to turn *indios* into citizens, particularly after 1877, when, along with forced-labor laws, the Liberal assault on communal land began prejudicing indigenous livelihoods.[14] This marginalization notwithstanding, the Liberal triumph sparked new demands for citizenship and genuine legal equality that reverberated into the twentieth century,[15] as *indígenas* who contested exclusionary definitions of citizenship and claimed the nation as their own demonstrate.

Like their Liberal counterparts elsewhere in Latin America, President Justo Rufino Barrios (1873–1885) and his successors championed the rule of law and state building as the keys to social order and material progress. To these ends, they rewrote the civil and criminal codes. As evidenced by civil codes addressing marriage, children, and parenthood and criminal codes concerning child abandonment, abortion, and infanticide, family preservation was paramount for Liberal nation builders.[16] In contrast to their Conservative predecessors who leaned on the Catholic Church to help preserve social order, Liberals envisioned individual families controlled by powerful patriarchs as the cornerstone of their new societies. In short, the male-headed household was foundational to state building.[17]

Guatemalans who contested ethnic, class, gender, and state-subaltern relations demonstrate that the nation was far from formed by the late nineteenth century. As a country predominantly populated by indigenous people but ruled by non-indigenous leaders, Guatemala offers unique insight into the study of nation formation. Seemingly characterized by strong-arm stable rule coming out of Guatemala's *caudillo* tradition of the nineteenth century, the first half of the twentieth century is a crucial period to examine because it sheds light on how authorities and marginalized peoples deployed notions of ethnicity, gender, and class differently to advance their agendas at a time when the nation was striving to portray itself as modern.

During the first half of the twentieth century, Guatemala was ruled by two of Latin America's most repressive regimes: Manuel Estrada Cabrera's (1898–1920) and General Ubico's (1931–1944). Since these dictators' rhetoric of progress and order was grounded in patriarchal notions of authority, both state and local indigenous male leaders had a vested interest in excluding women from political, economic, and social positions of power. Subordinated by authorities and ladino elites, indigenous men used their access to education, material resources, and leadership positions to buoy their stations. By circumscribing indigenous women's access to these opportunities, resources, and offices, Maya males perpetuated their privileges at the expense of their female counterparts in much the same way nineteenth- and early twentieth-century K'iche'-Maya (henceforth K'iche') elites helped the state to control and co-opt the indigenous rank and file.[18] As historian Cindy Forster argues, "The courts and the law under Ubico used the gender line to turn men into accomplices of the state."[19] This complicity aided the Estrada Cabrera dictatorship and the governments of the 1920s, too. Few indigenous women simply accepted this fate, however.

The judicial record reveals how indigenous and poor women recast the terms of accusation and incrimination into terms relevant to their own lives, livelihoods, and circumstances. Similar to the way recent books by Greg Grandin and René Reeves have eschewed the simplified state-versus-Indian dichotomy that has dominated Guatemalan historiography,[20] this book reframes the study of patriarchy and gender relations by demonstrating how indigenous women's varied responses to the state's and men's attempts to mold and control them shaped the contours of social, economic, and political life in Guatemala.

Poor, indigenous women often refused to succumb to the will of authoritarian regimes or the regional and local power structures that operated under them. If we accept French philosopher and historian Michel Foucault's assertion that power normalizes and disciplines a populace, then perhaps these women's acts disclose a weak state hiding behind a ferocious façade. Dictatorial rule often masked institutional weakness.[21]

Even as these despots dealt harshly with political dissidents and others who opposed them, some of the most marginalized Guatemalans like

Chonay routinely ignored dictatorial mandates, broke laws, and assaulted authorities. Some Mayas adapted to authoritarian rule, while others re-asserted their communities' traditional justice systems and moral econo-mies. As an example of the subtle, playful attempts to both avoid authorities' grasp and undermine their legitimacy, some defendants invented surnames such as Numak, which in Kaqchikel-Maya (henceforth Kaqchikel) means "my crime" or "my sin." Although defendants frequently used pseudonyms to hide their identities and whereabouts from authorities, it must have been particularly gratifying for those few who, after having hinted at a confession with their pseudonyms, heard a ladino judicial official declare their inno-cence. Such subtleties point to how Mayas used language to establish some autonomy in ladino-dominated state institutions.

Gender Relations and Power

In the central highlands of Guatemala, gender, ethnicity, and class shaped the judicial process. Steeped in indigenous customs and practices, Maya women had to navigate the legal system's and government's patriarchal manifestations and their communities' particular patriarchal tendencies, which among other things generally granted them more autonomy and mo-bility than their non-indigenous counterparts but also expected stoicism in the face of a certain level of domestic violence. This autonomy encouraged indigenous women to engage the courts directly with strategies that varied from appealing to paternalism based on their gender, class, and/or ethnic positions to demanding their rights as *guatemaltecas* and citing specific laws pertinent to their cases. In contrast, ladino gender norms generally sought to shield women from public life and thus discouraged their participation in the legal system. When not represented by their male kin, ladinas who appeared in court often did so with the written consent of their husbands. In a subtle manifestation of this gendered ethnic distinction, court nota-ries tended to refer to ladinas by their husbands' last names and indigenous women by their maiden names.[22]

In pursuit of their own agendas, which often differed from and at times were at odds with those of their male kin and representatives of the state, poor and indigenous women routinely subverted the patriarchal intent of laws. From victimization to empowerment, women's experiences shed light on the ways patriarchy in Guatemala was constructed and relativized through a multiplicity of social contexts (crime, markets, plazas, streets, marriage, families, and households) and venues (municipal hearings, department courts, and audiences with governors and dictators) in the first half of the twentieth century. A historically emergent construction, patriarchy was also shaped by (and shaped) culture, class, ethnicity, gender, power, and sexuality. Although my sources offer little insight into sexuality, the judicial record sheds light on the other varied and variable forces and factors that influenced gender dynamics.

Within the rich historiography of crime and social transgressions, gender and sexuality have attracted considerable attention.[23] Following the lead of colonial scholars, historians of the national era are increasingly examining how women used the courts.[24] Nonetheless, studies of gender-specific crimes in modern Latin America such as prostitution, infanticide, rape, and domestic violence generally focus on females as victims of laws and violence.[25] By framing indigenous and poor females as protagonists, I examine the ways an individual's subjectivity both bounded and sustained their agency.[26]

In the wake of historian Joan Scott's groundbreaking work, scholars have increasingly explored the ways gendered power struggles influenced the past.[27] Examining the relationship between legal manifestations of patriarchy and gender relations has proven a fruitful line of inquiry. Throughout colonial Mesoamerica, indigenous women availed themselves of the courts, largely to protect themselves and their property.[28] In the transition from colonial to national rule, however, Latin American legal systems often increasingly marginalized women.[29]

With its legislation, secularization of society, land privatization, expanding bureaucracy, and patriarchal nationalism, the Liberal state enhanced male privilege and increased inequalities between men and women.[30] To buttress the authority of fathers and husbands, Latin American liberals reinforced the subordination of women and children through legal codes.[31] Even as the authors of Guatemala's 1877 civil code assured citizens that it "conformed with the modern spirit that fosters the rehabilitation of the woman,"[32] a number of the articles explicitly recognized the father as the ultimate authority and head of the household.[33] By enshrining women's child-rearing responsibilities, laws like those incriminating child abandonment, abortion, and infanticide limited women's employment opportunities and linked their rights to their moral duties as mothers. When women broke these laws, they challenged the gendered power relations in their families that the state sought to maintain.[34] Never monolithic, static, or unchallenged, patriarchy was a Hydra-like process that depended on legislators, authorities, and institutions to constantly reconstitute men's power.

Popular practices often contravened or obviated these efforts, as historian Bianca Premo adeptly demonstrates. Even though *patria potestad* (paternal authority) gave fathers control over their children, for example, mothers as well as wet nurses and other surrogates often had far more influence over children through their day-to-day care for them. Female-headed households provide but one example of the multiple functional patriarchies whose character varied depending on the head of household's ethnic, class, and gender positions.[35]

Class shaped patriarchal processes in ways that offered poor and working-class women mobility and autonomy. Partly because poverty compelled their female kin to work outside the home, poor men seldom enjoyed the authority and control in the home that their elite counterparts did. Armed with this relative freedom, marginalized women turned to the courts, where they demanded their rights and appropriated elite discourse.[36] The law often served them well; when it did not, some women distorted or inverted its intention. The very gendered institutions that buttressed local patriarchies also provided women with the tools to challenge these conditions.

Access to these institutions was often obstructed, however. After an altercation on February 5, 1926, with Fernanda García and her daughter Ignacia, the illiterate widow Antonia Guerra intended to turn immediately to the San Martín Jilotepeque (hereafter San Martín) municipal court for redress, but her gender and class positions delayed her doing so. As she explained in her petition three days later, she first had to prepare provisions for "the man I live with," who was setting off to do his military service. She feared the delay jeopardized her case since "many times the first one to present their complaint receives justice."[37] Even though she lived in a village far from the municipal center, she knew much about the municipal legal system, particularly how to maximize her chances of success in it, but she had to weigh the potential benefits of getting there first against the risk of upsetting her male companion. As well as they understood the judicial system, many highland women faced obstacles—patriarchal pressures, distance, poverty, illiteracy, monolingualism—that prevented them from taking full advantage of it.

Punishment and incarceration, too, were gendered. When women were convicted, the consequences were often more dire for them than for men. Guards raped women in jail.[38] With assumptions that women were either raped or, according to some female elders, solicited sex in jail,[39] incarceration tainted women's reputations more than men's.

Figure 0.1. Guatemala City jail, ca. 1875. Photograph by Eadweard Muybridge. Image courtesy of Boston Athenaeum.

Like incarcerated men being pressed into road service, women's punishment furthered images of order and progress by contributing to public works and keeping the physical environment clean.[40] "If women committed a crime, they had to grind limestone. That is what they did in jail," explains one Kaqchikel elder.[41] As the sixty-four-year-old Ixpop recalled, another tactic that became increasingly common during Ubico's reign was public punishment: "When I was young, I heard that women who made *aguardiente* [distilled sugarcane spirits, or rum] went to jail. They had to sweep in front of the municipal building so everyone could see their faces and they would be embarrassed. That was the punishment of women."[42] As Foucault explains, such public punishments projected the cost of disrupting the state's goals back onto the populace. Criminals sentenced to public works bore the signs of their crimes and thus became signifiers of their transgressions. As a result, the power to punish manifested itself in the minds of community members.[43]

Nation Formation and the Guatemalan State

By exploring how domination, defiance, and accommodation shaped Guatemala, this study builds on the growing historiography of nation-state formation.[44] To my mind, state formation is the complex, interrelated process of the effective operation and extension of state institutions and authorities on the one hand and the internalization of state legitimacy on behalf of citizens and subjects on the other. Even as the personalized rule of dictators underinstitutionalized state rule throughout Latin America, individuals who participated in such institutions as the courts often internalized, to some degree, the legitimacy of state rule. At the same time, subaltern participation in state institutions did not necessarily mean co-optation. The recourses people sought through state procedures and institutions did not always coincide with the state's intended purposes.

As in any national context, defining the state in Guatemala is difficult. At one end of the spectrum, the elites who wielded national political and economic power were the primary stakeholders. Yet even as they considered themselves superior to both *indios* and ladinos, elites alone did not constitute the state. At times Guatemalan Indians were the state. To carry out its many functions, the national government relied on local leaders in remote communities to do its bidding. As a result, poor and indigenous people comprised the state, too.

Frequently these functionaries were more concerned with their own personal or community interests than they were about fulfilling their superiors' directives and upholding the national government's authority. Local officials who operated their own stills even as they were charged with stamping out the moonshine trade provide but one example of state authorities' complicit, conflicting, and contradictory roles. Municipal officials who refused governors' requests for *molenderas* or other laborers with explanations that their charges were ill or overworked offer another.[45] Marked by divisions and alliances along cross-cutting ethnic, class, and territorial (municipal, regional, and national) lines, the state in Guatemala was never the purview of any one ethnic group or class; who or what constituted the state was always in flux.

Multiple local corporate entities further complicated the Guatemalan state's composition. As in other western Guatemalan departments, most of the towns in the department of Chimaltenango had a *municipalidad indígena* (indigenous municipality) that operated alongside the municipal (generally ladino) authorities who served and reported to the department and national government. Although indigenous municipalities exercised direct local control during much of the colonial period, by the mid- to late eighteenth century, their influence began to wane as more ladinos inhabited western Guatemala and established their own municipalities in indigenous towns. Since department and national authorities preferred to exercise their power through ladino municipalities, this shift in authority became even more pronounced by the late nineteenth century. While some indigenous municipalities defied this trend, by the early twentieth century those in the department of Chimaltenango had generally been subordinated to local ladino rule in the national government's eyes.[46] In a reflection of the state's preference, President Lázaro Chacón (1926–1930) abolished indigenous municipalities in towns with large ladino populations. In a move similarly intended to marginalize *municipalidades indígenas*, Ubico appointed municipal *intendentes* (intendants) to replace elected mayors. Such national policies did not dictate practice in highland communities, however.[47]

Despite their lack of legal authority in the state's eyes, indigenous officials continued to exercise considerable local power.[48] Although Kaqchikel raconteurs generally portray *intendentes* as favoring local ladinos and responding mainly to Ubico, in some towns *intendentes* and other ladino officials appointed by the central government consulted with indigenous leaders before making decisions. At times, indigenous officials ruled alongside ladino authorities. As one Kaqchikel elder from Tecpán explained, "The judge was pure *natural* [native], an employee. He would tell the Kaqchikel people what to do. . . . The *intendente* was in another part of the building, one for the ladinos and one for the Kaqchikeles. The *natural* was the judge because in those days the *naturales* had more offenses."[49] In some communities, indigenous officials bypassed local ladino authorities by appealing directly to regional and national officials.[50] In another indication of how crucial they were to local governance, indigenous leaders regularly settled disputes among *indígenas*. Whether national officials were unaware of the extent of their power, as one contemporary ethnographer proposes, or accepted this competing sphere of sovereignty as governable is unclear;[51] perhaps, as Grandin suggests, this relationship was another example of the Liberal state's ability to advance its own agenda by allying with "popular" sectors.[52] Generally state authorities only intervened in local indigenous rulings when called upon by the community.[53] As William Roseberry posits, state hegemony is less a totalizing domination than a common ground, however asymmetrical, for assertion and contestation.[54]

Recent scholarship on the contested nature of social control and power has corrected Foucault's overstated emphasis on the power of the state, particularly as it operates through punishment and law.[55] Most notably, subaltern studies and women's history have demonstrated that even the most marginalized members of society can challenge and shape the underpinnings of political rule and race, class, and gender hierarchies.[56] Still part and parcel of the dominant power that initiates and sustains them, subordinates can alter the conditions of their subjectivity and thereby work the system "to its minimum disadvantage," as historian Eric Hobsbawm and others have argued.[57] Scholars have also become increasingly sophisticated in recognizing popular practices that were not expressed in clear political terms of resistance or accommodation. Marginalized peoples themselves were not always sure whether it was subsistence, defiance, or other factors that motivated their transgressions.[58] For these and other reasons, historian Lowell Gudmundson cautions against celebrating resistance, particularly when subalterns' lives did not improve.[59] Women who challenged men's power in the home by refusing to prepare meals, wash clothes, or clean the house, for example, often were victims of their husbands' violent responses. When they went to court to protest male abuse, they upheld the legal system's patriarchal practices; resistance and complicity often went hand in hand in the "complex interplay of assent and struggle," as historian Steve Stern, among others, has demonstrated.[60] Foucault reminds us, "Resistance to power . . . is [not] . . . inexorably frustrated through being the compatriot of power. It exists all the more by being in the same place as power."[61]

More to the point, rural Guatemala's economic, legal, social, cultural, and political systems did not develop as such simply because indigenous people resisted capitalism, acculturation, or the state. Often indigenous people adapted to these forces and found ways to benefit from them. Similarly women did not invariably oppose the different manifestations of patriarchy they faced. Relations between and among local, regional, and national authorities and indigenous, ladino, and Creole men and women were influenced as much by "a culture of resistance" as by "the resistance of culture," to borrow anthropologist Marshall Sahlins's turn of phrase.[62] As Sahlins points out, the latter involves "the assimilation of the foreign in the logics of the familiar—a change in the context of the foreign forms and forces, which also changes their values."[63] His conceptualization of the resistance of culture is neither dependent on "an intentional politics of cultural opposition" nor "confined to the reactions of the colonially repressed."[64] Government authorities, local officials, Creole elites, and middle-class ladinos and Mayas contributed as much to this process as poor *indígenas* who were as interested in finding ways to adapt to or co-opt state institutions and representatives as to resist them.

Since the government intended one thing by its law, judicial officials often another in their rulings, and litigants something else entirely when they initiated legal proceedings, judicial records and the exchanges contained therein are manifestations of the complex processes of state formation and subaltern agency. Although such scholars as Jim Handy, Carol Smith, and David McCreery have examined nation building in Guatemala, only McCreery consulted judicial records and even then only sparingly.[65] This surprising omission distorts our understanding of Guatemala's past, since competing views of nation, identity, and citizenship were contested in courtrooms.

Examining different areas of the judicial record opens a window onto the complex gender, ethnic, class, and state-subaltern relations in highland Guatemala. Some crimes like bootlegging tended to pit indigenous men and women against national or at least regional authorities. As such, the cases were adjudicated in the *juzgado de primera instancia* (court of first jurisdiction, or department court) even if they began in a municipal courtroom. In contrast, even though the national government's efforts to control highland markets were intertwined with and dependent on local authorities, most of the litigation concerning market exchanges took place in municipal courts, since municipal agents collected market fees and taxes.

As often as the national government and its authorities took the initiative, marginalized individuals turned to police, mayors, magistrates, governors, judges, and even presidents to achieve their goals. Although the state had a vested interest in criminalizing infanticide and abortion, indigenous women often used these laws to criminalize men's violent outbursts. While assault and battery litigation, too, served this purpose, state laws limited the extent to which men could be punished for these crimes and thus condoned a certain level of domestic violence. Unlike infanticide and abortion cases, which were almost invariably tried at the department level, seldom did domestic violence litigation go beyond the municipal courtroom. Often courtrooms and judicial authorities merely provided a venue and authorial audience for disputes between people themselves. Defamation plaintiffs, for example, largely used the courts for leverage against their opponents.

The fragmentary voices in the archival record that emerge from discreet narratives and disguised critiques unveil a counterdiscourse. Just as judicial authorities sought to shape litigants' worldviews, behavior, and thinking, litigants availed themselves of the opportunity to teach judicial officials and other authorities about their lives and logic. Contrasting what reformers construed as deviant with what indigenous people believed to be normal reveals the broader factors behind the tensions over behavior in society. To better understand the informal arena of power located in the web of quotidian life, I highlight the contingent process of the criminalization of everyday behavior instead of approaching that behavior as self-evidently criminal.

As a flexible instrument of social control, the law sought to extend and deepen the state's hegemony. Since transgressions that the law defined as crimes often stood in opposition to popular notions of criminality, courts attempted to co-opt and reconstitute expressions of popular justice within the state apparatus.[66] Few Kaqchikel considered vagrancy or the production and sale of *aguardiente clandestino* (moonshine) a crime, for example, yet many were punished for these acts. Punishment, Foucault argues, is a constant lesson in the government's perception of the nature of crime.[67] When judicial officials punished defendants more harshly for their outbursts in court than for beating their wives, the state clearly enunciated its priorities.

By establishing a permanent presence, engaging both men and women, and maintaining some legitimacy, courts were the state's most effective means of extending its influence into remote corners of the nation. Neither compulsory education nor military conscription enjoyed much success inculcating *indígenas* who, once their studies or training ended, returned to their families and communities, where local relations, identities, and institutions mitigated national initiatives.[68] Guatemala's mountainous topography and predominantly rural population meant that the central government's power waned quickly beyond the few major urban areas.[69] If, as Philip Corrigan posits, the question is not "*who* rules but *how* rule is accomplished," then the legal system figures prominently in the answer.[70]

As other scholars have noted, judicial systems allowed dictators to contain conflict and maintain order precisely when their legitimacy was most seriously questioned.[71] By providing a framework to articulate and defuse ethnic, class, and gender frictions in ways that reinforced the state's power,[72] the legal system was both an extension of the government's coercive and administrative apparatus and, ironically, one of the few escape valves available for popular dissent.

Methodological Considerations

Although I consulted an array of primary sources—police reports, official correspondence, newspapers, contemporary ethnographies, and oral histories—judicial records are at the core of this study. From the Archivo General de Centro América (AGCA) in Guatemala City, I collected 166 cases from Chimaltenango's *juzgado de primera instancia*. To understand how the legal system operated at the municipal level, I focused on two Kaqchikel municipalities in the department of Chimaltenango: Patzicía and San Martín. The AGCA houses litigation from San Martín from which I collected 339 cases and petitions; I read 322 cases and petitions from Patzicía's municipal archive.

Large swaths of the population were illiterate and thus only entered the archival record when they brushed up alongside or against the state. For this reason legal and criminal records are indispensable for writing social and cultural histories of Latin America. William Taylor's groundbreaking 1979 study *Drinking, Homicide, and Rebellion in Colonial Mexico* demonstrated how to use court records to gain insight into otherwise obscured aspects of rural social history. It also inspired and informed much of the historiography of criminality in Latin America. Yet the subsequent scholarship's tendency to focus on violent crime, particularly riots and rebellions, has exaggerated the role resistance and violence played in the lives of the poor and marginalized.[73] Negotiation, collaboration, cooperation, compliance, ambivalence, indifference, and other responses were just as important.

Since violent crime tends to involve exceptional behavior, reconstructing the texture of crime as experienced in everyday life through less sensational law violations offers a more comprehensive portrait of rural life. Mundane conflicts generated by the productive activity of vendors, *molenderas*, moonshiners, and other entrepreneurs accounted for much of the social tension in rural communities. Yet even nonviolent crime primarily provides a glimpse into life at its worst. By reading against the grain of litigants' testimonies, I have attempted to capture the texture of interpersonal negotiation and community sanction that took place outside the courtroom. Despite their extraordinary nature, trial records go beyond descriptions of exceptional events to offer insights into ordinary people's everyday lives, relationships, and expectations.

To compare violent and exceptional crimes to nonviolent and frequent ones, I focused on crimes that ranged from infanticide to insults. My study of different crimes depended on the extant documents. I collected all fifteen infanticide and abortion cases in Chimaltenango's *juzgado de primera instancia* legal record from 1900 to 1925. Of the thousands of cases involving gender-based violence at the state and local levels, I selected a sample of 102.

Rich as they are, judicial records pose serious interpretive problems. They tend to exaggerate litigants' attitudes about crime and law, underrepresent or misrepresent the very acts they purport to document, and elide transgressions that communities sought to shield from the state and activities that people but not the state considered criminal.[74] Much criminal behavior remained beyond the view of the legal system; rapes went unreported, thefts were hidden, domestic violence was obscured. Even though arrests generally only reflected a small percentage of those involved in illegal activity, for the historian, crime is what documents, oral histories, photographs, and other primary sources preserved.

With suspects seeking to deflect blame and victims trying to convince authorities of their accounts, litigants often subordinated facts to gain freedom or vindication. Regarding the testimony of his nemesis Abraham Luna, for example, the thirty-four-year-old ladino landowner Manuel Leonardo warned the Chimaltenango department judge in 1913, "He who is accustomed to lying lies shamelessly."[75] Yet litigants' goals also compelled them to maintain a level of veracity, as other Latin American historians have noted.[76] In Guatemalan courts, lying could be costly: sentences for giving false testimony ranged from five days to six months of incarceration. As Laura Matthew and Michel R. Oudjik insist, "It is not a question of who is telling the truth and who is lying. In history, everybody tells the truth and everybody lies, at least in some way."[77] Although I approach these testimonies cautiously and scrutinize them within the broader context of historical and criminal trends, much of what they contain reflects social norms and historical truths even if the specific descriptions of these exceptional and chaotic moments embellish or distort them. Taylor asserts, "It is primarily through the accumulation of individual coincidences that the delicate network of relationships and feelings can be made visible through written records by the social historian."[78]

I examine the particular practices, testimonies, and habits of individuals in these sources to identify patterns of how Mayas and poor ladinos adjusted to dictatorial rule. Since the voices that emerge in the documents conformed to and confronted authority, these partial bits of evidence provide a mosaic of indigenous people's relationships with each other, ladinos, authorities, the law, and the state. The challenge is accessing indigenous perspectives, particularly those of indigenous women, through such documents. Almost invariably, non-indigenous males created the documents upon which this study is based. When women spoke for themselves as litigants or petitioners, their voices were mediated through male notaries, scribes, and often translators. Even though scribes and court officers were the final arbiters of what survived in the record, we should not underestimate the ability of subordinates to inject their opinions and perspectives. By analyzing how litigants and raconteurs crafted their narratives instead of simply examining what they said, as historians Natalie Zemon Davis and Daniel James have modeled, I analyze the archival record and oral histories for nuances of how power, gender, ethnicity, class, and morality were constructed and contested.[79]

The state's legal culture, personnel, and methods of interrogation (particularly the formal question-and-answer structure) shaped indigenous people's voices and motives. As brokers and legal lubricators, the interpreters, notaries, scribes, lawyers, and clerks played crucial roles, but their influence is difficult to discern. Notaries were seldom identified; translators, legal counsel (few apparently had any formal training in law), and those posting bail were required to state their names, ages, occupations, places of birth and residence, and occasionally their ethnicity but little else. The historian is left to wonder whose interests these interlocutors had in mind: their own, the state's, *indígenas'*, ladinos', plaintiffs', defendants', witnesses'? Even though bilingual Kaqchikel were less marginalized than their monolingual counterparts, they too were constrained by what notaries deemed most relevant. Tempted to clarify litigants' narratives, translators and notaries did not always convey litigants' words verbatim, as testimonies penned in the third person attest.[80]

Distortions can be useful, however. Courtroom procedural regularities and the formulaic nature of court testimonies allow for anomalies and quotidian language to point to less adulterated indigenous perspectives.[81] Opening statements filed in court followed a standard format in which litigants were identified by their names, occupations, gender, places of birth and residence, and at times ethnicity. Notaries then penned the testimonies. When testimonies varied from the general format of court recordings or were transcribed verbatim, as is intimated by the presence of gendered, ethnic, or class diction specific to the deponent or such words as *pues* (well, then), *indígenas'* views emerge more forcefully.[82]

Composed in less intimidating environments, petitions to authorities provide better access to indigenous perspectives than court documents do since petitioners who hired scribes generally enjoyed greater control over the narrative than their counterparts whose words were recorded by court notaries. Well versed in the petition process, private scribes almost certainly offered advice that petitioners may have welcomed. Yet the frequent first-person voice in these petitions speaks to narrators' ability to dictate the content. Kaqchikel oral histories offer the least adulterated indigenous voices, but these too were conveyed through interviewers and translators. My goal is not to identify primordial, autochthonous indigenous views of justice or crime but rather to understand how Mayas approached these issues and how successful they were at crafting narratives that advanced their agendas.

The study of Guatemalan judicial records is further complicated by their incompleteness and equivocation. Often legal dockets end in mid-proceeding. Even when a notary recorded everything, judicial officials sometimes refrained from offering definitive rulings. Similarly, petitions readily record plaintiffs' complaints but less often authorities' responses. As such, assessing the efficacy of litigants' strategies is difficult. Because litigants did not always self-identify and/or notaries did not always ask, even ethnicity could be elusive. In some cases, a litigant's ethnicity became clear in the proceedings or could be surmised based on descriptions and surnames. However, this process is fraught with peril. At times, an individual's ethnicity was indeterminable.

While department litigation evolved from incidents that occurred in towns and villages throughout Chimaltenango, my decision to focus on municipal jurisprudence in Patzicía and San Martín was guided by these towns' histories, demographic compositions, and relationships to regional and national authorities and structures. Both towns were predominantly indigenous (respectively, 71 percent and nearly 82 percent in 1893 and more than 70 percent and almost 87 percent in 1921; appendices 1 and 2).[83] Subordinated to the ladino municipality, neither Patzicía's nor San Martín's *municipalidad indígena* left behind a written record of its proceedings, duties, or actions. Even without this documentary trail, however, it is clear from ladino-penned documents that *indígenas* in both towns shaped local, regional, and national politics, economics, and social relations.

The largest and fastest-growing municipality in Chimaltenango (from 10,393 in 1893, the population increased to 14,163 in 1921; appendices 1 and 2), San Martín often attracted the attention of regional and national leaders.[84] Close to the capital and known as a hotbed of bootlegging, it was regularly subjected to such state interventions as police raids and presidential visits.

Smaller and less fecund than San Martín, Patzicía had a population size and growth rate (from 4,434 people in 1893 to 5,355 in 1921; appendices 1 and 2) that were about average when compared to other municipal centers in the department.[85] Yet because their town was situated directly off the Pan-American Highway, fifteen kilometers (nine miles) from the department capital and seventy kilometers (forty-three miles) from Guatemala

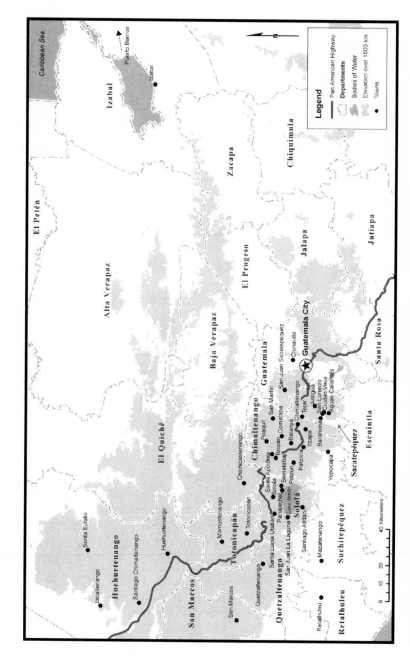

Map 0.2. Departments, cities, and towns mentioned in the text. Map by Rosemary Mosher.

City, *patzicianas* (residents of Patzicía) had more direct access to regional and national centers of power and their structures, for better or worse, than did many of their counterparts in the central highlands.

As the site where Liberal leaders formalized their overthrow of the Conservatives by signing the Acta de Patzicía on June 3, 1871, Patzicía has long been associated with Liberal and dictatorial rule. Indeed, the long succession of despots helped to contain ethnic strife there. Just a few days after the 1944 overthrow of the Ubico government—the last of these authoritarian regimes—ladinos from Patzicía and the nearby town of Zaragoza responded to Kaqchikel demands for land and other rights by massacring hundreds of *indígenas* in Patzicía.[86] This tragic introduction to democratic rule underscores the courts' crucial role in helping dictators mediate conflict in Patzicía by approaching the legal system as an arena of social contestation.

The archival materials from Patzicía and San Martín offer a unique opportunity to examine municipal judicial systems in indigenous communities and contrast the proceedings and procedures with those of the department courts. Like Patzicía and San Martín, the other towns—San Juan Comalapa (henceforth Comalapa), San José Poaquil (henceforth Poaquil), Tecpán, Patzún, Balanya, and Santa Apolonia—that frequently appear in Chimaltenango's *juzgado de primera instancia* records are predominantly indigenous (appendices 1 and 2). To broaden the geographic range of my study, I also consulted municipal proceedings in such predominantly Kaqchikel towns in the department of Sacatepéquez as San Antonio Aguas Calientes (henceforth Aguas Calientes) and Santa Catarina Barahona (henceforth Barahona). Although it is seldom explicit in the documentation, the census data and frequency with which *indígenas* in those towns had Spanish surnames suggest that litigants often dealt with indigenous municipal officials. With only ten ladino men in Aguas Calientes in 1893 and three in 1921, the town likely depended on Kaqchikel men to serve in municipal posts. (Barahona had just one ladino male in 1893 and two in 1921.)[87] Although little archival material remains in Sololá, the capital of the department with the same name, municipal proceedings there, too, shed comparative light on a town where the (Kaqchikel) *municipalidad indígena* was vibrant.

To contextualize this study within Kaqchikel reconstructions of the past and notions of crime, law, and judicial systems, I conducted and collected more than one hundred oral history interviews with Kaqchikel elders. Just as court records both inform and distort historical interpretations, partly because they are laden with asymmetrical power relations, so too are oral histories imperfect sources. Yet reading (and listening to) them as critically as one does archival documents enriches our understanding of how indigenous people experienced and conceived of economic, political, and social relations. However imperfect, these memories also shed light on intra- and interethnic relations and Kaqchikel perceptions of local, regional, and national authorities. In truth, I had only limited access to these historical perspectives since, except for a few topics such as moonshine production and consumption, Kaqchikel raconteurs were reticent regarding how crime shaped their pasts.

Like oral histories, archival research captures the past from the perspective of a contemporary moment in time. As repositories and inspirations for history, archives are not static.[88] This is particularly true in Guatemala, where documents at the AGCA disappear from one research visit to the next. The ground upon which historians conduct research in Guatemala also shifts as archives are discovered and closed.[89] Contingent upon timing and researchers' rapport with archivists and local authorities, any study of Guatemalan history is as much a reflection of the present as an inquiry into the past.

Hailed by the National Police as a first-rate periodical, *La Gaceta: Revista de policía y variedades* (henceforth *La Gaceta*) was a particularly rich source for police perspectives on crime and occasionally those of poor *indígenas* and ladinos. Judging from its advertisements, it targeted the literate upper to lower middle class. An instrument of public relations, propaganda, and investigative assistance for the National Police, it was the only newspaper that regularly reported on crime. In a reflection of dictators' efforts to portray Guatemala as a nation of law and order, other Guatemalan dailies only infrequently included short excerpts, let alone full-length articles about crime.

When trying to understand the broader contexts of people's lives, ethnographic studies of rural Guatemala conducted in the 1920s, 1930s, and 1940s by U.S. anthropologists also proved particularly insightful. Operating at the conjunction of anthropology and history, I use these studies of everyday life to explore the conditions and forces that landed people in court. The rich ethnographic descriptions that mark these monographs shed light on aspects of people's lives that complement the often laconic language in the judicial record. In his 1937 study of Santiago Chimaltenango, a Mam-Maya (henceforth Mam) community to the northwest of the Kaqchikel area that forms the core of this study, Charles Wagley found that the population was generally composed of two economic classes: "the wage earner and the landholder who may exploit relatively large areas by hired labor."[90] Although class relations in the Kaqchikel region were more complex than this binary suggests, the distinction is helpful in understanding the general economic position of most men who appeared in municipal and department courts. Notwithstanding the butchers, merchants, bakers, and storeowners who pervade the judicial record, the vast majority of male litigants were either *jornaleros* or *agricultores* (landowning farmers). Broadly speaking, the differential social and class positions of these two groups shed light on the root causes behind certain types of crime, especially gender-based violence. My goal is to use the social history embedded in the ethnographic record to contextualize what the judicial record teaches us beyond the individual trials at hand.

By offering an opportunity to evaluate what happened in the judicial record against what was happening outside it, ethnographies help to sharpen what people revealed—and what they did not reveal—to the state. Ethnographers' firsthand experiences in contemporary communities suggest the horizon of possibilities within which cases were initiated (or not). In a methodological and historiographical issue that extends beyond Guatemala, I want to explore what happens when we treat ethnographies as history and compare and contrast them with the archival record.

As with all sources, drawing from these studies demands close attention to the manner and time in which they were produced. (One scholar, Felix Webster McBryde, dedicated his monograph to Ubico!)[91] Instead of speaking the indigenous languages of the people they studied, these anthropologists conducted their research in Spanish. Like ladino judicial officials, they too needed interpreters at times. Their reliance on a few informants further limited their ability to fully comprehend local conditions, let alone access competing perspectives. To cite but one example, Ruth Bunzel's assertion that "with willing cooperativeness they [Indians] perform any task demanded by the government" stands in stark contrast to the record of *indígenas* petitioning to be excused from and others being arrested for failing to comply with their civic responsibilities or the state's myriad forced-labor mechanisms.[92] Most of these ethnographies are localized studies of individual communities, and any generalizations drawn from them must be approached with great caution, particularly in light of Guatemala's dramatic regional differences. As Wagley notes, "From one *municipio* [municipality] to the other, there is great variation and specialization of custom within broad common outlines of Middle American culture."[93] Further limiting the applicability of these manuscripts for my study, only two ethnographers worked with Kaqchikel speakers (McBryde and Sol Tax), and only one worked in a town (Sololá) that figures prominently in my study. Given these limitations, I am careful to avoid what I would call "side streaming," or using these studies of individual communities as emblematic of Maya experiences in early to mid-twentieth-century Guatemala.

Finally, with regard to orthography, almost invariably ladino scribes and notaries penned the documents I consulted. With few exceptions, I have modernized spellings and added accents to words and names found in archival records. If names are taken as Spanish, many require accents; if they are taken as indigenous, however, they do not. For individuals who could be identified as *indígenas*, I did not use accents in their indigenous surnames. For all others, I followed Spanish orthography.

When I use Kaqchikel-Maya pseudonyms and words, I adhere to the spellings and standardized alphabet promoted by the Academia de Lenguas Mayas de Guatemala (ALMG, Guatemalan Academy of Mayan Languages). In 1987 the National Congress approved this alphabet, which now is used for Guatemala's twenty-two official Maya languages. For Maya names such as K'iche' (instead of Quiché), I honor the ALMG spellings unless I am using a direct quote, in which case I use the author's spelling.

Book Structure

Courts and petitions were among the few forums for *indígenas* to position themselves as Guatemalans, insist on their rights, espouse their ideas of justice, and have their words recorded. With national politics largely closed off to them, what happened in the courtroom and how individual authorities responded to their petitions mattered more than the type of political system under which they lived. As one of the few institutions consistently open to all Guatemalans, courts were remarkably participatory—a characteristic that was even more pronounced during dictatorships.

The following chapters explore the process of everyday state formation by looking at different types of crime and the ways those who were victims or accused of these transgressions advanced their agendas through the legal system. *Indígenas* both used and were subject to the judicial system. To frame the tension between the limits of state rule and the state's ability to co-opt *indígenas* and poor ladinos, Chapter 1 sets up the comparison between criminal enforcement by authorities and voluntary suits initiated by people. After explaining the judicial process and its relationship to dictators in early twentieth-century Guatemala, Chapter 1 also contextualizes Guatemala's political, social, and legal history.

Chapters 2 and 3 examine how social constructions of race and crime affected bootleggers and market vendors. In outlawing extra-official alcohol production and sale, the state altered definitions of crime in ways that contravened indigenous conceptions of legality. By maintaining these cottage industries, bootleggers challenged definitions of deviant behavior. Their trials point to how people's socioeconomic positions influenced their interpretations of law and crime. As the conflicts between vendors and municipal authorities documented in Chapter 3 suggest, marketplaces were critical to *indígenas*' efforts to carve out spaces of autonomy and to elite efforts to mold the economy, society, politics, and *indígenas* to elite ideals. For these reasons, struggles over ethnic, gender, and state power were common in marketplaces. Like husbands' efforts to control their wives, women's responses to dictators' attempts to impose order and progress demonstrate that patriarchies were characterized by contestation.

Although legislators wrote laws that disadvantaged females, at times women inverted legislative intentions to their advantage. Chapter 4 contrasts women who accused fathers and husbands of reproductive crimes with national authorities who approached infanticide and abortion as crimes against motherhood committed by abjected women. Because pregnant women and new mothers broadened the popular definition of infanticide, in practice the litigation of reproductive crimes became less gendered than legislators had intended.

Building on the revelations in infanticide litigation, Chapter 5 explores gender-based violence. Similar to the way the Estrada Cabrera and Ubico dictatorships threatened Guatemalans by murdering political enemies, official indifference toward widespread violence against women perpetuated a sense of fear that these regimes used to keep people in line. By providing an outlet for male frustrations that undergirded local peasant patriarchies but did not challenge the state, gender-based violence helped to sustain these regimes.

Defamation litigation, too, served the state's interests by maintaining the rule of law, as Chapter 6 demonstrates. Since poor and working-class women faced fierce competition over clients, employment, and status in the communities, they—more so than men or elite women—had to constantly defend their honor even against the smallest slights. Their testimonies in municipal courtrooms tell us much about the ongoing disputes over the meanings of culture and the importance of reputations.

Despite the ways paternalism and patronage encouraged Guatemalans to appeal to authorities outside the legal system to right their wrongs, the courts remained vibrant venues for airing grievances, arbitrating differences, negotiating resolutions, and advancing agendas. By fostering and modeling particular types of conduct, the legal system and litigants helped the state maintain governability. In confronting the state and their antagonists through this process, litigants—even poor, illiterate, monolingual, indigenous women—shaped their lives, families, communities, and nation.

CHAPTER 1

Dictators, *Indígenas*, and the Legal System: Intersections of Race and Crime

More than any other institution—including schools and the military—courts were where competing views of nation, identity, and citizenship were contested. Although some historians have argued that early twentieth-century courts were illegitimate and anemic,[1] my study indicates otherwise. As one of the few venues that facilitated the integration of *indígenas* and poor ladinos particularly by instilling in them the habit of submitting their differences with each other to judgments by duly constituted authorities, courts were crucial for state building.

The courts can be used as an analytical tool to measure the balance of power between people and the state. Framing cases that resulted from the state's criminal enforcement against those initiated by people themselves allows for a nuanced understanding of the limits and persuasiveness of state power. In the state's campaign against moonshiners (Chapter 2) and its attempt to regulate highland markets (Chapter 3), the state—mainly represented by the police and other security forces, department judges, and local authorities—was enforcing its laws. Caught in the courts' clutches, defendants sought to mitigate their punishment by pointing out how officials had either overstepped their bounds or failed to build a state where the poor could thrive without breaking the law. The reproductive-crime litigation that informs Chapter 4 was also the result of the enforcement of state laws. Yet local indigenous and ladino women initiated this litigation as often as state representatives did. As such, the dynamics in these cases were more complicated than the state simply exerting its power and defendants trying to curb it; at times women used the courts for their own ends. The power relations and dynamics in the courtroom became even more equivocal in cases that were almost exclusively initiated by victims, such as litigation of domestic violence (Chapter 5) and defamation (Chapter 6). In these voluntary suits, plaintiffs used the courts to gain leverage against their aggressors or rivals. By inviting the intervention of judicial officials, victims acknowledged the court's and state's authority, even if only to settle disputes.

Although poor *indígenas* and ladinos who used the legal system provide one example of the state's ability to peacefully reproduce its legitimacy, their litigation was seldom an unqualified endorsement of the state. Even under its gaze, indigenous litigants pointed to the need to consider poverty and other social injustices when defining crimes. In their court testimonies, poor, indigenous, female bootleggers pointed out that they had little choice but to produce and sell moonshine to survive. While intellectuals and state agents asserted that *indígenas'* backwardness and culture explained their failures, indigenous litigants emphasized their diligence and adaptability to highlight capitalist modernization's shortcomings.

The laconic nature of most rulings makes parsing judges' perspectives difficult, but when examined collectively, the rulings suggest that judicial officials tacked between harboring a sense of despair because their judgments seldom changed people's behavior (as domestic violence litigation reveals) and a sense that their rulings could help keep peace among locals (principally when magistrates encouraged nonviolent responses to insults by upholding individuals' honor). Particularly when initiated by *indígenas* or poor ladinos, voluntary suits offer an opportunity to examine the balance between plaintiffs who wanted to use the state, via the legal system, and officials who may have wanted to take advantage of teaching moments to civilize *indios* or hegemonic moments to show poor and marginalized litigants who ruled. Understanding who is doing what to whom and who is using whom in judicial processes demands close attention to the shifting power relations and adulterated narratives in the judicial record.

Judicial Processes in Early Twentieth-Century Highland Guatemala

Often coexisting peacefully, indigenous and state-sanctioned judicial systems were not always at odds. For *indígenas* who felt wronged, generally the first step was to approach the local indigenous judicial system presided over by indigenous *alcaldes* (mayors) or *principales* (politico-religious leaders) in the *municipalidad indígena*. Generally conducted in their native language, indigenous municipalities' business, actions, and exchanges were seldom recorded, and thus historians have little access to them; oral histories and contemporary ethnographies provide a broad sense of the parameters but few specifics. The majority of complaints brought before indigenous authorities had to do with marital issues, particularly domestic violence and infidelity, and with drunkenness, land disputes, and long-standing frictions among community members that occasionally manifested as insults and violence. As was true in other indigenous communities, Maya justice systems sought communal harmony through damage compensation instead of punishment, a process grounded in consensus building as opposed to individual rulings.[2] By resolving many disputes and lending an air of legitimacy to cases that proceeded through the state's legal system, the indigenous judicial process performed a valuable service for the state and Mayas.

If the issue demanded or merited the state's attention, indigenous authorities referred it to the municipal court, at which point the historian gains a window onto the judicial process. After Ubico began appointing *intendentes*, indigenous mayors frequently referred cases to them.[3] For *indígenas* who lived in rural *aldeas* (villages), these referrals often compelled them to travel some distance to the more densely populated *cabecera* (municipal center)—Patzicía, San Martín, Comalapa, Tecpán, Poaquil, Chimaltenango—to which their *aldea* pertained. Oftentimes one and the same, the municipal mayors or justices of the peace who presided over these proceedings in the department of Chimaltenango were almost invariably ladinos.[4] At that level, authorities still likely knew or at least knew of litigants.

Based on their assessments of favorable rulings, some plaintiffs, particularly indigenous women who were disadvantaged in customary law,[5] bypassed the indigenous justice system and went directly to municipal or department authorities, as evidenced by petitions penned moments after alleged offenses. As historians have observed, these petitions are often the most valuable part of the judicial record since plaintiffs were conveying emotion-laden accounts before they had a chance to polish their narratives.[6]

If the Patzicía and San Martín municipal archives are any indication, like their indigenous counterparts ladino officials had few cases to adjudicate from one day to the next.[7] Such observations from the ethnographic and archival record remind us that judicial records only capture a fraction of life in highland Guatemala. The challenge is reading court cases for details that offer insight beyond the individual cases at hand. To a certain extent, the nature of judicial records facilitates this exercise. When courts were in session, both sides could give testimony, present evidence, and call witnesses, though defendants frequently remained silent.

Their interwoven and multifaceted subjectivities, identities, and positions shaped how litigants experienced the legal system. Moments after being accused of insulting her eighteen-year-old sister, for example, the thirty-three-year-old *indígena* Mercedes Tohom de Morales took advantage of being in San Martín municipal court to denounce her husband for beating and insulting her.[8] Although the record sheds little light on how or if the altercations were related, it clearly shows that Tohom was struggling simultaneously with contentious sibling and marital relations. Like their subjectivities, litigants' strategies for asserting their agency were varied. Depending on the circumstances, they might turn to the courts for redress and retribution (as Tohom did in response to her husband's abuse) or seek to settle their disputes extrajudicially (as she did by insulting her sister).

As Tohom learned, the judicial system could simultaneously punish and protect: on April 16, 1935, the San Martín *juez de paz* Arenas sentenced her to five and her husband to ten days in jail. Never omnipotent in these settings, municipal officials like Arenas risked open rebellion if their rulings appeared unjust or inequitable to their rural charges, particularly in highland communities remote from centers of state power. Justices had to use their power to condemn and vindicate wisely.

Although municipal judicial officials like Arenas disposed of many cases themselves, crimes like infanticide, murder, rape, and abortion required them to refer the cases and remand the offenders to the *juez de primera instancia*, or department judge. These decisions were not made lightly; department judges rebuked and fined municipal officials for referring cases such as assault and battery and defamation to them that could be handled locally. Once the case arrived at the department level, the *juez de primera instancia* had the final word. If litigants wanted to challenge his ruling, they could appeal to the Court of Appeals in Guatemala City.

As institutions of state power staffed by ladino men, courts could be intimidating venues for women and *indígenas*. The farther removed from their communities, the more foreign the court became. Once they left the indigenous authority, *indígenas* were compelled to communicate in Spanish in municipal court; many needed interpreters to do so. If their cases proceeded to the *juez de primera instancia*, exchanges between them and court officials became more formal and institutionalized, a world apart from their rural villages. At that point most plaintiffs retained lawyers, often provided by the court.

Where cases were tried and who presided over them affected the judicial process. Both figuratively and literally, the closer judicial authorities were to indigenous communities, the farther they were from national influences. Even though municipal ladino officials may have identified and allied most clearly with their superiors, they did not always or automatically comply with the bidding of the national government. Their rulings in cases involving *indígenas* and women had as much to do with maintaining their own local privileges, prerogatives, and prejudices as with propagating national power structures or patriarchal state practices. Depending on litigants' relationships with the justice of the peace, these ambiguities could work for or against them. Department judges, on the other hand, held positions that were more influenced by regional and national than local considerations and power structures. Recalling the Ubico era, Kaqchikel informants from San Andrés Semetabaj considered regional and national officials more impartial brokers than local ladino authorities.[9] Although they often were more evenhanded than their municipal subordinates, who may have had local stakes or interests in the rulings, department judges knew little of indigenous and poor litigants' daily conditions, struggles, and privations.

The absence of a jury system afforded judicial officials considerable discretionary decision-making power and encouraged litigants and judges to adhere to the clientelistic relations common in Guatemalan society. Aware that their fates depended on one man's ruling instead of a jury of their peers, litigants worked hard to endear themselves to judicial officials by singing their praises and promising eternal gratitude should they rule in their favor. Judicial officials seldom discouraged such adulations.

Adhering to proper language and comportment, most *indígenas* treated courtrooms as sacrosanct places—an indication that the state had habituated them to its expectations there. Crucial to gaining a favorable ruling, this behavior also can be interpreted as what James Scott calls "public transcripts." To frame their arguments "in close conformity with how the dominant group would wish to have things appear," indigenous litigants often reflected ladino rhetoric and Spanish legalese back to judicial officials.[10] Upholding these conventions and invoking these stereotypes in court did not necessarily mean acceptance of them, nor did addressing authorities in deferential tones convey trust or confidence in them; once in court, denying the validity of the legal system or insulting authorities only would have undermined litigants' fates. When the fifty-year-old illiterate *indígena* Petrona Tejax "lacked respect . . . [and] disturbed in this way public order with sulfurous words" in San Martín's courtroom on February 15, 1935, the *juez de paz* sentenced her to fifteen days in jail commutable by ten cents a day.[11]

As much as they were tools of oppression, courtrooms provided arenas for dispute and negotiation. Perhaps the best evidence of this and of Mayas' belief that the law could be an effective weapon for settling disputes was the frequency with which they engaged the legal system and found ways to defend themselves once forced to court. Indigenous men and women enjoyed considerable agency in the legal process. Some hired scribes and lawyers. Although marginalized groups often relied on obfuscation,[12] at times *indígenas'* critiques of individual laws and ladino exploitation were frank. Rather than being submissive, marginalized individuals confronted their rivals and even judicial officials through their testimonies. Even as a sense of alienation permeates many of their testimonies, indigenous people could be formidable forces in courtrooms. They respected the institution but seldom felt compelled to change their appearance or dress when appearing before it; out of necessity, some spoke their indigenous language in court. Injecting their own culture and characteristics in a physical space that was marked by ladino norms served their interests.

With the contrasting outlooks, experiences, and epistemologies that each party brought to the courtroom, court testimonies can be read as open-ended dialogues.[13] Operating on a number of levels—between judicial officials and litigants, between litigants themselves, and between the community and these groups—these exchanges helped to shape discourses that were constantly changing and adapting to the deployment of local strategies and the immediacy of contact with state power. Courtrooms were contact zones, to borrow Mary Louise Pratt's phrase.[14] Authorial tensions in court testimonies and the unequal relations between indigenous litigants and (predominantly) ladino judicial officials resulted in hybrid documents. In their multiple roles and uses, courts were combinations of institutions of state power, venues for popular demands, facilitators of governability, and forums for airing grievances.

The Evolution of a Hybrid Legal System

Rooted in the colonial period, Guatemalan law was marked by ethnic, class, and gender discrimination. Published in 1265 by the Spanish king Alfonso X, the seven-part compendium of laws titled *Siete partidas* informed colonial jurisprudence even after Spanish America's own *Recopilación de las leyes de Indias* (1680) established two sets of laws: one for indigenous peoples and the other for Creoles and mestizos, people of mixed European and indigenous ancestry. The office of Protector de Indios, which later became part of the office of Procurador de la Audiencia, assumed the role of protecting and delineating indigenous people's rights and obligations.[15] Despite its paternalistic and discriminatory nature, the law was an important tool for indigenous people. Their frequent use of the legal system earned them a reputation for litigiousness among Central American mestizos.

Following independence, Liberals sought to establish the principle—if not the practice—of equality before the law. To modernize the legal apparatus and rid Guatemala of Spanish colonial law, in 1836 the nascent Liberal state adopted the Livingston Codes, which established trial by jury and circuit courts in towns and regions previously isolated from the state, guaranteed habeas corpus, and abolished multiple courts, corporal punishment, and private *fueros* (privileges and immunities for certain social groups, some of which benefited indigenous people). Forced to help build new courthouses and jails, many Mayas resented this encroachment on their traditional systems of justice and viewed the new system and judges as corrupt. By the time Liberals repealed the Livingston Codes in 1838, Maya unrest—further fueled by state efforts to control the sale of alcohol and regularize landownership—was formidable. The emerging peasant leader José Rafael Carrera harnessed it to overthrow the Liberals in 1839.[16]

Absent the Livingston Codes, Guatemala, like other Latin American nations, continued to call upon colonial law. In a move that afforded considerable indigenous judicial autonomy, President Carrera (1844–1848, 1851–1865) reinstated the *Recopilación de las Leyes de Indias* and offices of the Protector de Indios in 1851. The guarantee of interpreters in court notwithstanding, the government's paltry finances and refusal to grant *indígenas* or women full legal rights as citizens limited the impact of these legal reforms.[17] Customary indigenous law often ruled the day.[18]

Not until the Liberals returned to power in 1871 did the Guatemalan legal system begin to break from its colonial vestiges. In his preamble to the 1877 civil codes President Barrios noted, "Until now the legislation in force in the Republic, most of which comes from old Spanish law, is incomplete, confusing, and difficult to understand and apply. . . . To replace those defective laws with codes that exhibit the heights of the era's advancement and the country's progress," the commission charged with writing the codes used "the principles of modern legislation."[19] Altered to include the civil, penal, military, and commercial codes, an image of Barrios republished during the Ubico regime suggests how proud twentieth-century Liberals were of Barrios's role in establishing Guatemala's modern legal system (figure 1.1).

Unlike their early nineteenth-century counterparts, late nineteenth-century Liberals approached reform cautiously, especially when it affected the majority population. The commission that codified Guatemala's penal codes both recognized how urgent legal reform was for "the progressive march of the Republic" and lamented that the new codes "did not define . . . or clearly establish with desired precision, many of the crimes to which it refers."[20] Although he recognized these shortcomings when he authorized the use of the new penal codes on March 15, 1889, President Manuel J. Barillas

Figure 1.1. General Justo Rufino Barrios, Guatemalan Reformer, *La Gaceta*, July 19, 1935. Image courtesy of Hemeroteca Nacional de Guatemala.

(1885–1892) echoed his predecessor when he insisted that the Código Penal "has filled a great social necessity [by] substituting the old laws."[21] Since Spanish paternalism and patriarchy remained deeply embedded in the new legal codes, *indígenas* and women faced significant obstacles in their quests for justice and fairness. As challenging as the process of writing new laws was, enforcing them proved even more difficult as *indígenas* and women negotiated the spirit and letter of the law in rural courtrooms.

Whether they worked through the legal system or appealed to other powers, *indígenas* deployed a broad range of arsenals in their petitions. In one crucial example of indigenous efforts to call upon Liberal rhetoric of equality, modernity, and progress but also to frame their arguments within Guatemala's reality, in 1886 a group of sixty-three indigenous men from Aguas Calientes petitioned the Guatemalan Legislative Assembly "to end once and for all this slavery to which we have been condemned."[22] The signatories invoked the very symbol of the nation's independence and effort to chart a just society: the constitution. "We approach the Respectable Legislative Body, to demand aid and protection, so that through a law and in harmony with the founding charter [*la carta fundamental*], we *los indíjenas* expeditiously have our rights to reclaim our freedom of work, whose limitations must be urgently defined and determined," they proclaimed. By identifying themselves as citizens who contributed to the nation, they used Liberal individualist discourse to reject the state's efforts to deny them citizenship: "If one looks to extend progress, before anything else he should improve the condition of the citizen . . . because each one, in the orbit of his intellectual and material faculties, can be useful to himself, his fellow citizens and the entire society." Exhorting legislators to live up to the nation's promise did not preclude appeals to paternalism, though; they also portrayed themselves as members of "*la raza* that until today [has been] helpless [*desvalida*]."[23]

Despite their marginalized position and Liberal efforts to exclude them, *indígenas* never relinquished their sense of citizenship. Even when they cast themselves as indigent members of the "Indian race," their very presence in court demonstrated their claim to rights as members of the national polity. Although often as a backdrop to plaintiffs' primary objectives, the struggle over citizenship and rights played out in the courts throughout the Liberal era. In the larger milieu of the Liberal agenda of social order and material progress, law and crime played significant roles. Just as the law provided representatives of the state with the opportunity to create certain types of citizens and subjects, litigants influenced interpretations of law, crime, and justice with their comments about constructions of race, gender, and class. When it served their needs, *indígenas* used rhetoric that reflected racist, sexist, and classist discourse. Whether they resisted, negotiated, or accommodated their conditions of subordination, they contributed to nation formation.

Even as the rules of the game changed during Liberal reign, Mayas adeptly navigated the murky waters of the legal system. Estrada Cabrera prohibited the use of indigenous languages in government documents or verbal legal transactions, though interpreters were provided in court. In turn, Ubico centralized local legal systems by personally appointing justices of the peace.[24] Despite these vagaries, indigenous practices, perspectives, and customary law shaped jurisprudence and judicial institutions. As syncretic and malleable as the Guatemalan legal system was, it was neither free from nonjudicial interventions nor the only avenue through which to pursue justice.

Dictators and Law

Estrada Cabrera and Ubico allowed the legal system to function because it lent legitimacy to their rule, yet their paternalism undermined the institutionalization of the courts. Historian Catherine Rendon asserts that during the Estrada Cabrera period the "law was the President."[25] Preferring not to appear in public, Estrada Cabrera generally conveyed his pardons and punishments through his agents.[26] Famous for traveling to rural communities on his motorcycle (figure 1.2) and imposing his own brand of justice, Ubico also sought to extend his rule of law beyond the capital.[27] Such direct interventions in people's lives and news of them reinforced clientelistic rule by encouraging would-be litigants to bypass municipal courts or to challenge their rulings by appealing to department judges or to circumvent the legal process altogether by appealing to the governor or president. Petitioners' reasons for doing so varied. As Anselmo and Josefa Mutzutz explained when they appealed directly to Chimaltenango's *jefe político* (governor) in 1939: "We are extremely poor and cannot sustain a costly and prolonged litigation."[28] Others approached superiors because local officials were unresponsive or corrupt. The result was a complex relationship between dictators and the rule of law.

When individual authorities entertained appeals from petitioners who either ignored the judicial system or wanted to overturn its rulings, they often subverted the legal system. To understand how rule was accomplished, I use municipal and department court records along with petitions to local, regional, and national leaders to particularize how state institutions and agents both buttressed and contradicted each other in response to *indígenas'* and poor ladinos' efforts to advance their agendas.

Early in his reign President Ubico went to San Martín, where he adjudicated a land dispute between the ladino municipality and the indigenous community in front of a packed courtroom. *La Gaceta* offers a rich description of the proceedings. Seated behind the bench, Ubico first called in the mayor representing the municipality, a "ladino by his appearance and dress . . . [and] soft spoken and courteous manner," and then the plaintiff, represented by "an *indio* with long black hair, [and] a goatee with white threads

Figure 1.2. "Presidential visits." General Jorge Ubico on his motorcycle. This image captures one of the many layers of justice in Guatemala: the president might appear suddenly, almost out of nowhere, on his fancy, powerful machine to render judgment. *La Gaceta*, November 10, 1940. Image courtesy of Hemeroteca Nacional de Guatemala.

that adorned his wild and rebellious face, which had never known a razor blade. His upper lip was split by a scar that formed two lobes. . . . In his coat pocket, a pencil was visible." Unable to control his first impression, Ubico said quietly to his secretary of state, "This is a shyster. I can smell it."[29]

The indigenous plaintiff spoke first, explaining, "The Municipality has stripped the *pueblo* of its land, appropriating parcels that always have been the patrimony of the *nativos* [natives] of the *pueblo*. [When] the mayor put up gates, no *indio* could enjoy what belonged to them because the Municipality appropriated what was the indigenous community's." When Ubico asked if the community had a land title, he replied: "Title? No, *tata presidento*; but custom." The mayor interrupted to deny the charges, but the plaintiff quickly retook the floor, insisting that "the Municipality has made itself owner of something that is not hers. Going back years, centuries, that land has belonged to the indigenous community and now the mayor does not leave the poor *indios* in peace."[30]

Since even sympathetic elites tended to discount indigenous agency, playing on stereotypes of poor, ignorant, helpless *indios* could be an efficacious strategy. Writing in 1931, the Guatemalan intellectual Flavio Guillén lamented, "Everything has died in the *indio* of Guatemala: his combatant's courage, his constructive intelligence, his landowner activity. . . . He lives in fear of the mestizo or white man, eyes timid, voice trembles. . . . This is our work; this is our crime. Our equality is hypocrisy and our religion is deception, while we do not elevate the *indio* until the hour of our fraternity."[31] For Guillén, the way ladinos, Creoles, and the government oppressed *indios* was a crime. If the judicial record is any indication, however, few *indígenas* were waiting for elites to "elevate the *indio*."

When Ubico asked the plaintiff what he farmed, "the *indio* looked confused for a moment," perhaps because the question seemed irrelevant to the proceedings. He replied that he was not an agriculturist but simply defending "his *compañeros*' and *camaradas*' interests and ancestral rights." The plaintiff's response and perhaps his pencil confirmed Ubico's suspicions, which in turn betrayed the dictator's stereotypical perception of *indios* as illiterate farmers and manual laborers and those who stepped outside these stations as suspect. "As I said, a shyster from head to toe," Ubico remarked.[32] In the minds of many Central American authorities, literate indigenous people were not true *indios*.[33]

Although the indigenous plaintiff's admission that he did not farm and intimation that he was literate undermined his standing in Ubico's eyes, it also suggests why his colleagues chose him: he likely had more education and mobility than most agriculturists. As a broker who represented a community straddling two worlds, the indigenous plaintiff recognized the importance of literacy, as his pencil suggests, and insisted that custom constituted a legal precedent.

Even as *indígenas* came to see education and other aspects of modernization as crucial to their ability to improve their plight, few perceived these

Figure 1.3. Indigenous authorities from San Martín Jilotepeque, 1907. Image courtesy of Colección Fototeca Guatemala, CIRMA (Centro de Investigaciones Regionales de Mesoamérica).

resources to be at odds with their culture or traditions, at least for males, as the 1907 photograph of five San Martín indigenous authorities indicates (figure 1.3).[34] The man on the left maintains a pose with a pencil and paper to convey his literacy even as he and his colleagues are barefoot and in their traditional dress. Clearly staged, the photograph celebrates the very adherence to their culture and customs that urban ladino and Creole intellectuals argued were signs of *indígenas'* backwardness. As Grandin notes, "Photography helped bring about the reconciliation of modernity and tradition, progress and stability."[35] Mayas sought to advance this reconciliation since at least the late nineteenth century, while not until the 1930s did urban ladinos and Creoles begin to embrace it. Such images and the indigenous people who embodied them upset the prejudices of authorities, intellectuals, and journalists who at best saw *indios* as *hombres de maiz* (men of corn) or farmers and at worst considered them retrograde, lazy drunks.

Since neither party could produce a land title, Ubico ruled that the land belonged to the nation, which would allow the ladino municipality to manage the forest and timber rights. The journalist concluded that the case demonstrated "the passivity of indigenous communities that accepted a good-faith ruling . . . convinced of the justice."[36] Though hardly passive, many indigenous people considered courts legitimate venues for settling their disputes. The very pliability that characterized a legal system that could survive such blatant dictatorial interventions without surrendering its credibility must have been attractive to indigenous people who saw in this same flexibility the opportunity to engage with a state institution and its agents without abandoning their own norms and perspectives. Instead of jeopardizing the very foundation of a nation ruled by the law of an independent legal system rather than a despot, Estrada Cabrera's and Ubico's interventions may have strengthened it.

The San Martín proceedings and photograph offer examples of the ways indigenous epistemologies, traditions, and cultural markers coexisted with and confronted ladino and state ideologies, institutions, and norms. Modernization and tradition were intimately intertwined in Guatemala; courtrooms were no exception. Mayas embraced such aspects of modernization as literacy and legal reforms even as they asserted ancestral traditions, rights, and customs. Since community-based "traditional" approaches were grounded in customary law and the counsel of elders, they often clashed with state-centered "modern" constructions of law. By documenting indigenous litigants who cited laws in their own language or highlighted their literacy even as they identified as *indígenas* and wore markers of their indigenous identity, the judicial record reveals what Sahlins calls the "indigenisation of modernity."[37] Without necessarily surrendering or subordinating their distinct worldviews, indigenous litigants co-opted aspects of modernization and the legal system. In this sense, the judicial record provides a window into the broader history of postcolonial Guatemala, where Creole and ladino leaders bent on identifying the nation with its European influences confronted their predominantly indigenous subjects at every turn.

Modernizing Dictatorships

When they came to power in the last third of the nineteenth century throughout Latin America, Liberals espoused modernizing reforms that generally combined positivism, social Darwinism, and science in an effort to bring about "order and progress."[38] Although many late nineteenth-century reforms were already under way during the Conservative regime's twilight in Guatemala, particularly those dealing with the economy and education, Liberals more actively promoted them.[39] By the end of the nineteenth century, manifestations of modernization were apparent in such large urban centers as Guatemala City and Quetzaltenango where electric lights, telegraph services, wide boulevards, refashioned central plazas, and indoor markets conveyed a sense of progress. Like their Liberal counterparts in other areas of Latin America, Guatemalan leaders called upon architects to design grand buildings and other public works that would invite tourism and attract foreign investment.[40] Both Estrada Cabrera and Ubico enjoyed some success with the latter.[41]

Instead of embracing capitalist modernization, however, Guatemala's economic systems were eclectic.[42] In addition to forced labor, which survived in one form or another through the 1940s, the state set prices and acted as the intermediary between producers and consumers for certain "articles of daily consumption."[43] The striking contrast between physical manifestations of progress and the labor gangs that built them hinted at Guatemalan dictators' a la carte approach to modernizing reforms. Rampant lawbreaking does not automatically signify failed social control,[44] yet some of the most frequently prosecuted crimes during the first half of the twentieth century betrayed national leaders' claims of maintaining order: public intoxication, scandalous behavior, vagrancy, fighting, verbal abuse, and bootlegging (appendix 3). Guatemala's experience with capitalist modernization was laden with ambiguities.

Ushering in the twentieth century as Guatemala's president, Estrada Cabrera sacrificed liberty and justice for order and progress. Through an extensive spy network, draconian police force, and *mandamientos* (forced-labor drafts), Estrada Cabrera curtailed individual freedoms. In an indication that those suspected of undermining or challenging his rule were punished harshly, political prisoners outnumbered thieves and murderers in Guatemalan jails—a telling comparison, given that theft was generally among the top three crimes for which perpetrators were tried in Chimaltenango during his regime (appendix 4). Trusting no one, he even turned his spies on the military. At the same time, he cultivated loyalists through personal favors such as making exceptions to government policies and pardoning criminals.[45] As one consequence of this selective impunity, many Kaqchikel associated his regime with "disorder, thieves, and delinquency."[46] Even as he used any means possible to prevent social unrest, Estrada Cabrera obscured such national shortcomings as penury, illiteracy, and racism.[47]

Historical narratives from Maya communities convey his tyranny.[48] Junlajuj Imox, a Kaqchikel elder from Comalapa, recalled,

A long time ago Manuel Estrada Cabrera was president and he would not let us go to school. He also did not provide food or clothing to prisoners or men in the barracks. They had to walk around barefoot and that really hurt. He really punished people. . . . Twenty-two years he was president, two more and he would have been king. . . . But he was overthrown in 1920; that is when slavery ended for our people. Before that people would hide from ladinos and ladinas because they made you work without pay. You had to transport goods long distances and never get paid—exploitation. They also liked to call you *indio* and *ixto*. . . . Cabrera really made our people suffer. 1920 is an important date because slavery ended for us. Before that, ladinos treated us badly.[49]

Complicated by Estrada Cabrera's combination of persecution and co-optation, historical reconstructions of his rule are complex. His distribution of land to residents of San Gerónimo in 1906 softened their otherwise critical recollections of his reign.[50] Although his contradictory interactions contributed to a sense of anxiety and disorder that belied his mantra of order and progress, the legal system mitigated these tensions. Perhaps for this reason, Estrada Cabrera did not modify either the penal or civil codes during his presidency.

Intended to mask corruption and his disregard for other branches of government, Estrada Cabrera's public displays and exhortations of respect for the law buttressed the legal system. Neither *indígenas* nor poor ladinos simply surrendered their rights or goals in the face of the pervasive fear and oppression that marked his regime.[51] If not progress, order often was facilitated by judicial rulings. The courtroom provided a peaceful, structured venue for litigants and authorities to argue, disagree, and negotiate.

During the 1920s the Carlos Herrera (1920–1921), José María Orellana (1922–1926), and Lázaro Chacón (1926–1930) administrations approached the law differently. Although twenty-two years of dictatorship had ill prepared Guatemalans for a transition to less authoritarian rule, the fall of the Estrada Cabrera regime and the national political conflicts that ensued allowed local leaders to reassert control over their communities.[52]

Faced with poverty, malnutrition, failing schools, and a faltering economy, Herrera had little time to right the nation's course. Making good on his promise to restore constitutional democracy and basic political rights, he created the conditions for the revival of the press, political parties, unions, and private interest groups within months of his inauguration. His attempt to reduce the size of the army and his inability to mediate between Liberals and Conservatives cut his term short, however.[53]

After Herrera's overthrow in 1921, Orellana quickly restored the power of the military. Three years after he assumed the presidency and invited Ubico to become part of his cabinet, Orellana suspended constitutional guarantees in response to popular pressure and critiques from the press. Friendly to U.S. business interests, he established the quetzal as the official currency in 1924 but did nothing to alleviate the forced-labor demands on *indígenas*.[54]

As the vice president at the time of Orellana's death on September 26, 1926, Chacón took over and immediately reinstated constitutional guarantees. Marked by an era of tolerance and corruption, Chacón developed strong relations with some Mayas while alienating others. Even as his efforts to understand indigenous people and their realities predated Ubico's close contact with rural communities, Chacón's national police criminalized indigenous livelihoods, which ironically weakened his rule by contributing to a sense of lawlessness in the countryside. What most consumed authorities' time, though, was the battle against public inebriation: they arrested an astounding 25,335 drunks in 1928 and 18,987 in 1929 (appendix 3). Ultimately, the economic depression and a stroke doomed Chacón's rule. After surviving a coup in early 1929, he succumbed to a cerebral hemorrhage on December 11, 1930, and died four months later.[55] His incapacitation and the economic crisis paved the way for Ubico's strong-arm rule.

Uncontested in the presidential elections, Ubico assumed power in February 1931. He subordinated the Supreme Court and legislature, but according to Kaqchikel raconteurs, his rule was far more just than Estrada Cabrera's. Yet even as his government came to play "an increasingly significant role in the ordering of social and economic life," as Maxine Molyneux has observed regarding Latin American states generally as the twentieth century progressed, Ubico's reign stands in sharp contrast to her assertion that these states became "less authoritarian and less patriarchal" over time.[56] Kaqchikel and other Mayas both praised and condemned his rule.[57] Ixjo'q, a Mam woman, captured these contradictions well: "There were advantages and disadvantages to Ubico's rule. . . . It was safe. But the government did not take good care of the people. . . . There were sicknesses . . . and there was no freedom. They were like slaves."[58] Like Junlajuj Imox's portrayal of Estrada Cabrera's rule, Ixjo'q evoked the suffering during Ubico's reign by associating it with slavery. Unlike Estrada Cabrera's regime, however, Ubico's reign was tempered by a sense of security. Infamous for his tough stance on crime, Ubico's harsh but transparent rule afforded *indígenas* new opportunities to contest their servitude even as it served the agricultural export economy.[59]

Figure 1.4. Indigenous military volunteers in the *plaza central* of San Martín Jilotepeque, ca. 1940. Image courtesy of Colección Fototeca Guatemala, CIRMA (Centro de Investigaciones Regionales de Mesoamérica).

Ironically, making Guatemala safer facilitated some crime. Ixsimïl explained:

> My grandparents prepared *aguardiente* only at night. They did not do it in the town or houses. They did it in the ravine. It was the same when I was preparing [it]; I would only bring it at night. At the same time, if you wanted to sell, it was always at night. They did everything at night. . . . Very late my grandfather would come down to town with vessels of *guaro* [moonshine]. He was not afraid during that time to walk at night . . . only that it was so late and he had to carry it on his back.[60]

Hiding under the cover of night, bootleggers took advantage of the very conditions that resulted from Ubico's campaign against crime.

Instead of simply approaching *indígenas* as a problem, Ubico—unlike his predecessors—sought to integrate Mayas and even celebrate their culture and customs when it served his interests, particularly for tourism.[61] Aware of the exploitive nature of his regime, many Mayas nonetheless embraced these opportunities; they too sought to balance tradition and modernization, as the images of the San Martín indigenous authorities (figure 1.3) and conscripts (figure 1.4) wearing their traditional clothing suggest.[62]

Partly because Ubico did not pit tradition against modernity or capitalism, most Kaqchikel agreed with his government's rhetoric, if not always its practice, of state building.[63] The formula for nation building as articulated by a *Gaceta* journalist in 1935 mirrored Kaqchikel raconteurs' ideas: "The life of order, respect for the law and honorable and meritorious disciplines is the most adequate [means] to the material and moral progress of the Nation."[64] These points of agreement notwithstanding, Kaqchikel struggled to be counted among people who mattered in a nation whose colonial vestiges largely discounted *indígenas*.

Racial Constructs

Although indigenous people comprised a majority of the population, elite Creoles and ladinos controlled most political and material resources in Guatemala. A sense of indigenous ethnicity is elusive in the documents, but by identifying or being identified as *indígena*, *natural*, *nativo*, *indio*, or *india*, Maya litigants acknowledged a mutual condition and thus a shared ethnic position, if not identity, in Guatemala.[65] In turn, the definition of "ladino" shifted during the colonial and early national eras but came to signify "non-indigenous" by the late nineteenth and early twentieth centuries.[66] Recent scholarship has corrected the ladino-Maya binary that has dominated much of the literature on Guatemala. Ethnographic, anthropological, and historical studies dating to the 1920s offer a rich sense of the diversity of indigenous people in Guatemala, while only recently have scholars begun to explore the heterogeneity of ladinos, Creoles, and other non-indigenous Guatemalans.[67] Ladinos who learned Kaqchikel and appear in the criminal record as interpreters offer but one tantalizing hint of the ways local ladinos acculturated to indigenous norms. Never fixed, ethnic identities depended on the circumstances and individuals involved.[68]

People who shared such ascribed terms as *indígena* or *ladino* did not necessarily constitute a united group. Whether they were ladino or *indígena*, for example, the rural poor often had more in common with each other than either group did with its ethnic elite counterpart in urban areas. As it did with gender and class, the legal system both strengthened and provided a means to question racial distinctions.

In a country desperately striving to count itself among the world's modern nations by using such tools of modernization as science and positivism to address its self-proclaimed "Indian problem," early twentieth-century Guatemala was bent on cementing racial and social hierarchies. Ignoring the diversity of more than twenty linguistic and ethnic groups and expand-

ing on previous associations of indigenous people with indolence and de-
generacy, turn-of-the-century intellectuals and leaders increasingly defined
indios as obstacles to Guatemala's social order and material progress.[69]

Stereotypes about *indígenas* and the attempts they made to both play
upon and dispel the stereotypes permeate the judicial record. The thirty-
four-year-old ladino farmer *don* Manuel Leonardo's accusation of slander
against two illiterate indigenous *jornaleros*, Guadalupe Chonay and Reyes
Coroy, offers an example of how the multiple manifestations of racial discourse were influenced by class. As a literate landowner who enjoyed the
honorific title *don*, Leonardo likely counted himself among a small elite class
in Balanya. Without land or an education, Chonay and Coroy were part of
Balanya's much larger contingent of poor and working-class residents.

In his June 14, 1913, petition to the Balanya mayor, Solomón M. Arro-
yaz, Leonardo claimed that since "*indígenas* . . . believe what you tell them,"
Chonay and Coroy were "just instruments of certain individuals."[70] Three
days later, on June 17, the mayor summoned them to municipal court. Suggesting that Leonardo's latter assertion had some merit, Chonay and Coroy
testified that Abraham Luna had warned them that Leonardo was usurp-
ing their lands. Chonay claimed "there was no offense in what Luna had
told him," but Leonardo insisted a rumor of this nature threatened his life
because *indígenas'* simple nature made them dangerous. As the aforementioned San Martín land dispute demonstrates, *indígenas* did not take encroachments on their communal lands lightly. Contemporary ethnographies also capture the critical and often contested role of land in highland
communities. In addition to poisoning filial and sibling relations, land tenure was a source of tensions among *indígenas*, ladinos, and authorities.[71]

Convinced justice would not be served because Abraham Luna (who had
fled) was a "close friend and dear acquaintance of the [municipal] Secretary
who records the proceedings," Leonardo appealed directly to the department judge on June 18. In an indication that he sensed the urban judge was
unfamiliar with rural relations, he said: "A statement of this type in a town
of innocent and uncultured *indígenas* such as this one could be the cause of
an attempt on my life, because as the saying goes, they defend their own."
Later that same day and fearful that "tomorrow I will awake murdered by
the *indios*," Leonardo penned another letter to the department judge after
he learned the Balanya *alcalde* had dismissed the complaint citing a lack of
evidence.[72]

Abraham Luna, too, appealed directly to the department judge. He explained in his June 17 petition that the mayor tried to jail him, "but hap-
pily I managed to escape, so that I could come and seek justice from your
honorable court." After insisting the mayor had "abused his authority" and

Leonardo was "seeking to cause me harm," Luna explained (and Leonardo confirmed) that Leonardo's brother, who was an engineer, had come to survey "useless and excess lands." Playing upon assumptions of *indígenas'* ignorance, Luna claimed that he explained this to Chonay and Coroy, "but since the *indígenas* do not understand what is said to them, they thought that [Luna] had said that Leonardo was claiming their lands."[73]

Undoubtedly aware of such stereotypes, Chonay and Coroy pointed out in municipal court that they spoke and understood Spanish well. Although his illiteracy suggested he did not enjoy the same privileged status as Leonardo, a ladino and an *agricultor*, the thirty-year-old Luna enjoyed racial and class advantages over Chonay and Coroy. Variations on a theme, Leonardo's claim that *indígenas* were gullible and Luna's claim that they could not understand Spanish speak to the way ladino litigants deployed racist discourse about ignorant *indios* to bolster their narratives.

After three days of incarceration, Chonay and Coroy dictated their own letter to the department judge, which also played upon assumptions of indigenous ignorance. "According to what we have been able to understand," they began, "we gather that we are under proceedings due to Luna's complaint and accusation, but the facts of the complaint . . . are unknown [to us]." Although they introduced themselves humbly, they insisted that their ignorance regarding the charges was not the result of an intellectual deficit but rather a lack of information and proceedings that were "unfair and illegal." Instead of allowing Leonardo and Luna to define them, Chonay and Coroy explained, "Your Honor, we are not delinquents; this remains on our conscience; we are honorable, peaceful, humble, hardworking men." Before asking the judge to free them, they cited a specific law and precedents that justified their release. Although the scribe may have suggested these references, the composition and strategic nature of their narrative stood in stark contrast to Leonardo's assertion that "*indígenas* . . . know nothing of the law."[74] Even when inaccurate, imaginations about race were informed by interracial exchanges, many of which took place in courtrooms between indigenous and ladino litigants and with predominantly ladino officials and lawyers.

Aware of Leonardo's and Luna's letters to the department judge, the Balanya mayor sent his own note assuring the judge the municipal investigation had been carried out impartially. Unconvinced, the judge ordered the mayor to send him the proceedings. Two days later, the mayor obliged and remanded Chonay and Coroy to him. By the time the court record arrived on June 21, the department judge had already received Chonay's and Coroy's petition.

Perhaps sensing that Chonay and Coroy were caught up in a feud between Leonardo and Luna, the department judge ordered their immediate release and summoned Luna to appear before the court. The judge also fined the Balanya mayor 25 pesos for arbitrarily imprisoning Chonay and Coroy, warning him that another abuse of his authority would result in legal action. As we will see, such tension between judicial authorities was not uncommon; state agents were not all of a piece. By the end of the month, the mayor had paid the fine and Luna had testified in department court, though it did not alter the judge's ruling.

With its multiple venues, litigants, and judicial authorities, this case provides an example of the often complex judicial process by which litigation initiated at the local level wound its way through municipal and department courts. Although Leonardo initiated legal proceedings in municipal court, he did not wait for that body to rule to initiate proceedings in department court. Convinced the mayor was either corrupt or incompetent, Luna skipped the municipal level altogether and appealed directly to the department judge. Seeing no crime in their actions, Chonay and Coroy likewise appealed directly to the department judge. Underscoring the extent to which petitioners enlisted the judicial system on their behalf, the subordinate and superior court were effectively adjudicating simultaneously instead of hierarchically. On one level the system worked as designed, with the mayor forwarding his proceedings to the department judge for a final ruling. On another level, the individuals involved ignored this protocol and appealed to the authorities they thought were most likely to assist them. By entertaining their petitions, the department judge undercut the municipal court, but he also buttressed the legal system more broadly by nurturing a sense among individuals that the state offered multiple recourses for addressing their concerns.

Cases like this also shed light on the ways ladino and indigenous litigants deployed racial stereotypes and the efficacy of such strategies. Unlike courts in contemporary Mexico City where prejudice often determined guilt,[75] in Guatemalan highland courts it was not unusual for indigenous litigants like Chonay and Coroy to enjoy success, if not justice, against ladino plaintiffs who accused them of crimes. In light of Guatemala's history of racism, the judicial system was often fairer than scholars might have expected.

By claiming certain aspects of ladino and state discourse, *indígenas* could elevate their own positions within social hierarchies. Some *indígenas* injected themselves into the national collective by identifying as *guatemaltecos* and *guatemaltecas* when they appeared before municipal and department courts. Despite being denied the right to vote, *indígenas* approached the construction of national identity and citizenship as a negotiated process. When he wrote directly to Estrada Cabrera in 1918, for example, Germán Medina identified himself as a member of the "indigenous race and citizen of the nation."[76] Although colonial- and national-era petitions reveal the way savvy indigenous progenitors learned to say what their superiors and authorities wanted to hear, Medina was not simply deploying Liberal rhetoric; like his nineteenth-century counterparts from Aguas Calientes, he seamlessly claimed what for many elites and officials were mutually exclusive identities: indigeneity and citizenship.

Although few engaged in discourses of rights, many *indígenas* claimed citizenship or national belonging to access such state resources and recourse as the courts and laws. As Florencia Mallon argues in her seminal work *Peasant and Nation*, to understand the consolidation of nation-states, scholars must take peasants' alternative nationalisms seriously. In a nation where, in the words of historian Arturo Taracena Arriola, "the Guatemalan was (and continues to be for many) the ladino,"[77] Mayas who identified themselves as *guatemaltecos* or *guatemaltecas* and as *indígenas* were conveying alternative nationalisms. Documentary evidence and Kaqchikel oral histories suggest that Guatemalan novelist and journalist Carlos Wyld Ospina's radical departure from the national narrative in 1936 was an accurate reflection of some indigenous imaginings. He considered "the *indio* more nationalist than the Ladino."[78] Even if *indígenas* only articulated this national identity during times of crisis or need, their alacrity in employing it to further their own goals intimates an awareness of the uses to which national belonging, if not citizenship, could be put. Claiming their stake in the nation had become part of their modus operandi.

On the other hand, for many *indígenas* the association between citizenship and communal or forced labor discouraged explicitly identifying as *guatemaltecos/as*. When he arrested the nineteen-year-old, illiterate, indigenous *jornalero* Vicente Xalin on April 8, 1935, for insulting him and refusing to complete his *trabajos de vialidad* (forced labor), the San Martín official Chicón explained that "instead of complying as a citizen, he [Xalin] has disobeyed [these requests] repeatedly and scorned the Authority [of the state]."[79] With good reason, Xalin and many other *indígenas* sought to distance themselves from citizenship and the obligations that accompanied it.

A number of sophisticated studies have pointed to the way multiple actors constructed citizenship differently in Latin America.[80] Yet often these scholars largely omit the role of popular legal strategies in shaping the nation-state and legal systems.

Indigenous litigants attempted to expand the notions and concepts surrounding race and indigeneity by injecting esteem into indigenous identities. For *indígenas*, demanding a sense of respect in courtrooms developed over time. Although indigenous litigants had been presenting themselves as *guatemaltecos/as* since the turn of the twentieth century, not until the 1930s did they claim such titles generally reserved for ladinos as *señora*. On April 10, 1935, the indigenous *jornalero* José Aceituj referred to his "enemy" Andrea Chali as *señora* immediately after the San Martín municipal court notary identified her as an *indígena*.[81] Although *indígena* was not a pejorative term, neither did it hold the same status as *señora* in the ladino system. In light of one Guatemalan ethnographer's observations in the 1940s that ladinos never "use *señor* or *señora* when addressing an Indian, even in official situations in the town hall," these linguistic subtleties are significant.[82]

By subtly suggesting terms of respect for their indigenous counterparts instead of confronting ladinos directly for disparaging them, indigenous litigants enjoyed some success. A little more than a week after Aceituj's use of *señora*, the San Martín notary identified two indigenous women as *señora* Dolores Sutuj and *señora* Luisa Can.[83] Two days after that, he penned "Señora Guadelupe Atz" and "Señor Félix Balan."[84] Using the archival record to determine how much of this language was intentional or even readily apparent to the parties involved is difficult, but ladinos and *indígenas* alike were keenly aware of the derogatory nature of such terms as *indio* and *indita* and the respect afforded such titles as *don* and *doña*. As the plethora of insult cases that came before the courts attests, highland Guatemalans had a sharp appreciation for the weight of words. When appearing before the court, indigenous litigants often sought to advance their agendas beyond the cases at hand.

Criminal Culture

Indigenous litigants who sought to subtly elevate the status of *indígenas* were struggling against a long history of denigration. Elite discourse of the late nineteenth and early twentieth centuries characterized indigenous people as lazy, drunken wards of the state; many intellectuals portrayed *indígenas* as degenerate because of their adherence to their ancestral languages, customs, and traditions.[85] As in Peru, cultural descriptions became part of criminal profiles in Guatemala as the National Police embraced positivist criminology in the early 1930s and increasingly associated indigenous culture with crime. Just as positivist criminology altered the relationship between the state and the working class in Mexico, Argentina, Peru, and elsewhere by redefining their rights and criminalizing their everyday practices, a similar process altered the relationships between indigenous people and authorities in Guatemala.[86] Akin to Foucault's analysis of how French penal reformers distinguished between delinquents and offenders to mark the former as dangerous criminals by their nature, authorities did not approach indigenous transgressions as criminal acts but rather attributed these acts to indigenous criminality.[87]

By defining as crimes what its officials knew to be everyday cultural practices, the Guatemalan state, like its counterparts in Mexico and elsewhere in Latin America, first illegitimatized and then criminalized activities that departed from what it considered modern.[88] Although efforts to turn delinquents into disciplined workers was most evident in campaigns against vagrants, the police used positivist criminology to extend their reach into other areas of modernization such as public health and trade to justify interventions aimed at controlling the lives of working-class, poor, and indigenous people. Guatemalan authorities were among the many Latin Americans who "embraced science as a form of progressive knowledge . . . and as a means of establishing a new form of cultural power," historian Nancy Stepan has pointed out.[89] In thinly veiled descriptions of indigenous customs, traditions, and livelihoods, the police identified midwives, *buhoneros* (long-distance or ambulatory merchants), and market vendors as suspects. As Foucault argues, to broaden the margins of criminality the state associated illegality with the lower strata's conditions of existence.[90]

The Guatemalan state's attempt to impose marketplace reforms in the early twentieth century offers an example of this process. When authorities tried to move indigenous vendors from public plazas to newly constructed market buildings, they betrayed an effort to claim public spaces for non-Mayas. In addition to suggesting that indigenous people were not culturally prepared to use urban space, authorities dismissed indigenous vendors' age-old practice of haggling as *acaparamiento*, that is, hoarding or stockpiling. According to the National Police, *acaparamiento* constituted "grave danger [*perjuicio*] for the whole population, but in particular for poor people, [who are] the majority."[91] By defending their long-standing locations and methods, *indígenas* rejected these aspects of the state's modernization program. As one of the many "unfinished conversations," (to borrow Paul Sullivan's term, between *indígenas* and authorities, the police were as convinced that certain traditional market practices jeopardized the lives of the poor as indigenous vendors were that certain state interventions undermined their ability to survive.[92]

Authorities similarly scrutinized ambulatory merchants. In 1928 the di-

Figure 1.5. *Buhoneros* arriving in the *plaza central* of Antigua, 1875. Photograph by Eadweard Muybridge. Image courtesy of Boston Athenaeum.

rector of the National Police, Daniel Hernández, said his institution had "moral reason to doubt the honesty and good customs" of *buhoneros*, whose goods were "almost always of the worst quality and of excessive cost."[93] Concerned that these "extortionists" were circulating in "our *pueblos*"—figure 1.5 shows *buhoneros* arriving at the very heart of such ladino and Creole urban centers as Antigua—Hernández launched a campaign against the livelihoods of many *indígenas*. In an indication that economic interventions were as much about worldviews and control as the law or market, authorities persecuted trades that Mayas considered honorable.[94] Authorities' campaigns against indigenous vendors and *buhoneros* were intended to establish national norms in opposition to Maya identities and practices.

In contrast to perceptions of urban order, rural Guatemala was associated with unrest and crime, which in turn reinforced assumptions about the relationship between race and crime. The very possibility of escape that the hinterlands promised came to establish its criminality. "The *fincas*, isolated communities, and mountainous places [provided] safe refuge to evade justice," noted director of the National Police Roderico Anzueto (figure 1.6) in 1932.[95] By pointing to such external factors as the environment in explaining crime, the police embraced aspects of criminal sociology.[96] "The particular conditions of the Guatemalan environment in the vast rural portions and even in inhabited [ones] where the indigenous element predominates . . . have come to constitute the urgent need for police action," according to

Anzueto.[97] To criminalize *indígenas*, the police crafted a unique combination of social and cultural determinism. Compelling some rural residents to turn to such livelihoods as bootlegging, poverty also contributed to rural Guatemala's image of criminality. Unlike Maya defendants or criminal sociologists in neighboring Mexico, however, Guatemalan authorities seldom identified penury as a contributor to crime.[98]

As authorities established the connection between race and place, the latter served to identify the former, thereby allowing them to critique indigenous practices, knowledge, and customs without referring to ethnicity. In 1937 National Police director David H. Ordóñez underscored the campaign against *curanderismo* (shamanism) and witchcraft by asserting that "superstition . . . principally occurs in the least civilized regions."[99] Borrowing a trope most famously espoused by nineteenth-century Argentinean Domingo Sarmiento, Ordóñez associated rural areas and their inhabitants with barbarism.[100] The association of *indios* with alcoholism and crime also facilitated the connection between race and place without explicitly mentioning the former. The following year Ordóñez claimed that "everyone knew"

Figure 1.6. "The General Director of the National Police, Brigadier C. Roderico Anzueto, in His Office." *La Gaceta*, June 30, 1936. Image courtesy of Hemeroteca Nacional de Guatemala.

Patzicía, departamento de Chimaltenango

Chorros de blancas sonrisas e impolutas simpatías en rostros de mujeres nativas

Ofreciendo la vendimia comercial en el típico cesto de confección primitiva y la vendimia de la gracia autóctona en un original ritmo confundido en rosas de atracción y de sonrisa, estas dos vigorosas mujeres del trópico guatemalteco encarnan todo un poema de trabajo, espontaneidad y pujanza.

El traje simbólico de la raza, con sus deleitantes colores hurtados al iris, complementa, en un complicado arrebato de luz, el hechizo hecho nota que escapa de los labios de las dulces aborígenes de chachal sonoro y güipil luminoso.

⁃ ⁃ ⁃

LA GACETA
REVISTA DE POLICÍA Y VARIEDADES

Guatemala, 16 de agosto de 1942

TOMO XX   AÑO XXII   NÚMERO 31

Figure 1.7. "Abundance of white smiles and pure charm on the faces of native women." *La Gaceta*, August 16, 1942. Image courtesy of Hemeroteca Nacional de Guatemala.

the most "sordid" cantinas and alcoholics could be found "principally in the neighborhoods isolated from the city."[101] Two years later he explained that it "has been necessary to persecute contraband and fraud in the most remote places of the country . . . where the recidivism of *clandestinismo* [moonshining] has been tenacious."[102] By associating certain behaviors or lack thereof with rural areas, authorities used place as a marker of race and crime.

By negating "Indianness" without explicitly referring to *indígenas*, authorities could introduce race in benevolent, if paternalistic, ways. The year after Hernández launched his campaign against *buhoneros*, his successor, Herlindo Solórzano recognized that there were "honorable exceptions" among them, "above all in the indigenous race."[103] Even as elites were using a discourse of modernization to scrutinize if not undermine indigenous livelihoods, at times paternalistic portrayals of race painted *indígenas* in a more sympathetic light. Some of these "honorable exceptions" appeared on the front pages of *La Gaceta*. Even during the campaign against indigenous merchants, the National Police celebrated them in photos and homages. The editor's description of the Patzicía vendors with their "white smiles and pure charm" on the August 16, 1942, cover of *La Gaceta* (figure 1.7) contrasted sharply with contemporary authorities' conceptions of indigenous female vendors as criminals. In Guatemala the reinvention of race and its association with crime was neither a linear nor uncontested process.

The chapters that follow explore how laws, crimes, and courtrooms helped to shape national development by bringing disparate parties together in exchanges that ranged from confrontational to cooperative. As biased and power-laden as it was, the legal system was one of the few institutions in which people and representatives of the state could learn about each other's goals, challenges, and worldviews in situations whose tangible outcomes compelled the parties to listen carefully. Even if they did not speak directly to each other, the parties had the opportunity to articulate their interests in ways that influenced judgments. By examining the litigation that resulted from the state's and Maya moonshiners' competing economies of alcohol production, the next chapter demonstrates how decisions, actions, and subsequent attempts to justify them were grounded more firmly in practical considerations than in ideal notions of justice. Rhetoric about crime, law, culture, and other social constructions often rang hollow in the face of people's daily lives and the state's goals.

CHAPTER 2

"Rough and Thorny Terrain": Moonshine, Gender, and Ethnicity

On December 3, 1932, authorities in Quetzaltenango discovered a clandestine still that was producing 250 bottles of *aguardiente* a day in the Administración de Rentas (Treasury Administration) building. Remarkably, this was not the first such offense. Perhaps surmising that such production was best disguised in the entrails of the very institution that was most concerned with stamping it out, other bootleggers had set up shop there, too. Their instincts may have been right; this latest distillery remained hidden in plain sight for more than a month before authorities found "a great quantity" of fermenting sugar "destined for distillation."[1]

In an effort to gloss over this scandal, less than a week after the director of Quetzaltenango's Administración de Rentas confirmed rumors of the operation, his office along with the Jefatura Política (Governor's Office) reported that the war against *clandestinismo* was going well: "The Treasury Police with the support of the department's military authorities make daily raids into different places in the region, inspecting with prudence and circumspection the houses that have had or have stills. . . . The telegrams that the press publishes daily about the capture [of moonshiners] in Quetzaltenango best demonstrate the actions of the Treasury Police and Jefatura Política."[2] Yet the telegram that reported the Treasury building distillery did just the opposite. If the Treasury Police did not even know what was going on in their own back storeroom, authorities were not likely to be able to curtail the moonshine trade throughout the countryside.

During the first half of the twentieth century, proceeds from alcohol sales filled government coffers, fueled local economies, and fortified family livelihoods. Despite national rhetoric decrying excessive alcohol production and consumption and Maya rhetoric lamenting the deleterious effects of alcoholism, neither the state nor local residents had the political will to eradicate *aguardiente clandestino*. While contemporary newspapers and monographs reveal the perspectives of Creole and ladino elites and oral histories provide a window onto Maya perceptions, municipal and departmental courtrooms were where state policies, reformist rhetoric, and lower-class realities clashed. Compelled to disguise their criticism of authorities, defendants nevertheless used these forums to call attention to the government's failings and society's injustices. Although they did not necessarily consider themselves guilty by their own definitions of crime, neither did they claim innocence. Since legal constructs deemed their actions criminal, indigenous moonshiners shifted the debate outside the confines of the law to consider the broader injustices of ethnic, gender, and class discrimination.

By pointing out that *aguardiente* was produced clandestinely to escape penury, some defendants let judicial officials, notaries, and police know that the state's failure to provide the conditions for subaltern survival, let alone success, was a greater offense than selling moonshine to feed one's family. Since the alcohol tax was regressive, it affected the poor more than other groups and therefore encouraged them to look for ways to circumvent it. As long as they remained mired in poverty and victims of exploitation, poor *indígenas* had no choice but to break the law to support and entertain themselves. Poor indigenous defendants knew ladino and Creole elites established alcohol laws to impose their moralistic musings and enrich themselves. Perhaps more than any other area of the judicial record, *defraudación al Fisco en el ramo de licores* (defrauding the Treasury of alcohol revenue) litigation pointed to how people's socioeconomic positions affected their interpretations of laws and crime.

Defendants who crafted compelling narratives convinced judges to reduce their sentences. Such negotiations are but one manifestation of the ways state representatives acquiesced to subaltern arguments to maintain order and a semblance of control. As was true during the Porfirio Díaz dictatorship in Mexico (1876–1911), the judicial system helped the Estrada Cabrera and Ubico dictatorships contain conflict precisely when their legitimacy was most seriously questioned.[3] Like the cat-and-mouse game played by authorities who enforced the state's liquor laws and *clandestinistas* (moonshiners) who tried to make profits extralegally, the exchanges in court between judges and *clandestinistas* demonstrate how state domination and subaltern resistance acted upon and limited each other. Whether they were in remote mountains or urban centers, *clandestinistas'* operations were evidence that the state and its authorities never dictated or controlled people entirely. In the courtroom, defendants exploited the state's need to maintain order by ensuring that rulings took into account the unique circumstances and privations that either led people to crime or necessitated their early release. The asymmetrical venues, conditions, and access to resources notwithstanding, subalterns were seldom powerless.

Based on judicial records, *aguardiente* was an equal-opportunity commodity and vice; neither ladinos nor *indígenas*, males nor females were excluded from the production, sale, or consumption of alcohol in Guatemala. Like their counterparts in other areas of Latin America (and the world), Guatemalan women played a prominent role in the alcohol economy, while the extent of their involvement varied depending on the region and time.[4] Of the 279 cases of bootlegging adjudicated in Chimaltenango from 1900 to 1925, nearly half of those tried (47 percent) were females (table 2.1). During the Ubico dictatorship of the 1930s and early 1940s, however, women comprised only 21 percent of those arrested by the National Police for moonshining (table 2.2). Although the distinct nature of these statistics (department versus national data) precludes drawing comparisons, authorities' gendered perceptions of women and criminals during the Ubico period blinded them to some women's extralegal operations. Even as they contributed to women's subordination, notions about motherhood and domesticity could serve women.

Legal or not, the sale and production of alcohol were among the few ways women could generate modest incomes without upsetting gender norms. As they operated their businesses in the domestic sphere of their homes, they also adhered to their traditional roles as purveyors of food and drink and as petty-commodity producers and vendors.[5] Although they risked losing their livelihoods, entrepreneurs who avoided the licensing fees and taxes—mainly because they could not afford them—could offer drinks at lower prices than licensed taverns. This savings appealed to lower-class drinkers who may not have been able to afford or willing to pay the sanctioned prices.[6] When the state cracked down on poor *clandestinistas*, it was responding to class and often gender and ethnic biases. *Clandestinistas* appearing in court often recast their incrimination into terms that were relevant to their lives by emphasizing their poverty and, in the case of women, their motherhood and domesticity.

This litigation consumed an inordinate amount of the Chimaltenango department court's time during the first few years of Estrada Cabrera's reign and continued to occupy that court throughout his rule. I selected a sample of twenty-six court cases to study closely (appendix 5). Nineteen women and ten men were defendants in these cases. Determining ethnicity was more difficult, five indigenous men, three indigenous women, and one ladina stated their identity for the scribe. Although ethnic identities of ten defendants remained obscure even after a close reading of each case, based

Table 2.1. Alcohol production and sale trials, Chimaltenango, 1900–1925, by suspect ethnicity and gender

Year	Number of cases	Ladino			Indígena			All	
		Male	Female	Total	Male	Female	Total	Male	Female
1900	70	24	33	57	10	3	13	34	36
1901	49	23	21	44	3	2	5	26	23
1902	32	9	17	26	4	2	6	13	19
1903	25	8	16	24	0	1	1	8	17
1904	15	7	4	11	2	2	4	9	6
1905	0	0	0	0	0	0	0	0	0
1906	6	0	5	5	1	0	1	1	5
1907	11	4	2	6	2	3	5	6	5
1908	2	0	1	1	1	0	1	1	1
1909	5	2	0	2	1	2	3	3	2
1910	1	1	0	1	0	0	0	1	0
1911	9	4	4	8	1	0	1	5	4
1912	5	2	1	3	0	1	1	2	2
1913	4	2	1	3	1	0	1	3	1
1914	1	1	0	1	0	0	0	1	0
1915	5	3	2	5	0	0	0	3	2
1916	5	1	2	3	1	0	1	2	2
1917	10	6	3	9	1	0	1	7	3
1918	11	8	1	9	1	1	2	9	2
1919	3	2	0	2	1	0	1	3	0
1920–23*	4	2	0	2	2	0	2	4	0
1923–25*	6	4	1	5	1	0	1	5	1
Total	279	113	114	227	33	17	50	146	131

Source: AGCA, *índice* 116, Chimaltenango department court, 1900–1925.
*The Chimaltenango crime index grouped data for the years 1920–1923 and 1923–1925.
Note: Ladinos are almost assuredly overcounted in this table. Except for individual cases that I examined and in which I could determine litigants' ethnicity, my research assistant Chriss Sutherland and I used defendants' surnames from AGCA *índice* 116 to surmise ethnicity. While many indigenous surnames stand out as distinctly Maya, many *indígenas* who identified as such had Spanish surnames.

on surnames and testimonies I could determine that six indigenous men, four indigenous women, two ladinos, and nine ladinas were defendants in this sample. Of those tried, only five were absolved (three indigenous men, one ladina, and one woman of unknown ethnicity). Ten were never caught; one (a ladina) escaped from jail.

Since most bootlegging defendants were caught red-handed, the high

Table 2.2. Alcohol production and sale arrests, Guatemala, 1932–1944, by suspect ethnicity, gender, and literacy

Year	Number of arrests	Ladino			Indigena			Male	Female	Literate	Illiterate
		Male	Female	Total	Male	Female	Total				
1932	614	—	—	—	—	—	—	456	158	—	—
1933	493	—	—	388	—	—	105	471	22	—	—
1934	3,265	—	—	2,138	—	—	1,047	2,919	346	—	—
1935	2,759	—	—	1,316	—	—	1,443	2,268	491	1,255	1,504
1936	2,441	—	—	978	—	—	1,463	1,800	641	683	1,758
1937	1,878	—	—	694	—	—	1,184	1,374	504	412	1,466
1938	2,289	—	—	—	—	—	—	—	—	—	—
1939	1,843	473	262	735	770	338	1,108	1,243	600	564	1,279
1940	2,399	839	198	1,037	1,006	356	1,362	1,845	554	986	1,413
1941	2,019	499	192	691	1,059	269	1,328	1,558	451	597	1,422
1942	1,659	393	117	510	939	210	1,149	1,332	327	416	1,243
1943	1,124	250	28	278	120	614	734	891	233	269	855
1944	689	143	68	211	364	114	478	507	182	184	505
Total	23,472	2,597	865	8,976	4,258	1,901	11,401	16,664	4,509	5,366	11,445

Source: Policía Nacional, *Memorias* 1932–1944.
Note: A dash (—) indicates that no data were available.

conviction rate (fourteen of nineteen, or almost 74 percent of those brought to trial) is not surprising. (One case record ended without noting the judge's ruling.) Of the fourteen people convicted of defrauding the Treasury, nine were women (four *indígenas*, four ladinas, and one of indeterminate ethnicity). Remarkably, in almost all the convictions (thirteen of fourteen, or almost 93 percent), the judges reduced the sentences and/or let the perpetrators out on bail—an indication that defendants', particularly women's, narrative strategies were efficacious. Demonstrating their discretionary power, department judges listened closely to even the most marginalized Guatemalans and often conceded some aspects of what they requested. As much as the courts allowed the state to penetrate marginalized people's lives down to the local level, they also allowed indigenous and poor defendants to educate judicial authorities about their plights.

Although few Guatemalans might have perceived it as such, the alcohol economy contributed to nation formation by facilitating communication among disparate parties. In judiciously handling rural residents, department judges strengthened the state's authority in places where its influence was attenuated. Indigenous and female litigants who expressed their deprivations and at times gained concessions came to consider themselves *guatemaltecos* and *guatemaltecas*, even if they were not treated as citizens outside the courtroom.

Although initially processed at the municipal level, most cases of *defraudación al Fisco en el ramo de licores* were tried in the *juzgado de primera instancia*. As a result, municipal archives contain little evidence pertaining to bootlegging beyond defendants' names and a sense of the broad range of reactions to the Treasury Police. For instance, in contrast to the Patzicía husband who attacked police with a knife while resisting his wife's arrest for *clandestinismo* in 1937, two years earlier the *señorita* Jesús Chamalé ran so quickly from Filiberto Sunuc's home when she saw the Policía de Hacienda (Treasury Police) coming that she tripped on a rock and cut her hand with the bottle she was carrying. Despite what her panicked flight might suggest, the San Martín authorities found no evidence of *aguardiente clandestino* in Sunuc's home or Chamalé's bottle.[7] These examples and a few others notwithstanding, however much people reviled the Treasury Police, once caught most suspects went peacefully with the officers.

In Latin American historiography, a focus on alcohol's relationship to violence, uprisings, and revolts has often blinded scholars to the more mundane ways alcohol producers, vendors, and consumers interacted with each other and the state. Because its sale, production, and consumption were steady throughout the year, excepting spikes during fiestas, alcohol more than any other commodity—including coffee, which generally involved *indígenas* only during the harvest season—was at the center of relations among *indígenas*, ladinos, and authorities in the highlands. By compelling disparate groups to interact, alcohol was paramount to Guatemala's nation formation.

The Economics of Alcohol

Prior to the Spanish invasions, Mesoamerican peoples including Mayas consumed fermented alcoholic drinks in their rituals. For their part, Spaniards followed the Mediterranean tradition of drinking wine as part of their daily lives. To control and profit from such practices during the colonial era, the Spanish Crown established a monopoly on the sale and production of alcoholic beverages. Because colonial legislation outlawed the production of *aguardiente* by males, women came to dominate it.[8] Revenue from alcohol continued to factor into the independent nation's budget. During the Central American Federation (1823–1839), such proceeds helped to fund militias.

While Conservative officials looked to the alcohol monopoly system as a primary source of income and dedicated increasing resources to repressing the prohibited production of alcohol throughout the mid-nineteenth century,[9] governors, local officials, *cofrades* (members of a *cofradía*, or religious confraternity), *indígenas*, and ladinos circumvented the state's mandate. To regulate and profit from the alcohol economy, the state auctioned off monopoly licenses for specific population centers. Although the highest bidders would be the sole licensees in small towns, larger towns like Tecpán and department capitals like Chimaltenango might have two to four monopoly licenses.[10] Ultimately, though, dependence on alcohol revenue undermined the Conservative government. Widespread resentment against the *aguardiente* police and broad opposition to the Conservative government's alcohol monopolies, which favored elites, helped to bring down the regime in 1871.[11] Yet almost immediately after their victory in June 1871, Liberals broke the spirit of their promise to abolish alcohol monopolies by establishing *aguardiente* licensing regulations, fees, and taxes that ultimately turned most small producers and vendors into criminals.[12] Even had they learned from recent history, Liberals had little choice: they needed alcohol income to govern the country.

Since local economies depended on this cottage industry and local officials were complicit with it, many *clandestinistas* went unpunished. The Liberals failed to eradicate the *aguardiente clandestino* trade largely because it was both ubiquitous and elusive. Perhaps because the government's efforts seemed futile at times, private individuals and institutions such as landowners and haciendas took it upon themselves to suppress bootlegging.[13] Not until the early 1880s did the Liberal state enforce alcohol laws in earnest.[14]

Coffee crises like the one set off when Brazil's 1897 record harvests depressed international prices underscored the advantages of alcohol revenue. Since alcohol consumption was relatively inelastic, its revenue was spared the volatility of other commodity markets.

Dependent on alcohol revenue, which in 1899 and 1900 was the government's largest source of income, to help create and maintain the first Guatemalan police state, Estrada Cabrera maintained the system of liquor monopolies (*estancos*) and continued efforts to stamp out illegal stills and, to a lesser extent, unlicensed vendors.[15] True to his paternalistic rule, he also granted exceptions and pardons to some bootleggers to earn their loyalty.[16]

Like Estrada Cabrera's government, Ubico's regime was dependent on alcohol income. The state could count on 200,000 quetzales annually from taxes on the sale of hard liquor, including legally produced *aguardiente*.[17] Because bootlegging detracted from this source of national revenue, authorities during the Ubico era were ever on the lookout for producers and vendors of *aguardiente clandestino*.[18]

At times, locals proposed controlling alcohol revenue. Drawing attention to Sololá's chronically empty coffers that stifled public works projects, in 1937 one licensed alcohol vendor proposed that the municipality take over the regulatory process and offer the National Treasury 20 percent of all license fees and fifteen cents for every eighteen-liter *garrafón* (large vessel) of *aguardiente* sold. Although the *intendente* promised to bring it up with the *jefe político*, the silence on the issue thereafter in the municipal record suggests the proposal fell on deaf ears.[19]

If the National Police obsession with filling state coffers is any indication, Sololá's *intendente* was wise not to advance a proposal that might reduce the national government's profits. The National Police often framed their hunt for moonshine in economic terms. When the Sololá police confiscated three stills and arrested their owners in 1931, *La Gaceta* hailed it as "one of the great . . . accomplishments by the police against the delinquents that hurt [the government's] fiscal interests."[20] After boasting about decommissioning "the best and most productive" stills in Santiago Sacatepéquez later that same year, the police explained, "We are auguring a formidable advance in the department's revenue. . . . [B]y diminishing this fraud, the sanctioned distilleries necessarily will sell more liquor and greater will be the taxes paid by them."[21] Guatemalan intellectual J. Fernando Juárez Muñoz exclaimed in 1931, "Alcohol! Alcohol is the vice that stimulates the state" and "maintains a great part of the bureaucratic machine of Guatemala."[22]

Elusive Enforcement

By the 1930s the state increasingly used governors to convey the importance of this campaign. Some enticed local authorities by pointing out that reducing illegal alcohol production would enrich municipalities. In one such exhortation on the eve of Ubico's rule, Chimaltenango's *jefe político* reminded mayors in his jurisdiction of

> the obligation you have to impose the liquor law to persecute actively and without rest contraband and fraud against the Treasury. Remembering at the same time that the Municipality should interest itself in the disappearance of this fraud. The more *aguardiente* consumed from [official] depositories, the greater the income the Municipality will receive from the taxes. For each bottle sold . . . its tax is evidence of the investment in works of progress and utility.[23]

Although such enticements did not ring hollow—the San Martín *alcalde* learned on October 31, 1931, that his municipality's account in the Banco Central had surpassed 2,000 quetzales thanks to *aguardiente* funds—plying local officials with promises of improved infrastructure and other public works highlighted the state's contradictory, if not hypocritical, stance.[24] While the Chimaltenango governor's memorandum explicitly encouraged authorities to crack down on bootleggers, it also implicitly encouraged leniency with drunks; after all, each bottle they purchased contributed to national income and thus progress. From this perspective, drunks were crucial to national development despite their reputations for disrupting public order. Three years after the Chimaltenango *jefe político*'s missive, his counterpart from Jalapa notified local leaders in his department that all government employees should "cooperate in the persecution of *aguardiente clandestino*."[25]

Working with local authorities both strengthened and weakened the national campaign against *aguardiente clandestino*. Given the diversity of players who constituted the state, it seldom presented a united front. Often local officials' cooperation was forthcoming. Such was the case in 1902 when two *indígenas* accompanied the Comalapa *regidor* (alderman) to arrest the fifty-eight-year-old, illiterate *indígena* Francisco Calel for bootlegging. Even during the more relaxed political climate of the 1920s, some local authorities vigorously pursued drunks and bootleggers. "In order to comply with the obligations that the laws impose," Comalapa's municipal officers charged "the Municipality with tirelessly pursuing inebriation, vagrancy, the movement of illegal arms, gambling, [and] fiscal fraud."[26] Fiscal fraud was largely the result of the *aguardiente clandestino* trade.

Not all municipal authorities were as accommodating as those in Comalapa, however. Frustrated by a pattern of noncompliance, the Chimaltenango governor reminded his mayors on September 10, 1926, that he needed monthly updates from each municipality regarding the status of and revenue generated by alcohol and tobacco licenses. If he did not have this information by the end of the month, he threatened to shut down any alcohol vendors in the delinquent jurisdictions.[27] Among the wayward authorities was San Martín's *alcalde*. Four days later, he added his own plea for compliance to the governor's letter and circulated it to the alcohol license holders in his jurisdiction.[28] Like so many ambiguous responses to superiors' mandates in highland Guatemala, San Martín's *alcalde* neither refused the request nor completed the task himself. In effect, he left compliance to the license holders themselves.

In another challenge to the state's efforts to maximize its alcohol revenue, often the very local officials charged with stamping out the extralegal alcohol economy were profiting from it. In Tecpán, a "famous great still" nicknamed "La Municipalidad" offers an example of how such complicity worked. As the nickname suggests, the owners were members of Tecpán's town council. In fact, the still was on the *alcalde*'s property. Although this operation was well known throughout Chimaltenango, the owners were so adept at shielding it from their superiors that ministry officials and the police believed its existence to be a rumor. When police finally discovered it in May 1931 they considered the operation to be "one of the largest that to this day has been decommissioned."[29] La Municipalidad still was but one manifestation of the ways local officials pursued their own interests in defiance of national policies and power structures.

Without the collusion of laconic locals, Tecpán's municipal authorities could not have duped their superiors. That national authorities believed the story to be a rumor underscores just how large the chasm between local and official realities could be. Remaining silent in the face of hegemonic inquiry and ignorance is akin to what James Scott calls "hidden transcripts" when marginalized populations build oppositional cultures without overtly confronting or challenging authorities.[30] By withholding information, locals could maintain a degree of autonomy. Knowledge was power, and national authorities did not have a monopoly on either.

In an attempt to curb the tendencies of complicitous authorities, Estrada Cabrera appointed outsiders to the various police and military forces charged with assisting the Ministerio de Hacienda (Treasury Ministry) in its campaign against *aguardiente clandestino*.[31] During his dictatorship, the *comandantes* del Resguardo de Hacienda (Treasury Police commanders) in Chimaltenango tended to be from other departments and linguistic regions. Because they did not speak Kaqchikel or know the area or local population well, *comandantes* like Valentino Gramajo, who moved from the K'iche'- and Mam-speaking area of Quetzaltenango to patrol the Kaqchikel town of San Martín, were dependent on their assistants—*indígenas* and ladinos— and the local population to guide their searches.[32]

Ubico, too, employed a strategy of bringing in outsiders to reduce corruption. The *Diario de Centro América* newspaper praised his finance minister for replacing personnel in charge of combating *clandestinismo* with "honorable and capable" men who improved the fiscal interests of "our country."[33] Armed and organized, the Treasury Police could be an intimidating force, as photographs of them in *La Gaceta* were meant to suggest (figure 2.1).

Whether these changes reduced corruption is difficult to discern, but regional officials' dependence on locals created tensions. After deserting the Resguardo de Hacienda in 1911, Froilán Ajsivinac was imprisoned for two weeks before his crime was even processed.[34] Some indigenous men took less confrontational approaches. In a typical scenario, the assistant Julián Catú frustrated officials who discovered a remote still in Comalapa in 1902 when he explained: "According to what you hear, the owner of the still is an individual from San Martín, but no one knows his name."[35] Based on Catú's recounting of community rumor, the only leads were based on geography and gender, and both may have been designed to derail rather than aid the search. Not surprisingly, officials never found the owner. As the still nickname "La Municipalidad" indicates, during the Ubico dictatorship locals continued to be reluctant to assist regional and national authorities.

Largely dependent on community members' tips to discover stills on private property such as homes or farms, authorities found it even more difficult to identify the owners of stills on communal land because locals often denied any knowledge of them. By setting up their operations there, moonshiners made it virtually impossible for authorities to trace stills back to them. When authorities found a still that could produce one hundred bottles a day in one of Comalapa's canyons in 1933, they admitted, "It was not possible to locate [the owner] because of the rough and thorny terrain."[36] The frequency with which authorities discovered stills on communal lands suggests another reason *indígenas* so fiercely defended their lands. Taking

TOTONICAPAN

Labor de la Policía de Hacienda en Beneficio de los Intereses de la Nación, Vulnerados por los Contrabandi...

(Fotos para "La Gaceta")

Decomisos llevados a cabo durante los primeros 20 días del mes de diciembre de 1932, por el Comandante de la Policía de Hacienda, ciudadano J. Dionisio Girón R., Sargento y demás personal a sus órdenes

Figure 2.1. Stills decommissioned by the Treasury Police in December 1932. The heading reads, "Totonicapan: Treasury Police's labor in benefit of the interests of the nation, vulnerable to contraband." *La Gaceta*, January 15, 1933. Image courtesy of The Latin American Library, Tulane University.

advantage of the central highlands' mountainous topography, sparsely populated rural areas, and *comandantes*' lack of familiarity with the region, many
moonshiners avoided detection. In a reflection of the geography of power,
one Kaqchikel word for *aguardiente*—*siwan ya'*, canyon water—suggests the
importance place played in helping moonshiners hide from authorities.[37]

Gender also influenced the location of stills. Men tended to set up their
operations in ravines, mountains, or forests far from the traveled routes of
authorities, while women often produced and sold moonshine in or around
their homes. Men's use of the most remote areas to establish their businesses speaks to a broader indigenous resistance to state incursions into
their daily lives. For ladino authorities, it provided a metaphor of barbarous
indios fleeing civilization.[38] In contrast, thanks to propriety and the notion
that women's activities in the home were beyond the purview of state officials, some *clandestinistas* remained hidden in plain sight. A Kaqchikel female elder explained one of the ways women avoided detection: "A long
time ago, over fifty years ago, women made *aguardiente* and then hid it in
the well with the water so when the *guardia* [soldiers] came they had no idea
and would not find it."[39] Although she was arrested in 1941, the *indígena*
María Baquiax (figure 2.2, bottom photograph) camouflaged her still in the
milpa (family cornfield) around her house.[40]

In an indication of how large a distillery could grow behind a gendered
veil, in 1933 a widow and three men operated a still that produced more
than six hundred bottles in the city of Quetzaltenango without arousing the
"least suspicion" of authorities.[41] Female *contrabandistas* (smugglers) similarly took advantage of gender assumptions to sell moonshine in such public
places as train stations and markets.[42]

Often it was drinkers themselves who broke these spells by leading authorities to vendors. The seventy-year-old *texel* (member of a religious sisterhood) Ixsub'äl recalled, "When a man asked for an *octavo* [an eighth of a
bottle], the ladina gave it to him. Then the soldiers arrived at her house to
take her to jail. Many days later the same thing happened to another ladina.
Later, women would not sell to drunks; they hid it from them and kicked
them out of their doorways so they would not cause problems."[43] By referring exclusively to them, Ixsub'äl emphasized the role of ladina vendors. Yet
while ladinas were more likely to run state-sanctioned operations, both indigenous and ladina women were arrested for selling *aguardiente clandestino*.
Unlike other areas of Guatemala where ladinos tended to dominate the alcohol trade,[44] in the predominantly Kaqchikel departments of Chimaltenango, Sololá, and Sacatepéquez indigenous vendors were not hard to find.
Ultimately as indigenous communities balanced a desire to keep outside in-
terference to a minimum with the need for government officials' assistance

Figure 2.2. Police with *clandestinistas* and their wares. Photograph 2 shows *clandestinista* Leonso Tohom (left). In photograph 3, the *clandestinista* María Baquiax (left) appears with a baby strapped to her back. *La Gaceta*, June 1, 1941. Image courtesy of Hemeroteca Nacional de Guatemala.

QUEZALTENANGO Y ZACAPA
LA POLICIA NACIONAL EN SU TESONERA LABOR
PRO LOS INTERESES DEL FISCO

(Fotos para "La Gaceta").

Defraudadores a la Hacienda Pública en el Ramo de Licores

Arriba.—(A la izquierda). Nº 1, Cleopatra de Egipto Mazariegos, mujer a la que le fué decomisada por la Policía Nacional, de servicio en la ciudad de Quezaltenango, una fábrica de aguardiente clandestina. El decomiso se efectuó en casa de Cleopatra de Egipto, ubicada en el cantón La Democracia, de la ciudad de referencia. Quedó consignada la reo y a disposición de Juez competente. Nº 2, agente Fidel Muñoz y Nº 3, agente Enrique Rodríguez, quienes laboraron para el buen éxito de la aprehensión.

Arriba.—(A la derecha del lector).—Zacapa.—La reo Rosa Morales, de 20 años de edad, soltera, originaria de Santa Cruz, de esta jurisdicción, hija natural de Cecilia Morales y de Francisco Aldana. Esta mujer, que había descollado como una de las

Figure 2.3. "Quetzaltenango y Zacapa: The National Police in Its Tenacious Work in the Interest of the Treasury." In the top left photograph, officers pose with *clandestinista* Cleopatra de Egipto Mazariegos. The top right photograph shows "one of the most audacious and dangerous *clandestinistas*," twenty-year-old *soltera* Rosa Morales. In the bottom photograph, agents stand behind three captured *clandestinistas*. *La Gaceta*, January 22, 1933. Image courtesy of The Latin American Library, Tulane University.

SOLOLA

Defraudación a la Hacienda Pública en los Ramos de Licores y Tabacos

LABOR DE LA POLICIA NACIONAL. GALERIA DE DELINCUENTES

VEINTISEIS CLANDESTINISTAS DE AMBOS SEXOS

Figure 2.4. "Twenty-six *clandestinistas* of both sexes." *La Gaceta*, January 8, 1933.
Image courtesy of The Latin American Library, Tulane University.

to maintain peace, resolve disputes, or seek revenge, community members more than authorities determined which bootleggers were caught.

To document their campaign and project an image of success, the National Police regularly used photographs like those of *clandestinistas* foiled by authorities in the January 22, 1933, issue of *La Gaceta* (figure 2.3). Susan Sontag and others have observed that photography facilitates an illusion of objectivity, possession, and control.[45] For police departments, photographing criminals and their wares projected an image of objectivity and efficacy. The mug shots of twenty-six *clandestinistas* in *La Gaceta* of January 8, 1933 (figure 2.4), celebrated the "labor of the National Police." Ironically, the same images police used to portray their successes often hinted at the futility of their campaign. Arresting twenty-six *clandestinistas* in one month in a single department, Sololá, betrayed how widespread the illicit alcohol industry was.

Ethnic Dimensions of the Alcohol Campaign

In contrast to the way indigenous people used alcohol as a form of payment,[46] the state's alcohol policies encouraged *indígenas'* integration into the national economy. By shutting down clandestine production, authorities hoped bootleggers would purchase licenses to continue their businesses or pursue other, presumably licit endeavors. By shutting down illegal vendors, the state hoped to compel poor drinkers to pay the higher prices at state-sanctioned venues (figure 2.5). At those prices, *indígenas* would have to engage more fully in the cash economy to support their habit. Ethnographic studies from the 1930s suggest that they did. "It is the desire for drink, more than any other need, that drives men to seek outside work," according to Bunzel in her ethnography of Chichicastenango, a town northwest of the Kaqchikel municipalities at the heart of this study.[47] In his ethnography of the Kaqchikel community of Panajachel in the late 1930s, Sol Tax estimated that purchasing alcohol for ceremonies accounted for 4 percent of all community expenditures and 11 percent of all expenditures made outside the community.[48] Like Bunzel and Tax, Wagley observed that most alcohol consumption was for ceremonial purposes. In his 1937 study of Santiago Chimaltenango, he found that in one Mam family, the father only drank alcohol during the three-day festival of Santiago, but that binge alone consumed 10 percent of the family's yearly income.[49]

Aware that alcohol flowed freely in the highlands, unscrupulous *contratistas* or *enganchadores* (labor brokers) used it to secure labor for the agricultural export economy, particularly the coffee harvest. Many indigenous men emerged from their drunken binges only to realize they owed their labor to a plantation whose representative had posted their bail or floated a loan so they could keep drinking. (In part to pay for alcohol, the Mam father in Wagley's study had to work on a coffee plantation.)[50] Exploitive *finca* owners and managers ensured that some laborers never escaped these debts.[51] According to one plantation owner, alcohol was crucial to the coffee economy: "Take *aguardiente* away from the Indian and what will become of coffee? Coffee plantations run on *aguardiente* as an automobile runs on gasoline."[52] An ethnographer working in highland Guatemala in the late 1920s

Figure 2.5. *Fonda de licores*, a state-sanctioned liquor dispensary, in Mazate-nango, ca. 1875. Photograph by Eadweard Muybridge. Image courtesy of Boston Athenaeum.

likewise reported that "work leads to rum, and rum leads to work."[53] Even as they defied the national economy by operating in the informal sector, moonshiners and clandestine vendors contributed to the coffee economy by facilitating campesino indebtedness.

To sustain their dictatorships and maintain an image of order and modernity, Estrada Cabrera and Ubico had to balance the demand to eradicate alcohol's social ills with the need for alcohol's revenue. As we have seen, the two despots sought to eradicate the extralegal production and distribution of alcohol. Since popular images and intellectual discourse associated *indios* with alcohol and its clandestine production, the government focused its efforts in the highlands.[54] By 1940 the National Police claimed success: Ordóñez boasted that his corps had decommissioned 243 stills between 1937 and 1940.[55] As further proof that illegal alcohol production was down, he asserted that in "the departments of Guatemala, El Progreso, Sacatepéquez, Escuintla, Santa Rosa, Suchitepéquez, Retalhuleu, Izabal, Zacapa, Chiquimula, Jalapa and Jutiapa . . . during 1940 NOT EVEN ONE clandestine *aguardiente* distillery was confiscated. And those departments that for their extension, topography, or whatever other circumstance are propitious for committing these crimes remain as orientation bases to reinforce future police action."[56]

By pursuing bootleggers, the state made getting a license more desirable—and lucrative. As one indication of the demand, in February 1927 alone there were twelve applications, at least five of them from women, for permits to sell *aguardiente* in San Martín, a town of about 14,000 people.[57] At times state-sanctioned operations seemed brazen by local standards. Kaqchikel of Comalapa decried ladinas who set up their stalls in front of the Catholic church on Sundays to offer libations to congregants as soon as they filed out of mass. Resistance to liquor dispensaries could be fierce. When Alfredo Letona Celada began to sell liquor in his Sololá home in 1942, his next-door neighbor started to insult and threaten him.[58] Although the costs were prohibitive for most *indígenas*, for ladinos who could afford it, the freedom to operate in plain view of the authorities increased their access to clients. Even as the minority, ladinos comprised the vast majority of liquor licensees in the central highlands.

The state's campaign against bootleggers similarly betrayed ethnic overtones. Most of the departments listed in Ordóñez's 1940 report were predominantly ladino areas, while those where the focus of police efforts would be reinforced were predominantly indigenous areas. Although the police were vague about what comprised "other circumstances" propitious for producing *aguardiente* illegally, clearly ethnicity was a salient factor. These findings resonate with historian Virginia Garrard-Burnett's study of alcohol-related crimes in Quetzaltenango, El Quiché, and Jutiapa; the ladino department of Jutiapa had far fewer arrests than the two indigenous departments despite being a transshipment point for contraband, including alcohol, from El Salvador. As she points out, these figures speak more to lax enforcement in ladino areas than to an indigenous propensity for alcohol production.[59] By pursuing indigenous bootleggers and turning a blind eye to ladino violations, the police were influenced by and perpetuated discourse that associated *indios* with alcohol and crime. Images in *La Gaceta* of indigenous bootleggers in their traditional clothing, such as Miguel Alonso Tin (figure 2.6) and Leonso Tahom and María Baquiax (figure 2.2, middle and bottom photographs, respectively), further cemented that association.

The state's expanding reach and shifting focus also reflected its growing strength. With its small and constrained institutions during the nineteenth century, the Conservative and early Liberal state struggled to control the ladino populations and their municipalities, let alone *indígenas* and their communities.[60] As the twentieth century progressed and the state apparatus gained power, the Estrada Cabrera and Ubico dictatorships could increasingly turn their attention to *indígenas'* institutions and affairs.

MIGUEL ALONSO TIN
exhibiendo parte de los
implementos incautados

Figure 2.6. Miguel Alonso Tin, *clandestinista. La Gaceta,* December 12, 1942. Image courtesy of Hemeroteca Nacional de Guatemala.

Public Critiques and Public Health

The state's antibootlegging campaign was not without its detractors. Guatemalan intellectuals regularly criticized the alcohol laws. In 1931 Flavio Guillén wrote,

> The distillation of intoxicating liquor is no longer a crime when it covers the fiscal rights; but confiscating apparatuses, closing down the still and imprisoning the producer, come down without mercy when the production takes place without the prior permission of the Treasury; this [money] is . . . given to the Treasury for official ostentation and waste. Therefore, drinking is not a crime, nor the sale of this lethal liquid, nor its distillation. The crime is in the government's refusal to part with the earnings from this brutish money. That is a despicable crime. . . . That is a crime of the state.[61]

Guillén's perspective differed from those of people involved in the clandestine alcohol trade in that he hoped to reduce alcohol production and consumption; however, he and *clandestinismo* defendants agreed that the state's stance was hypocritical. As an elite male who was not on trial, Guillén could be more explicit in his critique than could poor indigenous, female defendants. Oral histories reveal that few Kaqchikel considered producing and selling alcohol a crime. "The seller is not to blame. The one who looks for [*aguardiente*] is to blame," asserted the *texel* Ixsub'äl.[62]

To deflect criticism from such twentieth-century intellectuals as Guillén, Juárez Muñoz, and Jorge García Granados who claimed the government was poisoning the indigenous population to enrich its coffers, authorities highlighted the public health aspects of their work. Although the government established health standards for alcohol production as early as the Estrada Cabrera regime, not until the 1930s did the National Police begin emphasizing this goal in its rhetoric.[63] In his 1932 annual report, director Anzueto asserted, "Contraband in all its forms . . . jeopardizes the public health and the economic health of the country."[64] *Gaceta* journalists increasingly drew attention to the societal benefits of the campaign against *clandestinismo*.[65] After capturing members of the "powerful and famous . . . Barclay's Trust Inc.," an association in Petén that produced *aguardiente clandestino*, the National Police boasted that officers were combating "industries harmful to public health and fiscal interests."[66]

Kaqchikel descriptions of the production process suggest that such concerns and health regulations were warranted. Ixte' recalled, "To sell more *aguardiente*, women would heat it up alongside the bricks on the fire. Then they would put bricks right into the pot and heat it up that way. They would strain the bricks out of the pot, which left some residue that irritated people's throats so they would always ask for another cup to soothe their throats. In this way, women could sell three, four, five cups of moonshine."[67] According to oral histories, the method used to strain *aguardiente* could affect sales: "One *señora* strained the *k'uxa* [moonshine] with her underwear and that is why she sold a lot."[68] Accounts like these and reports of unhygienic equipment point to the health risks *aguardiente* drinkers faced, but compelling entrepreneurs to operate clandestinely increased such threats. When bootleggers buried their booze to hide it from authorities, bugs, dirt, and other organic matter could find their way into the brew. Consumers of such compromised drinks commonly became sick.[69] The police knew why: "The *aguardiente* drink made with poisonous substances, with poor hygiene, in coils and pots filled with rust and chemicals . . . causes . . . a slow but sure poisoning of the circulatory system and possible death by intoxication."[70]

This rhetoric notwithstanding, regular references to improved finances and the frequency with which authorities called upon locals to drink unidentified liquids suggests that public health was not a priority for officials. When the fifty-two-year-old carpenter Vidal Porras was arrested in December 1921 for selling *chicha*, he claimed his concoction was non-alcoholic. To determine its potency, authorities asked two local *cofrades* who happened to be in the mayor's office at the time to taste the brew. They agreed it was *chicha*. The judge must have respected their opinions even more than that of the court-appointed experts who judged the drink to be non-alcoholic; Porras remained in jail throughout the trial.[71]

Distilling Perceptions of Crime

Women's participation in the sale, distribution, and production of contraband *aguardiente* belied Liberal leaders' assumptions that men were the fundamental drivers of the economy. Although they were aware that women were crucial contributors to highland economies (authorities constantly arrested and harassed female vendors), officials never explicitly recognized the gendered component of Guatemala's economic development.[72]

Descriptions of such brazen female *clandestinistas* as Rosa Morales (figure 2.3) notwithstanding and despite women's prevalent role in the alcohol economy, authorities downplayed female infractions. The January 15, 1933, *Gaceta* article and photographs (figure 2.1) feature agents posing with male *clandestinistas* and their equipment. One of the celebrated captives ran "a copper machine capable of producing 75 bottles of *aguardiente* a day." Although *la indígena* María Chan's operation had the same capacity, authorities considered hers "a little machine." Apparently it did not warrant a photograph.

Wise to dismissive attitudes toward women, *clandestinistas* used such impressions to their advantage in the courtroom. In an attempt to absolve themselves or mitigate their punishment, female defendants and their lawyers played on images of women as meek and naïve. Some complemented these images with the gendered language of motherhood. Wearing her baby on her back (figure 2.2, bottom photograph) allowed María Baquiax to deploy the discourse of motherhood before ever saying a word. Beginning in the mid-eighteenth century in Central America and the early nineteenth century in Mexico, motherhood and the domestic, homemaking wife became increasingly prestigious stations "imbued with . . . important civic function[s]."[73] Female defendants who highlighted these aspects of their identities could reduce their sentences.

In a shift from the late nineteenth century, when women commonly used the gendered defense that being illiterate and living a sequestered life precluded knowledge of the law, by the early twentieth century female defendants increasingly embraced the law and developed narratives around their poverty to explain their transgressions, though they did not abandon the language of domesticity.[74] In this way, they shrewdly put the state on trial. If defendants were hardworking, as evidenced by their very crimes, who was to blame for their indigence? Through their testimonies and their operations, defendants demonstrated that it was not laziness that led them to poverty but rather a lack of opportunities, resources, and education. *Clandestinistas* who operated out of their homes, set up shop in government buildings, or enjoyed the collusion of local officials were defying the laws in plain sight. Defendants who voiced, however subtly, their disapproval of the state's hegemonic project in department courtrooms likewise challenged the state right in the belly of the beast.

Since their assertions could be subtle and ambiguous, often it is difficult to determine whether defendants were arguing that manufacturing *aguardiente* should be legal or that they were ignorant of the law. Even after trying to hide her bottles in a sheet and then stuffing them in a trunk when she saw authorities approaching her San Martín home on February 28, 1918, the ladina widow María Coroy de Zaragua insisted that "she believed she had not committed a crime."[75] She always kept her bottles in a trunk wrapped in a sheet. As for why she tried to bribe the officers, Coroy noted that being escorted from her house by them would have caused "grave damage," presumably to her honor. A person's reputation in highland towns and villages was paramount. Although she had held a license to produce *aguardiente* the previous year, neither of her explanations betrayed her perspective on moonshining.

In a clearer articulation of his reasoning than Coroy offered of hers, the forty-five-year-old *indígena* and day laborer Agustín Muj insisted he was unaware producing *aguardiente* was a crime. After he was arrested in Petrocinio Tortola's home in Patzicía on January 26, 1900, Muj admitted he had not asked Tortola's permission to produce *aguardiente*, thereby absolving him of any crime. Like many of his contemporaries, Muj complained that poverty compelled him to make liquor. He broke new ground in his defense, however, by relating his act to ethnic relations. The notary penned, "Since he saw ladinos doing it, he thought he would make a little."[76] In a nation that tended to idealize ladino behavior as the model of citizenship, perhaps Muj was suggesting that he, a simple Indian, did not suspect that following the example of a ladino would put him in such trouble with the law. Did not ladinos epitomize civilization and the rule of law? Surely this was not the form of ladinoization national leaders had in mind. He also may have been intimating that authorities looked the other way for ladino bootleggers or that because of their socioeconomic positions ladinos could afford the state's licensing fees. Whatever his underlying message(s), Muj drew the department judge's attention to injustices. Although he found Muj guilty, the judge set bail at only one hundred pesos and released Muj just two weeks later when the fifty-year-old farmer José Dolores Vela agreed to guarantee Muj's bond.

Compared to his contemporaries who set moonshiners' bails as high as 450 pesos during the Estrada Cabrera years, this judge's clemency indicates that he responded to some aspect of the overlapping disadvantages of poverty and racism to which Muj alluded.[77] At the very least, his ruling offers evidence that poor, rural, illiterate *indígenas* could sway middle- to upper-class, urban, ladino officials. Estrada Cabrera's pardons for bootleggers suggest that lenient judges were not breaking rank with but rather expressing the broader stance of national officials or at least the president.[78] By mitigating marginality, such gestures buoyed indigenous and poor litigants' sense that the legal system and by extension the state was compassionate, if not necessarily or always just.

Echoing the naïveté if not innocence of earlier bootleggers who claimed ignorance of the law, some defendants assured the courts that these were their first attempts to make moonshine; a few went so far as to claim they were not even certain they had done it correctly. No one wanted to convey expertise. When asked how many bottles she had produced prior to the rural guards' arrival at her home on September 14, 1902, the thirty-three-year-old (likely indigenous) widow Máxima Xical responded: "Not even one bottle. The first time I was going to begin, the *resguardo* prevented me."[79] Like so many other *clandestinistas*, Xical also noted that she had never before been arrested or convicted of a crime, let alone imprisoned. Despite her clean record, the department judge convicted her and set her bail at 450 pesos. Fortunately for Xical, the literate *agricultor don* Miguel Ruano posted her bail.

Portraying oneself as a novice who never before turned to crime was a common narrative strategy during the Ubico era, too. Some thirty years after Xical was arrested, police arrested Domingo Abac of Momostenango in a house he was renting; he insisted he was "a young pigeon" (*un pichón*) who had just begun learning the trade. The police quipped that now "his wings were clipped."[80]

Some described their first attempts as last-ditch efforts to survive. Since the forty-five-year-old widow Dolores Fiatz from the *aldea* of Chirijuyu was monolingual, she relied on an interpreter to convey her sense of desperation to Tecpán's *alcalde* in 1907: "Even though she had worked it [the still] one time, because she did not know how, she did not produce any *aguardiente*. Due to her poverty, she dared to do something that she had never attempted before."[81] Based on the evidence before him, the *alcalde* referred the case to Chimaltenango's *juez de primera instancia*.

By insisting they were first-time offenders, defendants demonstrated that their goal was never to manage a permanent operation but rather a desperate attempt to escape their indigence. As the twenty-one-year-old *patziciana* (and likely ladina) Adela Barrabute admitted, "It is true I was making moonshine. It is the first time I have experimented with making it . . . and I did not have the intention of establishing a business, only to succor my needs."[82] Valued at fifty-eight pesos, her confiscated goods were worth quite a bit more than Fiatz's. Nonetheless, Barrabute got out of jail a week after her arrest when a man posted her hundred-peso bail, while Fiatz languished in jail for a month and a half.

For poor *indígenas* and ladinos, the courtroom provided one of the only venues for them to inform authorities of their privations. To emphasize their poverty, most offenders claimed they were simply trying to support their families. In the same way "poverty pushed people to take extralegal measures to make ends meet" in eighteenth-century Ecuador, bootlegging was a survival strategy for some highland Guatemalans.[83] In 1901 the Chimaltenango department court notary recorded a twenty-year-old (probably ladina) woman's reasons for making moonshine in her father's home in Tecpán: "Her necessities are so dire that they obligate her to produce a little *aguardiente clandestino* to alleviate something. . . . [O]nly in this manner can she earn a living and provide for her family."[84]

In enlightening judges and authorities about the struggles of poor, rural residents, bootleggers pointed out that their behavior was rational and just. To survive in the highlands, they had to disregard alcohol laws. Read this way, defendants were doing more than just highlighting their inferior status to gain a judge's sympathy; they were arguing that the laws themselves were unjust and that the state's failure to provide for its citizens was criminal. These narratives resonate with Kaqchikel oral histories. A female elder recalled, "My father made *k'uxa* because we were poor. What else could we do? And he was taken away by the *guardia*."[85] Like the many defendants and witnesses who mentioned poverty but never explicitly articulated what the consequences of such oppression might be, she rhetorically asked, "What else could we do?" The answer authorities and ladinos feared most was revolt.

In a reflection of poor, indigenous, female plaintiffs' ability to alter penal decisions, judges found arguments about poverty compelling. After reading the *molendera* Dolores Fiatz's testimony about her poverty, the Chimaltenango judge allowed her to commute half of her three-month sentence and waived her legal fees due to her "highly evident poverty."[86] Unlike many of his contemporaries, however, he ignored her plea to be let out on bail; perhaps the forty-five-year-old widow Fiatz did not or could not claim she had young children at home who needed her maternal care.

Following the lead of her counsel, Fiatz pursued another strategy to reduce her sentence. "According to the experts," she noted, "the value of the objects that they apprehended from me was only worth seven pesos. The penalty that should be imposed on me would be two months less according to what is laid down in the precept of article 128 of the liquors law."[87]

For an illiterate, monolingual, indigenous woman, Fiatz was well versed in the details of the liquor law. Instead of claiming ignorance of it, Fiatz used her knowledge of the law to mount her defense and then negotiate her punishment. She worked closely with her court-appointed lawyer, who argued that "the crime for which you have processed my defendant is of such little importance that I believe that the prison suffered and the express circumstances in the first, third, and fourth clauses of article 125 of the liquor law call for her immediate release."[88] Fiatz and her lawyer insisted the punishment did not fit the crime. Based on the judge's detailed ruling, their references to the law did little to change his mind. After paying the commutable rate for half her sentence, Fiatz was released from Chimaltenango's women's jail on January 15, 1908.

By drawing attention to her poverty and the excessive nature of the punishment, Fiatz and her lawyer pointed out the injustice of a system that imprisoned poor people for trying to improve their lot. Other defendants also drew attention to the negligible value of the goods confiscated to emphasize the insignificance of their crimes. Even witnesses occasionally made this point. When he testified on María Coroy de Zaragua's behalf, Francisco Ruano implored the court "not to sentence her for the very little that they found; [moreover] she (*la* Coroy) has cooperated fully."[89]

As subjects of gender, ethnic, and class discrimination, some poor, indigenous women claimed they did not have access to the resources needed to commit the crimes. Lorenza Tuch's lawyer argued as much when he tried to convince the court that the still the police found in her home in June 1901 could not be hers:

> It is true they found the apparatus that produces *aguardiente*, but from this you cannot deduce that Tuch is the defrauder, because being *indígena* and a *molendera*, it would not make sense for her to do something that was outside of her station. Neither can you conceive that she would have the money to install a still. As you know, one needs many resources and knowledge. For these reasons, I think that Tuch is not guilty and in light of that I ask you to absolve these crimes that have been formulated, and set her free.[90]

In short, how could a person who was ignorant, poor, and lacking social capital establish her own business? The irony, of course, is that many women did. Even though the judge did not reduce the length of Tuch's three-month sentence, he cut the commutable rate in half to one peso a day and waived some of her legal fees due to her highly evident poverty. Such gestures were not insignificant. In 1909, when authorities arrested Ángel María Ruano and Eduardo Estrada for their *aguardiente* still, it cost them four hundred pesos each to get out of jail.[91]

Engendering Explanations

Most female defendants combined descriptions of their poverty with the gendered discourse of motherhood. In 1900 the municipal notary penned the forty-four-year-old, illiterate widowed washerwoman Petrona Espaderas's response to why she had a still: "As the defendant is a single woman with ten children all minors and crippled who live off the personal work of the defendant, she saw the need to establish a still to produce *aguardiente clandestino* in her house."[92] When she appeared before the department court three days later, she confessed to her crime and agreed to her punishment. Although her court-appointed lawyer, too, was illiterate, he helped Espaderas file a request that she be released on bail. Less than a week after her arrest, the judge freed her when Cecilio Echeveria posted her two-hundred-peso bail. If the rapidity with which her case progressed through the courts is any indication (many of her counterparts were imprisoned for weeks and even months before being released), Espaderas's reference to her crippled children served her well.

To get out on bail, women commonly appealed to their roles as mothers. After being incarcerated for a month and a half, María Coroy de Zaragua implored, "The prison that I suffer is great because my poor children, who are minors, are essentially abandoned [*abandonados*] because today they lack the mother who I am."[93] Two days later, the judge set her bail at three hundred pesos and released her when the *agricultor* Eladio Alburez posted it. She was wise to use the term *abandonados*. The state took child abandonment seriously, even if the underlying goal was often to compel mothers to stay with their families.[94]

In addition to motherhood, female defendants framed their testimonies in the broader discourse of domesticity. When authorities confiscated two pots with *chicha* dregs and some bottles of *aguardiente clandestino* in the forty-five-year-old *soltera* (single woman) Dolores Moya's home on May 17, 1907, she had a ready explanation for the Patzicía *alcalde*: one of the pots was "completely useless," and the other was for making non-alcoholic drinks. As for the bottles, the notary wrote, "they belong to her but what she is accused of is completely false, since she has always used the bottles for domestic uses."[95] Unconvinced, the *alcalde* sent the case to Chimaltenango's *juzgado de primera instancia*, where judge José Barrios promptly freed her. Although judges seldom referred specifically to gender issues, Barrios apparently found Moya's explanation compelling. That she, like Barrios, was ladino may have helped her cause.

Male defendants like the indigenous *jornalero* Agustín Muj likewise argued that poverty compelled them to produce *aguardiente clandestino*, but they crafted their narratives differently than women. As did some nineteenth-century Q'anjob'al-Maya males in Huehuetenango, early twentieth-century Kaqchikel men like Francisco Calel often related the production and consumption of alcohol to custom and tradition.[96] Aware that *aguardiente clandestino* was illegal, Calel hid his stash under some rags on his bed. When the *regidor* and two *indígenas* searched his Comalapa home on September 24, 1902, they found it. The notary recorded Calel's explanation: "About a month ago *su mujer* [his woman] Rosa Morales bought from an individual from San Martín Jilotepeque a *garrafón* containing *aguardiente*, for the price of fifteen pesos. They used the *aguardiente* in a wedding festivity that they had in their house . . . the little that was left over [was] what had been confiscated."[97] In his effort to subtly challenge the alcohol laws by pointing out *aguardiente*'s ceremonial use, Calel was careful to offer some specific details such as the alcohol's price (fifteen pesos) and origin (San Martín) while omitting others such as the individual's name and whether it was produced and sold illegally. Unfortunately for Calel, pointing out that authorities and laws criminalized indigenous customary practices held as little sway in twentieth-century Chimaltenango as it did in nineteenth-century Huehuetenango.

Calel's appeal to be let out on bail demonstrates another way men's narrative strategies differed from women's. He explained to the judge that his imprisonment caused "my small interests to be completely abandoned."[98] Instead of saying he was destitute, the fifty-eight-year-old self-described *guatemalteco* said he had humble yet important matters to tend. Rather than emphasizing the effect their incarceration would have on their families, most men warned of the damage it would do to their business interests. Seldom did they claim their crimes were insignificant, as women often did. Even though patriarchal power diminished as one descended the socioeconomic ladder, poor, indigenous men held privileged positions vis-à-vis indigenous women and therefore refrained from presenting themselves as powerless.

Such assertions had their drawbacks, however, since they generally precluded judges from waiving legal fees or setting bails low. Nonetheless, the judge must have been sufficiently impressed with Calel's testimony; he set bail at 150 pesos, which, though not the lowest (100 pesos), was more reasonable than others. When the thirty-one-year-old *agricultor* Laureano Mich posted bail on October 15, 1902, Calel was freed three weeks after he had been incarcerated. He was far from absolved, though. More than two years later, on May 2, 1905, the Chimaltenango department judge ordered Calel to return to court for further questioning regarding the case. As Calel's bondsman, Mich was responsible for making sure he showed up.[99]

More than any other type of litigation, bootlegging trial records conjure images of a relatively peaceful, stable, and orderly world that operated simultaneously outside and alongside the law-abiding one. For *indígenas*, it was not moonshiners but licensed *aguardiente* producers and vendors who destabilized the tranquility of rural communities; their businesses not only invited but in many ways were contingent upon state intervention.[100]

Courting the Law

To win in court, one had to know the laws and the legal system or be fortunate enough to have good counsel. Remarkably, some defendants convinced the court of their innocence without the benefit of literacy, Spanish, or a lawyer. Surrounded by Kaqchikel speakers in his remote village of Simaulew, Comalapa, Monico Mux spoke only Kaqchikel even though his license to sell *aguardiente* was in Spanish. On January 23, 1912, Mux asked his son to pick up a barrel of *aguardiente* on his way back from farming. Because the boy did not have the permit with him while transporting the liquor, the authorities arrested him and later Mux. Presenting his case through an interpreter and with the aid of his wife, who testified on his behalf, Mux convinced the court of their innocence.[101]

It took nearly three months for the court to free Mux, but his case was not nearly as complicated as the one in which Isabel Siquinajay and Lorenzo Tala were embroiled five years earlier. On March 23, 1907, these two illiterate, indigenous *jornaleros* set out for Antigua to purchase *aguardiente* for the celebration of Holy Week in their hometown of San Andrés Itzapa (henceforth Itzapa)—a common enough excursion in light of the social and ritual uses to which Mayas put alcohol.[102] When the Itzapa mayor stopped them at ten o'clock that evening, they did not have their permit to transport alcohol with them, so they met the same fate as Mux and his son.

With the confidence of a man who knows he is innocent, Siquinajay argued their case before the Chimaltenango department court. By pointing out that the very mayor who arrested them had granted them the permit, Siquinajay cast doubt on the mayor's motives and credibility. Saying "My imprisonment is unjust," Siquinajay reminded judge Barrios that he had filed and received the proper paperwork, purchased the *aguardiente* from an official vendor for twenty-five pesos, and had no intention of selling it; rather it was going to be used for a fiesta. Like Francisco Calel five years earlier, Siquinajay emphasized its customary use. He concluded, "I fail to see an illicit act in the purchase of this liquor. For believing this and considering myself without any responsibility, I ask you judge if you would deign to free me and return the *aguardiente* that was confiscated from me."[103] The judge granted both requests. After hearing from court experts as to the alcohol's composition, he also ordered that the vendor be brought in for questioning on the grounds that he was adulterating *aguardiente*—leaving open the possibility that Siquinajay might have his twenty-five pesos refunded.

Besides the vendor, the Itzapa *alcalde* fared poorly under official scrutiny as well. Underscoring Siquinajay's suspicions, Tala suggested that the mayor arrested them only because they did not purchase the liquor in Itzapa. Even the Chimaltenango *jefe político* reprimanded him. In his March 25 letter to the mayor, the *jefe político* underlined (three times!) his rebuke of the mayor for not following instructions. As this case and others in the archives calling for the censure if not dismissal of *alcaldes* demonstrate, local officials often failed to serve either their superiors or their charges well.

The odds against illiterate and oftentimes monolingual *indígenas* who had no formal education gaining the upper hand in court were considerable, but the Mux and Siquinajay cases demonstrate that *indígenas* enjoyed some recourse through the courts. In light of his admission that he was not registered "as a soldier or a citizen," Siquinajay's success was all the more noteworthy. Judicial triumphs were not contingent upon citizenship. Neither exceptional nor common, such victories occurred often enough to buoy marginalized and isolated people's belief that the legal system could work for them. The official recourse and responses were crucial to maintaining the state's legitimacy.

The alcohol economy helped to shape the nation by bringing disparate parties together through exchanges that were both confrontational and cooperative. Government leaders like Estrada Cabrera and Ubico considered alcohol revenue essential to creating a nation that could proudly portray itself as modern. Only with those funds could the state build infrastructure that would impress and attract foreign investors.[104] Numerous intellectuals decried the state's role in the alcohol economy; Juárez Muñoz, for example, wrote that if the state remained dependent on "money that brings with it so much misery," then "we will never be a nation."[105] Yet, national leaders refused to shake the government's reliance on alcohol revenues. The campaign against *clandestinismo* was intended to encourage the sale of liquor licenses and payment of the liquor taxes that filled state coffers. But it also was aimed at impressing upon people—especially monolingual indigenous speakers living in remote areas—the state's presence and power, however varied and contradictory such manifestations were in their lives. Without these interventions, how would people know they were being ruled?

The state's singular goal of enforcing the alcohol laws necessitated a broad array of agents, from the Treasury Police, National Police, military, and other security forces who looked for stills and persecuted bootleggers to the municipal and department judicial officials—mayors, justices of the peace, translators, notaries, and judges—who facilitated the judicial process. Captured *clandestinistas* came to know the state's multifarious nature via their contact with myriad representatives. Even through conflict, indigenous subalterns and ladino authorities were getting to know, if not respect, one another.

Since the state seldom achieved consensus regarding its hegemonic project among its own representatives, *clandestinistas'* pursuits were not always at odds with those of authorities. At times the relationships between moonshiners and authorities were akin to the "uncoordinated and accidental confederation" that historian Amy Chazkel describes between clandestine lottery vendors and police in Brazil, which created "a trade network that was only partially submerged."[106] The many municipal officials who ignored, encouraged, or engaged in the extralegal alcohol economy undercut the state's campaign against *clandestinismo*. Reeves similarly has found that this illicit commerce flourished in nineteenth-century Quetzaltenango precisely because so many municipal authorities "exhibited little zeal in persecuting *clandestinistas*."[107] Local authorities' attitudes toward *clandestinistas* had as much to do with maintaining their own privileges and prerogatives within their domains as with propagating national power and enforcing state laws.

Department judges seldom strayed far from the state's hegemonic project, partly because they were closely connected to national power, but they also enjoyed some flexibility in terms of how they interpreted and enforced the state's campaign against *clandestinismo*. Some judges empathized with poor, indigenous defendants, particularly when litigants demonstrated how poverty precipitated acts that the law considered criminal. Although they did not exonerate defendants because of their penury, judges frequently reduced *clandestinistas'* sentences and fees in light of their poverty.

In addition to referencing poverty, women effectively deployed the discourse of motherhood to reduce their sentences and expedite their release on bail. In at least one case, an explanation related to domesticity contributed to a woman's exoneration. That exoneration notwithstanding, in general those who fared best were women who related their motives to poverty and their appeals for leniency to motherhood. These exchanges and rulings suggest that at least some urban, ladino, male authorities understood the realities of poor, rural (particularly female) litigants.

Such rulings and exchanges buttressed the Estrada Cabrera dictatorship, whose pursuit of *aguardiente clandestino* represented an attempt to impose its order in the most remote and isolated parts of the nation. By the early twentieth century the state was becoming strong enough to begin contemplating shifting its focus from ladinos to *indígenas*, even if it was far from doing so with any success. Following the late nineteenth-century Liberal *reforma*, this effort coincided with a transformation in the definition of citizenship from the hierarchical caste system of the Conservative state to a more universal—and exclusionary—understanding of citizenship based on ladino identities and norms.[108]

Despite these prescriptive notions of citizenship, courtrooms offered litigants the opportunity to articulate their interests and critiques; some moonshiners challenged the hegemonic project by calling attention to the state's failings. Their testimonies in court and statements to authorities before arriving there can be read as efforts by poor *indígenas* and ladinos to let officials know they understood the system and often the laws; they also sought to inform judges about their own lives and ideas of justice. By emphasizing poverty, they drew judges' and other authorities' attention to what they considered to be one of the fundamental ills in Guatemalan society. The police, judges, and other officials who listened to these perspectives and at times acted in accordance with them helped to maintain social order. For it was through airing their grievances and at times gaining concessions, however limited, that indigenous women and other marginalized Guatemalans enjoyed a sense that they were part of the nation and held the potential to benefit from its institutions. Even as they decried injustices, defendants used the government's tools to further their own goals and thus buttressed the state's and the legal system's legitimacy. By dealing efficaciously with municipal officials and residents in remote regions, Chimaltenango's *juzgado de primera instancia* shored up the state's standing in places where it was otherwise relatively weak.

The many police and other personnel employed in the campaign against *clandestinismo* who all but admitted to its futility speak to the state's weakness in many parts of the country. When the Treasury Police reported in 1935 that they had reduced *aguardiente clandestino* to "its minimum expression," they conceded they would never eradicate it.[109] Moonshiners who established their stills in "rough and thorny terrain" constantly frustrated authorities. Even in regional centers of state power, moonshiners often held the upper hand. Women used notions of femalehood to operate out of their homes in busy towns. The most brazen offenders established their businesses in government buildings. By letting authorities know that no matter how powerful or fearful they appeared, resistance and defiance would accompany the state's hegemonic project; these acts helped to shape dictatorial rule.

Permitting a little resistance went a long way in letting off steam and preventing serious challenges to the state's power, as James Scott notes, and thus the state was served well by erratic enforcement.[110] Stills are a good example of this lower-level resistance. As Foucault asserts, "A penal system must be conceived as a mechanism intended to administer illegalities differentially, not to eliminate them."[111] Many functionaries pursued convictions with great zeal, while some officials understood that most *indígenas* and poor ladinos could not afford to purchase licenses or, for that matter, legal alcohol.

Removing *aguardiente clandestino* entirely would have caused a contagion of intended and unintended consequences, particularly for the economic system by which *contratistas* recruited laborers. The sale of *aguardiente clandestino* was an important source of revenue flow into local and regional economic systems, even if the state could not directly access it. The local collaboration and complicity that ranged from corrupt officials looking the other way to authorities establishing their own illicit operations was as much driven by personal interest as by an awareness of the bigger economic picture. Nonetheless, collusion also stemmed from the state's ambivalence about the efficacy of its alcohol policies, which in turn made enforcement spotty by design, as the aptly dubbed La Municipalidad still on the Tecpán *alcalde*'s property and stills in the Quetzaltenango Treasury building demonstrate.

The multiple and varied interactions inside and outside the courtroom contributed to an increased mutual awareness between marginalized people and state agents; in fact, many of the latter were not so removed from the reality they policed and judged. This growing experiential knowledge among subalterns, interlocutors, and hegemons contributed to the development of a nation that, if not united, was in some areas and at some levels getting to know its distinct features. Nation-state formation seldom reflected what subalterns or hegemons had envisioned. This ongoing process was full of fits and starts and disappointing, even tragic developments. The different perceptions of what was just and unjust, legal and illegal informed these interactions and shaped the nation. That poor, indigenous women were contributing to this process during two of Latin America's harshest dictatorships speaks to the influence of marginalized people during extraordinary times.

As significant as these exchanges related to *clandestinismo* were, they happened only intermittently, and most of the adjudications occurred in department courts far removed from defendants' rural villages and realities. For an exploration of how the state's attempts to criminalize indigenous livelihoods affected *indígenas* on a more routine basis and were adjudicated by authorities whom defendants likely knew or at least knew of, we now turn to the ways indigenous female vendors confronted the state's modernizing economic reforms at the municipal level.

CHAPTER 3

"Productive Activity": Female Vendors and Ladino Authorities in the Market

When a *regidor* caught Isabel Bajxac "monopolizing" fruit and other goods *en cantidad mayor* (wholesale) in the San Martín plaza early on the morning of February 11, 1935, the forty-eight-year-old, illiterate, indigenous vendor claimed she was unaware of the law restricting such sales to the afternoon.[1] A few months later, when the *regidor* arrested Bajxac for the same crime, he noted that "Bajxac has extensive knowledge [of the prohibition] as she has been punished repeated times now for the same reason." In her defense, Bajxac told the *juez de paz* that she engaged in these acts because she was "very poor."[2] Evidently, he had little sympathy; both sentences of five days in jail commutable by ten cents a day only compounded her poverty.[3]

Bajxac confessed to selling the goods but not to committing a crime. The first time she claimed ignorance and the second time poverty. Rather than brazenly flouting the law, she was simply trying to survive. Although she used the municipal courtroom to express her dismay with local authorities, neither the *regidor* nor the *juez de paz* acknowledged how the state's attempt to impose order condemned her—and other vendors—to destitution. Cases like these reveal the ambiguities and ambivalences in subalterns' efforts to understand, evaluate, and respond to asymmetrical relations of power. On one hand, *indígenas* recognized the authority of judicial officials and, to a lesser extent, of *jueces del mercado* (market inspectors and tax collectors), and at times they welcomed, even invited their interventions. On the other hand, vendors were quick to confront these officials when they thought their actions or the laws were unjust. As an enforcer of laws, the state was a powerful protectorate and a menacing nuisance. As Bajxac's testimony intimates, people were not necessarily proud of their resistance. She was choosing between feeding her family and breaking the law. Like moonshiners, Bajxac used her testimony to inform authorities that she had to disregard their regulations in order to survive.

As one of the few public spaces where indigenous women held sway in a nation governed by elite ladino and Creole men, marketplaces were contested terrains shot through with complex power relations. If the criminal record is any indication, clashes with state officials—aldermen, market inspectors, sanitation officers, judicial officials, police—were some of the most important relations Maya marketers experienced. Highland *indígenas* enjoyed control over an integrated rural marketing system, which in turn offered avenues for indigenous economic autonomy and upward mobility.[4] Partly for this reason, marketplaces became battlegrounds for the Guatemalan state's neocolonialist ambitions.

To advance its hybrid brand of capitalism and extend its vision of order and progress, the Liberal state sought to impose market principles and ladino norms in the marketplace. When indigenous women like Bajxac frustrated these efforts, whether intentionally or not, highland marketplaces were transformed into theaters of class, gender, and ethnic struggle. As Foucault's analysis of power suggests, domination and resistance were mutually constituted. Perhaps more than any other public space, highland marketplaces experienced the clash between the state's efforts to impose ladino nationalism and *indígenas'* and other subalterns' efforts to imbue the economy, society, and ultimately the nation with their own worldviews and modus operandi. Vendors who faced down market inspectors were not necessarily defying capitalism or nationalism because they knew where these experiments were headed.[5] Often the economic, social, and political realities of their lives compelled them to act in ways that contravened the state's laws. Vendors' public positions instilled them with a certain degree of influence and authority, but it also made them targets of authorities' attempts to reinscribe their and the state's power at the local level. Although the state's programs and policies shaped the possibilities and constraints of its citizens, even the most marginalized subjects could limit or expand state power.

By revealing how subalterns and authorities advanced their claims and agendas in shifting fields of power, the criminal record elucidates the clash between the state's ideologies, goals, and policies and local alternative practices and worldviews. Like courts, marketplaces were venues where the state asserted its power and where *indígenas* contested that power. The struggle over who controlled highland markets—those who participated in them or authorities—demonstrates that material cultures were part of "everyday forms of state formation."[6]

Gender and ethnicity mediated how people experienced Liberal rule in Guatemala and Latin America.[7] When women operated in such public positions as midwives, market vendors, and sex workers, the Guatemalan state attempted to regulate their activities to further Liberal conceptions of social control and national development.[8] Since highland markets were one of the few areas where officials could directly affect indigenous women, attempts to enforce domestic stability and gendered and ethnic morality were particularly intense there. According to national and local ladino authorities, women disrupted order and thus had to be controlled, and *indios* hindered progress and thus needed to be assimilated.[9] In the same way Yucatecan elites believed henequen haciendas would "civilize" indigenous "barbarians,"[10] Guatemalan officials sought to modernize *indios* by transforming highland markets.

In an effort to understand the interplay of state mandates, municipal and national authorities, and local (primarily indigenous female) vendors and consumers in highland markets, I closely examined thirty-one municipal judicial proceedings from Patzicía, San Martín, and Sololá (appendix 6). Fifty-six women and eleven men were cited for marketplace violations in these thirty-one cases; forty-five were identified in documents as indigenous women, four as ladinas, and nine as indigenous men. Based on surnames and such descriptions as a woman wearing a *güipil* (handwoven traditional Maya blouse), a total of forty-eight indigenous women, eight ladinas, ten indigenous men, and one ladino were arrested. Municipal justices of the peace absolved only two people (a ladino and ladina), and in both cases the accusations came from community members, at least one of whom was an indigenous woman. In every case in which a municipal market or health inspector, alderman, police agent, or other public authority accused someone of violating municipal or national market regulations, justices of the peace sentenced defendants to five days in prison commutable by a rate that ranged from five to twenty cents a day depending on their offenses and the goods involved. Subtracting the four cases for which the ruling was lost, the conviction rate was a staggering 96.8 percent!

Unlike defendants in *defraudación al Fisco en el ramo de licores* litigation adjudicated at the department level, those accused of market violations had little success in altering either the rulings or the sentences regardless of whether they referenced their poverty, motherhood, or ignorance of the law. Perhaps aware of this trend, a number of defendants simply remained silent or confessed. The distinct circumstances, laws, and enforcement related to liquor and market crimes notwithstanding, since defendants in both types of crime were almost invariably caught red-handed, these findings suggest that department judges were more likely to be swayed by defendants' testimonies than were their municipal subordinates. In turn, even though the judicial settings were further removed from their communities and realities, moonshine defendants were more likely to assert themselves in department court than marketplace violators were in municipal courts. Determining cause and effect is difficult, but department judges' clemency apparently encouraged debate, while the high conviction rate of marketplace defendants frequently squashed their motivation to contest rulings or sentences. Where one was tried mattered.

The marketplace interactions and exchanges of municipal and national authorities, vendors, and consumers involved far more than what survives in the judicial record. Assault and battery and defamation litigation also sheds light on conditions and relations in highland markets. Oral histories and contemporary ethnographies further flesh out aspects of this past. Finally, despite its scant detail on the arrests, *La Gaceta*'s police blotter was helpful in understanding how marketplace struggles played out on a national scale in Guatemala.

At the same time, this analysis of Patzicía, San Martín, and to a lesser extent Sololá should not be generalized to Guatemala as a whole. Across the highlands, markets and marketplaces varied significantly depending on who operated, frequented, and controlled them. Such an analysis goes beyond the scope of this chapter; distinctions appear, however, in comparing cities like Sololá and Totonicapán, where indigenous leadership held more sway, with towns like Patzicía and San Martín, where ladino surveillance was the norm. Based on fieldwork he conducted intermittently between 1927 and 1941, Felix Webster McBryde documented variations in highland markets. While ladinos tended to dominate the indoor marketplaces in the more urban and industrialized centers such as Guatemala City, Quetzaltenango, Mazatenango, and Huehuetenango, they did not have a monopoly on these markets. Some "well-developed" indigenous towns like Totonicapán and Santiago Atitlán had daily (as opposed to weekly, as in Patzicía and San Martín) markets that were effectively run and patrolled by *indígenas*.[11] Anthropologist Carol Smith found similar distinctions when she studied the 1893 and 1921 censuses that quantified Guatemala's predominantly rural, indigenous population. She has noted that department capitals, which exerted administrative control over their townships, tended to be predominantly ladino and "parasitic." These urban, nonagricultural, ladino populations "lived off the surplus exacted from the nonspecialized, Indian countryside."[12] Like McBryde, Smith has highlighted Totonicapán as an exception. Because the region's and capital's indigenous merchants were so successful in provisioning regional markets, the marketplaces therein enjoyed greater autonomy from ladino authorities than those in ladino-controlled departments like Chimaltenango. Chimaltenango's productive lands and close proximity to urban centers, particularly Guatemala City, and lowland markets facilitated its position as a major basic-grain producer for the region.[13] As we will see in Patzicía and San Martín, this crucial production intensified ladino authorities' surveillance, particularly during corn and other grain shortages.

Highland Markets, State Formation, and the Economics of Gender and Ethnicity

Throughout the pre-Hispanic, colonial, and national eras, markets facilitated the exchange of agricultural products, foodstuffs, textiles, pottery, firewood, clothing, medicine, and the like in Mesoamerica. Most goods came from the region surrounding each market, but long-distance merchants offered products from other areas. Particularly in indigenous communities, these markets had long been the domain of women. Since markets provided residents with most of their dietary staples, female vendors dominated one of the most crucial institutions of highland life.[14] As mosaics of distinct economic systems, markets were not timeless, autonomous, or homogeneous.

During the colonial era, indigenous communities were connected to the economy largely through paying taxes and fulfilling labor demands. While highland villages enjoyed considerable autonomy during the Hapsburg dynasty (1516–1700), by the mid-eighteenth century the Bourbons (1701–1823) were increasingly intervening in community life and attempting to draw indigenous people into the colonial economy. Partly because Mayas believed Bourbon economic reforms violated notions of reciprocity and the right to subsistence that were the pillars of a Maya moral economy, these reforms enjoyed little success in Guatemala. By the early 1800s Mayas openly defied colonial agents and tax collectors.[15] Because the Guatemalan state and the Catholic Church were relatively weak after independence in 1823, most highland communities and markets maintained significant sovereignty until the last third of the nineteenth century.[16]

Other relations of production notwithstanding, most indigenous communities relied on subsistence agriculture and petty commodity production for their livelihoods. Through such services as processing raw materials into finished goods and providing credit to clients, female vendors helped to connect subsistence and commercial economies. These hybrid highland economies became more complex as the nineteenth century progressed and indigenous communities' sovereignty diminished.[17] Yet not until the turn of the twentieth century did authorities earnestly attempt to impose capitalist relations of production and exchange on highland marketplaces.

For reasons that emanated from the top down as well as from the bottom up, the transition to capitalism never became a thoroughgoing market revolution. Market forces seldom regulated acquisitions of land or the movement of labor. The state privatized land to transfer communal holdings to agricultural export entrepreneurs at cheap prices. Many coffee planters similarly relied on the state's forced-labor mechanisms to supply field hands. In turn, many *indígenas* had access to land, though not necessarily as owners of it, that allowed them to produce much of what they consumed. In this sense, highland Guatemala was akin to a society with markets as opposed to a market society, to borrow Karl Polanyi's distinction between noncapitalist and capitalist societies. Instead of regulating social interactions and governing the social order as it would in a market society, a self-regulating market system or market economy only played a marginal role in social relations in highland Guatemala.[18]

By attempting to control rather than eradicate indigenous marketplaces, the state further promoted a hybrid economy. The syncretic and adulterated nature of economic forms in Guatemala did little to bridge the "profound cultural differences [that] arose" between subsistence and capitalist modes of production.[19] By the early twentieth century the complex power relations in highland markets made it difficult if not impossible for municipal or national officials to control and shape these sites.

Packaged with Liberal leaders' efforts to homogenize the nation, the market culture represented more than just an economic imposition. In an effort to establish a more united nation, Liberal governments denigrated indigeneity. In response to systematic discrimination and exclusion, most Mayas maintained an autonomous ethnic ideological system.[20] By approaching nationalism, economic development, and indigenous culture as interdependent, this alternative conceptual framework threatened the ladino nationalist project.[21] Walter Little suggests that Mayas who participated in Ubico's National Fair had a sense of how their ethnicity contributed to economic development by attracting tourists.[22] Maya notions of the complementarity of nationalism and indigeneity are also evident in oral histories, in which Kaqchikel define the nation as indigenous, and in court records, where litigants identify themselves as *guatemalteco/as* and *indígenas*.[23] To cite another example of this synergy, from the late 1920s to the mid-1940s, Comalapa authorities—indigenous and ladino alike—regularly secured labor for public works projects by appealing to *indígenas*' sense of patriotism and emphasizing the local and national economy's need for such infrastructure.[24] Indigenous men who voluntarily responded to this call acted on the potential symbiosis of nationalism, indigeneity, and development.

Despite the abundance of female vendors' infractions in the criminal record, neither national nor municipal authorities explicitly recognized local markets or female vendors as important contributors to the economy. Seldom did journalists or notaries refer to women's financial skills, resources, or contributions. As one manifestation of officials' and intellectuals' reluctance to recognize the importance of female labor, corvée labor legislation generally targeted male workers. The 1934 vagrancy law only applied to men. Most national officials were ignorant of or refused to recognize women's agricultural labor on coffee *fincas* and other farms.[25]

In addition to obstructing women's economic opportunities, men's privileged access to employment, education, and other resources often blinded them to women's economic ingenuity, success, and significance, which in turn fanned perceptions of their vulnerability. In 1931 professor A. del Vecchio warned that females were most at risk during times of economic depression:

> We have observed that the situation of the woman gets worse each day, because of the absolute ignorance of order and economics . . .
>
> Many women have the very bad system of acquiring all their articles through credit, spending in this manner twice the amount of the price, creating the illusion that everything is moving along marvelously without realizing that when it comes time to pay the bills, there is no money available.
>
> I do not think it is impossible to teach girls in the schools and in the homes how to organize the daily costs of the house so that when they come of age, they will know how to sustain themselves and contribute to the prosperity of *the businesses of their husbands* and the well-being of their children . . .
>
> These girls that now grow up coming from financial conflicts in the home, without finding any remedy, later will look for the easiest means to free themselves from these pains, compromising their reputation. But if there is a hand that guides them toward a good path and shows them that even in well-organized poverty they can find satisfaction and joy, they will become hardworking and orderly little women.[26]

Del Vecchio's comments reflect the Liberal state's concern that women—vulnerable and weak—needed to be nurtured or controlled, lest they fall into ruin and disrupt social order and national progress. If girls did not learn to manage their indigence, they would become lazy, unruly, and perhaps use sex to escape squalor. In advocating paternalistic guidance and celebrating well-organized poverty he heralded a Liberal vision of national development and social control based on gender and class hierarchies of material power.[27]

Informed by Guatemalan Liberals' tendency to discount women's economic contributions, del Vecchio attributed entrepreneurship to men. Such notions led officials to discount the economic importance of highland markets. Members of a commission in charge of introducing electricity to San Martín in 1935 informed government officials that they would have to charge a household tax to raise the funds necessary for the project. The commissioners explained their reasoning: "It is known that the commerce in this village is purely local and without any significance."[28]

In contrast, since males dominated long-distance trade, writers often conjured romantic images of that profession. In a 1943 paean and photograph (figure 3.1) titled "Our Powerful and Hardworking Native Race," a *Gaceta* journalist exalts indigenous men for facilitating trade (even while emphasizing their subordination):

Satisfied with their labor and always smiling before the difficult and daily fatigue of work, these aboriginal merchants take a break in the middle of the beatific peace of the road. Hardworking men of iron, bronzed by the luminous radiance of our tropical sun, they have honor for their guide, smiles for their balsam, and work for their religion. Anointed by the satisfaction that their productive activity creates, these contracted traffickers cross exalted paths in interminable excursions, transporting their original and curious products from one part of the country to the other, while the jungle seems to shelter them with an affectionate subjectivism that scatters about in whispers and joy.[29]

In juxtaposition to social constructions of gender like del Vecchio's that portrayed women as inclined toward indolence, disorder, and immorality, these indigenous male merchants were laborious and honest by nature.

Perhaps partly because the photograph and caption situate them in the jungle as opposed to ladino urban centers, these *buhoneros* were considered among the "honorable exceptions . . . in the indigenous race."[30] The National Police generally demonized *buhoneros* and encouraged local authorities to be vigilant around them. When Diego Toj Mejía was transporting goods without a license in 1941, the Sololá police arrested him. The record indicates that the municipal justice of the peace empathized with this

Figure 3.1. "Our Powerful and Hardworking Native Race." *La Gaceta*, January 10, 1943. Image courtesy of Hemeroteca Nacional de Guatemala.

indigenous vendor's plight and released him after Toj Mejia explained that he lacked the money to pay the licensing tax and agreed to leave his two *bultos* (packages) of chilis and other goods as collateral. Illiterate, Toj Mejia was unable to read the document that allowed him to ply his trade. None-theless, he returned two weeks later with a license to collect his merchan-dise.[31] If this proceeding is any indication, municipal authorities' perspectives of *buhoneros* were more akin to those of the journalists who celebrated them than of the police agents who sought to criminalize them.

Compared to his Patzicía and San Martín counterparts' consistent incarceration of indigenous vendors, this Sololá judicial official's leniency also hints at the effects of ladino as compared to indigenous surveillance. The Sololá *municipalidad indígena* was vibrant and influential throughout the first half of the twentieth century. Unlike Chimaltenango, where the department capital was more decidedly ladino, Sololá's indigenous population and leaders were more involved in the day-to-day operations of and proceedings in the city.[32] Even though the Sololá document does not betray the judges' ethnicity, his indulgence suggests that whether he was ladino or *indígena*, the city's distinct ethnic and marketplace relations influenced him. Sololá's municipal archive yielded other references to market relations, but they tended to be limited to market regulations and applications for licenses; no other economic crime proceedings emerged. Despite sparse documentation that precludes comparative analysis, Toj Mejia's case points to the variations in markets and marketplaces across the highlands.

In sharp contrast to the Patzicía and San Martín archival materials, which reveal ladino municipal authorities' preoccupation with predominantly indigenous, female vendors in local markets, *La Gaceta*'s focus on itinerant male merchants obscures indigenous female traders who traveled beyond their communities to sell their wares,[33] evidence of which appears in oral histories, criminal records, ethnographies, travel accounts, and even the police blotter. Authorities were generally wary of women who traded outside their communities.[34] A number of factors explain why many women were enjoined from long-distance trading. Their roles as childbearers and rearers as well as the daily demand for their family labor often compelled them to stay close to home. Nonetheless, women devised ways to expand their mobility and sell their goods in other towns.[35]

According to Liberal intellectuals and leaders, men were the drivers of the economy, and as such their diligence should be held up as part of the nation's pride. In contrast, while women could support male endeavors, their own economic activity was negligent. Gudmundson observed in his

Figure 3.2. "Work: The Faith and Religion of Our Autochthonous Race." *La Gaceta*, November 1, 1942. Image courtesy of Hemeroteca Nacional de Guatemala.

study of San Gerónimo, Baja Verapaz, Guatemala, "However great the private, productive, and even commercial powers of women . . . grossly unequal power relations based on gender would continue . . . when private and public spheres collided."[36] Another celebration of hardworking *indígenas*, which appeared on the November 1, 1942, cover of *La Gaceta*, documents this distinction (figure 3.2). The title, "Work: The Faith and Religion of Our Autochthonous Race," simultaneously acknowledged *indígenas*' agency by recognizing them as descendants of the region's original inhabitants and subjectivity by claiming they belonged to Guatemalans. Beneath the title a photograph shows indigenous men and an indigenous woman returning from a market. The author exalts the man for using his "virile shoulders" to carry merchandise but assumes that the woman, "submissive and comprehending that following her *compañero* is her duty, transports perhaps prepared food for the couple's daily sustenance."[37] While he associates the man with commercial activity, the journalist situates the woman firmly in the domestic sphere, devoid of economic value in the eyes of most contemporary Guatemalans and Latin Americans.

Contested Spaces and Perspectives

The Guatemalan government's campaign to move vendors from public plazas to enclosed buildings during the first half of the twentieth century was motivated partly by sanitary and visual ideals of cleanliness, civility, and progress. It was also an attempt to counteract the influence and control of indigenous women, who largely determined the modus operandi of public plazas on market days. Mayas did not necessarily see this program as a wholesale assault against them, however. "Ubico introduced 'order' in the plaza when he constructed market buildings and ensured that they were clean, just, and peaceful," according to some Maya elders.[38] Some municipal councils, such as Comalapa's, endorsed the national government's plan despite its elusive goal.[39] Faced with a shortage of materials and laborers, the Sololá municipal council proposed a public works tax and recommended that the *regidor de indígenas* (indigenous councilman) be charged with enlisting workers. Such shortages kept Sololá's marketplace in the planning stages for seven years before it was completed in the early 1940s.[40]

Some Mayas recognized the benefits of market buildings, but many female vendors claimed being enclosed in a building marginalized their sales.[41] By the 1940s towns throughout the western highlands had enclosed markets, but even in these communities and especially in the central highlands, public plazas remained the business place of many vendors, as photographs from the first half of the twentieth century illustrate (figures 1.7, 3.3, and 3.5).[42]

The control and use of public space was an expression of power. By spreading their goods on the street, vendors were not merely claiming the ground they occupied; they also were helping to create an environment where the marginalized could move about freely with a sense of propriety.[43] Some women defied the state's project right in front of its market buildings. On the left-hand side of figure 3.4, the nineteenth-century vendor has her wares spread out on the street across from the entrance to the public market in Guatemala City. In an indication of how valuable such spaces were, at times merchants physically removed shoppers and bystanders who crowded their vending areas.[44]

Greatly outnumbered in most highland towns, ladino authorities criminalized indigenous activities in the plazas and streets to establish control over these public spaces. For example, because upper- and middle-class ladinos associated *indios* with street life and generally considered the street, with its exposure to dust and air, to be contaminated and dirty—as they often described *indios* and their dwellings as well—local officials frequently arrested or fined *indígenas* for "dirtying the streets."[45] Since many ladino officials and medical professionals were convinced that *indios* were suscepti-

Figure 3.3. Mercado de Tecpán, ca. 1925. Image courtesy of Colección Fototeca Guatemala, CIRMA (Centro de Investigaciones Regionales de Mesoamérica).

Figure 3.4. Public market, Guatemala City, ca. 1875. Photograph by Eadweard Muybridge. Image courtesy of Boston Athenaeum.

ble to and propagators of disease because they lacked hygiene, modern notions of public health and biomedicine added an air of legitimacy to these arrests.[46] In ladino authorities' worldviews, market buildings facilitated a more sterile and organized environment and thus contributed to public health, national progress, and social stability. These structures could also help officials to reinscribe their power in public places.

Keeping marketplaces clean and orderly was a central concern for local authorities. It was not just women's prevalence in markets that gave these crimes a gendered component, however. When authorities extended the codes to the streets, they seldom cited men for sanitation violations.[47] Associating females with domestic labor, municipal officials expected women to keep public spaces, including streets, clean and almost invariably described offenders as *amas de casa* (housewives).

As evidenced by those arrested for soiling streets and markets, many of whom were recidivists, women readily disregarded cleanliness as part of their socially constructed identities.[48] An incident that occurred on September 2, 1935, is emblematic of these confrontations:

> Yesterday, during market hours, *señora* Catarina Estrada was busy expending *arroz en leche*, without any concern for the cleanliness of the stall's dishes; the cups as well as the wash stand in which she washed them were extremely dirty. For this reason, the person in charge of sanitation vigi-

lance, José Contreras, called her attention to this particular [problem]. And Estrada, instead of respecting the instructions of *señor* Contreras, verbally abused him.[49]

Informed by racist stereotypes about *indios*, authorities focused their efforts on the indigenous population, yet they were as likely to cite ladinas (such as the forty-year-old Estrada) as *indígenas* for public health violations. Women cited for sanitation violations were not necessarily rejecting social constructions of women's domestic responsibilities, the state's efforts to improve public health, or ladinos' attempts to exact their labor. Many were simply preoccupied with other tasks—ones that did not correspond to the priorities of municipal authorities.

Some vendors resisted or ignored public health encroachments, while customers often welcomed them. In October 1944 Emilia Ajquejay Bac took a butcher to San Martín municipal court, where she testified:

> With complete confidence I took them [the *chorizos* or sausages] home and prepared them for lunch, with the rest of my family members and domestic partner. . . . Immediately after [eating them,] I had an uncomfortable feeling of cold leaving from my heart and the rest of my body, [and] burning in my eyes, and headaches to the extent that I could not see. And that was how everyone else was, with stomach pains and burning lips. For that reason, I immediately presumed it was the effects of the *chorizos*.[50]

Already sick with parasites, her five-year-old daughter had not eaten any *chorizos* and "nothing happened to her," added Ajquejay.

Her son's testimony suggests that some *indígenas* placed great faith in the government's public health interventions. In confirming the family's sudden symptoms, Vicente Ajquejay noted that his mother was going to throw away the *chorizos* because they smelled so bad, but his father told her not to because "selling bad meat in the plaza was prohibited."[51] Perhaps convinced of the efficacy of the municipality's campaign against "merchants with few scruples [who] sell to the public articles in bad condition,"[52] Vicente's father could not imagine the meat was rotten even though it appeared to be. To his mind, state control as it manifested itself through public health regulations did not infringe upon citizens; on the contrary, it protected them. It is unclear whether the municipal magistrate's opinion was informed by a similar sense of confidence in the public health system or by his suspicion of the indigenous plaintiffs, who, he observed, showed "symptoms of intoxication" but otherwise appeared to be in good health, but he, too, doubted the *chorizos* were spoiled, and he absolved the butcher.

Figure 3.5. Kaqchikeles de San Juan Sacatepéquez, ca. 1910. Photograph by Alberto Valdeavellano. Image courtesy of Colección Fototeca Guatemala, CIRMA (Centro de Investigaciones Regionales de Mesoamérica).

In truth, local officials' vigilance of perishables, particularly meat, was motivated as much by financial as public health concerns; licenses generated income for municipalities. Earlier that year, a magistrate discovered that Sofia Tay had lard, *chorizos, chicharrón,* and other pork products in her home, and he arrested her for butchering a pig without obtaining a license or paying the corresponding tax. Tay explained that she could not have fulfilled the municipal requirements because her actions were not premeditated; the pig had drowned, so she had to butcher it immediately. Her appeal failed to impress the San Martín magistrate, who sentenced her to thirty days in jail.[53] In light of Tay's plight, the fifty-year-old indigenous widow Margarita García was wise to request permission in December 1944 to butcher her pig. The San Martín municipal secretary readily granted her a license as long as the lard and meat were for personal consumption, not sale.[54]

Butchers were not the only vendors who had to comply with local public health mandates. In 1935 the San Martín *regidor* Vicente Herrera arrested the thirty-year-old, illiterate, *indígena* Feliza Armira for "selling groceries without her corresponding medical certificate."[55] After Armira confessed, the *juez de paz* sentenced her to five days in jail commutable by ten cents a day. Documentation of failures to abide by the regulations as well as evidence of other residents' confidence that the system was protecting their health demonstrate that *indígenas* resented and welcomed government regulations.

The state's intervention went beyond interactions in marketplaces to the way space and vendors were organized within them. The Estrada Cabrera and Ubico regimes attempted to reorganize markets based on goods instead of people. Traditionally, vendors sat with their linguistic, ethnic, and community groups, and government officials sought to relocate them according to the products they sold. Since communities tended to specialize in certain goods, some traveling merchants could sit together without violating the state's organizational schema. Others resisted the proposed changes as infringing upon their businesses and worldviews.[56] In August 1944 Maximiliana Chonay "was in jail because she did not want to position herself in the place that corresponded to her in the market."[57] By defining such acts as criminal, the state sought to strip indigenous women's protests of their legitimacy.[58] Much like her contemporaries who undermined authorities' efforts to reclaim public plazas and streets, Chonay disrupted the state's attempt to impose its version of order and progress.

Contested Worldviews

Disagreements over modalities of production and exchange litter the criminal record. Since offenders were largely indigenous women and authorities were almost invariably ladino men, these interactions provide a window into gender and ethnic relations. Inspectors and police regularly arrested female vendors for *abuso mercantil* (commercial abuse) and for establishing "monopolies" on such goods as eggs, chickens, sugar, plants, maize, and beans. In the San Martín plaza on January 5, 1925, authorities arrested two illiterate, indigenous *molenderas* ages sixteen and fourteen "for monopolizing . . . articles of first necessity." Without raising "any objection in their favor," the girls confessed to their crime and were convicted.[59]

Their silence and that of many of their contemporaries stands in stark contrast to Kaqchikel historical narratives that decry ladinos', particularly butchers', efforts to prevent competition by establishing monopolies and threatening would-be indigenous rivals. According to the sixty-three-year-old Comalapa vendor B'eleje' Imox, "Only *mo's* [ladinos] would sell. They did not let *qawinäq* [our people] because they did not want *qawinäq* to succeed. That is what they did in the market."[60] A Kaqchikel ethnohistorian whose great-aunt (shown in figure 1.7) was a vendor in the Patzicía market in the mid-twentieth century was shocked to learn that Kaqchikel women were accused of monopolizing the sale of goods. He was sure only ladinas did that.[61] Oral histories and judicial records represent idealizations and thus distortions of the past; Kaqchikel informants' selective memories of unscrupulous ladinos who abused Mayas in marketplaces are informed by a broader history of ladino and Creole discrimination against *indígenas*, while the predominance of indigenous, female vendors in criminal records is partly a product of Guatemalan structures designed to exploit *indígenas* and privilege Creole and ladino elites. But oral histories and legal documents find common ground in their portrayal of highland markets as theaters of conflict among Mayas, ladinos, and authorities.[62]

Although the documents do not elaborate on what constituted *abuso mercantil* or how women established monopolies, authorities were explicitly concerned with food supplies. In 1933, San Martín officials explained that they prosecuted "monopolizers" because monopolies caused shortages in the market.[63] As the staple food of the majority of the population, corn preoccupied most officials. That same year Chimaltenango's Jefatura Política prohibited the wholesale exchange of maize.[64] The director of the National Police echoed these concerns in 1937 when he justified the campaign against hoarding (*acaparamiento*) by noting that "the shortage of maize is great."[65] On these grounds, authorities sometimes arrested consumers who they believed were hoarding. Such was the case when the chief of Patzicía's municipal police arrested Marcelino Ajquejay on February 2, 1943. In his defense, the twenty-six-year-old *jornalero* admitted that he purchased "a little more than two *arrobas* [of maize, about fifty pounds] . . . but it is for his consumption . . . not for business."[66] Confident of the evidence before him, the *juez de paz* sentenced Ajquejay to five days in jail commutable by fifteen cents a day. Two days later, Ajquejay commuted his sentence.

In contrast to the two aforementioned teenage girls from San Martín, another illiterate, indigenous *molendera*, Felipa Laria, denied hoarding chickens in the public market; she insisted she was selling them at a fair price. Patzicía's *juez de paz* was not swayed; he sentenced Laria to five days in jail commutable by five cents a day "for being known as a chicken hoarder."[67]

Cases like Laria's point to *indígenas'* and authorities' differing logic regarding marketplace exchanges. Authorities often related *acaparamiento* to selling goods above or below their "official" prices. Setting prices low could lead to monopolies,[68] but often wide price ranges were simply part of a long tradition of haggling whereby vendors set prices of certain goods such as fruits, vegetables, and chickens high knowing that consumers would negotiate them down. Sometimes vendors would sell their goods below the official prices because they needed to move their goods.[69] Yet San Martín authorities equated hagglers (*regatonas*) with monopolizers (*monopolizado-*

ras).[70] In truth, officials, not indigenous vendors, tried to control the market by setting prices, though as the ethnographic record shows, frequent price fluctuations and multiple media of exchange made establishing official prices nearly impossible for many commodities.[71]

At the same time, Kaqchikel were not naïve about the potential pitfalls of the traditional bargaining system. A Kaqchikel female elder recalled, "A long time ago, if women charged too much money in the market, they went to jail."[72] Confrontations over haggling could become violent. To cite but one example, when the thirty-five-year-old *indígena* Daniel Sirin from Itzapa refused to sell his avocados at the price Angela Morales demanded, she responded with what he described as an *aguacatazo*, or powerful avocado blow. Unfortunately for him, the Patzicía police officer Manuel de la Cruz only saw Sirin hit Morales, so he was sentenced to five days in jail commutable by ten cents a day.[73]

As the prodigious number of marketplace violations suggests, municipal and national authorities were increasingly inserting themselves into local economic relations. That police arrested *la señora* Francisca de Meneses of Patzicía for violating a gas-sale ordinance in 1937 and eighteen-year-old Faustina González Sazo from Santa Lucía Utatlán for violating a brown-sugar ordinance in 1943 speaks to the specificity of the state's regulations.[74] Such confrontations demonstrate the hybrid nature of highland marketplaces, where distinct economic and social relations of production, exchange, and circulation intersected.

These arrests reveal how the change from one market culture to another transforms a local economy and society. As an expression of what Sahlins calls "the resistance of culture,"[75] some vendors sought to maintain or adapt earlier modalities of production and exchange in the face of a new, disempowering system. By imposing new regulations on vendors, the state was not merely enforcing the transformation of indigenous markets in abstract economic terms but rather encroaching upon cultural traits by establishing ladino logic, worldviews, and behavior as normative in the structure and functioning of those markets. As in Argentina and other nations, elites conceived of the market as a way to integrate subalterns into Guatemala's national program of progress and thereby engender social harmony.[76] Tempting as it is to read vendors' violations as resistance to the state's hegemonic project, they can also be attributed to poverty, honest mistakes, "the ultimate dream of domination: to have the dominated exploit each other," or simply everyday behavior.[77] Forster has noted that participation in an underground economy was a form of working-class resistance,[78] yet it is also worth noting that often it was a survival strategy. Defendants like Isabel

Bajxac and the numerous bootleggers who claimed they disregarded laws to feed their families speak to this phenomenon.

Marketplace confrontations reveal the broad array of officials who patrolled local markets: inspectors, tax collectors, police, and other authorities. The state's campaign against *aguardiente clandestino* meant that the Treasury Police, particularly suspicious of vendors who sold sugar since it was one of the principal ingredients in *aguardiente*, perambulated municipal markets and public plazas as well. To cite an example of this vigilance, Treasury Police officer Víctor Muñoz arrested the thirty-year-old ladina Santo Rosales twice for selling *tapas de panela* (brown-sugar cakes or disks) below the regulated price of eight cents a *tapa*.[79] In both instances, indigenous men aided Muñoz. When Juan Xico Patzay approached Rosales in the municipal market on May 2, 1942, she sold him a *tapa* for seven cents. Denying the transaction ever transpired, she admitted she had no witnesses to prove it. So Patzicía's *juez de paz* fined her seventy-two cents and sentenced her to five days in jail.

Perhaps in an effort to avoid Muñoz's gaze thereafter, Rosales moved her business to the public plaza, but when she sold a *tapa* for seven cents to Rafael Samatz a few months later, Muñoz again arrested her and confiscated her *tapas*. Rosales again denied the charges, insisting that she only sold her *tapas* for eight cents each. In what was becoming a familiar pattern, the *juez de paz* disregarded her testimony, fined her, and sentenced her to five days in jail. Although she lost fifteen *tapas de panela* valued at eight cents each, for a total of slightly more than a quetzal, and accumulated fines of more than another quetzal, Rosales had enough money to commute both sentences. A note in the margins of the first case to alert the Jefatura Política suggests that these were not isolated events. At the very least, they speak to a broader phenomenon of Treasury Police scouring municipal markets for sugar vendors associated with the *aguardiente clandestino* trade.

The frequency with which female vendors appear in the criminal record suggests authorities were concerned about women's control in the marketplace. Barely three weeks after prosecuting the two teenage vendors mentioned above, San Martín officials arrested ten other women for monopolizing goods in the marketplace.[80] Their ages ranged widely, from fourteen to seventy; most vendors arrested for these crimes were illiterate, indigenous females. Since most towns, including Patzicía and San Martín, had only one major market day a week, vendors generally had other occupations; many were *molenderas*. Their responses to being arrested varied from confessions to declarations of innocence and the many shades of ambivalence and ambiguity in between. As Isabel Bajxac's violations revealed, some vendors were unaware of the state's mandates or were unable or unwilling to act in accordance with them.

Although the majority of women arrested were *indígenas*, authorities were not blind to ladina violations. In 1941 a Patzicía municipal official arrested the thirty-five-year-old ladina Micaela Escobar for hoarding eggs. Despite her insistence that she was not planning on selling them, the *juez de paz* sentenced her to five days in jail commutable by twenty cents a day.[81]

In addition to their efforts to extirpate monopolies and to protect public health, officials regulated media of exchange. Here, too, the Treasury Police played a prominent role. Since rural vendors used at least four systems of weights and measures (the English, the colonial Spanish, the metric, and the indigenous), authorities sought to standardize as well as police their interactions.[82] According to Tax, the government largely succeeded in controlling "merchandising by means of full-weight laws."[83] The judicial record and contemporary ethnographies reveal, however, that standardization was elusive. Even as scales became more common throughout the highlands in the 1920s, the unit of measure varied widely.[84] On April 19, 1925, three illiterate, indigenous *molenderas* were arrested in the San Martín market for weighing their goods with a rock.[85] Metal and brass cup weights were commonly used in highland markets by the 1930s, yet Tax and McBryde observed vendors weighing goods with stones and potatoes as late as the 1940s.[86] In 1943 Treasury Police officer Demetrio Gálvez arrested three indigenous vendors in Patzicía for using fruit to weigh their corn. In confessing, the accused explained they only used fruit because they did not have a *marca*, or more accurate unit of measure.[87] Unmoved by their lack of resources, the *juez de paz* sentenced them to five days in jail commutable by ten cents a day.

Many accused of such economic crimes pled innocence or ignorance, partly because in addition to being jailed or fined, they stood to lose their products and reputations. Accused of defrauding the public on October 30, 1935, the twenty-two-year-old, illiterate *indígena* Vicenta Pata told Patzicía's justice of the peace that she was unaware that her scale was inaccurate since she had borrowed it from another woman in town. Too poor to own her own scale, Pata pointed out that her incrimination was the result of her marginalization rather than a calculated attempt to break the law or deceive her customers. Her explanation failed to sway the municipal magistrate, who sentenced her to five days in jail commutable by five cents a day.[88] Eight years later, when the market inspector caught the forty-one-year-old Segundina Ajquejay selling maize with inexact weights and measurements, she similarly insisted that "it was not her intention to defraud the public."[89] Claiming he could see that the scale and weights before him were inaccurate, the Patzicía *juez de paz* sentenced her to five days in prison commutable by ten cents a day.

This struggle between the state's goals as articulated in its laws and indigenous practices was as much about economic privations as about distinct methods and logic. Some vendors may have claimed that poverty precluded their shift to the state's standardized measurements to mask their resistance to changing their long-accepted methods. Although the question begs further research, ethnicity and class almost undoubtedly shaped how vendors responded to officials' mandates. By 1944 a number of vendors who appeared to be ladinas preempted market inspectors' investigations by registering with the municipality. Updating their licenses periodically, they continued to return for official approval of their weights.[90] Whether ladinas were more likely than indigenous women to abide by the state's regulations because they had the means to do so or because these economic reforms resonated with them is difficult to discern. Whatever the explanation, municipal *jueces de paz* refused to allow *indígenas'* poverty or distinct market relations to influence their rulings. For vendors, local justice tended to be harsh.

Insolent *Indígenas*

That some women simply accepted their fate but did not change their practices, as evidenced by recidivism, while others sought to convince authorities of the legality of their actions hints at the diverse ways women claimed authority and contested power. Indigenous vendors were not always or necessarily surreptitiously trying to evade the state's mandates; some confronted local officials directly. Court and police records abound with indigenous women disobeying market regulations and more generally disrupting the peace by fighting, drinking, and yelling. These documents reveal what E. P. Thompson has called "working women's lack of deference and their contestation of authority."[91] As Patzicía's *juez del mercado* in the early 1940s, the *agricultor* José María Juárez from Patzún was regularly subjected to market women's abuse. In one case, Juárez tried to collect the *impuesto de piso* (municipal tax on a vendor's space) from *la indígena* Juana Coc on June 9, 1943; she refused to pay, so he took a garment from her as collateral. When she arrived to pick it up, she "insulted and disrespected him."[92] Comprising the vast majority of participants in highland marketplaces, indigenous women often felt emboldened there. Upon entering these places, ladinos, men, and municipal and national officials could no longer take for granted the privileged positions they generally enjoyed in broader Guatemalan society.

Poor, indigenous women who threatened and abused ladino officials challenged hierarchies of power based on gender, ethnicity, class, and state-subaltern relations. Simply put, upper- to middle-class ladino men were among the most privileged of the nation's citizens, while poor and working-class indigenous women were among its most marginalized. Furthermore, men, not women, were supposed to be aggressive and outspoken in public. But these female vendors often were brusque, bold, independent, and tough. As protagonists who initiated aggressive actions against ladino authorities, these indigenous women were breaking with normative constructions of gender and ethnicity, even if diverging from the conventions may not have been motivated by attempts to radically alter patriarchy, racist relations, state hegemony, or capitalist modes of production.

At times they insulted authorities simply because they considered the demands unjust. When Juárez charged the illiterate *indígena* Modesta Chirir the *impuesto de piso* on July 22, 1942, in the Patzicía plaza, she responded by calling him a "shameless thief [*ladrón*] . . . [who] collected money to rob her."[93] Although she was young (twenty-five years old), single, and far from her Itzapa home, Chirir did not cower in court. She admitted to her outburst, explaining that when "the collector" charged her two cents for her sale of tomatoes, she offered to pay one cent, but he declined. "That is what made her angry and provoked that word [*ladrón*]," the municipal notary recorded.[94] Chirir was not challenging the municipality's right to taxation; rather, she insisted the rate was too high (as did many of her counterparts) and became irate when Juárez refused to negotiate. Perhaps Chirir was simply lowballing Juárez. Ten years earlier the minimum market tax in Sololá was two cents, though McBryde observed frequent arguments between vendors and tax collectors there too. Like the plethora of *acaparamiento* arrests, Chirir's arrest emanated partly from a clash of cultures and the logics that informed them: Chirir was constantly haggling with customers, and Juárez never considered the tax negotiable.[95] That she paid fifty cents to commute her five-day sentence indicates she did not lack the money to pay the tax.

These interactions provide a window into perceptions of social status and the contested nature of authority. When indigenous vendors insulted Juárez, they effectively attacked his social position and mocked his authority. To defend these privileges, Juárez took them to court, where judges attempted to reinstate his status and reestablish his hegemony by punishing the women. Because these exchanges were also rooted in the regulation of public space—market inspectors like Juárez not only charged for the use of public space but also tried to establish what types of behavior would be tolerated in public markets and plazas—market inspectors were far from alone in this battle. The forty-five-year-old *indígena* Leona Esquit insulted

Juárez while he was collecting the sales tax on November 13, 1942; municipal police agent Alfredo Calderón arrested her, and his assistant Antonio Racanac testified on Juárez's behalf. With so many authorities pitted against her, Esquit's denial of the charges failed to impress Patzicía's municipal magistrate. He sentenced her to five days in jail commutable by fifteen cents a day.[96]

The frequency with which Juárez and other market inspectors brought such offenses to the court's attention indicates that indigenous women did not confer the same social status or authority upon these officials that they and the judicial officials did. Like their counterparts elsewhere in Latin America, female vendors were remarkably free to insult authorities and elites.[97] The divergent assessments of who deserved respect and obedience suggest that these vendors operated by different principles (and as Chirir's testimony implies, logic), which in turn underscores the state's failure to unite citizens around its national imaginary and impose its hegemonic project.

As arrests of outspoken vendors attest, authorities were quick to quell unrest in marketplaces and their environs. Since keeping the peace was good for business, some vendors appreciated these efforts. When a fight broke out causing a "great commotion" in the central plaza on September 29, 1943, a market day, Juárez and two assistants quickly arrested the offending parties. Later that day they whisked away a disgruntled military conscript whose yelling "disturbed order" in the central plaza.[98] Merchants also appreciated authorities' efforts to curtail theft.

Confrontations with local officials notwithstanding, the market afforded the chance for camaraderie in a largely female world. Even today, like domestic labor, selling is considered essentially female in nature in much of Latin America.[99] Tax found that the few males who sold in Panajachel's market were subject to criticism and ridicule.[100] Further fomenting female familiarity, a shared indigenous cultural category (as opposed to identifying as ladina), socioeconomic background, and occupation (*molendera*) characterized most highland vendors.

Yet female solidarity should not be overstated. A number of female vendors appeared before the court for hitting or insulting other women. At times, violence in the market was related to racism. Ix'ajpu', a seventy-seven-year-old Kaqchikel woman from Patzún, recalls, "If you were in the market where they sell cheap goods, ladinas . . . would hit you because they were ladinas."[101] The high incidence of female crimes in marketplaces as compared to other public spaces reflects women's significant numbers and the state's vigilance; it also indicates women's ease and freedom there.

As the domain of women, the marketplace was one of the few places where women became politicized. Reflecting on his boyhood, Víctor Perera remembers Maya market women as "a vocal and militant faction in the affairs of Guatemala City."[102] In some cases, relations were so inverted that in effect market administrators served vendors. As one ethnographer notes, local officials were careful not to antagonize politically powerful marketers.[103] Since women were denied leadership positions in such community organizations as the *municipalidades indígenas*, they had few structures through which they could advocate for themselves. Their public presence and stake in marketplaces encouraged them to be outspoken and confront authorities there.

Viewed in light of nineteenth- and twentieth-century policies designed to promote commercial coffee production through land divestiture and labor extraction, the attempt to alter highland markets can be seen as a continuation of the state's assaults on indigenous communities and economies. Prior to the state's interventions, highland marketplaces were complex indigenous institutions that had their own normative practices and moral economies within which indigenous women played a significant role. The shift from the end of the nineteenth century onward altered these conditions but not as a market revolution, according to abstract economic norms. Rather, liberal economic reforms were experienced via the state's intervention as an attempt to remake the market as ladino, not indigenous, controlled by males, not females, and regulated by state authorities, not local communities. With varying degrees of success, the state achieved this "modernization" of market structures, relations, and exchanges in Guatemala City, Mazatenango, Huehuetenango, and Retalhuleu.[104]

Regardless of their intentions, indigenous market women through their diverse actions and tactics confounded state efforts to transform central highland marketplaces in the ways it intended. They attenuated the effects of the market culture and ladino acculturation on indigenous economies and communities through their public presence and interactions with local officials. Poor indigenous women were perhaps the least able to control the circumstances of their lives, but they were not powerless.

As protagonists strove to maintain or adapt earlier modes of production and exchange when confronted by a different, disempowering logic, struggles in the marketplace were simultaneously rooted in class, gender, and ethnicity. The interplay of national agendas, laws (national and municipal), police (National, Treasury, and municipal), local authorities, vendors, and consumers demonstrates the complex, contradictory, and contested everyday process of marketplace and by extension nation-state formation.

In terms of the balance of power between authorities and delinquents, municipal officials who lived and worked alongside the people they arrested and tried had to constantly reconstitute their authority over community members whose lives were not much different from their own. Informed by dictatorial rule at the national level, municipal officials sought to implement their own versions of strong-arm rule, however attenuated, at the local level. In contrast, department judges worked and presumably often lived in the department capital of Chimaltenango, far removed—geographically, socially, and politically—from the rural villages and towns of many of the litigants they saw in court. In short, the high conviction rate of vendors in municipal courts as opposed to the frequent clemency enjoyed by moonshiners in department courts can be attributed, at least in part, to municipal judicial officials' greater stake in the outcomes of those particular rulings than their department counterparts had in theirs. Since municipalities collected and kept marketplace and licensing fees, municipal officials were keenly aware of direct benefits of enforcing marketplace regulations and laws; department judges had little self- or institutional interest in ruling against moonshiners beyond upholding the law because alcohol revenues were collected and disbursed at the national, not regional level.

Living and working in the same close-knit communities as the vendors they arrested and tried meant that municipal officials were also likely better informed about these violators' circumstances than department judges were of the lives of defendants who entered their courts. As evidenced by racial tensions in highland communities, this intimacy often bred cynicism and loathing. Defendants' attempts to reframe their incrimination by pointing to poverty or other conditions that predetermined their lives and livelihoods seldom swayed municipal judicial officials. Defendants who exaggerated their marginalization in hopes of reducing their sentences had better results in department courts than municipal courts, perhaps partly because municipal magistrates based their rulings on their own perceptions of litigants' lives.

Some officials patrolling highland markets, such as the Treasury Police, were connected to national power structures, and many municipal officials were attempting to enforce such national agendas as public health regulations and vendor locations; however, most municipal officials had decidedly local agendas. A study of these relations in towns such as Sololá, Totonicapán, and Quetzaltenango where indigenous leadership held considerable sway vis-à-vis ladinos and state authorities would undoubtedly reveal a broader range of responses to market regulations and violations.

The ethnic dimensions of state building in Guatemala reflected a broader trend in much of Latin America where national elites simultaneously incorporated and marginalized locally diverse, ethnically distinct, indigenous peoples in the march toward capitalism, modernization, and nationalism.[105] The paeans of indigenous merchants described earlier reflect this tendency by holding up "aboriginal" men as symbols of national diligence on one hand and depicting them as technology-averse beasts of burden who would never become full citizens on the other. As the struggles in the marketplace illustrate, this hegemonic process also had a gendered and class component. Guatemalan postcolonial elites sought to contain women's possibilities and channel women's contributions into patriarchal and non-indigenous visions of nation building. The increasing state regulation of the economy led in turn to greater interventions in the realm of public morality.[106] Despite being based on patriarchal notions of authority, these interventions offered women considerable space to contest male, ladino, and elite power.

As economic and cultural brokers, indigenous female vendors, like their nineteenth-century predecessors, enjoyed considerable influence, autonomy, and economic mobility.[107] Though it was two to three times the commutation rate assessed her contemporaries who insulted market inspectors, the forty-year-old indigenous *soltera* Timotea Miculax readily paid a quetzal and a half to commute her five-day sentence.[108] In her study of nineteenth-century Diriomo, Nicaragua, Elizabeth Dore found that independent female artisans and traders enjoyed significant wealth and thus freedom; some used their "economic wherewithal to postpone marriage."[109] Miculax and other successful senior *solteras* in the archival record suggest this was the case for Guatemalan indigenous women too. In the early to mid-twentieth century, ethnographers of Guatemala including Wagley found that married indigenous women enjoyed significant sway in their families as guardians of money and important papers.[110] The married *molenderas* and vendors who were often outspoken in highland marketplaces and courtrooms indicate their authority in community and familial matters.

Depending on their goals and circumstances, women engaged some aspects of dominant discourses and recourses and ignored or rejected others. By welcoming, accommodating, ignoring, or resisting municipal and national authorities, indigenous women were conveying different messages. Vendors who were arrested repeatedly for *abuso mercantil*, monopolizing goods, or sanitation violations let officials know, even in their silence, that the enforcement of those laws jeopardized their livelihoods and was generally regarded as a nuisance. On the other hand, by using the very institutions that criminalized vendors' activities to press for their own rights, some women invited municipal officials to be more interventionist. Such acts were not necessarily complicitous; on the contrary, as scholars of India and Africa have demonstrated, often subalterns retained their oppositional agency by invoking aspects of the dominant culture.[111] Indigenous women's sundry strategies for achieving their goals were informed by nuanced comprehension of the differing goals, agendas, and authority of the state's local, regional, and national representatives.

Authorities' dealings with market women were similarly ambivalent. In colonial Potosí, Bolivia, historian Jane Mangan asserts, the city council persecuted indigenous market women;[112] in contrast, municipal officials in highland Guatemala both plagued and protected indigenous market women. Patzicía's *juez de mercado* José María Juárez exemplified these interactions, from collecting taxes and arresting vendors to protecting their livelihoods by ensuring that the marketplace was safe and orderly.

Their broad range of roles and responsibilities can be attributed partly to officials' perceptions of women as both formidable and weak. By portraying women as vulnerable and susceptible to corruption, liberal leaders and intellectuals vested them with a certain degree of power, since these same characteristics made them a threat to national progress and social order. The very social constructions that constrained women's life possibilities also identified females as a force that had to be contained. Even though local and national officials largely downplayed or ignored women's economic contributions and emphasized and even celebrated men's entrepreneurship and labor, the number of indigenous female vendors who appear in the criminal record indicates that municipal and national ladino authorities perceived indigenous women as a threat to capitalist principles and Hispanic homogenization.

As in the state's campaign against *aguardiente clandestino*, its goal in highland markets was to impose its will. Since the goals, personalities, and perceptions of the various players who cumulatively constituted the state varied, the experiences of those who came in contact with authorities differed greatly. Just as the vendors who refused to pay taxes and insulted market inspectors reveal the limits of state power, consumers who turned to municipal courts to regulate marketplace exchanges disclose the state's ability to co-opt even its most marginalized charges. We now approach the balance of power between people and the state by examining the ways authorities and women deployed gendered legislation and discourse to radically different ends.

Unnatural Mothers and Reproductive Crimes: Infanticide, Abortion, and Cross-Dressing

The National Police and other authorities approached infanticide and abortion as crimes against motherhood, reflecting rhetoric elsewhere in Latin America, while highland women put fathers and husbands on trial for these acts. Of the fifteen cases of infanticide and abortion in the department of Chimaltenango from 1900 to 1925,[1] nine of the defendants were males and nine were females; in one case the police had no suspect (appendix 7).[2] The high rate of male defendants contrasts sharply with other areas of Latin America; in Argentina and Mexico, infanticide generally was committed by women to maintain their jobs or honor.[3] Although some Guatemalan women committed reproductive crimes for similar reasons, those who accused men of these crimes demonstrated how the same gendered institutions that buttressed local patriarchies provided women with the tools to challenge the men's perceived right to beat their wives.

In effect throughout the Estrada Cabrera regime, the 1889 penal code defined "infanticide" as a crime that only mothers or maternal grandparents could commit.[4] According to the law, infanticide litigation against men should have been tried as homicide. Yet as a manifestation of popular notions influencing Guatemala's legal system, municipal officials and even a few department judges approached these felonies as infanticides in response to the new mothers and their kin who employed a broader definition of the crime.

Using the legal system for their own ends, highland women complicated gendered notions of reproductive responsibilities and held men accountable for their violence. By accusing men of infanticide and abortion, women highlighted male reproductive responsibilities in a nation that, like most patriarchal societies, tended to view such responsibilities as primarily those of females. Remarkably, the women often did so by using legislation that underscored this view.

From 1900 to 1925, seven men and seven women were accused of infanticide in Chimaltenango (appendix 7). Of these, six identified as indigenous men, three as indigenous women, one as ladino, and one as ladina. The midwife and two other women who did not explicitly state their ethnicities all appear to have been ladinas. Including those whose ethnicities we can confidently infer, three ladinas and one female *indígena* were convicted of infanticide. By framing her act as a desperate attempt to protect her and her ladina matron's honor, the *indígena* had her sentence reduced. Because the judges changed the charges from infanticide to homicide, the two indigenous male defendants who were convicted served longer sentences than their female counterparts. Of the eight people acquitted, four were indigenous men, two were indigenous women, one was ladina, and one was ladino. With only ten cases to study, discerning a ruling or sentencing pattern based on ethnicity or gender is difficult.

The five abortion cases (one of which had no suspects) during this period make this challenge even more acute. Two men (most likely one was ladino and one *indígena*) and two women (one identified as *indígena*, and the other likely was) were defendants in those cases. None were convicted of abortion, though the indigenous male served a little over two years in jail as his case wound its way through the judicial system. As part of what emerged as a common theme in infanticide and abortion litigation, his incarceration provided his wife some respite from his physical abuse. Having lost a child or pregnancy, these female plaintiffs never won restitution, but by altering the intent of infanticide legislation and casting a broad net with abortion legislation, they often exacted retribution.

Women who used the term "infanticide" to label crimes by men that were homicide as defined by Guatemala law were not doing so in opposition to state power or patriarchy. On the contrary, they used the state's tools to criminalize individual men. With their own logic and worldviews and the help of municipal judicial officials who processed and referred the cases as infanticide to department judicial officials who often continued to consider them as such, female plaintiffs altered the context and confines of Guatemala's judicial system. Absent "an intentional politics of cultural opposition" on the part of female plaintiffs and with some officials' tacit approval, these reconfigurations of the law can be read as a "resistance of culture," to borrow Sahlins's turn of phrase, to the legal precepts laid down in Guatemalan criminal codes.[5] That poor, indigenous women could leverage the

Table 4.1. Infanticide arrests, Guatemala, 1927–1944, by suspect ethnicity, gender, and literacy

Year	Number of arrests	Ladino Male	Ladino Female	Ladino Total	Indígena Male	Indígena Female	Indígena Total	All Male	All Female	All Literate	All Illiterate
1927	2	—	—	—	—	—	—	—	—	—	—
1928	11	—	—	—	—	—	—	—	—	—	—
1929	7	—	—	—	—	—	—	3	4	—	—
1930	—	—	—	—	—	—	—	—	—	—	—
1931	—	—	—	—	—	—	—	—	—	—	—
1932	7	—	—	—	—	—	—	3	4	—	—
1933	7	—	—	1	—	—	6	0	7	—	—
1934	5	—	—	2	2	—	3	2	3	1	4
1935	17	12	0	12	5	0	5	17	0	4	13
1936	7	—	—	2	—	—	5	4	3	2	5
1937	8	—	—	5	—	—	3	4	4	4	4
1938	2	1	1	2	0	0	0	1	1	—	—
1939	22	0	8	8	2	12	14	2	20	0	24
1940	10	3	3	6	1	3	4	4	6	5	5
1941	12	1	3	4	1	7	8	2	10	2	10
1942	10	1	5	6	1	3	4	2	8	4	6
1943	6	0	3	3	0	3	3	0	6	0	6
1944	2	1	0	1	0	1	1	1	1	1	1
Total	135	19	23	52	10	29	56	45	77	23	78

Source: Policía Nacional, Memorias 1928–1945.

Notes: A dash (—) indicates that no data were available.

Neither National Police reports nor judicial archives suggest an explanation for why 17 men and no women were arrested on infanticide charges in 1935. I suspect the numbers were placed in the wrong columns. Subtracting this outlier from the data further underscores the gendered nature of infanticide charges.

judicial system against male aggressors with the aid—if only in the form of silence—of municipal and department authorities even as these strategies diverged from the intent of national legislation speaks to the state's limited ability to dictate the behavior of its representatives, let alone its charges. Ironically, this weakness facilitated the judicial flexibility that helped to sustain the Estrada Cabrera regime.

Reproductive crime litigation offers insight into the equivocal dynamic between people and authorities. As in bootlegging and marketplace litigation, the state's primary goal in reproductive crime litigation was to enforce its will. Yet reproductive crime prosecution differed from that of bootlegging and marketplace infractions in that the state was not intruding into people's lives; rather, women implored judicial officials to enforce the law. When they engaged the court for their own personal pragmatic reasons, they acknowledged the legal system's authority. As the six convictions suggest, judges asserted the state's hegemony in ways that were similar to the moonshine and marketplace rulings: courts reminded litigants who was boss. At the same time, indigenous and poor ladino litigants enjoyed teaching moments in the courtroom. Just as department judges learned about rural poverty through moonshine litigation, so too did they learn about the gendered contours of rural violence through reproductive crime litigation.

The shifting balance of power between judicial authorities and female plaintiffs evident in these cases stands in stark contrast to police officers' and journalists' unequivocal judgments of women who committed infanticide during Ubico's reign. By the 1930s authorities made a concerted effort to maintain infanticide as a feminine transgression. If *La Gaceta* is any indication, rural, female highlanders' perceptions and practices had little effect on urban authorities or journalists. During the course of the twentieth century, certain types of deviance became more heavily gendered. Men continued to be accused of infanticide, while the number of females tried for that crime nearly doubled that of men (table 4.1). Abortion litigation was even more starkly gendered; from 1927 to 1944, 110 women and only 5 men were tried for abortion (table 4.2).

Daily newspapers like the *Diario de Centro America* seldom reported reproductive crimes; *Gaceta* journalists sensationalized them. Referring to female perpetrators as *madres desnaturalizadas* (unnatural mothers) and *madres sin entrañas* (soulless mothers), these journalists generally highlighted mothers' shortcomings instead of addressing such issues as poverty and marginalization that the accused often identified as catalysts to their crimes. Harsh rhetoric, stiff sentences, and social exclusion were the norm

Table 4.2. Abortion arrests, Guatemala, 1927–1944, by suspect ethnicity, gender, and literacy

Year	Number of arrests	Ladino			Indígena			All			
		Male	Female	Total	Male	Female	Total	Male	Female	Literate	Illiterate
1927	0	—	—	—	—	—	—	—	—	—	—
1928	0	—	—	—	—	—	—	—	—	—	—
1929	4	—	—	—	—	—	—	0	4	—	—
1930	—	—	—	—	—	—	—	—	—	—	—
1931	—	—	—	—	—	—	—	—	—	—	—
1932	6	—	—	—	—	—	—	0	6	—	—
1933	12	0	3	3	0	9	9	0	12	—	—
1934	2	0	1	1	0	1	1	0	2	—	—
1935	9	0	9	9	0	0	0	0	9	4	5
1936	10	0	10	10	0	0	0	0	10	4	6
1937	7	0	7	7	0	0	0	0	7	6	1
1938	9	0	6	6	0	3	3	0	9	5	4
1939	10	0	7	7	0	3	3	0	10	7	3
1940	15	0	10	10	0	5	5	0	15	6	9
1941	6	2	3	5	1	0	1	3	3	6	0
1942	10	0	5	5	0	5	5	0	10	1	9
1943	9	1	3	4	1	4	5	2	7	4	5
1944	6	0	2	2	0	4	4	0	6	2	4
Total	115	3	66	69	2	34	36	5	110	45	46

Source: Policía Nacional, Memorias 1928–1945.
Note: A dash (—) indicates data were not available.

for female culprits of infanticide by the 1930s even as their testimonies implicated their communities and the state.

Heightened Suspicions

Community members' concern with reproductive crimes was inversely proportional to their occurrence. The low incidence of reported reproductive crimes in Chimaltenango from 1900 to 1925 was not unusual; the department court only litigated three infanticide and six abortion cases from 1926 to 1944 (appendix 3).[6] Between 1927 and 1944 the arrests by National Police annually ranged from two to twenty-two people for infanticide and from two to fifteen people for abortion (tables 4.1 and 4.2). The frequency of reported reproductive crimes paled in comparison to other crimes such as bootlegging, theft, and assault and battery (appendices 3 and 4), yet denizens were ever vigilant as the 1907 trial of an indigenous couple from Tecpán intimates. After burying their baby in a cornfield, they were subject to investigation until upon exhumation, the coroner confirmed the child was stillborn.[7]

A heightened awareness of infant deaths often conspired against innocent women. When Joaquín Torrez found a fetus in Tejar in August 1909, a number of community members including *la indígena* Dolores Baran de Ajche, who needed an interpreter to testify, insisted the twenty-three-year-old *soltera* Amelia Cabrera had been pregnant but no longer appeared to be. Her status as an educated ladina did little to protect her from incarceration or a gynecological exam at the hands of a male doctor, who concluded that she showed no signs of an abortion or recent birth.[8] By mandating gynecological examinations, authorities assumed ownership over female bodies and subjected them to "a legal act of forcible penetration."[9] The parents who fought hard to spare their daughters this procedure offer one indication of how much it marginalized women.[10]

At times suspicious conditions were enough to implicate innocent women, as *la indígena* María Peren learned after passing out on the kitchen hearth of an Itzapa cantina on the night of November 29, 1901.[11] When the cantina owner saw Peren's dress covered in blood, she assumed Peren had had an abortion. Peren only compounded the problem by telling the police as much in a drunken stupor. Once sober, she recanted her testimony and explained that excessive menstrual bleeding had so stained her dress that she was too embarrassed to go outside, so she just lay across the hearth.

Adding insult to her already compromised reputation, she was subjected to a gynecological examination by a military surgeon; he confirmed that she showed no signs of abortion, only "abundant menstrual flow," which he associated with menopause.

As defendants often pointed out, false accusations could destroy a person's reputation. Two weeks after Chimaltenango's *juez de primera instancia* found her innocent of having an abortion, Juana Cuxil sent him a letter to formally accuse her complainants of libel because they continued to call her a criminal and yell at her in the streets of Poaquil.[12] Forster notes, "The mere existence of laws against these acts kept women of childbearing age in perpetual anxiety over their reputations. Even rumors of infanticide or abortion destroyed reputations and peace of private lives."[13]

Men too were victims of false accusations. When their six-month-old daughter Sebastiana died in April 1914, Juana Xon and her husband, José Morales, got drunk together in Tecpán to drown their sorrows. In her stupor, Xon lost her "mental faculties" and accused her husband of infanticide in Tecpán's municipal court. Through an interpreter, she misidentified herself as Sebastiana and explained that her husband, enraged because she refused to let him sleep with her sister, hit Xon while she was holding their baby in her arms, thereby killing the child. Although the municipal *alcalde* continued to preside over the proceedings, Morales was questioned (also through an interpreter) in the *juzgado de indígenas*, or indigenous courtroom. Despite their pleas of innocence and a coroner's report that concluded the cadaver displayed no signs of injury, Morales and his brother Domingo spent ten days in jail before the department judge exonerated them.[14]

In an indication that Xon's drunken binge lasted a while, it took her five days to recant her inebriated testimony, by which time the case was before the Chimaltenango *juez de primera instancia*. Apologizing to the authorities, she absolved her husband by explaining that her daughter had suffered from an illness, crying almost constantly during her last few days. Her admission, "My extreme poverty did not allow me to cure my daughter," subtly informed the department judge that the government's failure to provide for its citizens resulted in the death of a baby girl.[15] In contrast to Estrada Cabrera's attempt to portray the state as powerful, she highlighted its weakness. How could the state pretend to be omnipotent if it failed to ensure such basic rights as access to food and health care? Even the notary's description of Xon as illiterate and monolingual spoke to the state's shortcomings and limited reach. As we will see, other marginalized women also reminded authorities that such social ills as poverty and unemployment engendered tragedy.

The Surprising Gender of Reproductive Criminal Litigation

As women's insinuations of the state's culpability in the death of children suggest, in Guatemala infanticide and abortion had a number of meanings. Women who approached infanticide legislation as a means to hold men accountable for violence provide but one example of the diverse perceptions of the legal system, justice, crime, and reproductive responsibilities in the highlands. Despite Guatemalan law that a homicide was only considered infanticide if the mother (or maternal grandparents) killed a child within forty-eight hours of birth, Juana Miculax accused her husband, José María Yal, of infanticide when he kidnapped and killed their two-week-old daughter on the way home from her baptism in 1911. As a seventeen-year-old, illiterate, indigenous woman who lived and worked on a *finca* some distance from her hometown, Miculax faced a number of obstacles in bringing the case to court. She was from Patzicía but initiated litigation in San Pedro Yepocapa (henceforth Yepocapa) to ensure that "the death of her daughter would not be in vain."[16]

With evidence mounting—the coroner reported that the bite marks, scratches, and bruises on the cadaver were evidence of physical abuse the baby "could not survive at her tender age"—and witnesses testifying against the father in Yepocapa's municipal courtroom, the thirty-year-old, indigenous *jornalero* admitted to killing the baby because "he was enraged she was not his daughter. When he got together with Juana she was already pregnant."[17] Yal conceded that when Miculax and her parents informed him about her pregnancy, he had assured them it was not a problem. Perhaps realizing this admission precluded a defense of offended honor that many men used to justify violence, Yal claimed he was drunk.

After hearing these testimonies, the Yepocapa *juez de paz* sent the case to Chimaltenango's *juez de primera instancia*. Reminding the department court of his poverty, Yal insisted he be provided a lawyer. The forty-four-year-old, literate farmer Pedro Ruiz, who agreed to represent Yal, played on racial stereotypes in his defense:

> Keeping in mind that *los indígenas* don't labor in their activities with full and complete discernment, since the shameful labors to which their lives are subjected; the precarious life they lead; the habit of inebriation and principles of doubtful morality that are inculcated in them from childhood make them beings very susceptible to crime. In them dominates instinct, not sane judgment; and one has to realize, as a general rule, this principle and not apply the penal law in all its rigor.[18]

Ruiz went on to explain that even though witnesses claimed Yal was sober, it "is inconceivable that *los indios* can give up getting drunk with any pretext and baptisms are always very festive occasions for them."[19]

Although the judge seemed to agree with Ruiz's characterization of *indígenas* as drunk, ignorant, and immoral, he condemned the "malicious attitude of the criminal . . . [who killed] the absolutely defenseless child," and he stressed that "our laws do not recognize any positive disposition that diminishes the punishment that any delinquent deserves, for being a fool or ignorant, or for not maintaining perfect control over their acts."[20] Ruling the crime a homicide, he sentenced Yal to fifteen years with time off for good behavior. Six months later, in February 1913, an appellate court reduced Yal's sentence to six years and eight months, though it did him little good, as he died in jail the following year, on October 16, 1914.

Since judges rarely referenced a litigant's character, this ruling is particularly revealing. When set against the life of an "absolutely defenseless child," the judge had little sympathy for the plight of *indígenas* whom, his judgment suggests, he considered fools and ignorant. A sense of frustration with his charges is almost palpable in his emotional judgment, which both condemned Yal's act and warned others about the consequences of not controlling theirs. He seems to have intended the ruling as a teaching tool and a display of the state's power. Perhaps the appellate court's ruling was partly an attempt to correct the judgment of an overzealous official.

Unlike Yal, whose self-proclaimed inebriation appeared to be a desperate attempt to explain his crime, many men accused of infanticide really were drunk. Such was the case in Comalapa when the *indígena* Florentín Roquel attempted to hit his twenty-five-year-old wife, María Jesús Saj, while she was nursing their infant son on April 8, 1904. Missing her, his blow struck their son, Santos, with enough force to knock him and his mother to the floor. The child of ten days lay lifeless for a few minutes, then regained consciousness only to cry until he died early the next morning. A number of witnesses corroborated Saj's account that Roquel had become upset when she refused to fund his drinking binge. According to Saj, Roquel knew he had committed a crime. The municipal notary wrote: "Roquel was preventing her from leaving the house yesterday, because he understood that she would come to ask for *justicia* against him for the act he had committed; but in a moment of [his] carelessness, she managed to escape."[21] When Saj went to visit Roquel in jail later that day to tell him their son Santos had died, he warned her: "If she mentioned anything about this, he would kill her with a knife."[22] It must have been chilling for her to learn that he escaped from jail that night. The proceedings against Roquel did not continue until he was captured nearly two months later, on June 8.

Since early twentieth-century judges often considered inebriation a mitigating circumstance, many men accused of violent crimes deployed it in their defense. Building on his character witnesses who testified he was a chronic drunk, Roquel explained that his inebriation was an attempt to drown his sorrows; only a few days before Santos died, the child's twin brother had died at the tender age of seven days. In an indication that some judges empathized with *indígenas'* alleged alcoholism, Roquel's strategy worked; though the department judge did not issue his ruling until May 1, 1906 (more than two years after the crime), he reduced Roquel's ten-year sentence by a third, to six years and eight months, and allowed him to deduct the time he had already served. Noting that Roquel was poor, the judge also waived the cost of the official paper upon which his case was documented, a considerable sum since his docket ran to almost seventy pages.

Before sentencing Roquel, the judge explained that the crime was homicide, not infanticide. Had he ruled the crime an infanticide, Roquel would have been subject to only four years in jail.[23] In accord with the law, trying such cases as homicides allowed judges to mete out stiffer sentences.

In light of infanticide's minimal penalty compared to homicide sentences, women's decisions to subvert the intent of the law are perplexing. Emotion-laden testimonies suggest that plaintiffs' passion as much as their logic determined legal strategies. Read another way, because it was directed at women and explicitly identified with killing a baby, infanticide held a greater social stigma than homicide, as the sensationalism with which infanticide was reported attests. The decreased sentence notwithstanding, in small communities where killing could be honorable and locals occasionally hid murderers from authorities, distinguishing between homicide and infanticide could have a lasting effect on a perpetrator's reputation. By initiating infanticide as opposed to homicide litigation against male murderers, women underscored that the victims were babies and perhaps in this way assured that their deaths "would not be in vain," in Juana Miculax's words. Such decisions open a window into the distinctions between indigenous and state conceptions of justice.

Despite the autopsy report that confirmed Santos died of a "mortal" blow to the head, Roquel never confessed. On the contrary, in numerous letters to the department judge he tried to convince the court of his innocence as he emphasized his faith in the legal system: "Resting always in the dominion of reason and justice for everyone in the law, I come before you with my petition."[24] Unsatisfied with his reduced sentence, the forty-year-old, illiterate *indígena* petitioned to retain his lawyer and appealed the ruling. Much to his dismay, the appellate judge increased the sentence to ten years. Yet here too Roquel enjoyed leniency. According to Guatemala's penal codes, those who killed their sons or daughters could serve up to fifteen years in jail.[25]

Male Reproductive Responsibilities

Unlike the infanticide law, abortion legislation explicitly identified men as potential perpetrators of reproductive crimes. By drafting the abortion law in such a way that fathers could be criminalized, legislators recognized at least one aspect of men's reproductive responsibility, that of not harming pregnant women, in the 1889 penal code. An abortion resulting from violence against a pregnant woman was punishable by six years in prison. In turn, a woman who induced her own abortion or agreed to allow someone else to was subject to three years in prison; that was reduced to one year in 1936. If she did so to hide her dishonor, the maximum sentence was two years in jail, reduced to six months in 1936. So great was the pressure to maintain one's honor that the law recognized it as an extenuating circumstance.[26] As in nineteenth-century Mexico, women who demonstrated their work ethic and honor generally enjoyed leniency from the judge.[27]

Like court-ordered gynecological exams, legislation criminalizing abortion established male ownership over women's bodies. Drafted in part to protect women from violence, this law ultimately violated women's privacy and infringed upon their rights. Nonetheless, women enjoyed some success in using it to hold men accountable for their transgressions.

By accusing men of infanticide and abortion, women reminded them and authorities of male reproductive responsibilities. At the very least, men should refrain from hitting their pregnant wives. Perhaps for this reason, from the perspective of most female plaintiffs infanticide cases were more closely related to abortion than homicide. Women who sued delinquent husbands for medical expenses associated with childbirth likewise drew attention to male reproductive responsibility. Conceived more broadly, women who took fathers to court to collect child support similarly highlighted this responsibility.[28]

Based on her study of contemporary San Marcos, Guatemala, Forster argues, "The fact that in Guatemala only women were charged with committing reproductive crimes is common in most societies that have largely discounted male reproductive responsibility."[29] Although reproduction was feminized, women who accused men of committing reproductive crimes and male officials who heard these cases ensured that men were not exempt from reproductive responsibilities. Municipal *jueces de paz* who forwarded homicide cases as infanticide litigation did so at some risk to themselves. If the *juez de la primera instancia* deemed the case misclassified or improperly handled by his subordinates, he could fine them. Perhaps the severity of these crimes emboldened local officials and softened department judges; the former readily forwarded such cases without redefining them, and the latter seldom rejected them. Through a combination of women's perseverance, legal codes, and amenable authorities, men's reproductive responsibilities remained apparent.

Violent Men

As with infanticide, abortion cases against men often involved violence against women. When Victoriana Mayzul had a miscarriage an hour after her husband, Alberto Sipac, beat her while drunk on August 19, 1912, she accused him of abortion in Patzún's municipal court. To prove her case she had to undergo a number of physical exams. The first person to examine the thirty-year-old, monolingual Kaqchikel speaker was also a woman who spoke no Spanish; *don* Alberto Méndez translated this midwife's description of Mayzul's bruises and "coagulated blood that indicated an abortion" for the Patzún notary. Although it is unclear if they were medical professionals, the two (likely ladino) men who next examined Mayzul confirmed she had aborted her two-month-old fetus and noted that her womb was "very inflamed" from being kicked. So grave was her condition that they recommended she remain in bed for at least nine days.[30] With the shift from an indigenous woman to ladino men, Mayzul must have felt increasingly alienated by these exams.

Despite his violent history, which included a conviction for attacking his sister-in-law, Sipac denied hitting his wife or knowing she was pregnant. According to him, she was already on the floor when he came home that day. As the eyewitness accounts mounted against him and the case moved to Chimaltenango's *juzgado de primera instancia*, he changed his strategy. Illiterate, he dictated a letter to the department judge from jail in which he claimed that his mother-in-law had drummed up the charges and his *mujer* (woman) would exonerate him.

When Mayzul appeared before the department court on January 31, 1913, officials turned to their prison for assistance; the twenty-four-year-old

San Martín *reo* (criminal) Venancío Tapáz acted as her interpreter. Admitting that she did not know if Sipac intended to cause an abortion, Mayzul maintained that he had beaten her over the sale of some land and that "he always has given me cruel treatment, hitting me always whether I was pregnant or not. The last time he hit me was after he got out of jail and he said he wanted to kill me." She had been trying to separate from him for three years and frequently escaped to her parents' house, but Sipac always followed her. The notary penned Mayzul's request that her husband be punished "severely because she fears that when upon leaving [jail] he will return to hit her or perhaps then realize his evil proposition whether it be with her or any member of her family."[31]

Her request undermined Sipac's subsequent petition to be released on bail "for my young children who I have left abandoned." Generally effective when deployed by women, Sipac's suggestion that he should be released because his children needed him failed to impress the judge. In response to his wife's description of his abuse and death threat, Sipac further implicated his parents-in-law. A few weeks after his wife's testimony, he explained that when he was seventeen years old they pressured him to marry their daughter, who was then twenty-five. After a seven-month "battle" he relented. From the beginning, his relationship with his in-laws had been antagonistic. "As a son-in-law, I had to do whatever work he [my father-in-law] wanted," Sipac complained. Worse still, they burned the house he inherited from his parents and began to spread rumors about him. What emerges from his letters is an image of greedy in-laws who, when they failed to acquire his wealth, sought to impoverish him. According to Sipac, the abortion litigation was another manifestation of his in-laws' "fatal revenge" and efforts to replace him with another husband.[32]

Although most of their studies were conducted some twenty or thirty years after this case, a number of ethnographers noted the tensions in indigenous family life, particularly among husbands, wives, and in-laws. Land pressure, inheritance, and the need for female labor were all sources of potential hostilities. Living within close proximity and often in the same compound if not house as one's in-laws amplified these strains.[33] The same intimacy that facilitated close bonds could escalate antagonistic relations. "The people who live together in one house are continually getting in each other's way and on each other's nerves . . . family life is invariably described as bitter and discordant," observes Bunzel.[34] As further demonstrated in Chapter 5, familial opprobrium could turn violent.

With his appeal to see his children, lamentation over his parents' deaths, and a detailed description of his inimical relationship with his in-laws, Sipac built many of his narratives around the theme of family. Losing his father and being deprived of a good relationship with his father-in-law, Sipac ultimately appealed to paternalism: "*Sr. Juez de Primera Instancia*, I beg you as our father . . . house me in your justice and protection."[35]

When his appeals failed, Sipac sent another letter on November 27, 1913, explaining that he had contracted dysentery in prison; to recover, he asked to be released on bail. After a doctor confirmed that Sipac's dysentery was unlikely to clear up in prison, the fifty-five-year-old farmer David Rodríguez posted Sipac's two-hundred-peso bail on December 1, and the judge released him. The slow judicial system never offered a ruling, but it documented Sipac's penchant for violence in vivid detail and provided a two-year reprieve from it for Mayzúl and her family. Such relief was no small measure. According to one Kaqchikel octogenarian from Patzún, her own husband's beatings and kickings resulted in four miscarriages.[36]

In an indication that gender-based violence cast a wide net, husbands were not the only male defendants in abortion litigation. On October 17, 1906, the thirty-one-year-old military commander and public school teacher Belisario Valdéz from Quetzaltenango accused Comalapa's mayor Abel Rayo of causing an abortion. Imprisoned in Chimaltenango, Valdéz wrote directly to the department judge. Valdéz explained that when his wife, Enriqueta Avendaño de Valdéz, asked Rayo why he had jailed her husband, Rayo threw her to the ground, saying: "Don't even talk to me about that *bandido ladrón*."[37] Immediately feeling the effects of Rayo's blow, Avendaño consulted a midwife, who helped her through the miscarriage or, in Valdéz's words, "abortion." Valdéz had the fetus and his wife's blood-stained clothes sent to Chimaltenango as evidence.

Unable to determine the cause of the miscarriage or even if she had one, the surgeon who examined Avendaño a week later noted: "If she had an abortion, [it] was spontaneous." Avendaño's gynecological exam demonstrates one of the ways the legal system victimized women even when they or their male kin employed litigation designed to protect them. This violation of women's privacy and affront to their honor suggests why so few such cases arrived before the courts.

Valdéz's persistence in the face of his faltering case suggests he was motivated as much by retribution for his wife and unborn child as by discrediting Rayo and perhaps exonerating himself. On November 14 he wrote another letter to the department judge with the names of four men who had witnessed Rayo hit Avendaño and asked that they be called to testify. If the court summoned Rayo or these witnesses, no record of it or the judge's ruling survives, but the broader judicial record suggests Rayo was a problematic official.

Two years later, the middle-aged farmer Paulino Ovalle accused Rayo of unjustly imprisoning him. In his letter to Chimaltenango's *jefe político*, Ovalle characterized Rayo as a corrupt and disruptive official who was chronically inebriated. According to Ovalle, Rayo's "abuses constituted a true scandal."[38] With such a reputation, it is not hard to imagine that Rayo had imprisoned Valdéz unjustly too. Although Valdéz was undoubtedly upset about his wife's miscarriage and Rayo's abuse of her, a history of animosity with Rayo also likely informed if not inspired Valdéz's suit. Despite its gendered nature, infanticide and abortion litigation often arose out of contexts that were broader than the lives, conditions, and concerns of female victims and their perpetrators.

As Valdéz's petitions demonstrate, crafting a narrative that convincingly related men's violence to infanticide, abortion, or miscarriage was difficult. Rosa Álvarez similarly struggled with this challenge in Patzicía's municipal court when she accused her son-in-law Federico Santizo Higueros of killing her six-day-old grandson on August 12, 1915. There were no witnesses, but she claimed Santizo repeatedly kicked her daughter Juana Tobar's womb a few days before the baby was born. Owing to the midwife Petronila de León's skilled delivery, the baby survived and recovered. Álvarez carefully described the bruises on the infant's back and lame leg. A few days after the birth, Santizo stormed into their home and threatened Tobar with a machete as she and the baby lay recovering in bed. "From that moment with the *susto* [fright] that her daughter Juana carried in her very delicate condition, the infant became ill and died," declared Álvarez.[39] Like her mother, Tobar explained how *el chiquito* (the little one) survived the blows in her womb only to die from the *susto* of her husband's fit and death threat.

Guatemalans and other Latin Americans sometimes attributed illness and death to *susto*, but the law did not recognize frightening someone as a crime. As ladinas, Tobar and Álvarez may have been comfortable offering this cultural explanation of her son's death to a local ladino official. It must have had some influence on the *alcalde*, who sent the case to the *juzgado de primera instancia* despite any compelling evidence to charge Santizo with infanticide or, more accurately, homicide.

Santizo's responsibility for the infant's death became increasingly tenuous when neither de León nor the midwife who performed the autopsy attributed the child's death to physical abuse. Both midwives claimed the bruising, discoloration, and misshapen shinbone was the result of a lunar eclipse. The unlicensed physician's assistant (*asistencia de empírico*) Manuel López Armas countered their claim, saying that although blows caused the bruises, he did not associate them with the baby's death. When the police finally captured Santizo on August 18, the twenty-one-year-old ladino *jor-*

nalero denied hitting his wife before his son's birth or threatening her afterward. Finding no grounds for conviction on infanticide, the department judge freed him after twelve days of incarceration.[40]

In addition to documenting perceptions of infanticide, this case reveals the coexisting and competing epistemologies and worldviews that surfaced in the courtroom and society more broadly. That rural litigants felt comfortable expressing such traditional perspectives as the physiological effects of *susto* and eclipses in court speaks to their sense of ownership or at least stake in the state's legal system. At the same time, initiating litigation was not necessarily a common or comfortable practice. When Patzicía's *alcalde* interviewed Tobar while she was still sick in bed, for example, he asked why she did not report Santizo's abuses to the authorities. "Since I was not summoned for the case, I forgot to do it," she responded.[41]

Even with witnesses, it was difficult to prove that men's physical abuse resulted in a baby's death. When the twenty-year-old, illiterate, *indígena* Raymunda Chonay claimed that violence at the hands of her husband, Demetrio Apen, ultimately killed their daughter Leona in July 1917, two witnesses testified on her behalf, saying that Apen had beaten her while drunk. When they tried to intervene, Apen attacked them too, giving one a bloody nose. Chonay testified in Comalapa's municipal courtroom that "Apen has done the same thing with another one of his little daughters who died about four months ago from *sustos* that she got every time he hit, as is his custom, the declarer."[42] Perhaps the twenty-three-year-old indigenous *jornalero's* apparent disregard for his daughters' well-being was related to his own less than ideal relationship with his father; admitting that he did not know whether he was an *hijo legítimo*, Apen intimated that his father never formally recognized him as his son. Whatever the cause of his frustrations, the relationship between Apen and Chonay resembled those of many other couples in the criminal record for whom domestic violence was routine.

Despite telling Comalapa's *juez de paz* he was too drunk to remember the incident, Apen assured Chimaltenango's *juez de primera instancia* in a typed letter that the crime was "truly imaginary" and that "only the slander of my woman could cast me in a crime so false and calumnious," since his daughter died of natural causes.[43] The autopsy neither incriminated nor absolved Apen. According to Comalapa's doctor Ernesto Celis, the pulmonary congestion, lockjaw (or tetanus), and other complications that killed the child were not the result of physical abuse, but they were preventable. "The girl was marked by a lack of care on the part of her parents whose impositions caused the death of their daughter," he concluded.[44] Neglect, not blows, had killed her. On November 24, 1917, the department judge released Apen.

The ladino doctor's judgment of this indigenous couple stands in stark contrast to the monolingual indigenous woman Juana Xon's assessment of why her daughter died in the neighboring town of Tecpán. As a mother who lived in "extreme poverty," Xon (and women in *La Gaceta*'s pages, as we will see) made the connection between poverty and illness explicit for authorities; in contrast, Celis ignored how poverty contributed to the conditions that led to the girl's death even though Apen was unemployed. Juxtaposing these perspectives reveals how class and ethnicity informed people's perceptions of mortality and crime. Middle- and upper-class ladino medical professionals and journalists blamed poor and indigenous parents for the deaths of their offspring, while marginalized mothers highlighted the social and economic conditions that condemned their children.

Reproductive-crime litigation provides a window into broader relations of violence in highland Guatemala. In an indication of the level of violence surrounding family and community life, the same day Apen was released from jail, his father-in-law, Trinidad Chonay, informed the Chimaltenango department judge that "with his freedom, the lives of my daughter and me are in danger, since he has offered to finish us off because his wife had to declare that Apen killed her daughter Leona."[45] The fifty-one-year-old farmer went on to explain that his son-in-law was a chronic drunk who lived as a vagrant "because he had no means of subsistence." Earlier that year, Apen arrived at their home with a revolver, threatening to kill Trinidad. The judge found the father-in-law's letter compelling enough to begin proceedings against Apen for these threats. In a chilling conclusion to Apen's file, written across the top were the words *sin captura* (at large).

Defense Strategies

Since pointing out the economic privations that led to their acts seldom won judicial sympathy in infanticide litigation, most female defendants pursued other narrative strategies. Some accused medical professionals of corruption. Others framed their acts as desperate attempts to preserve their reputations.

Women who committed infanticide tended to be more marginalized than men who were accused of it. Most were isolated from family networks, illiterate, poor, and monolingual. Such was the case for the twenty-year-old, illiterate, indigenous *molendera* Concepción Bajxac, who gave birth alone at four o'clock in the morning on May 8, 1912, in the house of her *patrona* (female employer), *doña* Jesús Martínez, *viuda* (widow) of García. When the baby began to cry, Bajxac threw him in the toilet. Noticing Bajxac bleeding later that day, Martínez called a midwife, who, realizing Bajxac had given birth, searched for the infant only to find him too late to revive him. Still shaken the next day, Bajxac gave testimony in San Martín's municipal court that was suspended because her "words were spoken with much exertion."[46] The trauma of giving birth alone and then disposing of the baby often manifested through women's "incoherent" testimonies.[47]

Bajxac retracted her initial testimony a few months later in Chimaltenango's department court, claiming the baby was stillborn. Too poor to afford a lawyer, she asked the court to appoint one. After consulting with her lawyer, *licenciado* Enrique Bocanegra, Bajxac changed her strategy. Insisting she was unaware her act was a crime, Bajxac explained in an October 7, 1913, letter to the department judge that she did not know whether the baby was born dead or alive. When she carried him to the bathroom, he did not move. Embarrassed and aware that her *patrona* was "very fragile," Bajxac put the baby in the toilet to hide her dishonor. To ensure the crime would fit into the law's most lenient category, a few months later Bocanegra wrote to the department judge noting that his client committed this act immediately after the birth to "hide her dishonor and avoid consequent embarrassment with her employers."[48]

In light of the midwife's and coroner's observations that the baby was born alive and showed signs of physical abuse, revising her narrative was wise. Mothers who killed their babies within forty-eight hours of birth to hide their dishonor were subject to a maximum of three years in jail.[49] Bajxac behaved well in prison, so the department judge allowed her to commute the last two-thirds of her sentence at two reales a day. Noting her poverty, he also waived her legal fees. *Don* Manuel Pérez Montúfar paid her bail of two hundred pesos, and she was freed on February 13, 1914.[50]

Bajxac's testimony reflects two broader trends common among the narratives of female perpetrators of reproductive crimes. First, many claimed they did not know their acts were crimes. Second, many pointed out the state's and society's complicity. Like female defendants who indicted the state by pointing to unemployment and poverty as catalysts, many women also implicated community members and society more broadly by alluding to the scrutiny to which women's reputations were subjected.

Since the law's recognition of dishonor as a mitigating circumstance and judges' corresponding leniency encouraged women to invoke this language in their defense, determining to what extent honor motivated women's acts is difficult. Honor was paramount for even the most marginalized Guatemalans. Often related to honor, practical considerations were also crucial determinants as the twenty-two-year-old *soltera* María Zuleta Salazar from Ciudad Vieja explained to the police chief of Antigua in October 1941. When her boyfriend was enlisted in the military, they decided to end their affair. Shortly thereafter, she realized she was pregnant. "For fear that her mother would kick her out of the house," she kept her pregnancy a secret. Remarkably, Salazar birthed, suffocated, and buried the baby without her mother or anyone else noticing. The journalist who described her as an "unnatural," "cold-hearted," "unloved," "incorrect," and "cruel" mother failed to acknowledge that her lost honor would have resulted in her homelessness.[51]

Less than a year later, the twenty-five-year-old maid María Lorenzo beat and suffocated her infant so "the different people that live in the house would not realize I was a mother."[52] For her, dishonor might have led to unemployment. Labeled a "wicked mother," Lorenzo never identified the father. If the broader historical record is any indication, he may have been one of the male members of the family that employed her. Although explanations that invoked concerns over one's honor could lead to clemency, a close reading of the criminal record indicates that tangible consequences, as opposed to abstract notions, motivated women's fatal acts.

Cases like these and the broader record of reproductive crimes reveal a striking intimacy and dependency among victims, perpetrators, and other community members. Despite being subject to beatings and threats from her husband, Florentín Roquel, as described earlier, María Jesús Saj brought him coffee in jail the day after she had him arrested for killing their son. When Roquel escaped from jail that evening, it was his mother, upon arriving with his dinner only to find him gone, who informed the jail keeper, who was his brother.[53] In these highland communities, people's lives were inextricably intertwined.

Unnatural Mothers

By positioning themselves as experts, Guatemalan police and journalists created the new social category of *madre desnaturalizada* or *madre sin entrañas*. As early as the 1930s, mothers who intentionally harmed or killed their children now assumed a subject position within the discourse of gender and power in Guatemala. Similarly, in Argentina and other areas of the Americas, medical professionals and lawmakers agreed, "only aberrant mothers consciously endangered their infants."[54] Guatemalan authorities drew special attention to the women who committed these crimes.

Número 1, ROSA ROGELIA PINTO URZUA. Número 2, LUISA URZUA DE PINTO. En la parte baja de la gráfica, sentada, en el momento en que desenterró el feto, aparece esta última persona.

Figure 4.1. Rosa Rogelia Pinto Urzúa (left) and Luisa Urzúa de Pinto. The inset shows Luisa as she exhumes the fetus. *La Gaceta*, March 16, 1941. Image courtesy of Hemeroteca Nacional de Guatemala.

Even though both men and women were accused of reproductive crimes, *La Gaceta* framed these felonies as feminine. An example from 1941 is illustrative. Two days after seventeen-year-old Rosa Rogelia Pinto Urzúa induced an abortion, she packed the three-month-old fetus in a shoebox and brought it to her mother with a "smiling and secure face," saying, "Mama, I bring you this so you can see what to do with it." Unaware that the police had followed her daughter, Luisa Urzúa de Pinto waited until nightfall to bury the fetus in a thicket behind their home. Shortly thereafter the police apprehended them and forced the mother to exhume "the nauseous remains of the product of the punishable abortion" (figure 4.1).[55]

The journalist's narrative reveals how the National Police and other authorities approached reproductive crimes. The false promises and irresponsible behavior of Rosa's lover, Gerardo Tela, figured prominently in the story. Despite his key role, however, the journalist depicted the crime in a feminized way by tracing its roots to Rosa's independence. As a washerwoman in the home of a banana-company manager, she earned five quetzales a month and her own room. The latter facilitated "a series of nocturnal romances without the least difficulty, since nothing could interrupt them." When Tela learned Rosa was pregnant, he fled. So Rosa sought an herbal remedy—a "fatal potion" that worked so quickly she had the abortion while standing. If not for the intervention of a female friend, she might have died. The reporter also cast suspicion on another friend who saw Rosa with the potent drink but failed to halt this "completely illicit end."[56] Even as he condemned Tela's behavior, the journalist portrayed women as the crime's protagonists.

Seldom dwelling on fathers', society's, or the state's role in pushing women to these extremes, journalists and police demonized female perpetrators of reproductive crimes. On occasion, the accused perpetuated these perceptions. When the police stopped María Ciani (figure 4.2) from strangling her baby in 1931, she insisted that since "the little one was hers, she had the perfect right to do with him what she wanted." Rich with suspense and horror, the journalist's description of the incident left little doubt as to Ciani's culpability. "Fearing that something grave was happening to the little one that gave such alarming screams," two police agents went inside and surprised Ciani "in the cavernous task of strangling her little son. . . . The agents immediately apprehended that *madre sin entrañas*, saving the little one from a horrible death . . . at the hands of the author of his existence."[57]

Ciani's statement aside, when their voices emerged in *La Gaceta*, most

SEÑORA MARIA E. CIANI

Figure 4.2. Señora María E. Ciani, "soulless mother." *La Gaceta,* March 29, 1931. Image courtesy of Hemeroteca Nacional de Guatemala.

mothers related such societal ills as poverty and unemployment to infanticide. "Tired of looking for work with which to support her son and not finding any, she had decided to abandon him to his luck, so that someone would take him," explained the police when they arrested Francisca Juárez in June 1931.[58] Like Juana Xon's testimony, Juárez's explanation implicated the state in her crime for failing to provide for its population.

A few weeks later, Juárez tried to kill her son. Evoking an image of a mother and child who loved each other, their photograph suggests a more complex explanation for her act than the police's assertion that she was a *madre desnaturalizada* (figure 4.3).[59] Labeling her a *madre sin entrañas* for abandoning her child and *madre desnaturalizada* for trying to kill him, the journalists downplayed the state's and society's responsibilities by drawing attention to Juárez with sensational labels. By identifying a few individual women as opposed to society's shortcomings as the problem, authorities deflected attention away from the state's inability to confront such problems as poverty, under- and unemployment, and illiteracy. Portrayed as outliers instead of emblems of larger social problems, *madres desnaturalizadas* and *madres sin entrañas* served the state well. The system did not need fixing; a few abhorrent mothers did.

By identifying such crimes as Juárez's as infanticide, the police sensationalized them. According to Guatemalan law, Juárez's act should have been labeled an attempted homicide. Like female plaintiffs who accused men of infanticide, the police stretched the term's application to serve their ends. Similarly, ten years later a *Gaceta* journalist highlighted another crime by mislabeling it infanticide. In February 1941 the twenty-five-year-old single mother Cruz Mendoza Ujpan of San Juan Laguna, Sololá, dislocated her five-year-old son's vertebral column by hitting him with a piece of firewood.[60]

The term *madre desnaturalizada* relegated female perpetrators of infanticide to what feminist theorist Judith Butler calls the "domain of abjected beings."[61] They were no longer even subjects, let alone citizens. In a country grounded in patriarchal norms and convinced that male-headed households provided social stability, this label represented more than simply a loss of maternal essence. Women who rejected traditional family structures and, worse, reproductive norms threatened the nation. Therefore, they had to be excluded from the nation-state, at least rhetorically if not physically. Anne McClintock's framing of abjection in her study of South Africa is helpful in understanding the relationship between state representatives and those rejected by the state. To identify multiple forms of abjection, she distinguishes

Francisca Juárez y su hijito Juan.

Figure 4.3. Francisca Juárez and her little son Juan. *La Gaceta*, June 7, 1931. Image courtesy of Hemeroteca Nacional de Guatemala.

between abjected groups and agents of abjection.[62] In Guatemala, journalists and the police were agents of abjection, and female perpetrators of reproductive crimes and sex workers were abjected groups.

In many ways, *madres desnaturalizadas* were the mirror image of feminized men: *madres desnaturalizadas* took on male traits of violence and aggression, while feminized men assumed female traits of passivity and subordination. Historian Robert Buffington points out that the labels for such groups were often gendered and sexed.[63] In much the same way that modern Latin American nations repressed and erased male homosexuals,[64] Guatemala repudiated female perpetrators of reproductive crimes by defining them as women who defiled the laws of nature.

Men who committed reproductive crimes were not excluded in this way, however; even when punished for these crimes and reviled for their actions, they remained part of the national politic. As horrific as these transgressions were, authorities and journalists never defined them as unnatural when committed by males. In the many examples in which men neglected, abused, and killed children, the term *padre desnaturalizada* never arose. Perhaps correspondents assumed violent men were exercising, not defying, their nature.

Similarly, for all their immorality and perversion, male rapists of young girls or pregnant women were never defined as "unnatural." On the contrary, their predatory nature could be related to male instincts. Despite being subject to forces of exclusion and abjection, rapists were never culturally unintelligible in the way *madres desnaturalizadas*, feminized men, or crossdressers (as we will see) were.

When Jorge Salán tried to rape a pregnant woman, *Gaceta* journalists referred to him as a "degenerate youth."[65] Salán's label identified him as abject but was not as damning as *madre desnaturalizada*. A degenerate youth held the potential to be regenerated. Similarly, when Humberto Villatoro lured a girl with money and toys, the police characterized him as "a satyr . . . who forgetting any idea of morality, was at the point of committing a horrendous crime with a six-year-old girl."[66] As much as *Gaceta* journalists and Guatemalan society more broadly reviled rapists like Villatoro, they were never portrayed as defying their nature.

The few instances in which male acts were defined as "unnatural" suggest that the term was deployed against those who upset patriarchal power relations. When Vicente Pirir attacked his father with a machete and cut him up so badly that he needed to be rushed to the hospital in Antigua, the journalist referred to him as an *hijo desnaturalizado*.[67] Sons were supposed to respect, obey, and serve—not attack—their fathers. By refusing to give birth to or care for children, women who had abortions, committed infanticide, or abandoned their children similarly undermined their perceived roles in Guatemala's patriarchal society.

Contrasting the frequency with which male journalists and authorities applied the term *desnaturalizada* to women against its scarce application to men throws into sharp relief how the process of human reproduction limited patriarchal power in Guatemala. To reconstitute the social and political order contingent upon men's privileged position vis-à-vis women, among other factors, authorities and intellectuals sought to control sexuality partly by criminalizing acts that interfered with human reproduction and by ostracizing women who committed them. An abjected group, women who defied their reproductive roles embodied one of the ways patriarchy in Guatemala was limited and distorted by other types of power relations.

As further evidence of authorities' preoccupation with reproductive crimes, *La Gaceta* routinely highlighted these feminine transgressions even though their incidence rate paled in comparison to other crimes, such as homicide, theft, and bootlegging (appendices 3 and 4). In a reflection of *La Gaceta*'s use of photographs as forms of authority, in some cases images appeared without any accompanying articles or even descriptions save the captions. Such was the case with Ángela Vásquez, who at age seventeen allegedly committed a "double infanticide" in 1931 (figure 4.4).[68] The National Police knew publicity could be a form of punishment, but as Foucault asserts, such displays were aimed more at the broader community than the individual criminal.[69] The point was not to learn about the individual lives of such criminals as Vásquez, who was denied a voice in *La Gaceta*, but rather to sensationalize their crimes. As they bore their transgressions through the publicity of their identities and images, public criminals became signifiers of their crimes.

In one macabre image from the January 8, 1933, edition of *La Gaceta*, authorities forced Ester Contreras Chavarría to embrace the infant she had strangled (figure 4.5). Poor and alone, she gave birth in her shack on a banana plantation in Izabal. When medical experts insisted the baby was born healthy, authorities dismissed her claim that "her economic circumstances" resulted in a premature stillbirth. Ironically, the father of the child was a nurse at a United Fruit Company medical dispensary. Compelled to hide her pregnancy lest she lose her job, Contreras Chavarría kept on working and going about her life so seamlessly that her roommates never noticed anything out of the ordinary.

ANGELA VASQUEZ, de 17 años de edad, casada, vecina de la finca "Pavón", término de Fraijanes, presa en la Casa de Recogidas como presunta autora de doble infanticidio.

Figure 4.4. Ángela Vásquez, "alleged perpetrator of a double infanticide." *La Gaceta*, June 14, 1931. Image courtesy of Hemeroteca Nacional de Guatemala.

SUCESO TRUCULENTO OCURRIDO EN MORALES, Departamento de IZABAL

UN GRUPO TOMADO INMEDIATAMENTE DESPUES DE DESCUBIERTO EL DELITO

Arriba.—El cadáver del niño es_
trangulado y que, extraído por los
perros del sitio donde había sido
sepultado, fue devorado a medias
por ellos.

Abajo.—Nº 1, don José Leiva, Juez
de Paz de Morales.—Nº 2, don Eduar
do Muñoz G., Secretario del Juzgado
de Paz.—Nº 3, agente de la Policía
Municipal, don Rodolfo Mayorga Ordóñez.—Nº 4, la reo ESTER CONTRERAS
CHAVARRIA, con el cadáver de su
hijito, en brazos.—Nº 5, otro agente
de la Policía Municipal.

Figure 4.5. "Gruesome crime in Morales." Top photo, the unearthed body of a strangled infant. Lower photo, the mother, Ester Contreras Chavarría, holding the body and surrounded by police and other authorities. *La Gaceta*, January 8, 1933. Image courtesy of Hemeroteca Nacional de Guatemala.

By using powerful images and forceful rhetoric, *Gaceta* journalists inflated readers' awareness of these infrequent crimes. Even in rural areas where few people had access to print media because so much of the population was illiterate, concerns about infanticide and abortion percolated. At times the National Police tapped into these preoccupations. When crimes were shrouded in mystery, they called upon the public to assist in investigations. Such was the case when the cadaver of a strangled baby boy was discovered in Guatemala City's San Sebastián Church (figure 4.6). "The profaning of the church and the magnitude of the crime has inflamed Guatemalan society with anger and disdain for good reason," the journalist noted. The police had no clues or leads, but they betrayed their presumption that the perpetrator was a woman when they offered a reward for any information that would help them catch "the unnatural mother" who committed the "doubly grave offense" of killing a baby and profaning a Catho-

Envoltorio en que se hallaba la recién nacida estrangulada que se encontró en la iglesia de San Sebastián.

Figure 4.6. Bundle containing a strangled baby. *La Gaceta*, May 24, 1931. Image courtesy of Hemeroteca Nacional de Guatemala.

lic church.[70] Infanticide had become so feminized that authorities could not imagine a man killing a baby.

Cross-Dressing

Like *madres desnaturalizadas*, female cross-dressers, too, rejected social constructions of their sex and gender and thus occupied what Butler defines as "'unlivable' and 'uninhabitable' zones of social life."[71] Even though they lived in a society where legitimacy, intelligence, and authority were associated with masculinity, attempting to access these characteristics by assuming male identities marginalized women. With gender codes embedded in clothing, most women who cross-dressed presumably did so to gain access to male power and privileges.[72] Because gender performance is "a negotiation between the individual and his or her society," some societies were more accepting of it than others.[73] The Mexican Revolution, for example, briefly created conditions whereby female cross-dressers and other gender benders could flourish.[74] Early twentieth-century Guatemala, in contrast, offered few such openings. As responses to cross-dressing attest, women upset local power and legal structures when they assumed patriarchal privileges.

These disruptions of norms and men's efforts to reinstate them were particularly pronounced in certain cases, as when the nineteen-year-old *indígena* Antonia Gos cross-dressed. Returning from Patzún's Sunday market on July 9, 1911, to find his daughter gone, Felipe Gos began a frantic search for her. When his relative Luis Maysúl escorted her home wearing men's clothes three days later, Felipe initiated litigation in Patzún's municipal court to investigate if "a crime has been committed in the person of his daughter Antonia Gos."[75]

Both the municipal and department notaries struggled throughout the proceedings to describe Antonia's act; the latter labeled the case one of "disappearance and disguise." Despite Antonia's male garments and admission that she wanted to and did "work as a man," the Patzún notary identified her as adhering to *oficios de su raza and sexo*, or occupations appropriate to her race and sex. Confused by her transgression, both men lacked the very words to describe it. In early twentieth-century Guatemalan society, female cross-dressing was unintelligible.[76] By disrupting restrictive labels, family structures, and social order, such acts and the women who performed them threatened the Liberal state's classic Positivist motto, "Order and Progress."

In an indication that these transgressions challenged local authority, Patzún's mayor was even more concerned than Antonia's father. Despite her insistence that she had not been raped, he commissioned a midwife and doctor "to prove whether any crime against [her] honor has been committed or if Antonia Gos suffers from mental derangement."[77] In other words, if she was not raped, she must be crazy. By attributing her act to insanity, the mayor effectively labeled Antonia abject and cross-dressers an abject group.

Like women accused of reproductive crimes, Antonia had to endure a gynecological exam that laid bare her subordinate and violable position as a woman. By consenting to this procedure her father essentially asked the mayor to reinscribe patriarchal power. Since perpetuating male privileges was one way subalterns could engage in nation building,[78] both men may have expected Patzún's patriarchal community to protect the social position of men and punish women who blatantly aspired to it.

In contrast, department authorities did not always uphold municipal officials' attempts to reconstitute their power over women. Failing to find any evidence of criminal behavior, the Chimaltenango judge set Antonia free. Unlike the mayor, as far as the judge was concerned, she could cross-dress again if she liked.

In a notable shift from the Estrada Cabrera period, during Ubico's rule department and national authorities sought to discourage similar transgressions, as the following incident attests. When Rosario Quib donned men's clothes, cut her hair, and changed her name to Cristino in 1940, the Alta Verapaz governor's office turned her over to the National Police, who subjected her to an invasive physical examination to determine her gender. Despite "unequivocal signs that she was not a man," authorities admitted "that strange woman had such a custom of wearing masculine clothes that her posture in the photograph would fool anyone."[79] Figure 4.7 demonstrates how Quib adeptly adhered to conventional gender distinctions. As a woman, she is looking down and away from the camera, with her arms folded around her. As a man, Quib displays more confidence, with her arms akimbo and torso extended as she looks directly at the photographer. Such gendered poses were common in early twentieth-century Guatemalan photographs.[80]

The "trick with which she disguised her true sex" was revealed when she could not complete the requisite road labor. Although authorities and the reporter attributed this failure to feminine weakness, it was more likely a "strong infection" that betrayed her. The doctor who examined her considered it serious enough to admit her to the hospital. The reporter considered the affair a "comical adventure," while he also noted that her "deceit engendered strong suspicions."[81] What makes this incident all the more remarkable is that authorities reprimanded Quib even as she was performing unpaid labor that she otherwise would not have had to do as a woman. Apparently order (maintaining gender norms) trumped progress (building roads).

Early twentieth-century judicial officials' validation of the conceptual framework within which otherwise marginalized women portrayed the deaths of their children stood in stark contrast to Ubico-era *Gaceta* journalists' depictions of *madres desnaturalizadas* and *madres sin entrañas*. Female litigants' stories helped them pursue their notions of justice via the state's

Figure 4.7. Rosario (above)/Cristino (below) Quib, cross-dresser. *La Gaceta*, January 5, 1941. Image courtesy of Hemeroteca Nacional de Guatemala.

institutions, while the *Gaceta*'s characterizations turned female perpetrators into abjected subjects who could never be part of the nation. For a state that was bent on maintaining social stability by upholding traditional family structures, women who contravened their biological and social roles as mothers were problematic.

The fates of cross-dressers and female infanticide perpetrators demonstrate how expectations surrounding motherhood could confine women's possibilities, yet many female plaintiffs deployed the discourse of motherhood to magnify the consequences of male violence. As we will see in the next chapter, some assault and battery victims emphasized their pregnancies to warn against the possibility of miscarriages. Ignacia Corominal complained of "pain all over her body and abortion symptoms" after her brother-in-law and his wife attacked her on June 19, 1933.[82] Framing their testimonies in the rhetoric of reproduction and motherhood, women used the heightened concern about reproductive crimes to capture authorities' attention.

In light of the prevalence of domestic violence in highland communities and the courts' inability to protect victims, women who pursued infanticide and abortion litigation against violent men may have been doing so partly for their own safety.[83] Often these crimes were manifestations of larger patterns of physical abuse. Even if men accused of reproductive crimes were ultimately absolved, they were imprisoned during the judicial proceedings, which in some cases lasted more than a year—far longer than the maximum sentence of ten days in jail for domestic violence, which many men commuted.

The disproportionate representation of men in reproductive crimes and the small number of these cases to begin with are also partly a reflection of people's reluctance to bring women to court for these crimes, particularly since trials meant shattered honor and potential jail time for women who already had suffered considerably. Men's accusations against men who allegedly induced abortions often emanated from long-standing animosities and power struggles between the men themselves. In contrast, to bring charges of abortion or infanticide against a woman, as Forster argues, someone in the community had to "judge the loss of pregnancy or infant more grievous than the woman's emotional pain."[84] Even exoneration came at a high price for innocent women who were dishonored by the state's gynecological exams or subject to rumors about their alleged crimes. Perhaps the string of witnesses who vehemently denied any knowledge of a discarded fetus in the fields of Itzapa in 1914 simply believed the author of the crime had suffered enough.[85]

At the same time, thirteen years earlier members of the same community told authorities they suspected María Peren of abortion when she had excessive menstrual bleeding. A few years later, a couple trying to bury their stillborn child were accused of infanticide. Although some people took pity on female perpetrators, legislation and media coverage prompted communities to pursue them.

The biological nature of reproduction, coupled with infanticide legislation's gendered language, established narrow parameters for women's defense. Faced with court-ordered gynecological examinations, most women who had been pregnant admitted to it. Like their bootlegging counterparts, infanticide defendants recast the terms of the accusations and incriminations into terms relevant to their own lives, livelihoods, and circumstances. Often informed by the advice of lawyers, women who claimed they committed infanticide to protect their honor generally enjoyed reduced sentences, though few Guatemalans might have agreed with their contemporaries in Buenos Aires who prioritized the mother's honor over the baby's life.[86] Most indigenous and poor female defendants in Guatemala explained their acts in the context of their poverty, unemployment, or risk thereof. Judges did not consider indigence a mitigating circumstance, as was true in bootlegging rulings, but they did waive court costs and reduce commutation rates if defendants' poverty was evident.

A life of poverty and marginalization had to be construed carefully, though. As the judgment in José María Yal's 1911 infanticide trial suggests, judicial officials were unlikely to empathize with poor, indigenous defendants they considered depraved. In an unusually candid response, the department judge expressed disgust with Yal's heinous crime. His perspective and even more so the lawyer's portrayal of indigenous inebriation intimates that some ladino judicial officials viewed indigenous people as savages who were unlikely to be rehabilitated through the law. In these instances, judicial officials' perceptions of how marginalized litigants were could work against them.

Because men were not beholden to gendered legislation the way women were, their legal strategies were more varied than women's, though no male defendant admitted to killing a child or inducing an abortion. Nor did any male defendant reference his honor to justify his act, as that would have been tantamount to an admission of guilt. Most claimed they were drunk; some denied their violence; others accused plaintiffs of lying.

Although few men were convicted of these crimes, a close reading of Chimaltenango's reproductive crime litigation suggests a more nuanced interpretation than one historian's argument that abortion and infanticide laws "functioned to heighten individual women's fear and isolation while enhancing men's power."[87] Some aspects of this legislation favored women, such as with shorter sentences than for men, and women often used the law to curtail men's power. In a reflection of the way poor, indigenous women could affect judicial proceedings and by extension nation-state formation, municipal and even a few department judicial officials conspired with female plaintiffs to broaden the parameters of infanticide litigation in ways that contravened the legislation. While some municipal judicial officials may not have been familiar enough with the law to know when charges should be changed from infanticide to homicide, department judges certainly did, yet only a few ultimately changed the charges to homicide. In addition to demonstrating the legal leeway judicial officials enjoyed, this pattern of flexibility suggests that at times department (and likely many municipal) judicial officials were not only sympathetic to female plaintiffs but also willing to follow their lead. Even as litigants experienced the legal system in ways that habituated them to the state, they educated judicial officials about their privations in ways that affected the process and outcomes in these power-laden situations.

Such malleable judicial procedures and rulings likely informed the elasticity that some litigants attributed to the law. The equivocal power relations that reproductive crime litigation reveals are even more elusive in the judicial record of women accusing their husbands of domestic violence. We now turn to the complex dynamics—both within and outside the courtroom—disclosed when women used the courts as leverage against violent spouses. Although the law's anemic punishment for these crimes limited judicial officials' ability to influence gender relations, by bolstering patriarchal rule the law undergirded their authority. As we will see, a broad range of social relations and conditions shaped power relations in ways that both constrained and emboldened men's influence in the home and authorities' ability to govern.

CHAPTER 5

Wives in Danger and Dangerous Women: Domestic and Female Violence

When the "Macheteador de Mujeres" struck in May 1931 (figure 5.1), the police described one of his victims as "a woman of indigenous race, with various grave injuries on the right side of her face and neck, similar to the way the forearms and hands were horribly slashed. It was clear that all the injuries had been caused by a machete."[1] The nickname and press coverage sensationalized the Macheteador de Mujeres's exploits, but the criminal record reveals that gender-based violence was not uncommon. When Tomasa Morejón denounced her husband shortly after he repeatedly hit her in the head with a rock on March 29, 1926, she told San Martín's *juez de paz*, "If he no longer wants to live in peace in his home, find a way to separate us, since to do otherwise from one moment to the next something more deadly could occur."[2]

Other women were even more explicit. Less than a month later in the same court, Alejandra Aguilar testified, "In addition to hitting me with a machete, my husband burned my face with a smoldering stick and just by that inhumane action, you can imagine *señor alcalde* what type of individual he is. He continually threatens me saying he is going to hack me into a thousand pieces and drink my blood."[3] A few weeks later, Juana Ajbal de Díaz appeared before the same municipal magistrate in a desperate plea to separate from her husband because she did not want "to continue living with a person who could kill me." She proclaimed, "My husband has become my executioner."[4]

The systematic impunity that accompanied the pervasive and myriad forms of violence against women speaks to the state's violation of women's rights. A close reading of the criminal record shows that victims often suffered from a combination of mutually constituted forms of violence including sexual, verbal, psychological, economic (restricting a woman's ability to

RAFAEL PIRIR, bárbaro ma-
cheteador de Cristina Chicoj

Figure 5.1. "Rafael Pirir, barbarous *macheteador* of Cristina Chicoj." *La Gaceta,* May 24, 1931. Image courtesy of Hemeroteca Nacional de Guatemala.

generate or control her own income), and patrimonial (violating a woman's property rights). Just like the Estrada Cabrera and Ubico dictatorships assumed control over Guatemalans' lives, local authorities and men often assumed ownership over women's bodies, incomes, and property. By referring to men's wives as "their women," the law did little to discourage the notion of ownership.[5] The extent to which gender-based violence had become normalized is evident in the perpetrators who insisted they got along fine with their wives on the one hand and the men who held themselves out as exceptions because they did not beat their wives on the other. Whether employed within the family or society more broadly, violence was a tool of governance.

Akin to the way the Estrada Cabrera and Ubico dictatorships threatened Guatemalans by murdering political enemies, official indifference toward violence against women reinforced what Forster calls "gendered terror." Even Ubico, who portrayed himself as protecting women, refused to address domestic violence. By providing an outlet for male frustrations that did not challenge the state and perpetuating a sense of fear and intimidation, this indifference helped regimes keep people in line.[6] Popular depictions implied that some judicial officials held a cavalier attitude toward violence. A cartoon appearing in the January 8, 1933, edition of *La Gaceta* shows a judge absolving an assailant because he gave his victim aspirin to alleviate his headache (figure 5.2). By framing violence as interpersonal, the legal system depoliticized it.[7] Anthropologist Deborah Poole has observed, "States have used terror and violence to construct . . . regimes of overt au-

thoritarian domination."[8] Women and children who experienced tyranny at
home had less trouble tolerating a tyrannical state.

As evidenced by the record of men who beat women for speaking their
minds, many husbands expected the same obedience from their wives that
authoritarian regimes demanded from their citizens. Such disregard for
women's self-determination was used to justify violence against women
who did not conform to men's wishes. These perceptions were but one of
the ways despotic regimes' concepts of power and use of violence to govern
manifested in everyday life in Latin America.[9] Feminist scholars have demonstrated how gender-based violence shrank women's freedoms and maintained their subordination in their families, marriages, communities, and
nations.[10]

Women's vulnerability was partly a product of social constructions. Despite the success and mobility of vendors, midwives, and other entrepreneurial women, in general men and the law typecast women in domestic
roles of household and social reproduction. To enforce these norms, men
beat women who failed to fulfill their domestic duties. The courts did not
openly condone these responses or reprimand female plaintiffs for bringing
their cases forward as was true elsewhere in Latin America,[11] yet by refusing to rebut men's justifications for hitting their wives and assigning minimal sentences for these crimes, judicial officials and the law, respectively,
victimized women. The judicial rulings reflected a broader acceptance in
Guatemala and Latin America generally that dated to the colonial era of using violence against women to uphold patriarchy.[12]

Figure 5.2. "Before the Judge." *La Gaceta*,
January 8, 1933. Image courtesy of The Latin
American Library, Tulane University.

Customary law in many indigenous communities recognized a man's right to hit his wife. When couples married, elders informed new husbands that they must control their wives, as could be achieved with restrained levels of corporal punishment. In turn, women learned that they had to obey their husbands and endure occasional blows.[13] In his 1932 study of the predominantly Q'anjob'al-Maya community of Santa Eulalia, Oliver La Farge learned: "A man . . . should beat his wife if she 'gets above herself' and should not accept 'impudence'."[14] Such counsel was part of the social process that sustained violence and reified highland men's gendered power. Among some Mayas, religion buttressed gendered customs. In his 1937 study of Santiago Chimaltenango, a Mam community, Wagley observed: "Any married man, although sometimes himself dominated by his father, theoretically rules supreme in his own household. It is thought that God will punish any wife or child who acts contrary to his wishes."[15]

Sanctioned by God, government, and custom, the ideal of male omnipotence was always elusive, as Wagley suggests. As such, gender-based violence was not always or necessarily rooted in men's attempts to reconstitute their authority over their female kin. Perpetrators often lashed out in response to their subordinate positions, poverty, exploitive working conditions, low wages, unemployment, landlessness, and other forms of marginalization. Partly for this reason, the judicial record captures more incidents of domestic violence among poor, landless men than their wealthier, landed counterparts.

Class influenced gender-based violence and its reporting. Unlike early twentieth-century elites who seldom allowed these transgressions to be dragged into public arenas, the poor and working class led very public lives. The very mobility that characterized poor and working-class women's lives exposed them to the dangers of public life more frequently than elite women. Similarly, when their male kin migrated for work, poor, rural women were vulnerable in their own homes.

In stark contrast to Central American historiography, (particularly regarding indigenous peoples), contemporary ethnographies, and Kaqchikel oral histories,[16] judicial records are replete with reports of gender-based violence. According to Kaji' Tz'ikin, an indigenous *alcalde* who served during the Ubico years, the most common crime reported during his term in Sololá was domestic violence.[17] Since amicable marital relations seldom made it into judicial records, the sources are biased toward violence and abuse. Yet as the broader judicial record reveals, particularly in abandonment and reproductive crime cases, gender-based violence was underreported because many women shied away from using the courts to address it.[18]

Of the thousands of assault and battery cases involving women, I chose a sample of 102 to study closely: 49 from Patzicía's municipal court, 40 from San Martín's municipal court, and 13 from Chimaltenango's department court, where judges were either petitioned directly by victims or had cases referred by municipal authorities if the violence was extreme or related to another, more serious (in the eyes of judicial officials) crime. Of these cases 78 involved men attacking women; among the 24 cases in which females were the aggressors, only once was the victim a male. Since evidence of gender-based violence permeates the judicial record, dozens of other related cases also inform this chapter. Even assuming that contentious gender relations were not the norm, the incidents preserved in the criminal record provide a window onto how the violence that buttressed the authoritarian regimes of Estrada Cabrera, Orellana, Chacón, and Ubico both informed and was influenced by community and family relations.

In addition to the ways class influenced domestic violence reporting, my findings suggest an ethnic component to this litigation. Of the 78 cases of men attacking women I examined (appendix 8), only four plaintiffs were likely ladinas (5 percent). Fifteen plaintiffs' ethnic identities remained elusive (19 percent); twenty-one women identified as *indígenas* and thirty-eight others likely were (almost 76 percent). (In one case, a man attacked an indigenous couple.) Even accounting for their minority status in Chimaltenango's municipalities—ladinos comprised 22 percent of the population in the department, 30 percent in Patzicía, and 13 percent in San Martín, according to the 1921 census (appendix 2)—ladinas were far less likely to report domestic violence than were indigenous women. Despite this reporting bias, ladinos were defendants twice as often as ladinas appeared as plaintiffs. Among the eighty-one perpetrators, which included two female accomplices, three identified as ladino and six others probably were (11 percent), while seventeen identified as *indígena* and another forty-three most likely were as well (74 percent); twelve perpetrators' ethnic identities were unclear (almost 15 percent). Comprising at least 76 percent of the plaintiffs in this sample, indigenous women readily brought both indigenous and ladino men to court for hitting them.

If the Patzicía and San Martín municipal court records are any indication, female plaintiffs were extremely efficacious. Three cases in the Patzicía sample offer no clue as to the ruling, but in all thirty-four others, municipal justices sentenced male offenders to between five and twenty days in jail. No one was acquitted. Only nine of the thirty-four rulings in San Martín's sample survive; all were convictions. Chimaltenango department court rulings were similarly evasive; only once did the judge offer a sentence (a conviction), but of the other nine defendants, four were incarcerated as judicial authorities slowly gathered and examined evidence. Ironically, the department judicial system's glacial pace served victims of domestic abuse; their alleged attackers were imprisoned for months longer than they would have been had the judge immediately convicted them of assault and battery.

At the municipal level, however, the maximum sentence of ten days in jail for domestic violence offered victims little protection, and often justices of the peace doled out sentences of only five days. In an indication of the extent to which physical intimidation of women had become part of the fabric of everyday life, seldom did cases come forward as a result of public scandal. Most plaintiffs initiated litigation themselves; some described witnesses failing to come to their aid. Unlike bootleggers and vendors who almost invariably ended up in court as a result of their contact with one or more of the myriad authorities and officials charged with imposing the state's will, domestic violence victims generally first came in contact with representatives of the state when they petitioned judicial officials to impose the state's will. Besides engaging with fewer state agents before they arrived in court, these plaintiffs' experiences with judicial officials were qualitatively different than those of their counterparts who were defending themselves against moonshine or economic charges.

When domestic violence victims used the legal system as a lever against their assailants, the balance of power between female litigants and authorities shifted favorably toward the former. The high conviction rate (100 percent of the extant municipal rulings) must have buoyed plaintiffs, but the negligible sentences (some men commuted their sentences and left the courtroom with their wives) suggest this litigation was about more than just incarcerating the attackers. Once in court, female plaintiffs informed officials charged with maintaining social order about the terror women faced in their homes. In effect, they associated their interests with those of judicial authorities.

Particularly in light of recidivism, the cumulative effect of this litigation undoubtedly made municipal officials aware of the limits of their judgments and authority. As we saw in the previous chapter, when violence against women resulted in a miscarriage or a child's death, department judges imposed harsh sentences. When violence against women was tried as a crime in and of itself, however, the case generally was adjudicated in municipal courts by authorities who had fewer resources and less power than their department superiors. Comparing infanticide with assault and battery litigation reveals the critical difference between the nature and extent of power between municipal and department judicial officials. Confined by a maximum sentence that failed to deter perpetrators of domestic violence, municipal judicial officials had little power to protect women, let alone curb domestic violence. Although the department court afforded judges greater opportunities to protect individual women, even if just by slowing the proceedings, they too failed to arrest the broader phenomenon of domestic violence.

In a legal system established and presided over by elite men, individuals who challenged state authority were punished as harshly and often more so than perpetrators of gender-based violence, perhaps because such violence buttressed state authority. Underscoring judicial officials' priorities and the denigration of women during Estrada Cabrera's reign, Patzicía's magistrate sentenced the thirty-two-year-old *jornalero* José Coc to fifteen days for "disrespecting the authority . . . in the *tribunal* [court]" and only five days for hitting his wife![19] Similarly during Ubico's rule, Pedro López received the same punishment for failing to appear in San Martín municipal court as he did for hitting his sister-in-law: five days.[20] If, as Foucault posits, punishment reveals the state's perception of the seriousness of crime,[21] then the Guatemalan state—or at least these municipal agents of it—had little concern for gender-based violence. Since it generally carried the same sentence as most other common crimes short of murder, lawmakers apparently did not consider gender-based violence a greater threat to society than, say, theft, corruption, adultery, or defamation.[22]

Authorities' unwillingness and inability to address gender-based violence undermined their credibility, influence, and even relevance in the eyes of many highland women who turned to their families instead of the police or courts for protection. Even then, patriarchal protection was not absolute; a number of women were attacked in front of their husbands, and others were abducted from their fathers' homes. Most often, women were married to the men who hit them. The problem was that their communities were the very sources of violence. Indigenous and ladino men and women, customary and state law, and local and national authorities all perpetuated gender-based violence by upholding the vulnerability and subjugation of females in family and intracommunity relations.[23]

The collusion of state institutions with local cultural practices sustained violence in highly gendered ways. In contrast to men, when women lashed out authorities depicted them as simpletons who could not be held responsible for their actions or as immoral, savage "cave dwellers" who "drank the blood" of their victims—discourse that perversely justified their subjugation by rendering women as less than human.[24] Guatemala's overlapping patriarchies privileged male over female violence.

Root Causes and Multiple Forms of Violence

Class shaped the contours of gender-based violence. As the Patzicía and San Martín judicial records reveal, far more *jornaleros* than *agricultores* or merchants were arrested for beating their wives. Of the seventy-nine men on trial for beating women, thirty-three identified as *jornaleros*, seven were *agricultores*, and three were merchants. Thirty-six men did not name their professions (appendix 8). In other words, of the forty-three male defendants whose professions were identified, a staggering 77 percent were landless day laborers. In highland agrarian economies landless men enjoyed little prestige, independence, or security. As Bunzel found in her 1930s study of Chichicastenango, "The poor man works for others, the rich man works for himself; he is exempt from the more unpleasant kinds of labor . . . his advice is sought by his neighbors and his voice carries weight."[25] Poverty undermined men's ability to assume local leadership positions so crucial to status in their communities. Relating their frustrations to marital relations, Wagley observed that land-poor men "find it difficult to secure or keep a wife. . . . She knows that a husband, if poor, can hardly divorce her; he will fear, instead, her leaving him."[26] The multiple manifestations of patriarchy frustrated rural, poor, landless men who found it difficult if not impossible to fulfill the ideals of urban, elite, male-headed households. Although Bunzel and Wagley both discount gender-based violence,[27] my findings suggest poor, landless men's insecurity contributed to a higher incidence of domestic violence among them.

Another indicator of socioeconomic position in the judicial record highlighted male perpetrators' marginalization: illiteracy. Only three men said they enjoyed a formal education. Thirty were characterized as *sin instrucción*, without schooling, and thirty-four others could not sign their names or otherwise indicated they were illiterate. Twelve male defendants offered no clue as to whether they were literate (appendix 8). Of the sixty-seven men whose education level was apparent, more than 95 percent were illiterate. Inebriation, too, played a role. In twenty-one of the seventy-eight cases (27 percent), men who attacked women were drunk at the time.

According to my sample, the three most common characteristics among men arrested for beating women were their education levels (illiterate), professions (*jornalero*), and ethnicity (*indígena*). Indigenous women's penchant for engaging the judicial system compared to ladinas' reluctance to do so partly accounts for the higher percentage of indigenous than ladino men being tried for these crimes; the socioeconomic indicators suggest other factors. Scholars have noted the direct links between structural violence (structures, institutions, and other entities that oppress people almost invisibly) and interpersonal violence.[28] Drawing upon this theoretical framework, gender-based violence in Guatemala during the first half of the twentieth century can be traced to poverty, especially that caused by an exploitive land tenure system, low wages, and unemployment; to racism; and to an abysmal education system characterized by personnel, policies, and curricula that discounted and denigrated *indígenas*. Forced-labor mechanisms such as Estrada Cabrera's hated *mandamientos* and Ubico's vagrancy law can also be added to this list.[29] Designed to punish the more visible interpersonal violence, the judicial system helped to deflect attention from the multiple, interwoven, systemic inequalities that undermined people's well-being on a daily basis.[30]

Brief references to daily life in archival documents and fuller descriptions in contemporary ethnographies and oral histories suggest that the circumstances in which poor and indigenous men and women lived undermined their self-confidence by constantly compromising their ability to survive, let alone thrive. This was especially true for men whose self-esteem was largely related to their ability to provide for their families. Even after they headed their own households, many indigenous men continued to be dominated by their fathers and *patrones*. At times discord between fathers and sons, most commonly over when landholdings would be passed from fathers to sons, escalated into bloody battles.[31] Family life was stressful for poor and indigenous people.

When husbands suffered from some combination of a lack of land, unemployment, and alcoholism, women often had to survive on their own labor or off their families' largesse. Victims regularly identified these circumstances as catalysts of violence. Some highlighted their husbands' jealousy. Almost universally, victims asserted that they had done nothing to provoke male violence.

In a narrative that captured the way different sources of marginalization were mutually constituted, Benita Caja wrote to the San Martín *juez de paz* in 1926 asking to separate from her husband, Eulogio López. When they first married three years prior, she wrote, "we lived under the aid of my mother Teresa Sunuc who furnished everything so we could subsist."[32] According to contemporary ethnographies, this arrangement flew in the face of Maya custom, whereby a woman generally moved in with her in-laws after marriage and in some cases was "cut off from her blood kin."[33] As Bunzel explains it, "She is discouraged from visiting her parents, and . . . [i]t is assumed that she will never again return to their house."[34] Although patrilocal residence was the preferred practice, at least among men, at times economic and other circumstances compelled a couple to live near or with the wife's parents. Whether or not matrilocal residence tempered the violent tendencies of husbands who feared retaliation from their wives' kin is difficult to discern in the archival record; undoubtedly, living with and being supported by his mother-in-law was a blow to López's self-esteem.

Perhaps to escape this emasculation, López insisted they move to a *finca* where he found seasonal work. Caja explained that he earned less money than she had and shortly thereafter began to "grossly beat me saying I had a lover." To her mind, López moved them to the *finca* to "get back at me for my personal work."[35] Maybe he feared what one Chichicastenango man posited in the early 1930s: "the woman will have no respect for the man if she has her own money and does not depend on him."[36] By restricting her ability to generate or control her own income, López subjected Caja to economic violence.

Despite López's efforts to reduce his wife's income, Caja continued to be the breadwinner. When López brought home a goat from his mother, Caja paid one hundred pesos for it and lent him another two hundred pesos. Eight days later, they bought two kids, and he took all the animals to his mother's house. By depriving Caja of the goats purchased with her money, López violated her property rights and thus made her a victim of patrimonial violence. Asking for her animals back, Caja stated, "I separated from him because he has threatened many times to kill me and even lacks respect for my mother as is evident [when] he hit her."[37] By juxtaposing her independent income with his inability to provide for the family, Caja, like other plaintiffs, intimated that her husband's violence against his female kin emanated partly from their financial support of him.

Throughout Latin America, poor men often attempted to establish their precarious grip on household authority by undermining women's independence. Domestic violence was a means to this end.[38] Exerting one's physical strength was one of the few ways lower-class men could distinguish themselves from their female kin within the home. Several scholars have asserted that men's attempts to reinscribe patriarchal authority and their justifications for gender-based violence can be traced to their efforts to buttress their manhood.[39] As Butler argues, "One of the anxious aims of his desire [to be a man] will be to elaborate the difference between him and her, and . . . to discover and install proof of that difference."[40] For many poor *guatemaltecos*, the proof was in the beating.

Plebeian men's ability to wield power in the home was paramount to subaltern masculinity, but that alone does not explain the epidemic of gender-based violence. Buffington encourages historians to explore "the psychological processes that 'sparked' the violence in the first place: . . . individual fears of self-annihilation."[41] Unemployed, land-poor, or otherwise marginalized men like López who could not support their families or control their wives suffered crises of self-confidence. If they could not or would not perform the gendered domestic chores so crucial to family survival, what were they contributing? Some turned to alcohol, which often compounded problems of poverty and violence.

Living with a wife who provided income and domestic labor, moved freely about the community and ruled the roost, and disobeyed him *and* pointed out his failings even if only by her own endeavors, a husband could fear "self-annihilation." A few said as much in their testimonies. After his wife left him in 1914 because of his abuse, the twenty-year-old, illiterate, indigenous *jornalero* Pedro Patzán admitted that the "destruction of his marriage" had left him and his "small interests" in "complete ruin."[42]

Struggles of Labor and Love

Attempts to reconstitute elusive authority and threatened masculinity via gender-based violence also indicate the ways suspicions of infidelity were related to struggles over the control of women's labor and income. The Guatemalan case bears out Piccato's point that manhood was gained, secured, and, I would add, threatened "with the participation of men *and* women."[43] By fueling fears of infidelity, poor women's mobility and autonomy added to men's sense of vulnerability. Twenty-four-year-old, illiterate *indígena* Leoncia Bálan de Ruiz, whose husband hit her weekly with a machete, explained in 1931: "His jealousy has no limits [reaching] the extreme of judging my brother, my lover."[44] Her husband's accusation of incest betrayed his insecurity.

In an indication that judicial officials often affirmed men's sense of ownership over their wives, women accused of infidelity could be incarcerated. In fact, Bálan de Ruiz dictated her petition from the San Martín jail, where she was serving a ten-day sentence because her husband claimed she had cheated on him. Noting that it was the third time he had taken her to court, she insisted it was "truly slander." His physical, psychological, and patrimonial (he stole and sold her chickens and pig) violence made her life "unbearable."

Victoria Sutuj de Cumatzil likewise was a victim of jealousy. Married only eight months, she moved in with her parents and petitioned the San Martín municipal court on July 14, 1933, because her husband, Víctor Cumatzil, was giving her "a very bad life [*muy mala vida*]. He comes home from work with death threats, without my knowing his motives, saying to me that my life is not my own . . . well we have not had even one day of peace, he even forbids me to comb my hair because he is so jealous and moreover he tells me I am a lazy woman who does not even deserve food or clothing."[45] Motivated by jealousy, indigenous men like Cumatzil discouraged potential philanderers by refusing to let their wives maintain their appearance. In acts that contravened highland notions of female beauty, some men cut their spouses' hair. A few went so far as to disfigure their wives. Historian Richard Boyer demonstrates that in colonial Mexico, women used the phrase *mala vida* to describe privations that ranged from physical abuse to their husbands' failure to contribute economically, often because the men were having affairs.[46] In early twentieth-century Guatemala, women who complained of *mala vida* emphasized domestic violence as the main, though not only, source of their suffering.[47]

In a request that betrayed how the interplay of violence and notions of honor could limit Guatemalan women's freedom, Sutuj asked the San Martín *juez de paz* to approve her "provisional deposit . . . in the house of *don* Ismael Gálvez, an honorable and well-known person."[48] Uncommon in Guatemala, such arrangements occurred more frequently in Argentina, among other nations, where husbands put their wives on "deposit" in the homes of third parties while the couples worked out their differences.[49] Asking the *juez de paz* for a restraining order, Sutuj hinted at her reasoning: Cumatzil would have been less likely to bother Sutuj at the home of a well-respected ladino than the home of her (apparently indigenous) parents. If the criminal record is any indication, arrangements of this nature were made informally and could afford women some protection. The *juez de paz* rejected her request, but Sutuj insisted, "I am not considering living any more with that man who gives me an atrocious life."[50]

Sutuj's well-crafted narrative suggests that her husband's jealousy emanated partly from his sense of ownership over her. According to female plaintiffs, husbands often treated their wives as property—a perception that was reinforced by the exchange of land, animals, cash, or other resources that accompanied wedding rituals.[51] Unable to secure the authorities' protection, Sutuj returned to court three months later because Cumatzil threatened her with a knife when she refused to move in with his mother. Sutuj again fled to her parents' home. After submitting the knife as evidence, she declared, "I am the companion not the slave of my husband."[52]

The frequency with which victims of domestic violence used the word "slave" suggests the diminished status many women held in their spouses' eyes. Victims' descriptions of corporal abuse—being whipped, slashed, even branded—conjured images of slavery. When the daily beatings with a machete and stick that characterized her "very bad life" reached the extreme of her husband's "inhumane action" of branding her face, Alejandra Aguilar asked San Martín's *juez de paz* to explain to him that "he does not have the right to do whatever he wants with me. . . . I am not his slave but his wife."[53] Like her choice of the word "slave," the permanent scar on her face suggested her husband wanted to establish his ownership of and control over her.

Hinted at in the Maya tendency toward patrilocality, the ways men sought to establish control over their wives can also be glimpsed in struggles between sons and fathers-in-law. Since a Maya father could "retrieve the daughter if the son-in-law did not live up to his obligations," much was at stake in the transition from filial to marital life.[54] Throughout Latin America during the colonial and national periods, husbands concerned about the authority and influence of their fathers-in-law sought to limit the interactions between wives and their parents.[55] For Guatemalan men like Cumatzil who resided with or on the property of their in-laws, imposing such restrictions was nearly impossible. The clashes that ensued lend credence to the assertion that men often viewed their wives and daughters as property.

In an allegation that discounted his wife's agency, Cumatzil attributed her intractability to his father-in-law, who regularly arrived at their home to insult, hit, and run him off. He did not admit as much in court, but Cumatzil's insistence that he and his wife move in with his mother was likely motivated by his desire to vacate his father-in-law's house. "My father-in-law has introduced disorder into my home, poorly advising my wife so that she disobeys me in everything and offering that when something happens to her, she let him know so he can defend her," he explained. For this reason, Cumatzil called upon San Martín's *juez de paz* to "order his father-in-law Sutuj to abstain from guiding his daughter who is my wife down the bad path, since he is the cause of his daughter's bad way of living." He also asked that the judge compel Victoria Sutuj to "continue their common life" in the house Cumatzil had prepared, presumably his mother's, and obey him. He specifically requested that "without my permission, she not return to visit her relatives who far from giving her good advice, only inculcate her with things that threaten our tranquility."[56] As a *jornalero* living on his father-in-law's property, Cumatzil had little he could claim as his own, which undoubtedly made his father-in-law's attempt to protect Sutuj all the more menacing.

Cumatzil's petition provides a rare glimpse into how perpetrators of domestic violence framed their actions. Few denied hitting their wives, but Cumatzil's narrative thereafter reflects some common strategies. As other defendants did, he established himself as a hard worker who in turn expected his wife to perform her duties. When she failed to, he reserved the right to reprimand her. Since he judged her too simple to disobey him of her own volition, he identified a third party as the source of their marital discord. After defending himself against his wife's charges, Cumatzil asked the authorities to intervene on his behalf in the struggle over who controlled his wife. To add gravity to his petition, he invoked the regime's discourse of order. Like citizens who fomented and facilitated unrest in the nation, his father-in-law had sown disorder in his home and therefore should be punished. In turn, just as citizens should know their place and obey authorities, his wife should be put back in her place (literally his home) and obey him.

Although rare, fathers who initiated litigation on behalf of their daughters provide a different perspective on these struggles. On June 27, 1933, the literate and likely indigenous father Julián Balan reported his son-in-law Fidel Sutuj's offense to San Martín's *juez de paz*. Arriving at her parents' home that morning to borrow some corn, his daughter Gregoria Balan found her mother overwhelmed by the task of preparing lunch for their workers. So she stayed for a few hours to help. When Gregoria returned to her home, Sutuj beat her so furiously with his staff that it left bruises on her face and back. After showing them to the judge—bruises were crucial evidence in assault and battery litigation—Julián explained that this was not the first beating by Sutuj. Julián considered this attack "an ingratitude . . . because he [Sutuj] wants her to support him by force, that is to say that my daughter obtains corn and beans, while he occupies himself with getting drunk, spending the little money he earns. He says that I give advice to my daughter, I want him to say what this advice is."[57] For Julián, Sutuj's beatings and failure to provide for his family were far greater injustices than any fatherly advice could be.

Even as it demonstrates that his daughter's labor was valuable to him, Julián Balan's petition also intimates his love for her. Although assault and battery records focus on violence and abuse by their nature, petitions like this point to the deep concern family members and neighbors had for each other. The twenty-five-year-old *jornalero* Pedro Pérez's testimony in Patzún municipal court offers another example. The "instant" he heard Avelina Saguach's husband attack her with a machete in 1917, Pérez "immediately" ran out of his house and disarmed him.[58] Another neighbor accompanied Saguach on the two-kilometer walk into town to get medical care. If not for the help of her neighbors, Saguach may have died.

Examining the accounts of relatives, neighbors, and others who intervened on behalf of domestic violence victims provides a window into the broader cultural understanding of the limits of violence against women. While restrained corporal punishment was acceptable to maintain the household, violent men transgressed community codes of conduct when they crossed that threshold. The *indígena* Isidrio Xajil said as much when he surmised that Pedro Patzán's wife "left him because of the bad treatment that, contrary to expectations, her husband Patzán gave her."[59] Indigenous men should neither accept impudence nor be excessively violent.[60]

At times the judicial record yields manifestations of love. To cite an example that hints at these tender emotions, even three and a half months after the sixty-year-old indigenous *jornalero* Patricio Culajay found his wife bleeding on the floor of their home on March 11, 1902, the image haunted him. He told the department court notary that "as he was so tormented at the sight of his wife thrown to the floor and injured," he immediately pursued, captured, and turned over to the authorities her attacker.[61] Since they seldom demanded authorities' attention, expressions of love, compassion, and solidarity only inadvertently made it into the judicial record. Their intermittent appearance reminds us that marital, familial, and neighborly relations were often benevolent and caring.

Gendered Expectations

Not surprisingly, men and women had different expectations and interpretations of each other's roles, responsibilities, and positions in the family. In her study of gender negotiations in late twentieth-century Chile, historian Heidi Tinsman found that women and men interpreted the ethos of gender mutualism in contrasting ways: husbands expected their wives to support and obey them, and women expected their husbands to afford them respect and autonomy.[62] The gap between these and other conflicting expectations often led to discord.

The case between Victoria Sutuj and Víctor Cumatzil concerns this kind of discord. In contrast to his wife, Cumatzil said their altercation was the result of her disobedience, as she "had not done what I had . . . ordered and for that she yielded to my repression."[63] He denied brandishing a knife or hitting her but admitted to reprimanding her. Margareta Hydén finds that since "fights," as opposed to "assaults," were compatible with married life, men often sought to portray incidents as emanating from an argument or mutual aggression.[64] Tellingly, Cumatzil's narrative reinforced Sutuj's claim that he treated her like a slave rather than a companion. Like many of his contemporaries, Cumatzil appeared to believe his power included the right to punish his wife for insubordination. And as did many of her contemporaries, Sutuj challenged her husband's authority by not doing what he commanded.

Defendants who contested assault charges against them often called attention to their victims' failings. Among the most frequently cited justifications for striking a spouse was her failure to keep the house and children in order. A Poqomam-Maya (henceforth Poqomam) mayor affirmed these responses by suggesting that a woman's protection under the law was contingent upon her completing her domestic duties: "If a woman takes care of her husband, prepares the tortillas, washes his clothes, and attends the children, the husband has no right to punish her. If, owing to a bad temper, he beats his wife, she has the right to come to me."[65] Wagley, too, found that in addition to a woman's alleged infidelity and gossiping, laziness was among the most common alleged causes of domestic violence in Santiago Chimaltenango.[66]

In turn, indigenous women pointed out men's failings but seldom questioned the enormity of their own labor and reproductive responsibilities—some of which the Poqomam mayor delineates above—as compared to those of their mates.[67] Scholars have attributed this acceptance to ethnic solidarity and the complementary and interdependent roles of women and men particularly in indigenous communities;[68] however, the Nobel laureate economist Amartya Sen suggests another explanation. In a condition he refers to as "cooperative conflict," Sen argues that the division of benefits and chores in working families involves both conflict and mutual interest. Since maintaining family harmony discourages dwelling upon such conflicts, most are resolved implicitly rather than explicitly. The result is an acceptance of "the systematic deprivation of females vis-à-vis males in one field or another."[69] That so few domestic violence victims requested a separation or divorce and some wanted to save their marriages suggests how limited their options were. In the effort to contain conflict and maintain harmony within the family, "customary patterns of conduct are simply taken as legitimate and even reasonable."[70] Even women who were outspoken about male violence and ineptitude generally did not critique inequality in their marriages or family lives.

While male litigants implicitly highlighted complementary gender relations in indigenous domestic economies, women simply insisted that men's expectations of their domestic partners should be matched by fulfillment of their own responsibilities. In another manifestation of the imbalance of

gender power, they had to tread lightly when doing so. When María Gó-
mez reproached her husband for not providing for the education of their
two children and generally neglecting them, he hit her twice. In his defense
in Patzicía's municipal court on June 4, 1929, the twenty-three-year-old, illiterate, indigenous *jornalero* denied neglecting the children, though he admitted to slapping his wife "for disobedience in family affairs."[71] For his
aggression, he was sentenced to ten days in jail commutable by fifty cents
per day.

Seven years later, when Martina Mayzúl chided her husband for failing
to provide firewood, he hit and kicked her. According to Mayzúl, she had
suffered his abuse and attempts to run her off for a long time. Admitting to
hitting his wife in the head, the fifty-three-year-old, illiterate *jornalero*, who
identified as *indígena* and *guatemalteco*, said it was in response to her accusation that he was having an affair instead of working. Whatever the motive,
Patzicía's *juez de paz* Martínez sentenced him to ten days in jail commutable
by twenty cents a day.[72]

These two sentences reflect a trend in Patzicía in which male perpetrators of domestic violence enjoyed increasing leniency as the twentieth century progressed. Since at least 1916, Patzicía's municipal judges almost
invariably imposed the maximum sentence of ten days in jail for domestic violence. By 1935, however, Martínez and other municipal judges frequently sentenced men to only five days in jail. When they imposed ten-
day sentences, their commutable rates were often lower than those of their
predecessors', thereby increasing the likelihood that perpetrators would not
serve out their full sentences. This pattern of leniency reveals how individual justices undercut even the minimal protection afforded domestic violence victims under the law.

Sexual Violence

The legal system similarly exacerbated the plight of rape victims.[73] Of the
15 rape trials from Chimaltenango Juzgado de Primera Instancia I studied
closely (out of a total of 119 from 1900 to 1925), only 1 ended in conviction
and the charge was reduced to *rapto* (abduction). Even during the reign of
Ubico, who cast himself as a protector of women, perpetrators of sexual violence generally enjoyed impunity.[74]

In an indication of women's marginalization, all but one of the victims
in my sample were illiterate. Poverty both contributed to and compounded
women's vulnerability. With their families dependent on them to perform

numerous tasks and errands, poor and working-class females led precarious, ambulatory lives.[75] With good reason, when Kaqchikel girls set off on an errand, their fathers spat on the dirt floors of their homes and demanded that they return before it dried. At times, women were vulnerable in their own homes, as Andrea Caná learned on June 15, 1910, when Juan Mux broke into her house in Comalapa as she lay sleeping and raped her in front of her five-year-old son; her husband was away working in the capital.[76] Although at least one neighbor heard her screams in the middle of the night, no one came to her aid. The subsequent trial demonstrated how rape litigation disadvantaged women.

Because Mux threatened to kill her if she went to the authorities, Caná did not immediately report the rape; nor could she tell her husband, Felipe Colaj, until he returned in August. Even then it was not until the following April that Colaj brought the case forward. Intentionally or not, waiting this long obviated the need to undergo a court-ordered gynecological exam. After being raped, most victims were subject to this invasive procedure at the hands of someone who was neither female nor indigenous—a fate that often further alienated rape victims from the judicial process and reinforced their feelings of powerlessness.

Although Caná was spared the state's physical (if not verbal) probing, her husband ultimately dropped the charges of "adultery" against Mux. By redefining the crime, Colaj intimated that in his mind his wife had gone from being a victim to being a suspect. Class may have played a role in his change of heart: both men were literate, but Mux was a landowner, while Colaj was a poor *jornalero*.

As much as the rape underscored Caná's vulnerability and marginalization, the court proceedings deepened them. Three days after Colaj dropped the charges, the judge released Mux. Even in the face of strong evidence, such impunity was not unusual, as an incident from Yepocapa ten years earlier demonstrates. Although a midwife and unlicensed doctor confirmed the rape of a girl four and a half years old who took authorities to the scene of the crime, where they found imprints from a man's knees and her blood, the suspected rapist, who had mud on his knees when the authorities caught him, was set free.[77]

In addition to the low conviction rate, authorities' perverse responses to rape also must have discouraged many victims from coming forward. Homeless and suffering from elephantiasis, María Eligia Hernández became pregnant when José Toj raped her in 1933. If the Sacatepéquez *jefe político* refused to arrange for her hospital care, the San Lorenzo el Cubo municipal tribunal proposed that "the one who caused her damage [*daño*], José

Toj, should take responsibility for her."[78] Such chilling solutions were not uncommon in Guatemala, Mexico, or Peru, where rapists could avoid incarceration if they married their victims.[79]

In the face of threats of sexual, domestic, and political violence, women responded creatively and often efficaciously to the conditions that marked their marginalization. As we have seen, some did so by turning to the courts for redress; others publicly shamed perpetrators. To cite one example of the latter from 1923, *doña* Nicolasa Corona denounced Manuel E. Meneses in front of the clientele at her Patzicía cantina for raping María Corona while she was drunk. If Meneses's reaction is any indication, the rebuke achieved its intended effect; he took Corona to court for slander, insisting that her "accusation threatens my . . . social position."[80] Just as rumors of sexual impropriety infringed upon a woman's reputation, accusations of sexual violence could undermine a man's social position.

Constructions and Uses of Gendered Identities

With its laws, lawyers, judges, and notaries, the legal system perpetuated domestic notions of women. Court notaries generally described female litigants with such terms as *oficios de su sexo* (occupations appropriate to one's sex) or *oficios feminiles* (feminine occupations) even if the woman was a farmer, *buhonero*, or otherwise held a position generally associated with men. Though gendered, these labels did not carry racial or class stereotypes; indigenous, ladina, poor, middle-class, and elite women alike were identified by them.

When municipal magistrates based their rulings on gendered assumptions, female plaintiffs often were disadvantaged. To cite an example from 1916, the fifty-year-old indigenous farmer Felipe Lacan hit his forty-year-old wife, Petrona Perón, while he was drunk, and Patzicía's justice sentenced both parties to ten days in jail commutable by twenty reales a day. Since punishing assault victims was rare, he must have found Lacan's confession compelling: "The reason [he hit her] is that she was drunk, failing her domestic obligations and she had addressed me with some insults and dirty words and I ask that you punish . . . my wife for these transgressions."[81] The judge did not explain his reasoning, but the message was clear: behavior unbecoming in a woman—inebriation, domestic failings, insulting her husband—warranted punishment. As the record of female cross-dressers and infanticide perpetrators demonstrates, disciplining women's transgressions had strong social supports.[82]

At times the courtroom itself was an incubator of male privileges. The 1929 trial of José Sisimit shows how prerogatives of gender-based violence were modeled and reproduced. His wife explained that "he hit her in the face . . . because she did not give him money to continue drinking *aguardiente*." Patzicía's notary then penned, "Sisimit, confirming his offense, put forth as an exception that he had hit his wife . . . to correct her because of her disobedience in everything that he ordered."[83] As a fifty-year-old man it must have been especially humiliating for Sisimit to be rebuffed by his wife in front of his drinking buddy Eduviges Miculax, a twenty-two-year-old bachelor. Their one quetzal commutable rate was the same, yet Sisimit and Miculax were sentenced to ten and five days in jail, respectively.

Even if Miculax was too drunk to remember the evening, as he claimed, listening to the municipal court proceedings before him informed his understanding of marital relations. As illiterate indigenous *jornaleros*, Sisimit and Miculax shared a socioeconomic position. So Miculax could expect his life experience to be similar to Sisimit's. Should he decide to marry, Miculax already had developed a sense of the gendered roles, responsibilities, and power in the relationship. Viewed from this perspective, the court record indicates one of the ways men normalized their power over and even right to hit women.

Instead of allowing gendered conventions to confine them, some women manipulated these assumptions. To borrow Butler's conceptualization, Guatemalan women realized that "the name one is called both subordinates and enables" when they used notions encoded in such terms as *oficios de su sexo* and *oficios feminiles* to produce "a sense of agency from ambivalence, a set of effects that exceed the animating intention of the call."[84] For example, some female litigants invoked assumptions about the sexual division of labor to defend their refusal to perform certain tasks. Tomasa Morejón did just that when she explained to the San Martín *juez de paz*, "Today at eleven a.m. my husband lashed me in the head with a stone as you can see, only for not having retrieved a large log of corresponding weight from a distance of *una media legua* [two kilometers, more than a mile]. Not only am I sick, but *that work does not correspond to me*; he should send my oldest son to get the log. In light of this, my husband Ramon Díaz became angry and punished me in this barbarous manner, well [*pues*] repeatedly."[85]

Accustomed to associating women's labor with domestic duties, the magistrate would have been hard pressed to disagree that dragging a heavy log two kilometers would be women's work even if, in reality, many did perform such labor. As Morejón implied, by the court's standards Díaz's beating was unwarranted. Unfortunately, the judge's response is lost. Using social constructs to strengthen their cases perpetuated notions of women's domesticity and vulnerability. Women's agency was bound up in and often reinforced their subjectivity.[86]

Courageously ignoring her husband's threat to shoot her if she told the authorities that he had whipped her, María Francisca Rumpich, too, deployed the discourse of the sexual division of labor in her May 22, 1901, petition to Chimaltenango's department judge. He did not rule on the case, but in skipping the municipal judicial system and hiring a scribe to write her petition, this monolingual, indigenous woman enjoyed more control over her narrative than her counterparts who appeared in municipal court did over theirs. She noted that her husband not only "does not perform any of the housework . . . I maintain and dress him."[87] She effectively fulfilled the responsibilities of both husband and wife. According to Rumpich, her husband's most damaging violence was patrimonial: burning the title to her house and land. She asked that he be punished and evicted from her home so she could return to it.

Another way women used "the name one is called" to strengthen their positions was to invoke the tropes of motherhood to combat perversions of patriarchal power. Like women who accused men of reproductive crimes, domestic violence plaintiffs could highlight their status as mothers to underscore the depravity of violent husbands. Women throughout Latin America efficaciously deployed this strategy in courtrooms and other public venues partly because many Latin American nation builders considered the qualities of motherhood crucial to maintaining a peaceful society.[88]

When the thirty-year-old, illiterate *indígena* Lorenza Elías de Tun went to San Martín's municipal court in 1931 offering the bruises on her face as evidence of her husband's abuse, she crafted a narrative around her role as a mother:

> Without giving me the least consideration of my sex—I am sick from having recently given birth just as I am nursing my small son—my husband, after having served him dinner yesterday around seven p.m. despite my poor health, hit me in a cruel and impious manner protesting my failure to send his lunch to where he was working. But the fault was his. Since he did not tell me where he would be working. . . . I did not know where to send his food.[89]

Even though she was breastfeeding her son and recovering from childbirth, she did not contest the expectation that she cook and deliver her husband's meals. Accepting those tasks as legitimate aspects of "customary patterns of conduct," she decried the injustice of being beaten in her condition, particularly when blame for the failed delivery lay with her husband. If officials sanctified motherhood, she implied, then a nursing mother recovering from childbirth should enjoy a privileged and protected position.

In addition to vivid images of motherhood, Elías played upon assumptions about women's vulnerability. In light of her husband's improprieties, she asked for the authorities' protection and assistance in separating from him because "he has repeatedly abused my womanly weakness." Set against the description of her life and labor, Elías's reference to female fragility belied her character and industry; she invoked her "womanly weakness" to highlight her husband's ability to overpower her physically. Lest San Martín's *juez de paz* harbor any lingering doubts about her situation, she added, "My life is intolerable alongside my husband."[90]

Women were wise to deploy the discourse of motherhood. Municipal judicial officials responded decisively to mothers in distress, particularly when their sons were a menace. Even just the threat of violence could land a son in jail, as Cornilio Xavix Esquit, an illiterate *jornalero* who self-identified as a *guatemalteco*, learned in 1942 when he threatened his mother with a machete over a disagreement about inheritance. After the indigenous woman lamented her son's lack of "respect for his mother," Patzicía's magistrate sentenced him to ten days in jail commutable by twenty-five cents a day.[91] When sons hit their mothers, their sentences were even harsher. Coupled with ethnographers' observations in other Maya communities where custom expressly prohibited men from hitting their mothers, judicial responses to such attacks further flesh out the limits of gender-based violence in highland society.[92]

A powerful tool, the discourse of motherhood did not necessarily overdetermine women's narrative strategies and wishes, as Manuela Umul de Can's petition to Patzicía's municipal *intendente* on February 24, 1936, demonstrates. Married to Lucas Can for twelve years, she explained that during the previous five years he routinely abused her. She regularly reported these offenses to the municipal authorities, but her "ungrateful" husband never corrected his ways. "Most recently he had threatened to kill me and since I have tired of suffering from him and the law supports me in this case, I come to let you know that I will not return to my husband," Umul maintained.[93] Had this illiterate (and likely indigenous) woman felt a favorable ruling depended on her image as a mother, she probably would not have insisted that her two daughters would stay with her, but her husband should keep their three sons. Unfortunately, the archival record offers no hint as to the *intendente*'s ruling.

In contrast to litigants who played upon gendered stereotypes, some women exploded these categories and assumptions with their descriptions of marital and family life. By outlining their agricultural, marketplace, and other endeavors or providing specifics about the physical and technical nature of their tasks, a number of women used their narratives to highlight their diligence, intelligence, and skills. Even in calling attention to their physical weakness compared to men, victims often emphasized their integrity and productivity. After the third time her husband beat her, Julia Hernández de Camey complained that he was "abusing my womanly weakness." She also said, "My husband claims to give me tasks that are only for the home," but her labor covered the "daily expense of family subsistence" since he did not give her any money for her or their children's food or clothing. Like Morejón and Rumpich, Hernández de Camey suggested that her husband responded to his failure to provide for the family by overburdening her. In light of these perversions of the marital contract, she insisted, "The authority is obligated to help me in the legal manner."[94] The San Martín *juez de paz* agreed; he sentenced Camey to five days in jail commutable by one quetzal a day—a considerable sum in 1927.

Despite evidence to the contrary, officials generally accepted the notion that women were weak and vulnerable. With her thumb dangling from her hand after she was attacked with a machete on April 11, 1909, the forty-year-old *indígena* María Concepción Cujcuy consulted an *empírico* (unlicensed physician) who concluded that she would lose the thumb and need twenty days of medical care, during which time she should not work partly because of "complications related to her age, sex, and weak constitution."[95] His diminished view of her gender, seniority, and constitution stood in stark contrast to her ability to fend off her attacker, immediately report the incident, and testify in municipal court the next day.

Violence as a Means of State Power and Social Governance

Never as powerful as the Estrada Cabrera and Ubico dictatorships conveyed, the early twentieth-century state used gender-based violence to uphold its rule. Even though ladino officials' authority emanated from the state, they had to appease their indigenous charges who ultimately granted municipal magistrates local legitimacy. If communities deemed rulings to be unjust or punitive, revolts could ensue. Read this way, domestic violence victims were the sacrificial lambs who kept quotidian tensions at an acceptable level. Forster argues that by diverting "the anger of men into 'nonpolitical' channels . . . Ubico was served admirably by male violence against women."⁹⁶ In an indication that gender-based violence "was an eminently political phenomenon,"⁹⁷ it similarly served the Estrada Cabrera, Orellana, and Chacón administrations. Partly stemming from their recognition of *potestad marital* (a man's right over his wife's person and property), legislators' and judicial officials' reluctance to assertively address domestic violence was an exercise of state power.

That some perpetrators did not perceive a need to justify and others failed to see any "unpleasantness" in their actions speaks to the extent to which violence became embedded in everyday gender relations as mundane if not banal.⁹⁸ The record of recidivists and patterns of abuse evident elsewhere in the archives suggest that some highland women lived in terror because violence was the rule, not the exception. Typical was the experience of Rosana Elías de Tun. The twenty-six-year-old indigenous woman explained to San Martín's magistrate that her twelve years of marriage had been unbearable: "My husband has hit me, wounded me, and injured me innumerable times."⁹⁹ Prior to her husband's latest drunken blows and threat with a knife, on March 8, 1925, she had already complained to the authorities on six other occasions. By not adequately punishing men's violence against women, the judicial system reinforced violence as a mechanism of social governance.

Court rulings and the laws and belligerent men who precipitated them did not exist in a vacuum. Violence was a means of state rule for much of the first half of the twentieth century when the Estrada Cabrera and Ubico governments systemically employed intimidation and fear. To cite how these tactics and concepts were disseminated, a man who was drafted into Ubico's military recalled:

> [T]hey enforced a truly strict discipline in military service. They gave it to us really hard, just like [they expected us] to give it to civilians. You see, a soldier had the duty to take a thief prisoner without anyone's authorization. But if that same soldier were caught stepping even a foot beyond the post where he was stationed on guard duty, they'd give you forty lashes with a leather strip.¹⁰⁰

As harsh, obedient rule permeated Guatemalan society and patriarchs from the national to familial level employed violence to resolve conflict and to discipline, women suffered the consequences.

In the face of authorities' impotence some women pursued other ways to address domestic violence. Rosana Elías fought off her husband's attack until a neighbor responded to her screams and disarmed him. "It is dangerous for me in the house. I have been a victim of his bloody instincts and drunken tendencies without [his] heeding the restrictions that the authority has repeatedly established. I wish to place myself definitively under the full protection of the law, in its virtue. I want a divorce," she insisted.[101] As aware as Elías was of the inadequacies of the judicial and police systems, it must have been disappointing for her to learn that since the municipal court could not process divorce proceedings, she had to appeal to yet another authority: the department judge. Nor would she have been surprised that her husband commuted his ten-day sentence and walked out of the courtroom a free man. What is remarkable about this case is not the state's inability to protect domestic abuse victims, but Elías's belief despite all her experience to the contrary that at some point it would.

Perpetrators who commuted their sentences and left the courtroom in the company of their victims revealed the extent to which the state abdicated its responsibility to ensure the safety of women. With such short reprieves, in some cases only hours, it is remarkable that women turned to the courts for protection at all, especially considering that some perpetrators threatened to kill them if they did. The record of female fatalities is a testament to the seriousness of death threats that men used to gain power over women. Recidivists proved that ten-day sentences failed to deter violent men.

Elías's case also underscores the complexity of men's marginalization. Unlike most perpetrators of gender-based violence, her husband, the thirty-year-old Venacio Tun, was an *agricultor*, not a *jornalero*. Owning his own land undoubtedly facilitated his ability to pay the twenty-real commutation and additional 150-peso fine the judge assessed for other *faltas* (misdeeds). In contrast to his financial security, Tun's inability to sign his name must have been particularly frustrating in light of his wife's "elementary" education and literacy.[102]

Unlike Elías, most domestic violence victims were poor and thus had to weigh the financial burden of bringing their husbands to court. Besides the cost of purchasing municipal stamped paper and hiring a scribe, the money to commute sentences depleted household incomes. Just appearing in court often meant litigants lost a day of labor and the earnings associated with it. Putting aside for a moment the perilous nature of extrapolating subalterns' motivations from archival documents, particularly those produced in venues that disadvantaged poor, indigenous women, perhaps these female plaintiffs were hoping that public shame if not state authority would curb their husbands' penchant for violence. When it did not, the costs incurred exacerbated their plight.

Despite the risks and costs of litigation, even a brief incarceration could provide the space and security victims needed to address larger issues. While her husband was in jail for beating her in 1931, Luz Guerra de Luch asked San Martín's magistrate to send her appeal for a divorce to the higher court. She said that in addition to her own failing health, "my children are in a deplorable and grave state, and we have not even one cent."[103] Her situation remained dire, but her husband's imprisonment facilitated the process of extricating herself and her children from an abusive relationship.

Tired of retribution without long-term protection from the courts, some women chose instead to flee to the homes of relatives, neighbors, or friends. Many employed both strategies. Frequently fleeing to her mother's house to escape her husband, the twenty-four-year-old *indígena* Victoriana Miculax asked her mother to serve as a witness in Patzicía's municipal court on December 17, 1943. Despite Miculax's regular appeals to the *juzgado de paz* and her husband's subsequent convictions, he continued to beat her. In a statement that related authorities' impotence to the underreporting of domestic violence, she explained through an interpreter that "her husband [Mateo] Muy is a recidivist in abusing her," much of which she did not report.[104] In his defense, the twenty-three-year-old, illiterate *jornalero* admitted that he had been convicted previously for domestic abuse, but he denied hitting his wife on this occasion. He explained that he "always reprimands her because she is very neglectful in the home." The *juez de paz* sentenced him to ten days in prison commutable by fifteen cents a day; ten days later, Muy was released from jail.

More directly disregarding state authority, some men hit their wives in the presence of officials. Such was the case when the thirty-two-year-old *jornalero* José Coc kicked his wife and pulled her hair in front of the *alguacil* (bailiff) Agustín Esquit on July 30, 1916.[105] Perhaps owing to his inebriation, Coc tried to hit his wife again when he was brought into the courtroom. More concerned with maintaining order inside than outside the courtroom, Patzicía's *juez de paz* sentenced Coc to five days for hitting his wife and fifteen days for disrespecting the *tribunal*. The sentence did little to deter Coc, who was in municipal court again a few months later for whipping his wife. Even with no witnesses, Coc readily confessed his crime.[106]

Wittingly or not, domestic violence victims who kept returning to court made municipal justices aware of the limits of their judgments and authority. Clearly convictions failed to intimidate the many litigants who simply waited before beating their wives again. With such tenuous grips on power, most municipal judicial officials could do little more than keep gender-based violence at a level that allowed men to blow off steam but not compel women to flee their families or communities. When that happened, the balance of power shifted and judicial officials more readily upheld women's rights, as the record of *abandono* (abandonment) litigation reveals.[107]

Salvaging Marriages and Families

Given the municipal court's limitations and priorities, it was better suited for women like the twenty-five-year-old *indígena* Juana Ávila de Lool who hoped to right, not end, their marriages. Rich with descriptions of spousal negotiations, beliefs about child-rearing, and exchanges and considerations that precipitated court visits, her March 29, 1926, letter to San Martín's *juez de paz* is worth quoting at length:

> Today early, at six a.m., my husband Apolinaria Lool arrived at my home after suffering the punishment that you imposed upon him for hitting me last Sunday, for which I brought forward a formal complaint. Upon penetrating my home, which is my exclusive property via inheritance from my dead father *don* Manuel Ávila, my husband categorically said that he no longer is disposed to live in my company, that I should leave my house and leave my one-year-old daughter Benita Lool in his power. [By] threatening me [he has] compelled me to return before you another time to state, in use of my rights, that: I am not disposed to separate from my legitimate husband, since in addition to the matrimonial life that we have made, we are connected through our daughter, who needs the care of us both. With the fruit of our economies, we have purchased a small parcel of land. He has his land apart from what I inherited from my father that legally forms the patrimony of the family.[108]

Reluctant to surrender her marriage and family, Ávila was likely aware that, as Bunzel reports, some men abused their wives to break up the marriage,[109] so she developed a contingency plan. If Lool insisted on a divorce, Ávila wanted alimony and custody of her daughter, who needed "maternal care . . . and finally it is he not I who should leave the home, since as I have said, I am the sole owner."[110] The custom in some Maya communities was for fathers to keep the children unless they were very young when couples separated,[111] so she was wise to deploy the discourse of motherhood. Her press for financial support spoke to the reality behind women's narratives about the sanctity of marriage: single mothers often struggled to support themselves and their children.

The ambiguous nature of gender relations in poor, rural, indigenous families can best be understood in the context of ethnic and class domination. Faced with these forces of oppression, husbands and wives had to collaborate as couples for the survival of their families. Indigenous women who put up with a certain level of domestic violence or appealed to the judicial system to arrest it were not ineluctably complicit with patriarchal, state, or ladino power; they simply had to carefully calculate what aspects of power structures they would contest and which they would submit to. Knowing that they depended to some degree on their husbands' labor and income and that court costs and fines undercut familial finances, victims of domestic violence were in contradictory and ambivalent positions.[112] Neither fully rejecting nor accepting men's privileged positions and prerogatives, women sought to establish reciprocal relations and better conditions; historian Steve Stern calls these arrangements "contested patriarchal pacts."[113] Women who confronted or defied their husbands tended to do so when their husbands' failings infringed upon familial survival and success.

Keeping the family together compelled many women to put up with emotional and physical abuse. Antonia Cumatzil de Balan explained to San Martín's *juez de paz* in April 1933, "A long time ago my husband Lorenzo Balan began to give me a bad life, as much to me as to my family . . . but to maintain the harmony that should exist in marriages when the family is big like ours, I had resigned to suffer with patience all of the abuses of which I was the object, begging at the same time my children to have patience."[114] Not until he kicked her children out and began beating her more frequently did she leave him. Indicating that she doubted municipal authorities could stop her husband's violence, Cumatzil did not ask that her husband be punished for his crimes but rather that the court preside over their separation and divide their holdings equally.

For many women, the tipping point was losing their children. On December 6, 1926, the twenty-three-year-old (likely *indígena*) Francisca Chiroy de Sutuj explained to the San Martín *juez de paz*, "Today in the middle of the night . . . my husband arrived drunk and without cause or reason hit me in the face and used a machete to direct other blows at me that did not leave signs on my body because I defended myself with my night clothes. When he finished attacking me with the machete, he told me that if I complained to you, he would return to kill me and grabbing my two-year-old son, he left my house."[115] Underscoring "his indolence and failure to care for the home," she remarked that their clothes were gifts from her father. She asked that her husband be punished and "forced to surrender their small son who needs as yet maternal care."[116]

As many did to denounce their husband's violence, women also deployed the discourse of motherhood to rescue their children. As in Ávila's and Cumatzil's cases, the efficacy of Chiroy's narrative strategy is impossible to gauge absent the justice's ruling; yet by emphasizing her husband's drinking habit and failure to provide for the family, Chiroy asserted that she was more qualified than he to care for their son. By highlighting his violent streak, she suggested that her son was in danger with him. In contrast to the detailed description of her husband's failings as a father, Chiroy did not need to list her attributes as a mother. The name she was called did that for her; she simply reminded the judge that her son needed "maternal care."

Violent Women

While Guatemalans came to accept a certain level of male violence, they deemed violent females feral or irrational. Because their behavior defied social norms, accounts of female aggression were almost invariably accompanied by attempts to explain it. In contrast, excepting homicides, authorities and journalists seldom felt compelled to explain men's violent outbursts beyond attributing them to drunken rages. As the tragic events of April 8, 1914, demonstrate, women, too, became violent when drunk. Already inebriated when she arrived at the home of *la indígena* Vicenta Luis at 11 a.m., Regina Taquiej demanded a drink. Luis's twelve-year-old daughter informed Taquiej that Luis was sleeping, and Taquiej pulled a knife out of her belt and stabbed Vicenta Luis in the throat. Taquiej was still at large a month after the murder.[117]

This incident notwithstanding, female violence was far less likely to involve drinking than was male violence. Of the twenty-nine women and two male accomplices accused of assault and battery whose cases I examined (appendix 9), only two of the perpetrators were drunk. Far more frequent were attacks provoked by insults, jealousy, and economic competition. Subtracting the six female perpetrators whose ethnicity was indeterminable, the mix of seventeen indigenous (74 percent) and six ladina (26 percent) female perpetrators reflected local demographics. In contrast, eleven victims identified as *indígenas* and nine others likely were (83 percent), while only four victims were likely ladinas. Considered alongside the domestic violence data, these results indicate that indigenous women were more likely than ladinas to be victims of violence and then denounce their male or female assailants in court.

Relating notaries' descriptions of defendants to the structural conditions that precipitated interpersonal violence is less straightforward for women

than it is for men. Racism often informed their outbursts—some *indígenas* responded violently to racial slurs—but indigenous women were not arrested for assault and battery in numbers that were disproportionate to their
representation in municipal and department populations. Poverty also marginalized them, but only four women—a *tortillera* (tortilla maker and vendor), two *molenderas*, and a merchant—were identified by their professions.
The one characteristic among female defendants that stands out most clearly
in identifying poverty and marginalization is educational level. Fourteen
were characterized as *sin instrucción*, and nine others could not sign their
names or otherwise suggested they were illiterate.[118] Only one woman said
she was literate. Five female defendants' educational levels remained elusive.
At once a consequence and cause of their subordinate positions in relation
to men, women's lack of educational opportunities was a form of structural
violence that had become normative.

As in other societies where power and wealth were unequally distrib-
uted, a culture of violence permeated Guatemala; the few cultural spaces
where women could be violent were gender-specific. During childbirth in
Santiago Chimaltenango, women could hit and even wail on their husbands, who had to absorb the blows without responding.[119] Dominated by
women who were engaged in the often tense process of bartering and providing credit, highland marketplaces were sites of female violence. In private homes and courtyards, as well, commercial interactions turned violent.
Fights that erupted over payments, credit, and clientele suggest that often
violence between women was as much about economics as it was about enmity. When Francisca Choy did not have the money for the maize she had
purchased on credit from Ramona Porras in 1942, the latter gave the former
a bloody nose. As a merchant, the thirty-one-year-old, literate *soltera* readily
commuted her five-day sentence.[120]

A willingness to fight was a valuable tool for poor women, particularly
because it discouraged potential rivals from infringing upon their livelihoods, marital relations, and honor; they therefore tended to disregard
elite characterizations of females who brawled as disrespectful, dishonorable, and unnatural.[121] Women could justify violence and even murder if
they were defending their honor, as infanticide legislation suggests and the
broader judicial record bears out. Though uncommon in a society that expected them to protect their families, men occasionally admitted that their
female kin defended them; more frequently mothers defended their children from violent fathers.

As in the United States and elsewhere, the Guatemalan press sensationalized portrayals of violent women. When the domestic servant Agueda

1925 — ASESINATOS DE LA CALLE MARCONI — 1933

AGUEDA NORIEGA

Busto. Cuerpo entero. Perfil.—(Prófuga desde el 27 de febrero de 1926)

Figure 5.3. "Marconi Street Murders: Agueda Noriega." *La Gaceta*, March 12, 1933. Image courtesy of The Latin American Library, Tulane University.

Noriega (figure 5.3) was captured in 1933, nine years after she murdered the family for whom she worked, *La Gaceta* printed a story that ran more than forty pages, almost as long as its normal editions.[122] Even given the unusual and violent nature of the crime, the attention afforded it was excessive.

Like criminal anthropologists and journalists elsewhere, the Guatemalan police and *Gaceta* reporters often portrayed violent women as savages.[123] When bringing Magdalena Siquibache and Gregoria Boor before the court for fighting in the street in 1931, the police exclaimed that "so furious was Magdalena, she wanted to drink the blood of Gregoria."[124] In another report titled "For unconfirmed jealousy, a woman becomes bloodthirsty," the police graphically described Juana Francisca Carrera's response once she became convinced that her lover was having an affair with Julia Ávila: "Juana Francisca converted into a troglodyte, armed herself with a stone with a sharpened edge. . . . Ávila's blouse, as a result of her rival's casts, became a heap of useless rags."[125] Police reports that perpetuated depictions of women as irrational beings and bloodthirsty cave dwellers dehumanized them.

In contrast to its obsession with violent women, *La Gaceta* generally downplayed and even ignored the more common and pervasive male violence against women. When reading the police blotter, the reader is left to infer incidents of domestic violence from the copious reports of male inebriation and disorderly conduct. That newspapers including *La Gaceta* rarely reported domestic abuse demonstrates how normalized domestic violence had become. When journalists covered these incidents, their silence about the details spoke volumes. Compared to the graphic descriptions of Siquibache's and Carrera's crimes, for example, by ignoring the condition in which Abraham Pelo and Gerardo Sequen left *la indígena* Juana Vásquez after attacking her with a rock and machete, the *Gaceta* reporter sanitized the account that appeared in the paper on February 8, 1931.

Gendered dynamics of violence were already present in highland communities, but the police and the courts expanded the boundaries of acceptable male violence and constricted those of female violence. As in other patriarchal societies, in Guatemala violence was a male domain. If society expected men to establish their masculinity through violence, as several scholars have argued, then violent women blurred gender lines.[126] By portraying female aggressors as deviants, authorities and journalists implicitly condoned efforts to keep women in line. Like *madres desnaturalizadas* and cross-dressers, fierce females were ostracized and relegated to the domain of abjected beings.

The denigration and marginalization of violent females influenced and was reinforced by the law and those who presided over it. Judicial officials rigorously scrutinized violent women.[127] Regina Taquiej was never apprehended for the attack described earlier; in the other two cases of female violence tried at the *juzgado de primera instancia* that I examined, both female defendants were incarcerated for months before being released on bail. In 1902, Manuela Paredes was incarcerated for three and a half months for hitting Francisca Ardón, a crime for which, Paredes explained, she should have been sentenced to five days in jail.[128] In all eighteen rulings that survive in the municipal record, violent women were sentenced to between five and twenty days in jail.

Some municipal magistrates meted out greater punishments to female than male aggressors, as two cases from 1935 demonstrate. On January 14, Patzicía's *regidor* Ernesto Ávila arrested the thirty-year-old, illiterate, *indígena* Juan Martín for hitting Anselma Musia. A *jornalero* on *don* José Escobar's *finca*, Martín confessed his crime to Patzicía's *juez de paz* Roca later that day, explaining that he was drunk when he hit Musia. Whether Roca considered inebriation a mitigating circumstance is unclear; according to a 1927 decree, judicial officials were no longer supposed to do so. Still, his punishment was relatively light: five days in jail commutable by twenty-five cents per day.[129]

Roca did not preside over another trial until three days later, January 17, when the *regidor* arrested twenty-five-year-old Raymunda Miculax for hitting her domestic partner—Juan Martín. This altercation, too, occurred on Escobar's *finca*—a day before Martín hit Musia—but it was reported later. Perhaps Martín's inebriation and violent outburst were in response to his beating at the hands of his *concubina* (domestic partner). If his ruling is any indication, Roca considered Miculax's offense more serious than Martín's; he sentenced Miculax to ten days in jail commutable by ten cents a day and assessed her an additional one-quetzal fine to cover Martín's medical costs, despite the *empírico's* insistence that no medical care was necessary.[130] Justice Roca in his rulings downplayed violence against women with a reduced sentence for Martín, and he spurned violent women by imposing the maximum sentence and a stiff financial burden on Miculax, assessing her seventy-five cents more than Martín at a time when the daily wage was ten cents (for men and generally less for women). In doing so Roca reinforced the web of gendered social practices that sustained violence.

In addition to demonstrating one justice's apparent prejudices against violent women, these two related cases reveal the ethnic and class overtones of policing and judging. Like Ernesto Ávila, most *regidores*, municipal police, and *jefes de ronda* (patrol chiefs) who appear frequently in Patzicía criminal records bore ladino surnames: Ochoa, de la Cruz, Santizo. The notary's identification of the *finquero* (finca owner) José Escobar suggests that he had called upon the *regidor* to arrest both Martín and Miculax. Similarly, Roca, whose name suggests he was ladino and position suggests he enjoyed a comfortable class position comparable to Escobar's, may have fined Miculax (who was likely indigenous) because the *empírico* recommended Martín rest for six days to recover from his wounds. If Martín followed this recommendation, Escobar would have lost a week of work. Given the back-to-back violent incidents on Escobar's *finca*, Roca may have punished Miculax in excess of the norm to send a message to families there to pursue more tranquil and thus more productive relations. The sentences might also betray the notion common in contemporary highland Guatemala that male labor was more valuable than female labor.[131] Roca condemned Miculax to twice as much time in jail as Martín. Beyond the evidence and specific penal codes to which he referred, Roca's rulings offer few other clues as to his reasoning; the circumstances and relations surrounding these cases suggest that gender, class, ethnicity, and local economic concerns influenced his thinking.

Perhaps his relative leniency with Martín betrayed Roca's sense that domestic violence was normative and unlikely to be discouraged by a stiff sentence. In contrast, as an indigenous woman Miculax broke gender and perhaps ethnic, if Martín was ladino, norms with her violent outburst and
therefore merited the maximum sentence and a more significant fine. Considering Roca's and his colleagues' tendency toward lighter sentences for
male perpetrators of domestic violence during this time, her punishment
seems especially harsh.

Interestingly, the same social constructions that downplayed women's
humanity also held the potential to exculpate them. Two years after Ubico's
overthrow, an unnamed writer in a Guardia Civil (National Guard) publication contended that because women were inferior to men due to their
"economic dependence, diminished culture and general preparation . . .
[and] passivity, morals and customs," they could not be held responsible for
committing crimes. Conceding that society oppressed women, the writer
argued that "the woman has been unable to develop her mental faculties nor
form a clear and precise conscience . . . finding herself with an enormous
lack of preparation in the moment of having to make a decision. This is the
origin of innumerable crimes that are not anything more than the incapac-
ity to look for solutions other than the ones that instincts dictate."[132]

Referring to but never producing or citing statistics, the writer argued
that female crimes were never the product of premeditation, intelligence, or
deceit. Most were petty. Even those that were more serious, such as homicide, could be attributed to self-defense, revenge, or in rare cases the desire
to be with another man. The writer concluded that

> most female crimes lack the basic elements of imputableness: intelligence
> and freedom . . . [and] free will. Because for free will to exist requires the
> intelligent capacity to elucidate between good and bad, the capacity to con-
> ceive the results of an action and all the possible consequences. Most female
> delinquents—and this has been proven—in addition to their mental deficit,
> find themselves with numerous natural afflictions . . . making mental clarity
> and serenity even more difficult. . . . These circumstances have impeded the
> woman from participating in society with a sound, disposing mind.[133]

Put simply, the very condition of being female explained women's crimes.
Although expressed in a more sympathetic tone than those evoked in police
reports, this writer also judged women to be less than fully developed—an
impression that reflected criminal codes enacted in the late nineteenth cen-

tury throughout Latin America that considered women "irresponsible" for crimes because of their "naturally emotional" state.[134]

Ethnographies describe household tensions among in-laws and between fathers who controlled their sons' labor by holding on to family lands and sons who wanted their fathers to divide properties among them so they could strike out on their own.[135] Set against these studies, a close reading of court testimonies and male defendants' characteristics suggests that men's socioeconomic positions and early forays into married life frustrated their masculine aspirations in a society that expected patriarchs to be omnipotent in the home. Most perpetrators identified themselves as *jornaleros*, indicating that they did not own their own land; *sin instrucción*, indicating they had little if any access to education (few could sign their names); and between the ages of eighteen and twenty-five, indicating that they were just beginning their conjugal lives. As further evidence that they had few resources, most lived with or were supported by their parents or in-laws. Some were unemployed and many were dependent on their wives' incomes to some degree. Alienated from power and prestige, these perpetrators had much to anger them. Partly stemming from efforts to reinforce male supremacy in the home, their violence was also a response to their fears of self-annihilation, as Buffington suggests.[136] To buttress their self-esteem and establish a semblance of authority, many young, illiterate, landless, and/or unemployed husbands demonstrated their physical strength over their wives.

Other studies, too, point to men's marginalization as a factor in gender-based violence. Andean scholars have argued that in close-knit, interdependent family units, men chafed under the power women wielded in the household since it flew in the face of the broader national patriarchal system. Although they do not agree as to the causes of gender-based violence, many scholars recognize that labor conditions compound feelings of insecurity. Indigenous men often were paid poorly and exploited in their work, which at times necessitated long absences from home. Infidelity and suspicions thereof, poverty, indignities from their local superiors, and inverted gender power in the home often pushed anger and frustration to the point of violence.[137]

Victims of this torment had little recourse; few options delivered cessation of or long-term protection from domestic violence. Women who decried male violence in court and the friends, family, and neighbors who came to their aid speak to what Scott terms "a venerable popular culture of resistance" against wife beating.[138] Most women adhered to community expectations and stoically endured violence until it became extreme or routine. When they broke their silence, their communities generally rallied around them; when women reported gender-based violence, the accused were arrested. After the Macheteador de Mujeres had "so savagely slashed" Cristina Chicoj, the police pursued him from his highland village near San Juan Sacatepéquez to the Guatemala City train station from where, as they correctly surmised, he was headed to Puerto Barrios to work in the banana industry.[139] Yet women could count on little else to curb violence against them. In the context of the repressive regimes and forced-labor mechanisms that marked Guatemalan class and ethnic relations from 1898 to 1944, more often than not the state abdicated its responsibility to guarantee women's—and men's—safety.

Culturally supported through the promotion of unequal gender roles and portrayals of women as minimally human, gender-based violence came to find legal and social acceptance in the first half of the twentieth century. In one manifestation of the disciplinary aspect of domestic violence, women who failed to live up to society's expectations of them as diligent, docile producers and reproducers could be beaten. Men said as much in the courtroom. Municipal judicial officials did not explicitly affirm these notions, yet neither did they contradict them or impose the maximum sentences with high commutation rates; thus they contributed to the conditions whereby gender-based violence could propagate. Unlike parts of nineteenth-century Mexico where adjudication apparently arrested domestic violence,[140] in Guatemala the judicial system did little to stem men's sense of entitlement to beat their wives.[141] This legal leniency was both informed by and fostered more generalized violence in Guatemalan society.

Customary and state laws mapped different aspects of women's subordination to men. These cultural and legal premises helped the Estrada Cabrera and Ubico dictatorships and the less authoritarian governments of Orellana and Chacón to legitimize violence over less powerful groups. Just as attempts to undermine the government were dealt with harshly, so too was female insubordination in the home. An active participant in the promotion of violence against women, the state used women's bodies to legitimize and uphold its power by allowing men who were frustrated by their own anemic authority to vent their frustrations on females. Legal historian Douglas Hay argues that state violence and private violence are reciprocal and reinforcing.[142] An instrument of governance and tool to control men and women, gender-based violence was a critical part of the exercise and reproduction of power.

Even as gender-based violence served the state's interests, many victims educated judicial officials about the gruesome reality of this abuse. While male defendants sought to associate their power in the home with authorities' power outside it, female plaintiffs sought to portray the savagery that marked their conjugal lives as an affront to the order authorities purported to maintain. Both men and women underscored their analyses of their private lives by connecting them to authorities' public roles and responsibilities.

As with infanticide litigation, domestic violence trials reveal the equivocal relationship between judicial officials and litigants specifically and between authorities and people more broadly. When women used the court as leverage against their attackers, they initiated litigation that in some ways measured the power of the judicial system and its officials. Department judges who assigned lengthy sentences to men convicted of killing children felt the power of their authority; municipal magistrates who meted out inconsequential sentences to recidivists came to know the limits of theirs.

Regardless of their inability or unwillingness to curb domestic violence, judicial officials buoyed women's stake in the nation and its institutions by overwhelmingly ruling in their favor in these cases. In turn, the mere act of appearing in court reaffirmed that institution's legitimacy and by extension the state's as well. The long record of domestic violence litigation speaks to women's belief that judicial officials had the potential to help them in some way (for example, by restoring property rights or initiating formal separation proceedings) and suggests that female resistance to abusive relationships encouraged other victims to come forward.

In stark contrast to their willingness to listen to women whose use of the legal system pointed to the state's weakness and lack of control, authorities marginalized women who operated outside the limitations that the state and society placed upon them. Depicting fierce females as social deviants instead of as reflections of the nation's broader violent streak and punishing them more harshly than their male counterparts condoned efforts to keep women in line. Contrasting the acceptance of male violence with the vilification of female violence reveals one of the ways patriarchies were constituted and reconstituted in Guatemala.

Perhaps because they witnessed how poverty, unemployment, illiteracy, and landlessness undermined men's ability to exercise patriarchal power, domestic violence victims seldom challenged the patriarchal principles that subordinated women to men. Instead by critiquing abuses of patriarchal authority, their petitions were aimed at establishing the limits of male prerogatives. Even women who shattered the dichotomous division of male and female labor did so to highlight their contributions rather than to critique the reification of male privilege.

Women's reluctance to critique the patriarchies that enveloped their lives speaks to the complexities of systems that both subordinated and empowered them. Men were not the only challenges in poor, indigenous women's lives. Among other trying circumstances, entrepreneurial women—vendors, midwives, bootleggers—squared off against authorities; women as well as men competed against each other for scarce resources in their highland communities; and illiteracy and racism limited their possibilities. Women and men spoke articulately about the injustices of the larger social, economic, and political structures in Guatemala, yet the grinding challenges of quotidian poverty left little time to address them.[143] In this way, as Erin O'Connor argues in her study of postcolonial Ecuador, nation builders used ethnicity and gender to subjugate indigenous people and women.[144]

These social constructions did not invariably marginalize people, though; women deployed the very assumptions that undergirded Guatemalan patriarchies for their own ends. Some female plaintiffs shrouded themselves in the discourse of motherhood or domestic responsibilities; others played upon stereotypical notions of a woman's weakness and ignorance. Patriarchy served them well. Already having demonstrated they could survive and in some cases thrive without their husbands, many women who asked for separation or divorce were negotiating from a position of strength. Even those who hoped to salvage their marriages and families seldom surrendered the possibility of abandoning their husbands should the circumstances call for it. This too was a powerful negotiating chip.

As much as violence and intimidation buttressed the Guatemalan state during the first half of the twentieth century, its ability to instill fear was never absolute. To maintain the rule of law, authorities tapped into what Piccato calls "the tyranny of opinion." Judicial rulings in favor of even the most marginalized people's reputations helped these regimes to integrate indigenous people and poor ladinos into the nation-state. We now turn to the ways people facilitated this aspect of state building by going to court for vindication.

CHAPTER 6

Honorable Subjects: Public Insults, Family Feuds, and State Power

To read Guatemalan criminal records from the first half of the twentieth century, one gets the impression that highlanders—*indígenas* and ladinos alike—were both extremely foul-mouthed and excessively sensitive. Defamation and slander cases consumed an inordinate amount of the municipal legal system's time, and many such exchanges never made it to the courts. Chimaltenango department authorities too dedicated considerable resources to this litigation. Although they handled only 36 instances of slander (*calumnia*) between 1900 and 1944, they dealt with 523 insult and *injuria* (offense) cases—the seventh most common type of crime during that period (appendix 4). From 1932 to 1944, the National Police arrested 19,264 people on charges of *injuria*—the fifth most common crime during that period (appendix 3).

Despite dictators' efforts to buttress the authority of the state by instilling fear in the general population, locals directed choice words at each other and such agents of the state as market inspectors and police officers. Even as people who insulted each other and authorities seemingly upset portrayals of social order, defamation litigation helped the Estrada Cabrera, Herrera, Orellana, Chacón, and Ubico governments maintain the rule of law by upholding Guatemalans' reputations and punishing those who offended them.

By providing a language that linked personal reputations with national politics, honor became a medium through which authorities could exert their control and power. The November 10, 1942, *Gaceta* cover of Ubico and the term *honradez* (honesty, honor, integrity) offers one example of the ways dictatorships sought to associate themselves with notions and characteristics of honor (figure 6.1).

By outlining the boundaries of acceptable behavior and respected reputations, honor regulated social interactions. Whether they took their offenders

Figure 6.1. *Honradez* (Honesty, honor, integrity). *La Gaceta*, November 10, 1942. Image courtesy of Hemeroteca Nacional de Guatemala.

to court or responded extrajudicially, those who reacted sharply to insults were not simply defending their personal reputations, they were also policing their communities. Their responses indicate that as in Mexico, the political history of Guatemala likewise was not simply one of power and resistance; each individual's preoccupation with his or her reputation and honor meant that for authoritarian regimes, the tyranny of opinion was as valuable a tool as the combination of persecution and co-optation.[1]

If we recognize insults as central components of what historian David Sabean calls the "language of argument,"[2] then court testimonies from defamation litigation tell us much about the ongoing disputes over the meaning of culture and the importance of reputations. Honor signified dependability, resourcefulness, honesty, and integrity, and thus rural residents constantly had to buoy public perceptions of their individual value. One's reputation affected everything from selling and purchasing property and goods, particularly on credit, to finding a spouse, keeping custody of or adopting children, and maintaining good relations with kin and neighbors. In small rural communities where job loss or crop failure were often all that separated families from destitution, honor was a crucial component of people's lives and values, yet it has received surprisingly little attention in postcolonial Guatemalan historiography.[3]

Based on the eighty-eight department and municipal cases I examined, defamation litigation involved Guatemalans from most walks of life: men and women, ladinos and *indígenas*, the educated and illiterate, and those who were single, married, and widowed; their professions varied from *molenderas*, vendors, and *jornaleros* to school principals, tailors, butchers, *agricultores*, and municipal officials (appendix 10). Regardless of one's social position, everyone was subject to and could deploy the tyranny of opinion. As a cornerstone of quotidian relations and livelihoods, honor and the protection of it cut across class, gender, and ethnic lines.

As recent studies of honor have demonstrated, plebeians' lives, livelihoods, and perceptions shaped their constructions of honor more than elite notions did.[4] Definitions of honor varied across place, time, class, gender, and ethnicity, while popular and state perceptions dovetailed around its intrinsic value. As forms of social capital, honor and reputation were defended like goods.[5] Influenced by positivists like Herbert Spencer, Latin American legislators of the late nineteenth and early twentieth centuries came to see honor as a commodity worthy of legal protection.[6]

Since more people gained access to the rights and liberties of citizenship after independence, honor became more relevant for a broader swath of the population throughout Latin America than it had been in the colonial period. As honor shed its hereditary and elite characteristics and was increasingly based on merit and virtue, even those who were not recognized as citizens could portray themselves as such by tapping into honor.[7] Scholars disagree over whether this conceptual shift was precipitated by elite machinations or popular pressure, but by the nineteenth century Latin American states embraced a more inclusive definition of honor.[8]

Throughout the first half of the twentieth century, the extent to which relations between women and men changed in Guatemala depended mainly on ethnicity and class. Despite popular notions that equated a woman's honor with feminine obedience, by the early twentieth century poor and working-class indigenous women frequently defended their honor in court independently of their husbands—an indication that they had shed the colonial and early republican gendered restraint that folded women's reputations into family honor.[9] In contrast, ladinas' autonomy expanded more slowly. Elite ladinas seldom appeared in court; their middle- and lower-class counterparts generally did so only with their husbands' permission. When Jesús Morales insulted *doña* Gricelda Cabrera de García in early June 1929, for example, only her husband testified in court.[10]

Denoting elite status, the title *doña* points to the role class played in determining women's presence in court. Shielded from public confrontations (Cabrera was in her home when Morales knocked on her door), elite women became symbols of a proud nation. According to one journalist, "The *criolla* woman is distinguished by her refined *honradez*," the very characteristics of which were "healthy expressions of the country."[11] As was true elsewhere in Latin America, working-class women, in contrast, constantly had to defend their honor because their lives were so public and their livelihoods so dependent on their reputations.[12]

People constantly reconstituted honor's meaning and reevaluated its importance depending on the complex social relations and circumstances in which they found themselves. Struggles over the meanings and uses of honor in the court record are illuminating, but just as enlightening are the absences of such struggles. The youths, women, and *indígenas* who did not respond to offenses against their honor tell us much about the contours of honor's subcultures. Youths fought each other over insults yet had little recourse against offensive elders. Similarly, women used their fists and the courts to defend their honor against other women but seldom brought foulmouthed men to court. Finally, in light of the extensive accounts of ladino affronts against Mayas in Kaqchikel oral histories and the archival record, the paucity of *indígenas* who accused ladinos of offending their honor is noteworthy.[13] These patterns suggest that arguments about honor were most important when the parties involved considered themselves equals.

This selectivity was not so much an indication that certain parties considered themselves less honorable than their offenders but rather a sign that they shaped their own definitions of honor and recognized the limitations of the court's power. People had a keen sense of what the legal system could and could not do for them.

For the most part, insult and *injuria* accusations were handled at the municipal level. To adjudicate such cases department judges had to be convinced that the defamation constituted slander or libel or was accompanied by another crime. Five ladinos and three *indígenas* were plaintiffs in the eight cases from Chimaltenango's *juzgado de primera instancia* I examined (appendix 10). Six dockets ended without a judge's ruling, while on three occasions judges absolved defendants (one female and two illiterate male *indígenas*). In a reflection of department judges' preferences, one judge returned a case to the municipal court to be adjudicated there.

Some offended parties appealed directly to department authorities. When the director of the San Miguel girls school, Eugenia Girón, called Felipa Oj a "prostitute and other phrases that I will not allow myself to repeat" and then threatened her with a knife on April 2, 1901, Oj petitioned Chimaltenango's department judge, instead of initiating litigation at the municipal level, probably because Girón was "one of the [community's] principal people."[14] Absent a ruling, the efficacy of Oj's strategy is difficult to ascertain, but the alacrity with which municipal officials responded to the judge's order to summon the parties involved suggests that she at least succeeded in compelling authorities to take her complaint seriously. The case contravenes the general trend whereby *indígenas* seldom accused ladinos of insulting them, but Girón's death threat escalated the severity of her transgression. That an illiterate and likely indigenous domestic servant could marshal department and municipal officials to her cause against an influential educated ladina suggests why the judicial system so appealed to indigenous, poor, and other marginalized people.

Like women who accused men of reproductive crimes and domestic violence, most defamation plaintiffs used the courts for leverage against or to intimidate their opponents. Seeking retribution or restitution did not preclude plaintiffs from communicating directly with judicial authorities, however. Pasanala Xajil's petition to the San Martín *juez de paz* on May 8, 1933, offers an example. Two days earlier, as she was watering her tomato plants with her daughter, two drunken women approached them armed with a rock and a club and accused them of having affairs with their husbands. To Xajil's mind, the accusation was worse than the physical attack that ensued, particularly because Xajil's and her daughter's husbands were away working at a *finca*. She insisted that the two women be punished because "similar calumny can bring fatal consequences. . . . What will become of us when our husbands return if we have not asked for justice?"[15] In other words, if the magistrate wanted to maintain order, he had better punish those two women; unaddressed, their false allegations could wreak havoc in Xajil's and her daughter's marriages and, by extension, the community and nation. The ruling is lost, but if his counterparts' record in defamation litigation and the judge's response to Oj's petition are any indication, the San Martín magistrate likely acted upon Xajil's interests.

Those who took their offenses to municipal court trusted judicial authorities to vindicate their honor, which they often did. In the forty-five defamation cases I examined from Patzicía's municipal archive, only two people—both men, one of them likely an *indígena*, who allegedly insulted indigenous women—were absolved. Municipal justices ruled in favor of defamation plaintiffs (fifteen *indígenas*, seventeen ladinos, five of indeterminable ethnicity) thirty-seven times, a 95 percent conviction rate of the extant rulings (the outcomes of six cases were lost). Although the thirty-five defamation cases from San Martín municipal court yielded fewer judgments, officials there ruled in favor of plaintiffs (ten *indígenas*, seven ladinos, four of indeterminable ethnicity) in all twenty-one cases for which the rulings survive (appendix 10). By encouraging people to settle their disputes in court instead of extrajudicially, the rulings buttressed the authority and control of local and, by extension, department and national officials. In contrast to domestic violence litigation that exposed the limits of individual authorities' ability to maintain social order and protect women, defamation litigation disclosed one of the ways judicial officials succeeded in preserving public peace.

To understand the differing ways indígenas, ladinos, men, and women constructed defamation and honor, in this chapter I explore the processual variables that underlay judicial interventions and in so doing demonstrate how the judiciary integrated *indígenas* and poor ladinos into the state-building process. Just as judicial officials responded to popular notions of honor, they also imparted the state's sense of honor to litigants. Out of respect for the decorum of the courtroom and to reinforce their own sense of honor, most plaintiffs refrained from repeating obscene language in court. Lest any party ignore these cultural norms, judicial officials charged those who failed to speak or act deferentially in court with disrupting public order.

Insult litigation points to one of the crucial ways the state exercised power. Unlike in other areas of Latin America, Guatemalan judicial officials seldom dismissed or discouraged defamation plaintiffs, as the high conviction rates suggest.[16] In addition to recognizing how vital maintaining a good reputation was to the lives and livelihoods of rural residents, their rulings assured that the state's presence would be felt in the country's most remote quarters. Such concern with individual reputations contrasted sharply with the state's negligence in other areas of the rule of law such as indigenous land rights and gender-based violence. For the totalitarian regimes of Estrada Cabrera and Ubico, whose legitimacy was often suspect, honor and its legal protection was paramount to their stability and longevity.

Violence and Honor

Often provoked by insults, violence demonstrated actors' readiness to defend their honor. Of the 169 municipal cases I examined that entailed physical violence or verbal abuse, 23, or 13.6 percent, involved both. This number would be higher still if we include the many defamation cases that involved threats of violence. *La Gaceta* captured the relationship between insults and violence. When "words turned into actions," Ceferino Portillo stood little chance against his three brothers and two brothers-in-law, who were all brandishing knives.[17] Such altercations were not a new phenomenon; in the colonial and modern eras in Mesoamerica, insults against one's dignity often led to fights among the poor and duels among elites.[18] The professor of arms Pietro Lanzilli noted in 1898, "Very respectable people" generally preferred to use the courts, "but these same people, if victims of an insult, do not follow their own counsel, rather they seek justice through the hand."[19]

Since few things were worse for a man than to be publicly mocked by a woman, indigenous women who besmirched men's reputations were subject to violent responses. On April 25, 1929, the forty-year-old indigenous *jornalero* Miguel Cua hit Benita Ajsivinac in front of her husband, Félix Xicay, because "she made fun of him."[20] A few months earlier, another illiterate *jornalero*, Julio Merece, hit Francisca Xico in front of her husband, Luis Xicoy, because she ridiculed Merece for being drunk.[21] The Patzicía *juez de paz* sentenced both Cua and Merece to ten days in jail commutable by a half-quetzal per day.

By addressing these women directly and in front of their husbands, Cua and Merece conveyed that they did not expect indigenous men to control, let alone represent, their wives. These indigenous women's autonomy was also apparent in the judicial record; they, not their husbands, who remain silent in these records, brought the cases to court. In contrast to their ladina and other Latin American counterparts, assertive, outspoken, and even combative indigenous women apparently did not threaten the reputations of their husbands.[22]

Early twentieth-century highland Guatemalans accepted both the gavel and their fists as means of settling disputes. It is seldom clear whether those who preferred extralegal responses did not trust the legal system or think they would be successful in it, wanted to forgo the risk of additional stains on their reputations that recounting insults in court promised, or simply did not consider involving authorities honorable.

For many rural residents verbal abuse was as tangible as physical abuse. Plaintiffs often equated offenses against their honor with attacks on their bodies and property. Some claimed, and at least one doctor agreed, that they became sick in response to being insulted.[23] Recall María Francisca Rumpich's 1901 domestic violence case. Her husband had threatened her, burned her land title, and forced her to flee their home, and yet she insisted that the interpreter also explain to the judge that her husband had insulted her. To her mind, these forms of psychological, patrimonial, physical, and verbal abuse were all grave offenses that merited punishment.

In general, Guatemalan jurisprudence approached honor as a public, not private good. According to most judicial officials, punishable insults were spoken in public places—streets, markets, plazas, watering holes, washing stations, schools, cantinas, and even courtrooms. Absent witnesses, municipal magistrates seldom convicted defendants. Aware of this, when Juana Savín insulted her with no one else around, the twenty-eight-year-old illiterate *indígena* María Loch did not take her to court. Instead, ten days later "in revenge . . . she pushed her lightly," accidentally breaking Savín's *tinaja* (large earthen jar).[24] For that offense, the Patzicía *juez de paz* sentenced Loch to five days in jail commutable by fifty cents a day and ordered her to replace the *tinaja*. This incident points to indigenous women's preference for using the courts (she intimated she would have gone to court if there had been a witness to the insult), awareness of legal practice (Loch knew that without a witness she could not win), willingness to respond extrajudicially and physically when necessary, and fierce protection of their reputations (Loch could not let the insult go unanswered).

Family Feuds

At first glance, an insult, like Louise White's observation regarding gossip in colonial Africa, appears "more aural than oral; the fact that it is heard is more important than the fact that it is spoken."[25] Yet a close reading of the criminal record reveals that for most justices of the peace, insults did not need to be heard but merely witnessed to infringe upon a person's reputation, as seen in events that transpired on April 26, 1929, in Patzicía. Shortly after Isabel Escobar arrived at the home of Teresa Galvéz de la Cruz to collect a debt, the latter denounced the former in municipal court for "lightly insulting her with words that don't bear repeating."[26] Two witnesses testified they saw the exchange, but neither of them heard the insults. The thirty-six-year-old Escobar denied the charge, claiming it was a pretext to avoid paying the debt. If it was, the ruling bought Galvéz de la Cruz some time: justice César García sentenced Escobar to five days in jail commutable by twenty-five cents a day. For highland judicial officials, witnesses, not words, mattered.

Popular and legal notions of honor differed. If some people brought their cases to court knowing there were no witnesses, they must have perceived honor to be more than just a public affair. Some dueling parties served as witnesses to each other's insults, and thus both were punished. Such was the case on February 4, 1935, when the illiterate, indigenous couple Gregorio Patzan and Fermina Chacach appeared in San Martín municipal court to "mutually complain of being mistreated in word and act in the home that they have formed."[27] Since both admitted to insulting and hitting the other, they were each sentenced to ten days in jail commutable by twenty-five and twenty cents a day, respectively. The different commutation rates may have reflected justice Arenas M.'s assumptions about gender. Nine years her elder, the forty-five-year-old Patzan was a *jornalero*, while Chacach identified herself as adhering to *oficios feminiles*; perhaps Arenas surmised Patzan could afford to pay more than Chacach.

For Patzan and Chacach, their honor was as much about respect inside as outside the home. The judicial record of women insulting and hitting their husbands suggests that gender relations behind closed doors were not as inexorably unequal as is often assumed.

The courtroom's public setting and financial costs meant the decision to pursue litigation was not taken lightly, which explains why some may have preferred to settle their disputes extrajudicially. Individuals who initiated intrafamily defamation litigation generally came from humble means. Offended parties also had to weigh potential vindication against the risk of diminishing their reputations in front of yet another audience. By publicizing personal conflict that led to litigation, the court was a central source of information for community members.

In light of the fragility of family reputations, the frequency with which families aired disputes that otherwise could have been kept private is surprising.[28] If an insult rendered in private during the colonial era and even into the nineteenth century could be ignored without a loss of honor in much of Latin America, what motivated twentieth-century Guatemalan family members to make their altercations public?[29]

As historians of the public sphere in Europe have demonstrated, capitalism exposed households to public scrutiny.[30] With its diluted effects in rural Guatemala, however, capitalism alone does not explain why families invited the state into their private lives when the costs of doing so ranged from surrendering their privacy to incarceration. The construction of honor in highland Guatemala appears more complex than in Argentina, where, historian Sandra Gayol argues, honor was "based on conscience and not on reputation."[31] Court testimonies from Patzicía and San Martín that indicate self-esteem was as important as public opinion demonstrate that highland Guatemalans' conceptions of honor were more akin to those in Mediterranean culture, where, according to Julian Pitt-Rivers, honor was the value of a person in his or her own and in society's eyes.[32] In *La Gaceta*, professor of natural law Enrique Ahrens argued, "Man could have honor in front of God, in front of men and in front of his own conscience."[33] Victims initiated litigation to restore their reputations and to buoy their self-esteem. Regardless of the rulings, their willingness to press charges demonstrated to their antagonists and communities that plaintiffs valued their honor.

Often the result of men's inability to maintain family continuity and control, intrafamily defamation litigation generally hurt the reputations of patriarchs. With the exception of wives who accused their husbands of insulting them, the absence of patriarchs in the court record of most internal family honor disputes is telling. In contrast to other areas of Latin America where people resisted the state's attempts to usurp patriarchal authority in the home,[34] in early twentieth-century Guatemala some family members who deemed the patriarch to be weak, unresponsive, or unjust invited judicial intervention. Ethnographic descriptions of matriarchs' unchecked and at times abusive authority over their daughters-in-law in the households suggest why the latter might take the former to court.[35] As the indigenous woman who in 1919 shot at her mother-in-law in response to her request to sweep the floor demonstrates, some sought to level the playing field extrajudicially.[36] In communities where social order was largely contingent upon filial obedience,[37] new wives who disobeyed, let alone assaulted, their mothers-in-law were problematic.

Private exchanges that escalated into public humiliation could alter power relations. María Xicay insulted Petrona Ordóñez in the privacy of their home; once in court Ordóñez not only recounted the offense but added that her mother-in-law was a thief. This accusation so infuriated Xicay that she had to be escorted out of the courtroom and detained. Despite sustaining more public damage to her honor than Ordóñez did, Xicay was sentenced to five days in jail commutable by twenty-five cents a day.[38] Far from their own fathers, lower-class daughters-in-law routinely turned to the courts for redress. When they did, the courts shaped the relationships and reputations of those involved.

Ordóñez was wise to wait until she was in court to insult her mother-in-law. Doing so in private settings could be dangerous, as the *indígena* Agustina Martín learned on February 19, 1935. After disrespecting her mother-in-law while they were grinding corn, her brother-in-law beat her.[39]

For those whose familial (especially in-law) relations were contentious, practical considerations and tangible effects often trumped ideal notions of honor. It is unclear whether the thirty-five-year-old Petrona Ajquejay was aware that a police officer was present in the Patzicía plaza on September 29, 1943, when she "verbally abused" her son-in-law Francisco Sisimit Cujcuy, but she denied offending his honor, noting that she does not get along with him "because I am his mother-in-law."[40] According to Ajquejay, a woman's relationship with her son-in-law was invariably contentious, so insulting him was not an affront against his honor but rather part of daily life.

Cujcuy did not necessarily disagree. Claiming that Ajquejay advised her daughter to disobey and even leave him, he was more concerned about his marriage than his honor. Without clarifying which offense he found more problematic, the magistrate sentenced Ajquejay to five days in jail commutable by twenty-five cents a day.[41]

Similarly concerned about how her in-laws were disrupting her marriage, Petronila Luis wrote to the San Martín *juez de paz* on January 22, 1927, to explain that her sister-in-law Anita Ávila was "sowing discord between us with gossip [and] bad advice to her brother of which I am the victim, my husband has beat me four times for no reason."[42] Luis noted that the daily beatings began when she stopped lending Ávila money. As a merchant, Luis knew her livelihood was dependent on maintaining a good reputation. In an indication that marriage too could be a material asset, her complaint was not that her honor had been sullied but that her sister-in-law was destroying her marriage. Even as such hostility between sisters-in-law was evident in the broader archival record and Bunzel's observations of family life, Luis's testimony suggests other possible sources of her marital discord.[43]

Since her husband was landless and homeless, they lived in her grandfather's house, where Luis was the sole breadwinner. She explained to the *juez de paz* that her husband "knew nothing about daily expenses, much less expenses for clothes for her and her children," yet she insisted they "can live tranquilly" if her sister-in-law left them alone.[44] The numerous examples of men who turned to violence in response to landlessness, poverty, unemployment, suspicions of infidelity, and other forms of marginalization suggest otherwise. Luis's plan to move in with her parents would do little to buoy her husband's self-esteem, so perhaps she reasoned that their presence might discourage his violent tendencies.

Commercial Respect

The shared aspects of honor among indigenous men and women suggest honor was not as strictly gendered in highland Guatemala as it was in other areas of Latin America. Most studies of postcolonial honor portray honorable men as those who were fair, honest, and able to control their families, particularly their wives and daughters. This explains why they could ill afford affronts against their female kin's honor.[45] In turn, honorable women were those who maintained sexual purity and monogamy.[46] Although insults were gendered in highland Guatemala, the androgynous nature of much offensive language points to the ways men's and women's reputations were similarly constituted and vulnerable. Vague enough to apply to both sexes, the term *sinvergüenza* ("shameless" as an adjective, "scoundrel" as a noun), for example, was directed at those accused of theft, rape, loose morals, deceit, and gossiping. Since a strictly gendered view of honor fails to explain poor women's penchant for litigation, Piccato suggests analyzing the intersections of gender and class (as well as ethnicity, I would add) to identify the shared and divergent meanings of honor.[47]

At times elite and popular notions of honor were in accord. For example, though they manifested in different ways, honor was tied to trust. On the other hand, qualities like industriousness and humility were more important components of working-class than elite honor, as evidenced by the frequency with which poor plaintiffs began their testimonies with descriptions of how they were hard at work (drawing water, washing clothes, farming, selling in the market) and minding their own business when they were insulted.

In a marked departure from other studies of honor in colonial and modern Latin America where accusations of theft or dishonesty in business dealings were mostly directed at and most damning for men, Guatemalan women responded swiftly and forcefully to such allegations. To defend her honor and business against an aggressors' claims, the vendor María Justa Xajil de Atz Morales appealed to San Martín's *juez de paz*, with the full authorization of her husband, on May 29, 1931:

> Isabel Atz with her sisters Lucila and Catarina Atz slandered me yesterday in the public plaza at two in the afternoon. I was sitting selling a few *milto-mates* [tomatillos] that I brought from my village [when] Isabel and her sisters approached me with a threatening attitude, and with their words they provoked me into a fight in this public place, saying among other aggressive words that I was a woman sinvergüenza, thief, that the [*tomatillos*] that I was selling were from their harvest. These words and others that decency and morality oblige me to refrain from recording on paper, compel me, for my offended honor, to sue Isabel and her relatives. In addition to offending me, they have slandered me [by] treating me as a harvest thief, something that is not true since with my husband we grow all kinds of goods in our lands and we also plant *miltomates* that we don't only sell in this market but also take to the capital. As this is not the first time, *pues* this is the third time Isabel Atz slandered me with the simple act of discrediting me publicly, I can't take any more of her offenses; for this reason . . . using my rights and the justice that aids me . . . I beg you Señor Juez de Paz to proceed in justice.[48]

Like other plaintiffs, Xajil distinguished between insults and slander.

Despite the notary's description of her as a twenty-three-year-old, uneducated, rural, indigenous woman who dedicated herself to feminine tasks, Xajil presented herself as sophisticated, intelligent, and worthy. She pointed out that her business was national, not just local in scope. She also venerated the written word by refusing to allow foul language to sully the court record. Xajil further underscored her respect for the court by explaining that she did not come forward impetuously but rather only after two other offenses; the emerging pattern demanded judicial action. Confident in her rights, Xajil demonstrated that her sense of honor was not deflated by her humble position within Guatemalan society. Even if the Ubico government did not recognize her as a citizen, she wanted the court to see her as a respected member of society who contributed to her community and nation.

Like accusations of theft, affronts against one's financial credibility could be devastating, especially in the highlands, where pawning and informal lending were crucial to the economies of working-class households. In his study of the Kaqchikel town of Panajachel from 1935 to 1941, Tax observed: "Loss of face is probably worse for most people than loss of money."[49] For creditors and debtors alike, their reputations were paramount. When the thirty-two-year-old, illiterate, ladina Rosela Santizo told the *indígena* Jeronima Choy she lacked the four cents she owed her for milk, Choy insulted her. Santizo responded in kind and hit Choy. Since an indigenous woman corroborated Choy's account, Patzicía's *juez de paz* sentenced Santizo to five days in jail commutable by ten cents a day. Despite her claim to be broke, Santizo immediately posted bail.[50] *Indígenas* rarely took ladinos to court over insults; therefore, Choy's motivation was more likely to collect the debt and to impress upon Santizo and others the consequences of defaulting on Choy's loans. Although the court did not facilitate the debt collection, at least it provided a public forum where *indígenas* could reproach delinquent ladinos and expect tangible outcomes.

Because their livelihoods necessitated maintaining public trust, vendors, business owners, and entrepreneurs were particularly sensitive to insults. Selling in Patzicía's public plaza, José de Mata knew his success depended largely on his public persona. So he took Elena Per to court when she insulted him because he refused to take back meat that she had purchased "a long time" prior.[51] Based on her confession, the municipal magistrate sentenced Per to five days in jail, thereby buoying Mata's reputation and business.

Tensions quickly rose when economic competitors exchanged insults. The record of women insulting and hitting each other demonstrates that stiff competition over clients, status, and even men in their communities often inhibited female solidarity. A fight on October 14, 1935, between the neighboring *molenderas* Elena Mayzul and Juana Coc was loud enough to prompt the Patzicía police officer Manuel de la Cruz to enter their private patio and arrest them. Since the twenty-two-year-old Mayzul was married, she was particularly offended when the seventeen-year-old *soltera* Coc accused her of having "ladino and native lovers." The notary recorded Coc's response: "As Mayzul hit her, she saw herself obliged to give back as good as she got, since in that act she showed how two-faced she was."[52] As the criminal record indicates, toughness was especially important for working-class women. But so too was modest behavior. As this case demonstrates, it was difficult to balance the two. Coc's statement about giving "as good as she got" established her refusal to back down, but she also used Mayzul's aggression as evidence of her lack of honor.

As illiterate indigenous women, Mayzul and Coc were among the most marginalized in Guatemala, yet they both fiercely defended their reputations. Their sentences and the broader archival record suggest that Guatemalan authorities, like their counterparts elsewhere in Latin America, understood that even the most marginalized people had reputations to uphold.[53]

Mayzul was the first to strike, yet the municipal magistrate came down harder on Coc. Both received five-day sentences; Mayzul's was commutable by fifteen cents a day, Coc's by twenty cents a day. The latter's more punitive fine points to the *juez de paz*'s recognition of the power of words, particularly insults, and one's right to defend her honor. Since they competed for clientele, upholding their honor and trustworthiness as businesswomen was crucial to their livelihoods. Claiming that Mayzul had multiple partners across the ethnic divide was incendiary. As one student of Latin America has surmised, perhaps Coc hoped to expand her business by elevating her own status and reducing that of Mayzul.[54] Yet more than economics was at stake for Mayzul.

Damaged reputations could destroy marital harmony. If her aggression was in response to the power of rumor, Mayzul's fears may have been warranted. A little over a month later, her husband hit her in the mouth with a stick for "being an impudent prattler."[55] Judging from men's reactions to their wives' infidelity, women were wise to respond quickly and convincingly—whether through the courts or extrajudicially—to the accusations. Pasanala Xajil's rhetorical question in response to her and her daughter's alleged infidelity was "What will become of us when our husbands return if we have not asked for justice?" The implications of illicit relations, whether real or imagined, were heavily gendered and at times fatal. Santos Sian suspected his wife had a child with another man in 1908 and killed her, explaining "that for his jealousy he believed it was very just that he killed his wife."[56] In light of the findings described in the previous chapter, Sian's response can be read as an extreme manifestation of the more common beatings to which men subjected their wives whom they suspected of infidelity. Even as indigenous women defended and defined their own sense of honor, some aspects of their reputations remained inextricably tied to their male kin. Similarly, Coc's actions affected her father's honor by suggesting that he was unable to control her.

Men did not always presume the worst of their partners, however. A washerwoman accused José León Capir's wife, María Ambrocio Estrada de Capir, of having an affair with Julián Sunúc, and Capir set out to prove her fidelity and restore his and his wife's honor. The multiple and layered incendiary accusations—that Estrada's father was an *alcahueta* (pimp) who sold her body to Sunúc, who not only continued to call on her at night but also was the father of her child—necessitated a six-month investigation by Capir to gather all the "concrete facts." A literate *jornalero*, Capir assured San Martín's *juez de paz* on May 14, 1931, that this information would prove the "dishonor committed against his wife."[57] To add gravity to the case, he explained that Sunúc's wife and mother-in-law had threatened to kill Estrada. Hinting that the court, too, would have blood on its hands, Capir insisted "that if something unpleasant should happen to his wife," those women would be responsible.[58] In his concluding remarks, he encouraged the justice to show that the legal system was more powerful than gossip. Unfortunately, his ruling is lost.

The Power of *Puta, Sapa,* and Other Gendered Discourse

As the Capir and Mayzul versus Coc cases indicate, women bore the burden of defending their sexual honor. Often overemphasized in historiography, sexual purity as girls, monogamy as wives, and chastity as widows were not as inextricably linked to poor and working-class Maya women's identities as other Latin American women's identities, particularly those of elites.[59] Yet even as some Maya women enjoyed sexual freedom, sex remained intimately tied to female reputations.[60] The widow Siona Xajil articulated as much when Antonio Estrada attempted to rape her at machete point in 1927: "[He] wanted to use me, offending, in this way my condition as an honorable woman."[61]

Xajil's testimony also evoked how bodies communicated. Though she thwarted his efforts, Estrada found another way to attack her honor: "In his shame, he stole a green *güipil* from me."[62] As markers of ethnicity and class, Maya clothing embodied honor and conveyed social meaning. Whenever *güipiles* were torn or damaged during altercations, women specifically mentioned it.

Less verifiable but more damning than ripped clothing were accusations of sexual impropriety. As with rape cases, defamation litigation often revealed explicit connections between women's reputations and their sexual activity. Like theft, what was important was not so much the veracity of the accusations but rather their ability to shame. The mere imputation of sexual misconduct could damage a woman's reputation. When Luisa Can took her sister-in-law Mercedes Choy to court for saying Can had another lover,

Choy refused to withdraw the statement, insisting it was true. The twenty-five-year-old, illiterate *indígena* assured Patzicía's *juez de paz* that she only divulged this information because Can had insulted her first. The court did not attempt to establish the veracity of Choy's statement. Whether or not Can had another lover, Choy was punished for saying she did.[63]

Unlike their married counterparts, ladina *solteras* accused of sexual impropriety routinely used the courts independently of their male kin to defend their honor. When Amelia Juárez de Meneses and Elena Cabrera de Mendez spread a rumor in February 1943 that the nineteen-year-old *soltera* Angela Morales was having an affair with Juárez's husband, Morales took them to court. Juárez denied trying to discredit *la señorita* Morales, adding that if her husband were having an affair, "it would not be in her interest for people to find out."[64] In other words, why would she spread a rumor that would tarnish her own reputation?

The judicial record suggests one explanation: some women buttressed their honor by publicly acknowledging what others in the community were whispering. Perhaps aware of this strategy, Patzicía's *juez de paz* convicted both Juárez and Cabrera, and both commuted their sentences. Like Juárez, many women who addressed their husbands' infidelity extrajudicially were convicted of verbal and physical abuse.

Partly because their very independence cast them in a morally suspicious hue, single women like Morales went to great lengths to defend their sexual honor. While married women enjoyed a respectable position and well-defined, albeit subordinate, legal status, Latin American spinsters often were deprived of their civil rights, though not necessarily the right to own property or run businesses.[65] Ignoring such social constructions, many poor, single, highland Guatemalan women approached the court with the expectation that they would be treated as citizens.

The twenty-seven-year-old, illiterate *soltera* Felipa Argueta did just that when she asked the San Martín *juez de paz* to punish Agustina Camey de Car, Isabel Camey, and Carlota Car for "offending her honor" by "directing injurious words at her." The verbal attack began in the public plaza and continued into the streets, where they called Argueta a *sinvergüenza*, *mula* (mule) who was sleeping with and financially supported by Camey de Car's husband. "In addition to this being a great slander it also offended my honor, for I am known publicly as an honorable woman occupied exclusively with work . . . these insolent women have offended my reputation," Argueta protested.[66] Since any subsequent proceedings are lost, the ethnicities of those accused of the crime remain obscure, though their surnames and that of Camey de Car's husband, Pedro Car, suggest they were *indígenas*. Argueta was likely ladina. Having earned her financial and sexual independence through hard work, the claim that she needed a man (who was likely indigenous) to support her was as infuriating to Argueta as the accusation of an affair.

At times, sexually charged language was unrelated to sexual impropriety, however. Since poor and working-class highland residents shared and competed for such vital natural resources as water and land, contested access to them often led to insults and slander. Such was the case on November 30, 1900, when Silveria Racanac's cattle wandered into Zoila de León's *milpa*. Josefa Nájera was washing her clothes in the public basin nearby and told Racanac to remove her cows at once lest they destroy de León's harvest. Racanac responded with "injurious and dirty words . . . even saying '[Nájera] was a great *put* . . .' [*puta*, whore] and that Zoila 'was a big babbling fool, [a] big-eared *sapa* [gossip].'"[67]

The next day Racanac continued her verbal assault in the street: "That *puta* Josefa Nájera only Zoila de León can control her, since she is a *palineca* who came out of a whorehouse, and Zoila does not know her face from her ass. . . . Josefa has slept with everyone in town."[68] Nájera exclaimed that Racanac used "many other dishonest words that are too numerous to recount," and she asked Patzicía's mayor to incarcerate Racanac. The woman's verbal assault aptly demonstrates anthropologist Mary Weismantel's point that insults are intended to simultaneously "enrage one's opponent" and "amuse and delight an audience."[69]

To undermine her rival's credibility, Nájera repeated Racanac's claim "that there would not be any justice for her because all those who comprise the municipality are drunks." Perhaps that affront and the women's economic mobility—de León was a literate landowner and Racanac owned at least five cattle—explains why this defamation case, unlike so many others that never went beyond their respective municipalities, appeared before the Chimaltenango department court. After the mayor referred the case to the department judge, de León penned a letter for Nájera in which the latter reiterated that she wanted Racanac punished "for this crime of profound and grave injury to my honor."[70] The department judge ordered a *conciliación* (mediation) at which the accuser and accused appeared face to face in the Chimaltenango court; the two women failed to reconcile their differences. If the judge ruled on the case thereafter, the notary did not record it.

In cases like this, the multiple meanings and implications of such sexually charged language as *puta* can be discerned. Often accompanied by intimidating gestures like spitting and shoving, these visceral insults reinforced an honor system that privileged men even if choice words were not meant to reflect specific sexual misconduct. Pitt-Rivers observes, "Every quarrel, once inflamed, leads to imputations of acts and intentions which are totally dishonorable and which may well have nothing to do with the subject of the quarrel."[71] Women competing for the same man, for example, often accused each other of sleeping around. For her part, Nájera was not so much concerned that community members would believe she was a sex worker or had "slept with everyone in town" as she was that they might question her integrity or honesty more broadly. Piccato argues that terms like *puta* suggest "a woman's duplicitous relationship with neighbors, family, and men."[72] Because such insults undermined an individual's value in the eyes of the community and "impugned their right to circulate freely," responses were aimed more at buoying one's threatened social capital than denying certain sexual practices or relationships.[73]

Like the discourse of sexual propriety, the term *sapa*, or gossip, also revealed the gendered nature of honor and insults. Racanac faced charges for calling de León "a big-eared *sapa*." Insulting and defaming a rival were powerful weapons, especially in small highland communities where few people were strangers. One to whom the label "gossip" adhered paid a high social cost. Intended as an alternative to physical aggression in many societies,[74] gossip often incited violence in Guatemala. On a number of occasions, men like Elena Mayzul's husband claimed they beat their wives because they were gossips—a pattern that lends credence to historian Tanja Christiansen's assertion that some men believed gossip challenged their authority but also explains why some women explicitly stated they did not meddle in other people's affairs.[75]

The November 27, 1935, ruling on a case between two illiterate and likely indigenous *molenderas* suggests that some judicial officials recognized *sapa* as a hazardous term. Twenty-one-year-old Teresa Telan called twenty-three-year-old Petrona Esquit a *sinvergüenza* and *sapa* "among other things"; the following day Esquit returned the favor by passing Telan's home and calling her a *sinvergüenza*. Because they had "mutually insulted each other," both were sentenced to five days in jail, though Telan's bail was set twice as high as Esquit's.[76] Absent the Patzicía *juez de paz*'s explanation for the different bails, the historian is left to wonder if Telan's standing as a married woman compared to Esquit's as single and Telan being from the neighboring town of Comalapa (Esquit was from Patzicía) and the one who initiated the riposte influenced his decision or if he simply thought the term *sapa* was more offensive than *sinvergüenza*. If the archival record is any indication, the last explanation has some merit.

Women's Words as Weapons

As the fifty-one-year-old tailor Hipólito Arriola Argueta's suit against his neighbors the widow Aparicia Escobar and her daughter Alicia Furlán de Arriola demonstrates, poor women could use language to disrupt patriarchal and class power. Whether Arriola's family and his neighbors were relatives is unclear, but like other insult parties, these ladinos had a history of bad blood. During the second week of July 1940, Hipólito sued the two women for libel and slander in Chimaltenango's department court. In the interest of avoiding further rancor with them, he agreed to drop the charges "on the condition that they cease to sully my dignity as a honorable and upstanding man; that is to say, these individuals were not in any way to continue messing with my person or family. But . . . my good intentions . . . failed and my hopes were dashed because the aforementioned ladies did not refrain from bothering me and my family."[77] As Hipólito explained events in his second petition to the department judge on July 22, Alicia in particular refused to relent:

> On Thursday the eighteenth of this month, around eight o'clock, my wife Virgilia López de Arriola was milking a cow in the yard of our family home, the stated Alicia Furlán de Arriola, who lives . . . very close, with only a street separating [her house] from ours, she stood at the edge of her property, that is to say some twenty *varas* [about sixteen meters or fifty-two feet] from where my wife was milking the cow and said to her: "THAT SHE, that is to say MY WIFE AND I, as well AS OUR CHILDREN, WERE GOAT AND CHICKEN THIEVES and that my spouse and I additionally, WE WERE OLD SONS OF A GREAT WH . . . (a strong word)."[78]

Because "she spent almost the entire day insulting us," a military officer overheard the insults, as did a municipal court clerk who encouraged him to bring the case forward.

The department judge's ruling sheds light on the distinctions between municipal and department proceedings. "Due to their vagueness," he opined, "the insults uttered by the defendant do not constitute the crime of slander . . . but in the eyes of this Court, such insults do constitute the crime of minor injury, and therefore [it] is not within the jurisdiction of this court, but rather the Minor Jury of Patzicía."[79] Although the record of the municipal court ruling is lost, this judgment all but guaranteed Hipólito victory there.

This case demonstrates the ways honor in Guatemala differed from that of some other postcolonial nations; in Uruguay women's insults did not challenge men's honor, and in Argentina superiors simply ignored insults from lower classes because their words were inconsequential.[80] In Mexico and Peru as in Guatemala, however, poor women's voices could damage reputations and businesses.[81]

Most scholars have approached honor as an intraclass phenomenon, a contest among social equals, but in Guatemala it cut across ethnic, class, and gender hierarchies. By documenting the considerable power two poor women's words exerted over a middle-class tailor in the presence of two men who shared his social standing, the case of Hipólito versus the two women reveals how honor mediated interclass and gender relations. People navigated multiple interactions with subordinates and superiors on a daily basis, and arguments over honor were not only between social equals.

As offended as Hipólito, other plaintiffs, and some local authorities were, few expressed surprise at the female offenders' comportment or language. Outspoken poor and working-class women were not uncommon in highland Guatemala or other areas of Central America.[82] Unfettered by elite social norms, working-class women enjoyed a more expansive verbal arsenal than that of their wealthy counterparts.

Ethnic Nuances

Despite the ample documentation of the gendered aspects of honor, its ethnic contours are more difficult to discern through the written record. Ethnic labels like *india* and the more derogatory *indito* were deployed as insults but more commonly appear in defamation litigation when ladinos belittled other ladinos. In 1941 the widow Francisca de Mata brought Catalina Martínez to Patzicía municipal court for insulting her by, according to Mata's sixteen-year-old niece, calling her "*india* and other words even more vile."[83] Sentenced to five days in jail, Martínez commuted her sentence with one quetzal. That a sixteen-year-old ladina knew *india* to be a vile insult speaks to the extent to which highlanders availed themselves of racialized language. As was true in the Andes, indigenous and non-indigenous people deployed race words in their arsenals of epithets.[84]

In a revealing example, the *indígena* Ventura Quirac refused to sell her lemons at a reduced price on January 14, 1928, so Ramona Esquit de Rivera called her an *indita*.[85] Esquit de Rivera said the altercation began when Quirac grabbed and inspected her basket, presumably to check for stolen goods. In Patzicía municipal court, Quirac accused Esquit de Rivera of hitting her in the mouth but not of offending her honor. Since plaintiffs, whether indigenous or ladino, in assault and battery cases generally highlighted offenses against their honor as well as their bodies, Quirac's omission of this aspect of her exchange with Esquit de Rivera points to a different conception of honor. If Quirac considered Esquit de Rivera indigenous, the term *indita* may not have had such strong racial overtones. The notary did not record her ethnic identity; her family name, Esquit, suggests she was *indígena*, while her husband's name, Rivera, suggests he was ladino. Or perhaps Quirac simply ignored it to eviscerate its sting. Whatever Quirac's thinking, Patzicía's *juez de paz* sentenced Esquit de Rivera to five days in prison commutable by a half-quetzal a day.

In light of evidence of ladinos disparaging Mayas by calling them *indio/a* and *indito/a* in the archival record and Kaqchikel oral histories, the lack of insult cases brought by *indígenas* against ladinos is conspicuous. The seventy-seven-year-old Kaqchikel widow Ix'ajpu' recalled the litany of insults she frequently heard: "*ixta, idiota* [idiot], *india burra* [stubborn Indian "donkey"], *indio macho* [stupid, rude Indian]."[86] Since *indígenas* successfully used the courts for insult cases against other *indígenas*, thereby acknowledging their sense of honor, and brought ladinos to court for other offenses, thereby acknowledging the court as an efficacious institution for redress against ladinos, this glaring omission in the jurisprudence of highland honor cannot be attributed to a lack of experience or confidence in the legal system.

Ladino slurs were grounded in the colonial caste system and notions of cultural inferiority, and as such they do not appear to have undermined *indígenas'* perceptions of their own resourcefulness, honesty, or integrity. Since their livelihoods did not depend on ladinos, many *indígenas* could create an economic and social world alongside ladinos' that "operated by a different set of principles," as U.S. and Guatemalan scholars have demonstrated.[87] Emboldened by this autonomy, *indígenas* held notions of honor that allowed them to disregard ladino insults. As Forster argues for mid-twentieth-century San Marcos, "Elite values condoning race hate never became hegemonic and a majority 'counter politics' of ethnic pride emerged in indigenous women's refusal to relinquish their claims to personal dignity."[88] When Francisca and Ancelma Jala insulted the eighteen-year-old, illiterate, *indígena* Juliana Azurdia as she walked by their house on March 30, 1902, she "ignored them and continued on her way."[89] Accompanying Azurdia on that Sunday afternoon, her (likely indigenous) friend Paula Cuat later testified in Itzapa municipal court that she advised Azurdia to ignore them. Bunzel's observations in Chichicastenango suggest another reason for this strategy: the K'iche' there considered any contact with ladinos "a great disgrace."[90]

Some indigenous women limited their contact with ladinos because they feared sexual violence. Ladinas likewise feared *indígenas* would rape them, but judging by my sample of fifteen rape trials and the broader historical record, ladinos committed these crimes more frequently than *indígenas* did. A case from 1914 reveals the complex manifestations of ethnic relations in highland Guatemala.

When the fifty-year-old ladina merchant Luz Medina returned from a business trip to learn that her twenty-year-old daughter, María del Socorro Medina, had been raped, she accused her hired hand Marco Tobar of the crime. As an illiterate, indigenous, small-scale agriculturist, Tobar had few resources at his disposal. Too poor to afford a lawyer, he asked the department court to appoint him one. Tobar denied the charge and explained that Luz incriminated him because she was angry that he was "living conjugally" with the thirty-four-year-old *molendera* Mercedes Fuentes. As Luz's niece, and thus likely ladina, Fuentes waived the right not to testify against a relative. She explained that Luz was upset with them both because prior to their common-law marriage, Tobar stayed in Luz's house, where "Luz took advantage of his services without remunerating him in full or in part; these services were very useful for Medina and all the better because they did not cost her anything."[91] Even as she embodied the potential for interethnic harmony, as evidenced by her marriage to Tobar, Fuentes decried the far more common ladino exploitation of indigenous laborers.

In addition to enjoying a higher socioeconomic position, as a ladina and merchant, than Tobar, Luz played upon ladino fears of *indios* raping ladinas. She insisted a midwife examine María "to establish the truth." Whatever "the truth," justice was elusive. Despite the midwife's confirmation that María had been raped, no one was convicted of the crime. Yet Tobar languished in jail for almost a year before Francisco Turcios posted his bail of three hundred pesos—far longer than other alleged rapists who generally gained their freedom within a few days.

As the common-law marriage between Tobar and Fuentes suggests, re-

CIUDAD DE GUATEMALA   30 DE JUNIO DE 1940

Celebraciones del LXIX aniversario del
triunfo de la Revolución Liberal de 1871.

Desfile de las Compañías de Voluntarios hacia el Campo
de Marte y cuyos componentes, sobre sus trajes típicos
y regionales, portan con marcialidad destacada y disci-
plina, los arreos militares.—Nota importante fué ésta
que causó entusiasmo y cautivó cuantos presenciaron
el desfile de la columna, el Día del Soldado.

Figure 6.2. "Volunteer [military] Companies' Parade . . . [with] their typical and regional clothing . . . that enraptured and captivated those present . . . on Soldier's Day." *La Gaceta*, November 10, 1940. Image courtesy of Hemeroteca Nacional de Guatemala.

lationships between *indígenas* and ladinos could be cordial. After she was raped by Luis Escobar in a forest outside Patzicía on February 28, 1917, the twenty-year-old ladina Manuela Lima went to Victoria Esquit's home, where the fifty-year-old indigenous widow cared for her for three days.[92] Some *indígenas* and ladinos found ways to develop caring, loving relationships despite the ethnic tensions and often hatred that permeated their lives.

Even if Mayas did not internalize it, however, racism retained its power. Kaqchikel historical narratives criticizing such racist labels as *indio* and *ixta* suggest that ladino insults affected Mayas' self-esteem. Most Kaqchikel sought to eviscerate the power of such discourse without resorting to the courts. After they completed their military service, for example, Kaqchikel conscripts found that ladinos no longer spat at or tried to intimidate them. Since courage and physical combat training were attributed to soldiers, their military experience kept ladino affronts at bay.[93] That national leaders exalted and the press celebrated indigenous soldiers during the Ubico administration (figure 6.2) further mitigated local ladinos' slights.[94] Some Kaqchikel confronted ladinos directly, as Ix'ajpu' recounted:

> They would make fun of you. They handed you abuse. Some even continue to do it today. . . . "You are *ixtas*, *indios brutos* [ignorant, rude, immoral Indians]," they said to us one time.
>
> So I responded, "I am *indio* but of pure red blood. I am not mixed. Excuse me, I am not wrapped like you. I knew your mother; she was *natural*. Your mother wore an *üq* [indigenous skirt] when she arrived here [in Patzún]. . . . She did not have sandals; [she wore] a blue *üq*, brown *po't* [indigenous handwoven blouse] . . . You too wore a *maxtate* [indigenous loincloth wrap] when you arrived here.
>
> Then he told me, "You are an *ixto bandido* [Indian crook]."
>
> So I said, "You come to steal something from me when you call me a *bandido* to my face and that is not all you said. Okay, you are ladino, but pure shit, nothing. You are a ladino, but you are worthless in my mind."[95]

Taking pride in her indigenous identity and heritage, Ix'ajpu' was more insulted by *bandido* than by *indio*. By pointing out the clothing—*üq*, *po't*, and *maxtate*—and lack of footwear that marked her offender and his mother as *indígenas*, she criticized him for giving up his indigenous identity to become a ladino. Armed with ethnic pride, *indígenas* had multiple strategies for confronting racism.

Maintaining a separate set of values did not preclude deploying opposing principles, however. By not challenging disparaging perspectives of *indígenas* in court, indigenous litigants could harness ladino racism to their advantage. Some indigenous defendants introduced themselves as poor, ignorant *indios* to increase their chances of favorable rulings. As seen in previous chapters, sometimes it worked.

At first glance, embracing racist stereotypes suggests that *indígenas* internalized hegemonic discourse, but highlighting their disadvantages in Guatemalan society could reinforce indigenous litigants' understanding that their status was based on external prejudices rather than their self-worth. In this way, *indígenas* could maintain their own principles even while they advanced their legal claims by deploying ladino denigrations of them. Infinitely prolific, identities cannot be captured by any one word; indigenous litigants did not allow *indio* or other race words to define them.

Deploying racist discourse differently, some Kaqchikel used derogatory terms to distinguish themselves from their rivals and ally themselves with ladino authorities. After Bernarda Satz and Patrocina Yol accused Tranquilino Sunuc of being a thief and *sinvergüenza* in 1902, his mother, María Sunuc, explained her reason for testifying: "It was not my intention to complain, because it would never end if for each misdeed of *esas indias* [those Indian women] I bothered the authorities, but knowing that in addition to the daily repeated offenses, they also want to incarcerate my son for nothing," she had to come forward.[96] In one deft sentence, Sunuc demonstrated her deference to the court by lamenting having to bother its officials and then attempted to ingratiate herself by assuming or acknowledging their prejudices. Although she too was *indígena* and illiterate, Sunuc carefully wove her narrative to set her and her son apart from *esas indias* and their "perverse spirit." By using *indio* and *india* to describe their rivals and themselves, indigenous litigants disrupted the terms' power.

Ladinos did not enjoy this same emancipation from *indígenas'* insults. On a number of occasions ladinos brought *indígenas* to court for offending their honor. In 1943 the thirty-year-old *soltera* Irene Aguirre complained that the forty-five-year-old Antonia Esquit de Racanac insulted her every time Esquit passed in front of her house on the way back from the market. In Patzicía municipal court, Esquit claimed the opposite was true: Aguirre insulted her every time she saw Esquit in the street. Although Esquit did not think the insults warranted the court's attention, once accused she used them to justify her actions. Without any witnesses, both were punished—an indication that the magistrate believed honor cut both ways across ethnic lines.[97] Neither could sign her name, and each paid fifty cents to avoid incarceration, suggesting they shared a similar class status. Betraying Aguirre's belief that she enjoyed a superior status, Esquit more easily dismissed Aguirre's insults than vice versa. Contemporary ethnographies, too, point to ladinos' sense of superiority. In his 1940s study of a Poqomam community John Gillin notes, "Whatever anxiety a Ladino may feel regarding his status within his own caste, he can always derive some satisfaction from the feeling that he is at least better than an Indian."[98] Excluded from access to power and resources in many aspects of Guatemalan life, *indígenas* wielded words as weapons against ladinos who particularly smarted at insults from people they considered inferior.[99]

When *indígenas* disrupted ladinos' sense of entitlement, ladinos quickly sought to reestablish it. The *indígena* Juliana Azurdia mentioned earlier was incarcerated because Francisca Jala's father, an illiterate *jornalero*, and another witness claimed they heard Azurdia call Francisca a thief. After reading Azurdia's and her friend Paula Cuat's accounts portraying Azurdia as the victim of insults, the Chimaltenango department judge absolved her. Particularly since department judges were almost invariably ladino, rulings like this buttressed the legal system's legitimacy by conveying to *indígenas* that neither race relations nor racism overdetermined judicial procedures and outcomes.

This case also underscores generational differences among ladinos. Francisca's father was upset enough about the alleged insults to hire a scribe to petition the *juez de primera instancia*. Francisca, a nineteen-year-old *soltera*, testified in Itzapa municipal court, where the department judge sent a note asking municipal authorities to investigate the incident, that she was in her home on March 30 when she heard someone calling her name, and "seeing it was Azurdia who was speaking, she ignored her."[100] Francisca apparently was content to simply disregard Azurdia; Francisca's sixty-year-old father, however, considered the alleged offense so egregious that he bypassed local authorities and appealed to their superior in his attempt to put Azurdia in her place.

When indigenous women insulted ladino men, they upset both gender and ethnic norms. In one crucial example, on August 2, 1929, Estanislao Escobar brought Catarina Quiej and her daughter-in-law Micaela Callejas to Patzicía municipal court for "insulting him with expressions that offended him."[101] The two women denied the charges, but after Angela Morales testified that she had heard the insults they were sentenced to five days in jail commutable by fifty cents a day. That both Quiej and Callejas were formally married at a time when few indigenous women were must have further inflamed Escobar's sense of injustice at being insulted by them; their marital status adhered to ladino social ideals, and thus they were less easily dismissed than most *indígenas*.

Ladina Litigation

Honor was central to working-class women's aspirations and reputations throughout Latin America, but in Guatemala ethnicity largely determined whether females engaged the legal system to uphold it.[102] Throughout Latin America, women who adhered most closely to elite traditions depended on men to defend their honor.[103] Maya women's relatively autonomous reputations freed them from this dependency. In the few cases where their husbands intervened on their behalf or authorized their litigation, indigenous women still had a voice in court. This autonomy allowed poor, indigenous women to shape the meanings and contours of honor. By embracing the court's patriarchal authority as a legitimate means of defending their reputations, indigenous women ensured that the ethnic differences between indigenous and ladino gender regimes continued to coexist.[104]

Intent on distinguishing themselves from *indios* and hopeful of improving their status within Guatemala's social hierarchy, ladinos adhered more closely than *indígenas* to elite notions of gender relations and honor. As a result, ladinas seldom defended their honor in court, in contrast to the corpus of litigation initiated by indigenous women. The ladina moonshiner María Coróy explained in 1918 that just appearing in court could cause "grave injury" to their honor.[105] Suggesting that they had no legal personae in the public sphere, some ladinas were so sheltered from the public scrutiny of the courtroom that affronts against them only landed their husbands in court. If ladino husbands did not represent them directly, they often authorized their spouses in writing to represent themselves. Adhering to the discretion expected of elite women, ladinas tended to be reserved in their testimonies.

Even when they represented themselves in court, ladinas' honor was inextricably tied to that of their husbands. At times this association was explicit. The twenty-two-year-old Anita Burgos de Portillo testified that when she stepped out her front door on July 27, 1917, Eulalio García said that "the man who had gotten involved with me was *sinvergüenza* because I was a tomboy [*machona*], *puta* and other things." Making "the present accusation . . . with the authorization of my husband *don* Guillermo Portillo" because she did not want the "crime . . . to go unpunished," Burgos de Portillo also pressed charges against Marcelina and Patrocinia Barrios, who happened to be walking by and advised García "not to get mixed up with me because I was a whore."[106]

When the Chimaltenango municipal magistrate referred the case to his superior, Burgos de Portillo altered her accusation. On August 11 she wrote a letter to department judge Rubén Flores explaining that she had accused the Barrios sisters of offenses (*injurias*) against her and García of insulting her husband, not her. It is unclear whether Burgos de Portillo considered a favorable ruling more likely if the offenders were females or she perceived her subordinate position to include enduring insults from men. As this and other cases indicate, women were more likely to pursue defamation litigation against women than against men.

Before she and her husband signed the letter to the department judge, Burgos de Portillo expressed her concern that the case had stalled because the municipal secretary was the brother of the Barrios sisters, who in turn brought charges against Burgos de Portillo and her mother, husband, and brother-in-law. To ensure "impartiality," Burgos de Portillo asked that the secretary recuse himself, "since to do otherwise would result in us being the delinquents." Only after the fifth summons did the Barrios sisters appear in department court, for a September 6 *conciliación* with Burgos de Portillo, who refused to pardon them because their *"injurias* offended her honor."[107]

As the municipal secretary, José Barrios was in a good if conflicted, as Burgos de Portillo noted, position to represent his sisters. In a letter to judge Flores, Barrios critiqued the "unjust accusation" on technical and legal terms. He said that since Burgos de Portillo had not dated her initial letter, the municipal magistrate should have dismissed the suit. Barrios further suggested that it was Burgos de Portillo, not his sisters, who was using her personal relationships to influence the case. Asking Flores to absolve his sisters, Barrios concluded, "I hope your judgment will be a true ray of justice." Ironically, Barrios also failed to date his letter.[108]

Even without a record of the ruling, the case highlights that honor was as important to middle and upper-class ladinos as it was to poor *indígenas.* None of the litigants identified her or his ethnicity; their surnames and positions suggest they were ladinos. The lengths to which Burgos de Portillo went to punish the Barrios sisters for a public slight was matched by their and their brother's efforts to defend themselves against her accusations.

Cases like this demonstrate the ways status—whether it be based on gender, class, ethnicity, generation, or marriage—established the parameters of honor, which in turn determined how and if people responded to insults. Even into the twentieth century, colonial notions of status persisted alongside republican constructions of honor grounded in merit.

Certain circumstances unfettered ladinas' customary restraints. By definition widows and spinsters were largely free from male restraints, as litigation introduced by ladina *solteras* demonstrates. Such was the case in September 1943 when the sixty-nine-year-old widow *señora* María de la Cruz brought her nephew Juan de la Cruz to court for insulting her. She and the Patzicía notary both hinted at a sense of propriety that shielded ladina widows from affronts when she insisted and he recorded that Juan had no reason for insulting her, "much less if you take into consideration that the speaker is not only the offender's aunt, but also a single woman."[109] In contrast, single, indigenous women, young and old, appeared before the court as perpetrators and victims of insults with no indications that the exchanges were unusual.

Seniority facilitated ladina litigation as well. Juan's defense betrayed his subordinate position vis-à-vis his aunt. The notary penned the counter-charges Juan made: "As the aforementioned *señora* insulted the declarer, he also insulted her since he had no other recourse."[110] In light of the dearth of cases in which younger plaintiffs accused elders of offending their honor, Juan's assertion that he had no other recourse against her insults suggests that elders enjoyed considerable leeway in their words and actions. Age mattered. Juan was sentenced to five days in jail.

When the offenders were females, as Burgos de Portillo's litigation indicates, ladinas more commonly invited authorities to intervene. The case of two illiterate ladinas provides another example. On June 17, 1929, Mercedes de Escobar took Dolores Escobar to court for insulting her in the street in front of the mayor of Patzicía. Admitting to this transgression, Dolores attributed it to the "bad blood" between them.[111] After commuting her five-day sentence, Dolores was back in court two days later because Mercedes had "verbally abused her by means of rude insults and by ridiculing her publicly for the fact that she had caused them [authorities] to punish her."[112] With two witnesses confirming Dolores's account, Mercedes received the same sentence Dolores had.

This case demonstrates how the weapons and recourses people deployed to advance their agendas could be used against them. When insulting another, one always had to beware and perhaps even expect that the offended party would see "herself obliged to give back as good as she got," to borrow Juana Coc's phrase. Similarly, while the court held the allure of restoring one's wounded honor, it often found plaintiffs guilty of the same crimes for which they accused their rivals. As Mercedes learned, gaining the upper hand one day made one all the more vulnerable the next.

Mercedes's use of Dolores's incarceration to insult her also reveals how legal culture influenced popular culture. As in other areas of Latin America, judicial rulings in highland Guatemala "made their way into the repertory of street-corner insults."[113] A sentence, particularly incarceration for women (given that women were suspected of being raped or soliciting sex in jail), could be used as fodder for the next insult.[114]

The very act of taking their disputes to court demonstrated plaintiffs' virtue. By allowing judges instead of their own responses, be they verbal or physical, to reestablish their reputations, they could claim the moral high ground. Unlike poor Brazilians whose definition of honor included protection from impersonal state power, many highland Guatemalans called upon the court to uphold their honor.[115] The goal was to ensure that people were held accountable for their words.

Early twentieth-century defamation and slander legislation and litigation in Guatemala and other Latin American nations suggest that capitalist modernization was unfolding more slowly than national leaders might have liked.[116] In nations where large percentages of the population were illiterate and lack of infrastructure and banks, particularly in rural areas, meant that economies still depended heavily on reputations, honor was crucial to local economies and national development. As late as 1941, professor Enrique Ahrens argued in *La Gaceta* that the legislation and prosecution processes surrounding honor were insufficient. Like Lanzilli before him and in a reflection of Uruguay's creation of a tribunal in 1920 to deal specifically with honor, Ahrens advocated expanding the courts that dealt with honor.[117]

Courts were central sources of information, yet historians have largely neglected them as components of public life. Despite facing punishment, few people denied having insulted the offended party, as if admitting to it allowed them to revisit the stain placed upon their opponent's reputation. Because it was fragile, honor was an easy target for disrupting a rival or official. But it was also durable and elastic. Even if never fully restored, it could be reshaped and reclaimed.

The way people defined, experienced, and acted upon honor differed based on gender, ethnicity, age, class, and relationship to the community. Reputation and self-worth mattered deeply, but what impinged upon them and warranted a response varied widely. In an indication of the centrality of individualism in Guatemalans' lives and the limits of what they could convey about their worldviews to authorities, municipal magistrates did not pretend to understand or even know the many nuances of each person's definition of honor; as long as witnesses verified that something *was* said, the plaintiffs' assertions that their honor was offended sufficed. Because each group shaped its own notions of what constituted honor, even when subordinates insulted superiors to remind them of their tenuous privileges honor tended to reinforce rather than restructure social hierarchies.

Defamation litigation must be understood in the larger context of the social relations and conditions in highland Guatemala, where conflict was the norm. If, as Sabean argues, "culture is a series of arguments among people about the common things in their everyday lives,"[118] then insult and assault and battery cases tell us much about how people negotiated social relations. Paramount to economic security and tied to one's self-esteem, conscience, and public persona, honor was a critical component of these negotiations. The constant barrage of cases from poor, indigenous women reminded authorities that even the most marginalized were not, in contrast to one historian's assertion, "bereft of the right to protect their honor."[119] As was true elsewhere in Latin America, everyone in Guatemala was entitled to have and defend honor,[120] even if many *finqueros* and foremen discounted claims of honor from their race, class, and gender subordinates.[121]

As agents of the state, judicial officials' legitimacy emanated partly from their willingness to allow litigants to define, claim, and expect honor. As with domestic violence litigation, municipal magistrates ruled overwhelmingly in favor of plaintiffs. Although they were motivated by bruised reputations instead of bruised bodies, like domestic violence plaintiffs, defamation plaintiffs taught municipal judicial officials much about local social relations. Even as litigants' participation in the legal system represented a tacit acceptance, if not approval, of the state's authority and agenda, by listening to these testimonies, judicial officials gained a greater understanding of the social foundation upon which they were building the state.

Associating republican honor with citizenship held the potential to unite the nation by bridging ethnic divides, yet *indígenas*' and ladinos' differing notions of honor suggest some seemingly insurmountable ethnic rifts. Ladinos' perceptions of *indígenas* tended to be negative, and their insults reinforced that norm. The perceptions obstructed *indígenas*' economic, political, and social mobility and at the same time freed *indígenas* from having to defend their honor in the ladino world. Interethnic commercial exchanges were seldom significant enough to compel *indígenas* to defend their creditworthiness in front of ladinos. Nor were forced-labor mechanisms contingent upon good reputations. Often desperate for workers, *contratistas* who hired or shanghaied Kaqchikel for seasonal work on coastal coffee plantations cared little about their local reputations.[122] As *indígenas* strove to improve their lot in their communities and the nation more broadly, relations among *indígenas* were generally a more crucial determinant of their livelihoods and self-esteem than were their relations with ladinos.[123]

Ladino and indigenous worlds were intricately but not intimately tied in highland communities, and therefore *indígenas* had an easier time distancing themselves from subordinate relations with ladinos than women did in distancing themselves from subordinate positions with men. Based largely on subsistence strategies, a family's daily survival was contingent upon the contributions of men and women. This economic interdependence meant that gender relations were marked by contestation and solidarity in ways that ethnic relations were not. Responding to ideals of patriarchal authority, men more readily brought women—whose supposedly subordinate positions made their insults of men all the more powerful—to court for insulting them than vice versa.

Wives who charged their husbands with insulting them were demanding respect if not equality. Indeed, the judicial record of disputes among couples, particularly those emanating from exchanges of insults or women's refusals to adhere to their husbands' demands, suggests that women had more power in the home than most scholars have recognized. Historian Kathryn Sloan found that in nineteenth-century Mexico, no matter how insignificant elites perceived working-class women to be, the women "considered themselves to be part of the social contract or body politic."[124] Indigenous women and ladina *solteras* used modern notions of honor to increase their social agency.

With greater freedom—and need—to circulate publicly than middle- and upper-class ladinas, working-class indigenous women appeared and represented themselves in court more often than their non-indigenous counterparts. Their public roles, particularly as proprietors and entrepreneurs, compelled indigenous women to defend their social and moral capital in court. For poor indigenous men, this litigation was a reminder that exercising patriarchal authority in the home by restricting their wives to the domestic sphere was far less feasible for them than it was for middle- and upper-class ladinos. Confined to elite constructions of gender that circumscribed women's public roles and voices, middle- and upper-class married ladinas shied away from the public scrutiny of the courts.

To counteract Guatemalan elite efforts to exclude them from citizenship, *indígenas* and women defended their honor in court while also extending claims of citizenship. Indigenous and female plaintiffs insisted that they deserved equal rights by identifying themselves as *guatemaltecos/as* and convincing judicial officials of the importance of their reputations despite their poverty, illiteracy, ethnicity, or gender. By upholding their honor and treating them as citizens in the courtroom if not beyond it, judicial officials integrated *indígenas* and women into the nation-state.

Defending honor by duels, fights, or loud arguments undermined the state's project of order and progress, and offering a peaceful venue to reestablish social status and defend reputations facilitated the elite project of state building. Because adjudicating disputes helped the state foster compliance, maintaining the honor of lower-class indígenas and ladinos was as important to the Estrada Cabrera, Herrera, Orellana, Chacón, and Ubico governments as it was to the plaintiffs. Honor encouraged people to behave in an orderly and peaceful manner. Judicial officials' rulings in their favor affirmed plaintiffs' honor and buoyed their confidence in the courts, which in turn reinforced the state's institutional legitimacy by discouraging extrajudicial responses to disputes. Despite operating under dictatorships that exacted land and labor and curtailed other freedoms, the legal system encouraged *indígenas* and poor ladinos to perceive the state as an entity that could meet their needs if not consistently mete out justice. The extensive defamation and slander record speaks to an even more formidable, pervasive, and constant force in highland communities than these totalitarian regimes: public opinion.[125]

CONCLUSION

Emboldened and Constrained

The legal system and particularly criminal litigation reveal much about the governments under which they operated. To encourage the populace to embrace the mantra of order and progress, dictatorial governments in Guatemala engendered a desire for order by creating threats of disorder. Decrying and criminalizing the methods and in some cases even the very existence of certain indigenous livelihoods did just that. As the twentieth century progressed, the state increasingly deployed criminology, biomedicine, and other modern "sciences" to embolden its position. Convinced that *indios* were susceptible to and propagators of disease because they lacked hygiene, for example, authorities used modern notions of public health to add an air of legitimacy to their campaigns against bootleggers, midwives, and market vendors.[1] When authorities arrested these entrepreneurs for plying their trade while only lightly reprimanding men for beating their wives, they established the state's priorities in opposition to the needs of local communities and individual freedoms. Adjudicating these forces of state rule, the courts were crucial to the government's legitimacy.

Guatemalan historiography, Kaqchikel historical narratives, and novels like Miguel Ángel Asturias's *El señor presidente* depict Estrada Cabrera's regime as a time without law,[2] yet the legal system was functioning and helped to maintain social stability during his reign. The judiciary similarly served Ubico, even though he, like Estrada Cabrera, was more interested in maintaining the rule of order than the rule of law. Couched in the discourse of modernizing and moral reforms, the state established the parameters for what constituted legal and illegal activities. The impulse for action based on these laws, however, was as likely to come from subalterns as state agents.

By affording multiple avenues to restitution and retribution, the very lack of a clear, standardized judicial process that held the potential to destabilize Guatemala's legal system instead buttressed it. Even though Estrada Cabrera and Ubico risked underinstitutionalizing the courts when they intervened in, overruled, or disregarded the legal system, *indígenas* and poor ladinos perceived the judiciary to be legitimate. As the archival record demonstrates, *indígenas* understood the state to be multifarious, complex, and contradictory. When they did not achieve their goals in one venue, they knew they could approach another. For every department judge who returned a case or redirected a petition to the municipal court, there was another (or a *jefe político* or president) who entertained petitions that had bypassed local procedures. Instead of undermining its legitimacy, the malleability of the system bolstered it.

In light of historian William Stuntz's critique that the U.S. justice system's preoccupation with procedure often precludes justice, the Guatemalan judicial system's pliability may have made it more just.[3] If a victim knew local officials to be corrupt or in cahoots with her offender, she could appeal to their judicial or political superiors. The sixty-year-old widow Tomasa Pérez did so in 1931 when she learned that the man who raped her daughter had arranged with the *alcalde auxiliar* (assistant mayor) of her village to block the case from getting on the local court docket.[4]

As in other areas of Latin America, the arbitrary nature of Guatemala's legal system likely informed both the elasticity that some litigants attributed to the law and the exaggerated sense of optimism that some poor, indigenous, and female plaintiffs held toward the eventual outcome of legal procedures. The law was "an ambiguous, malleable, and slippery arena of struggle" where the rules of the game were defined not just by legislators and judges but also by litigants whose perceptions of crime, legality, justice, and rights were far from static.[5] In an indication of how litigants and their stories could influence decisions, at times plaintiffs, such as women who accused men of infanticide, reworked the law to advance their agendas and in doing so shaped how judicial officials conceived of justice.

Any study of crime invariably discloses the difference between de jure and de facto reality. As was true elsewhere in Latin America, tensions between the two often arose when the state attempted to legislate, litigate, and explain differences such as those based on gender, race, and class. Codified laws more closely reflected national leaders' and legislators' ideals than reality.[6]

The *indígenas* who persevered as bootleggers, market vendors, *buhoneros*, and in other trades that attracted authorities' attention demonstrate how little laws affected some practices and how weak the state was, particularly in areas remote from the nation's capital. That the state could neither curtail nor reform poor *indígenas'* or ladinos' behavior, much less eradicate the causes of their disputes or transgressions, speaks to how little or at least how selectively subalterns were listening to it. With its vast geography and topographic diversity, Guatemala was a difficult nation to rule. The department of Chimaltenango's proximity to Guatemala City enhanced local and regional authorities' power and presence and facilitated a functional legal system, in sharp contrast to regions farther north and west.[7] Still authorities' ability to enforce state rule in most of Chimaltenango's *municipios*—including Patzicía and San Martín—was limited and became increasingly attenuated as one left the *cabeceras* for the *aldeas*. These findings resonate with other studies of rural Guatemala and Latin America that demonstrate that central state authority is difficult to enforce in remote and rural areas.[8]

Set against the backdrop of despots who used spies, security forces, governors, local officials, and presidential visits to extend the state's reach, the opportunity to speak in court was crucial for people's sense of inclusion. In light of the failure of schools, military conscription, market reforms, and many public health initiatives to bind rural *indígenas* to the state's nationalism, definition of citizenship, and modernization programs, the courts were one of the best venues for *indígenas* to shape national mores, development, and priorities. As the *indígenas* who learned Spanish, became literate, and/or deployed legal precepts in their testimonies attest, indigenous people were not always opposed to the state's overtures. They were, however, more likely to have an open attitude toward them in venues where they were respected and afforded civil liberties.

Because they believed these institutions could solve their problems, *indígenas* and poor ladinos often used municipal or department courts as sounding boards for their struggles. For example, some litigants highlighted how the state's shortcomings—such as its inability to curb poverty, unemployment, and discrimination—often precipitated transgressions and tragedies. As Sen reminds us, the conditions of societies themselves are as important as institutions and laws in determining justice.[9] During dictatorial rule, the legal system offered one of the safest means for *indígenas* to push the state for reform. Despite the significant disadvantages that awaited them, *indígenas* often entered courtrooms with the hope that they would leave having achieved their goals or at least having minimized their marginalization.

As arenas of social contestation, courts could be instruments of subaltern power, particularly if we accept Foucault's definition of power as actions that act upon the actions of others.[10] Often, judicial officials afforded Guatemalan litigants considerable sway. When municipal magistrates ruled in defamation litigation without knowing what the insult was, they accepted litigants' and witnesses' ability to determine acceptable social behavior. When they reduced sentences and waived legal fees in response to defendants' "highly evident poverty" and efforts to recast the terms of accusation and incrimination into terms relevant for their own lives, department judges demonstrated that even the most marginalized litigants could influence them. By demonstrating that rulings were often more ameliorative or resolution-oriented than punitive, these responses contributed to litigants' sense that justice, however incomplete or ineffectual, was done in court.

Approaching laws as weapons, plaintiffs used the courts to inflict damage upon or exact retribution or restitution from their adversaries. As was true in colonial Ecuador, instead of being autonomous from the conflicts and negotiations that ran parallel to the legal system, courts were mirrors of and oftentimes hosts to the quotidian struggles in communities and the nation.[11] By submitting their claims to the court, defamation and domestic violence plaintiffs enlisted the aid of local authorities to protect their reputations and bodies, respectively.

Courts played many different roles in Guatemala, as instruments of state and subaltern power, release valves for popular pressure, and venues for negotiation, contestation, and grievance. If we cannot definitively articulate what courts were in early twentieth-century Guatemala, then perhaps we should approach other government institutions the same way: as organic entities that assumed multiple roles, were used in various ways, and hosted multifarious power relations and negotiations.

The Equivocal Nature of State Building and Power in the Courts

By binding people to the state, reinforcing uniformity at the same time it entertained alternative viewpoints, and providing even the most marginalized people an audience with local and national officials, the legal system was an important part of state building in Guatemala and elsewhere in Latin America.[12] As instruments of state power where judicial authorities imposed the state's will upon and conveyed the state's procedures, norms, and worldviews to some of the most isolated rural residents, Guatemalan courts were vehicles for integrating *indígenas* and poor ladinos.

The judiciary's power to effect assimilation should not be overstated, however. The extensive record of bootlegging, for example, indicates that the state's alcohol laws did little to integrate *indígenas* and poor ladinos into the national economy. Indigenous vendors' rejection of economic reforms that contradicted their own knowledge and practices similarly suggests the state's limited influence in that realm. Indeed, the legal record abounds with examples of the state's failure to unite *indígenas* around its national imaginary and impose its hegemonic project. If we accept Roseberry's conceptualization of hegemony as a "framework for living through, talking about, and acting upon social orders characterized by domination," these outcomes are not surprising.[13] Hegemony seldom meant subalterns' total acceptance or submission.[14] Domination and resistance were mutually constituted.

Because indigenous litigants often said what they thought authorities wanted to hear, the legal record probably overstates the state's influence. Indigenous plaintiffs employed pithy, judicial Spanish to diplomatically underscore their perspectives and demands. When exhorting judges to rule in their favor, they might insist that their offenders be punished *en conformidad a la ley* (in conformity with the law). Perhaps more than any other type of litigation, defamation and assault and battery cases demonstrate the extent to which litigants learned about the legal system and adhered to its norms. With few exceptions, defendants stood reverently before judicial officials and refrained from the vile language or violent behavior that had landed them in court. The few who did not observe these expectations were punished.

When it suited them, *indígenas* availed themselves of the malleable inventions of race and nation. Like other Latin American indigenous people during the colonial and early national periods, instead of identifying themselves by their particular linguistic, ethnic, or community group, Mayas adhered to Spanish conceptions of *indígena* or *indio* that homogenized indigenes. By the late nineteenth century, however, "Mayas were . . . becoming Guatemalans, increasingly affected by and responsive to politics and power outside their communities," as Taylor and other historians have noted.[15] When indigenous men and women identified themselves as *guatemalteco/as*, they were not necessarily demanding legal citizenship and suffrage but rather insisting they be included in the national polity as members who enjoyed basic civil, political, economic, and social rights.[16] Although this positioning resonated with other Mayas, such as nineteenth-century K'iche' elites in Quetzaltenango, most non-indigenous elites considered nationalism and indigeneity mutually exclusive.[17] Aware that the legal system was not immune to racism, classism, or sexism, indigenous litigants generally approached the courts as institutions where their rights were most likely to be upheld.

Courtroom contexts are crucial to understanding a litigant's position, strategy, and likelihood of success. Unlike their female counterparts who aggressively defended market rights, domestic abuse victims often played upon the weakness and ignorance state agents commonly assumed of women. How and why one arrived in court also influenced the outcome. Unlike the wily defendants who crafted narratives to dismiss their rivals' accusations, suspects caught red-handed by authorities had little chance of exoneration. Defendants were more vulnerable than plaintiffs, yet at times the latter were sentenced for their transgressions too. Deborah Poole points out in her study of Peru that the state was a guarantor of rights and an enforcer of law. This arbitrary power meant litigants entered the courtroom cautiously.[18] Taking such risks demonstrates how much was at stake.

Despite settings where judicial authorities and most litigants were male, women often approached the courts with a confidence that defied the gendered nature of the judicial system. The effect the masculine nature of law and courts had on female litigants was largely determined by the litigation in which they were embroiled. For example, the gendered dynamic of the courtroom weighed less heavily on female bootleggers or vendors than on victims of rape or those accused of abortion or infanticide. Ethnicity, too, affected litigants. More than marital status or class, ethnicity determined which women initiated litigation and appeared in court. Despite—or perhaps because of—their diminished social position, indigenous women enjoyed more legal autonomy than ladinas.

Given the critical difference between the degrees and types of power held by rural justices of the peace and urban department judges, the venue—which depended largely on the classification of the crime—also mattered; this helps to explain why some plaintiffs bypassed the local judicial system and appealed directly to the *juzgado de primera instancia*. For instance, given the maximum ten-day sentence for assault and battery tried at the municipal level, *jueces de paz* were hard pressed to protect women from their attackers. When women filed infanticide charges, however, department judges could incarcerate violent men for years. Even when lesser charges of assault and battery made it on their dockets, department judges could protect domestic violence victims by delaying the proceedings as the accused waited in jail. On the other hand, although both crimes undercut state revenue, department judges were far more likely to be lenient with bootleggers than were municipal magistrates to reduce the sentences of renegade vendors. In contrast to findings in Guatemala and elsewhere in Latin America, municipal magistrates' hard line with tax evaders suggests they were not always less powerful than their urban superiors when dealing with local issues.[19]

The high conviction rate in municipal market crimes seemed to discourage debate among female defendants, who more often than not simply accepted their sentences with little more than confessions. Compared to the *clandestinistas* who, by way of explaining their transgression and reducing their sentences, decried poverty and/or their struggles to support their children, the reserved responses of some otherwise outspoken female marketers suggests that despite their formality and physical and cultural distance from most litigants, department courtrooms could be more welcoming than municipal ones.

Comparing litigation that resulted from criminal enforcement by the state with cases that were brought by people themselves to the courts offers further insight into the balance of power between people and the state. While the myriad state representatives—national, treasury, and municipal police, market inspectors, *regidores*, judicial officials—who enforced liquor and market laws were predominantly attempting to impose the state's will, victims of violence and insults drew upon the state's laws and courts as levers against their opponents. This changed the dynamic between judicial officials and litigants in the courtroom. By asking the court to enforce the law, plaintiffs hinted at authorities' failure to do so without outside initiative. The state's ability to impose its will was less commanding when judicial officials adjudicated conflict between subalterns than when they ruled on issues between the state and subalterns.

In another manifestation of the complex power relations at play in the legal system (and beyond it), the mere act of initiating litigation could curtail judicial officials' power. Some petitioners did so intentionally in efforts to remove corrupt officials. As examples of department judges reprimanding and fining municipal magistrates for unnecessarily referring cases to them attest, often plaintiffs unwittingly upset an authority's standing. Department judges, too, had to answer to their superiors, most notably when the court of appeals reversed their decisions. At the same time these checks against individual authorities' power served to legitimize the judicial system, they also revealed that the various officials who personified the state in the legal system, not to mention those outside it, seldom represented a united front.

Poor *indígenas* influenced the criminal justice system as mediators who were as likely to help prevent crime as to deflect authorities' attention from transgressions they did not consider criminal. The frequency with which the topic of bootlegging emerged in Kaqchikel oral histories, particularly when compared to the paucity of discussion about other types of crime, suggests that Maya notions about deviance were at times at odds with the state's. When the criminal record captured such extrajudicial strategies as people obscuring moonshiners' identities and parents protecting daughters from abusive spouses, it revealed the ways individuals and communities intervened to bring about justice on their own terms.

Indígenas knew what the state would and could do for them. They refrained from initiating defamation litigation against ladinos who called them *indios* or *ixtas*, but they readily brought ladinos to court who infringed upon their rights in other ways, say, by assaulting them or failing to pay debts. Indigenous women in particular refused to allow the state's limits to frustrate them. When they denounced male violence, they simultaneously pointed to the state's inability to maintain order in their homes and, by extension, communities and nation and conveyed confidence that authorities would ultimately uphold the law. Even though municipal justices' handling of domestic violence litigation tended to perpetuate official indifference toward widespread gender-based violence, women continued to reject the dictates of patriarchs—whether in the home or the presidential palace—that they deemed excessive or unjust.

Courting Gender and Patriarchy

Like their counterparts elsewhere in Latin America and Europe, Guatemalan leaders considered patriarchal, if not peaceful, families crucial to social order and economic progress.[20] Many men held similar beliefs. Interpreting their responsibility to maintain order in the home as an indication that their power there should be absolute, men beat their wives for disobeying them even as they insisted, as did the forty-three-year-old, illiterate, ladino farmer Esteban Ordóñez, there was "no unpleasantness" between them.[21] In petitions that suggested local patriarchal power and national order were symbiotic, men used the legal system to discipline females.[22] Despite indigenous women's attempts to disassociate the rights afforded Guatemalans from men's patriarchal powers, the legal record demonstrates that many local patriarchs related their authority to their sense of national belonging.

As historically contingent processes constructed in different ways through multiple social contexts and legal venues, patriarchies complemented, contrasted, and even contradicted each other. Although generally impotent when set against state bureaucracy,[23] peasant patriarchy often benefited from the legal system. Even when they ruled against men, judicial officials seldom undermined patriarchal power. In response to verdicts that did little to undercut countervailing social pressures that discouraged women from leaving their spouses, for example, domestic violence offenders frequently commuted their sentences and returned home with their victims.

Patriarchy at the state level did not require the protection of women from all violent men, just those whose excesses threatened to destroy family life. Evidence of family, friends, and neighbors who intervened to protect women suggests indigenous communities had a lower threshold for violence against women than the state did, yet in many ways the state's official indifference toward gender-based violence reflected Maya notions that women must endure some corporal abuse from their male kin. From the local to the national level, violence against women helped patriarchs assert their authority. By providing an outlet for male frustrations that undergirded local patriarchies but did not challenge the state, gender-based violence helped to construct and sustain these regimes. In contrast to the often very public and raucous disputes over reputations, husbands who beat wives behind closed doors did not disrupt images of an orderly nation. The role of the judiciary, police, and other institutions of social control was not to eradicate but to manage violence against women. For this reason, the same judicial officials who doled out minimal sentences in domestic violence litigation often ruled in favor of women who fled their homes when abuse became intolerable.[24]

Overlapping patriarchal systems seldom resulted in male omnipotence, however. Despite widespread gender-based violence and such legal manifestations of patriarchy as *patria potestad*, the court record suggests that men did not necessarily dominate highland households. Wives who insulted and hit husbands in the privacy of their own homes or simply refused to meet their spouses' daily demands offer evidence of women's ability to shape gender relations even as overarching political, social, and economic structures tended to diminish their agency vis-à-vis men. Similarly, the frequency with which indigenous women initiated litigation reveals their independence from their husbands. In turn, as historian Eugenia Rodríguez Sáenz argues, men who initiated litigation against their wives often betrayed a sense of "masculine frustration" at not being able to exercise authority in the home. Social ideals contradicted quotidian realities.[25] This frustration can also be read in the domestic struggles within the home that could be traced to women's mobility, autonomy, and relationships outside it.[26]

Denied access to community organizations such as *municipalidades indígenas* and often even schools, indigenous women had few institutions through which they could advocate for themselves and be recognized as Guatemalans. Their public presence and stake in highland markets encouraged them to be outspoken and confront authorities there, but their very defiance meant that these markets largely operated outside state control. In contrast, courts offered an official venue where women's voices could be heard. By initiating litigation, women both invited the state into their lives and presented themselves as members of the national polity. Most female defendants would have preferred to avoid the state's gaze, but they often asserted their rights in court as well.

Regardless of the circumstances surrounding their litigation, women assumed a degree of agency by addressing their marginalization in court. While it provides evidence of the ways women were exploited, violated, and abused, the judicial record also documents women who refused to let victimhood define them. Using the courts as much for retribution as for vindication, women defended themselves and their properties, businesses, children, and reputations.

Their positions were assumed and reinforced immediately upon presenting themselves to the court through some variant of the formulaic identifying phrase *oficios de su sexo y raza*. Yet indigenous women revealed more complex identities and realities through their testimonies when they spoke of their agricultural work, entrepreneurial endeavors, long-distance travel, independence from men, and other descriptions that shattered ladino if not indigenous gender norms. By demonstrating that poor, indigenous women's lives rarely conformed to the rules of patriarchal propriety, indigenous female litigants laid claim to the same rights that men enjoyed. These repeated performances of denaturalizing gender challenged the assumptions upon which patriarchies were based.[27] On the other hand, few men departed from their prescribed identities as *jornaleros* or *agricultores* in their testimonies. Women's descriptions of their labor and lives attest that men seldom performed domestic duties or followed orders from their wives. The few who did were loath to reveal as much in court. Because of their subordinate position within the gender and ethnic scheme, indigenous women were more likely than men to upset gender norms and later admit to it in court.

Female litigants shaped ideas of citizenship, motherhood, and ethnicity as well as gender through their testimonies. Kaqchikel women insisted they could be indigenous, poor, single mothers who engaged in premarital sex and still be virtuous, intelligent, and productive. Their strategies varied, yet female litigants almost invariably presented themselves as honest, hardworking, honorable women. Those who identified themselves as *guatemaltecas* buoyed their positions and maximized their security by suggesting that the civil liberties and legal rights granted men should pertain to women, too.

Women's interpretations of gender codes and the law altered their relationship to society and the legal system. Their courtroom narratives help us weigh the ambiguities of when subalterns took recourse to state procedures for other than state-intended purposes. By accusing men of breaking laws generally designed to subjugate women (such as infanticide or abortion), women used the state's apparatus to curtail men's power. That judicial officials entertained such cases and at times prosecuted men for these crimes is an indication that even disenfranchised Guatemalan women, like their counterparts elsewhere in Latin America, affected the operation and formulation of law.[28] By ruling in their favor, judges buttressed women's sense that the legal system was efficacious if not always just, which in turn encouraged them and their counterparts to use it. Although the letter of the law favored men, in practice it often helped women.[29] At the same time, some types of litigation, most obviously for rape, so decidedly disadvantaged women that their attempts to gain justice were almost invariably fruitless.[30]

If the best defense called for conformity, women framed their testimonies in the language of domesticity and motherhood to request protection based on their conditions as females and mothers. Female litigants who explained their victimization or criminal activity by associating it with their presumed weakness and ignorance as women enjoyed some success with legal authorities who were more likely to consider women degenerate than criminal. Emphasizing feminine roles and responsibilities in some ways perpetuated such gendered violations as court-ordered gynecological examinations, yet the discourse of motherhood could influence judicial outcomes and underscore the depravity of violent men.

Appealing to gendered notions of womanhood did not always reinforce female subordination. Since the state, authorities, and society generally accepted that women's reproductive capacity had to be protected,[31] women who requested aid based on their social function as mothers did not have to denigrate themselves. Embracing what were for many contradictory ideas, some women identified themselves as *guatemaltecas* and mothers who deserved rights and special protection. Womanhood was never fixed in legal testimonies because women manipulated their identities according to their purposes and audiences.

Similar to what Stern found in late colonial Mexico, instead of challenging men's "right to patriarchal authority," twentieth-century Guatemalan highland women shaped gender relations by contesting "patriarchal pacts."[32] Any strategy they invoked to counteract their oppression was a product of the conditions, expectations, and norms that such power brokers as authorities and elites established.[33] For these and other reasons, historians of women and gender, particularly those studying the law and legal systems, struggle with how to interpret women's positions. When women initiated domestic violence litigation against their husbands, were they manifesting their strength and initiative by engaging the legal system, or did the very need to seek outside help betray their diminished status and weakness within the home?[34] To my mind, framing historical actors in a weak/strong binary occludes many of the exchanges, motives, and actions that were not informed by concerns about power. Power was present everywhere, but people were not always obsessed with attaining, maintaining, or expanding it.

Women's nuanced strategies and narratives suggest they were more interested in reciprocity than equality. Even in light of the extraordinary nature of criminal documents, the legal record indicates that conflict was not the exception but the norm in everyday life. Like other Latin American women, most Maya women accepted this aspect of gender relations, but they also expected men to fulfill their duties and respect them.[35] When men did not, women took them to court, fled, or fought back. Indigenous women resisted, adapted to, reinforced, and even benefited from the gender-based power imbalances in their families, communities, nation, and legal system.

What's in a Name?

In countries with large indigenous populations like Guatemala and Ecuador, nation builders used ethnicity and gender to subjugate indigenous people and women.[36] In Guatemala, indigenous and female litigants used these notions to their advantage in highland courtrooms. In so doing, they compelled judicial officials to negotiate the very discourse the state deployed to control indigenous people and women.

Historians have adeptly analyzed the various ways Latin American women used arguments that ranged from lamenting their feminine weakness to celebrating their reproductive capacities,[37] while few have explored how postcolonial indigenous women deployed ethnicity in the courtroom to their advantage. Alan Knight, among other historians of modern and particularly revolutionary Mexico, found that indigenous complaints and demands were "usually couched in class rather than caste terms."[38] Guatemalan *indígenas*, however, frequently framed their grievances in terms of class and ethnicity. Like their male counterparts who portrayed themselves as indigent, helpless members of the "Indian race," some indigenous women sought to convince authorities they deserved special consideration as *indias* who were disadvantaged by discrimination, illiteracy, and poverty. This strategy could backfire, as it did when a lawyer attempted to portray his indigenous client as a product of *indígenas*' "habit of inebriation and principles of doubtful morality that . . . make them beings very susceptible to crime" and instead seemed to convince the judge of indigenous depravity and the defendant's guilt.[39]

In testimonies that contravened indigenous disparagement, some indigenous litigants used the courts to challenge prevailing notions of *indígenas*' proclivity toward drunkenness, indolence, and crime. Bootleggers and market vendors who insisted they only broke the law to feed their families were among the many *indígenas* who defined themselves not as a race of criminals but rather as individuals who were handicapped by discrimination, poverty, and illiteracy. In this way they used Liberal, individualist discourse to their own ends. Even as their need for translators underscored their ethnicity, indigenous women defied stereotypes of lazy, ignorant *indios* when they highlighted their economic contributions or cited specific legal codes. Their arguments were grounded in rights and merit. Some associated their ethnicity with patriotism by identifying themselves as *guatemaltecas* and *indígenas*. The judicial record reveals that whether they appealed to a sense of paternalism, individual rights, national belonging, or some combination thereof, narrative strategies that evoked ethnicity enjoyed some success in mitigating sentences.

Since idealistic definitions of citizenship often masked the ways gender, race, and class shaped individuals' relationships with the state and their access to rights, groups that historically suffered discrimination and exclusion often fared worse when the principle of individual equality was rigidly applied.[40] From that perspective, indigenous litigants were wise to play on ladino stereotypes by identifying themselves as *indios* who needed special treatment from the state to countervail the injustices done to them.

Throughout the Americas, working-class men and women employed similar narrative strategies with varying degrees of success.[41] Butler notes that such language should not be read as internalizing discrimination: "To take up the name that one is called is not simple submission to prior authority. . . . The word that wounds becomes an instrument of resistance in the redeployment that destroys the prior territory of its operations."[42] Even as *indígenas* described themselves as ignorant *indios* or *indias* and females portrayed themselves as weak to evoke sympathy in court, the very act of claiming these stereotypes aloud dislodged them and at times diminished their power.

Tapping into these discourses did not reify them. As Michael Herzfeld notes, subalterns' use of official discourse was often "serendipitously subversive of accepted meanings."[43] *Indígenas* who identified themselves as *indios* and *indias* in the legal record often explained that their diminished social position was related to poverty and discrimination. Instead of saying they were *indios* by nature, or more accurately by culture, as elite connotations of the word suggested, indigenous litigants asserted that the struggles they faced as *indios* were a product of social conditions. Many elites purported that *indios* could alleviate their plight through assimilation, while *in-*

dígenas indicated that they could maintain their ethnic identity and improve their lot if the state addressed their lack of economic, political, and social resources. Their everyday use of the term *indio* eroded its fixity and rejected elites' assumptions about their ethnic identity and social position.[44]

However unequal the power relations between ladino authorities and *indígenas*, the judicial and broader archival record indicates that *indígenas* knew far more about ladinos and the state than officials knew about them. To navigate the courts and manipulate authorities, *indígenas* had to know them both well, while authorities had less immediate need to understand their charges. State representatives who were oblivious to such indigenous marketplace logic as vendors' locations and haggling contrast sharply with illiterate women who cited legal codes in their defense.

In addition to exchanges within the courtroom, the legal record also offers a window into the complexity of social relations in highland Guatemala more broadly. Resonating with Guatemalan historiography, the judicial record abounds with evidence of ladinos exploiting, hitting, and insulting *indígenas*, and *indígenas* abused each other in these ways too. Yet courtroom narratives also hint at cooperation, even solidarity across ethnic lines when, for example, indigenous women stayed with their ladino *compadres* or neighbors for extended periods to avoid violent husbands. In turn, ladinas relied on indigenous women for shelter and protection at times. Relationships with in-laws similarly could be marked by contention and enmity. Husbands who were convinced their fathers-in-law were destroying their marriages and wives who complained of abusive mothers- and sisters-in-law permeate the judicial record, but evidence of women and men who defended their daughters- and sons-in-law can also be discerned. In short, ethnicity, gender, class, age, and kinship all influenced the ways individuals interacted with each other.

What these relationships and the broader judicial record reveal is that the law mattered. No matter how intimate and private personal relationships were, the individuals involved in them often felt confident they could use the courts to resolve their disputes or exact restitution or retribution. In this way, far from being undermined during authoritarian and interventionist rule, the legal system was essential for maintaining order during two of Latin America's fiercest dictatorships and the less authoritarian regimes that governed during the 1920s. Crucial to subalterns as well as to authorities, courts and law became a means of communication between them and among subalterns themselves. As often as defendants sought to educate judicial officials by highlighting how their alleged crimes were related to their privations, disputants informed each other about how seriously they approached offenses and the extent to which they would go to defend themselves and their property, reputations, and families.

Since it offered the potential to both strengthen and question gender, class, and race relations, hegemons and subalterns alike approached the legal system as a venue that could serve their needs. Its ambiguous, malleable, and at times even arbitrary nature facilitated these perceptions. As described in the introduction, the same system his *patrón* deployed to persecute him for fleeing his debt allowed Lorenzo Chonay to precipitate an investigation into the alleged incompetence of the authorities who had arrested him. Exchanges in courts and the insights testimonies offer into what happened outside them shed light on the myriad ways indigenous and poor men's and women's seemingly small gestures shaped the course of nation formation and day-to-day governance in twentieth-century Guatemala.

Appendix 1. Population 1893, by race, gender, and literacy

| Department/ Town | Total | Ladino | | | | Indio |
		Male	Female	Total	%	Male
Chimaltenango	57,177	6,980	7,347	14,327	25	21,794
Balanyá	797	4	13	17	2	393
Chimaltenango	3,749	603	635	1,238	33	1,165
Comalapa	4,796	111	173	284	6	2,366
Itzapa	2,359	475	494	969	41	659
Patzicía	4,434	633	656	1,289	29	1,476
Patzum	5,932	645	737	1,382	23	2,437
Poaquil	2,109	9	8	17	1	1,133
San Martín	10,393	837	1,068	1,905	18	4,213
Santa Apolonia	929	34	53	87	9	437
Tecpam	7,602	1,197	1,209	2,406	32	2,643
Yepocapa	2,908	307	325	632	22	1,124
Sacatepéquez	42,713	6,463	9,398	15,861	37	13,878
Aguas Calientes	2,012	10	14	24	1	936
Barahona	1,015	1	27	28	3	540
El Cubo	524	21	31	52	10	229
Sololá	70,039	4,251	4,087	8,338	12	31,610
Sololá	7,627	1,026	1,056	2,082	27	2,686
Guatemala total	1,364,678	235,981	245,964	481,945	35	441,491

Source: DGE, *Censo . . . 1893*.
Note: I adhered to the spellings (e.g., Tecpam) and classifications (e.g., *Indio*) in the 1893 census.

Indio			All				
Female	Total	%	Male	Female	Illiterate	Read only	Read, write
21,056	42,850	75	28,774	28,403	50,682	3,502	2,993
388	781	98	396	401	781	8	8
1,346	2,511	67	1,768	1,981	2,981	428	340
2,146	4,512	94	2,477	2,319	4,405	212	179
731	1,390	59	1,134	1,225	1,955	220	184
1,669	3,145	71	2,109	2,325	3,951	251	232
2,113	4,550	77	3,082	2,850	5,177	410	345
959	2,092	99	1,142	967	2,081	14	14
4,275	8,488	82	5,050	5,343	9,112	685	596
405	842	91	471	458	835	50	44
2,553	5,196	68	3,840	3,762	6,977	343	282
1,152	2,276	78	1,431	1,477	2,768	77	63
12,974	26,852	63	20,341	22,372	34,925	1,063	6,725
1,052	1,988	99	946	1,066	1,729	1	282
447	987	97	541	474	961	8	46
243	472	90	250	274	436	18	70
30,091	61,701	88	35,861	34,878	67,593	323	2,123
2,759	5,445	71	3,712	3,915	6,974	55	598
441,242	882,733	65	677,472	687,206	1,240,092	25,033	99,553

Appendix 2. Population 1921, by race and gender

Department/ Town	Total	Ladino			
		Male	Female	Total	%
Chimaltenango	88,030	9,064	9,840	18,904	22
Balanyá	1,071	38	37	75	7
Chimaltenango	6,264	754	877	1,631	26
Comalapa	9,379	172	208	380	4
Itzapa	3,822	484	535	1,019	27
Patzicía	5,355	759	825	1,584	30
Patzum	9,912	668	889	1,557	16
Poaquil	3,234	125	109	234	7
San Martín	14,163	891	1,010	1,901	13
Santa Apolonia	1,974	74	81	155	8
Tecpam	9,219	1,121	1,410	2,531	28
Yepocapa	5,082	591	527	1,118	22
Sacatepéquez	46,453	8,755	10,175	18,930	41
Aguas Calientes	1,536	3	5	8	1
Barahona	616	2	4	6	1
El Cubo	648	15	14	29	4
Sololá	104,283	5,834	5,845	11,679	11
Sololá	11,319	593	708	1,301	12
Guatemala total	2,004,900	342,456	362,517	704,973	35

Source: DGE, *Censo . . . 1921.*
Note: I adhered to the spellings (e.g., Tecpam) and classifications (e.g., *Indio*) in the 1921 census.

Indio				All	
Male	*Female*	*Total*	*%*	*Male*	*Female*
35,027	34,099	69,126	79	44,091	43,939
465	531	996	93	503	568
2,337	2,296	4,633	74	3,091	3,173
4,136	4,863	8,999	96	4,308	5,071
1,399	1,404	2,803	73	1,883	1,939
1,873	1,898	3,771	70	2,632	2,723
4,229	4,126	8,355	84	4,897	5,015
1,477	1,523	3,000	93	1,602	1,632
6,130	6,132	12,262	87	7,021	7,142
897	922	1,819	92	971	1,003
3,355	3,333	6,688	73	4,476	4,743
1,838	2,126	3,964	78	2,429	2,653
13,344	14,179	27,523	59	22,099	24,354
725	803	1,528	99	728	808
313	297	610	99	315	301
272	347	619	96	287	361
46,265	46,339	92,604	89	52,099	52,184
4,714	5,304	10,018	89	5,307	6,012
649,440	650,487	1,299,927	65	991,896	1,013,004

Appendix 3. Selected crimes, Guatemala, 1899–1900, 1927–1944

Crime*	1899	1900	'27	'28	'29	'32	'33	'34	'35
Abandono de hogar	0	0	53	0	111	115	178	182	172
Abandono de menor	0	0	0	27	16	14	44	14	14
Aborto	0	0	0	0	4	6	12	2	9
Adulterio	0	0	37	60	32	40	61	52	30
Agresión	187	249	—	—	1,521	1,171	—	1,214	1,050
Allanamiento	8	7	—	132	130	111	156	155	77
Amenaza y coacción	—	—	—	—	418	341	—	296	285
Asesinato	—	—	—	—	98	25	—	85	117
Calumnia	—	—	—	12	5	38	—	62	4
Corrupción de menor	—	—	—	—	12	—	3	13	7
Defraudación, licores	101	47	85	188	171	614	493	3,265	2,759
Ebriedad	5,347	4,596	5,170	25,335	18,987	8,818	6,905	6,974	7,697
Escándolo	—	—	—	1,133	2,606	738	640	762	507
Estafa	25	14	—	—	290	288	533	—	308
Estupro	—	—	—	43	30	41	53	62	60
Homicidio	17	9	—	74	64	21	—	102	123
Hurto	462	567	—	—	2,035	1,163	1,636	—	1,412
Infanticidio	—	—	2	11	7	7	7	5	17
Infracción, ornato	—	—	—	—	34	22	—	11	2
Infracción, sanitaria	—	—	—	—	106	71	—	131	278
Injurias	494	17	—	—	708	976	2,079	233	1,737
Lesión	—	—	—	—	651	316	—	592	539
Mozo fraudulente	—	—	—	—	396	45	—	173	216
Parricidio	—	—	—	—	—	—	—	—	2

'36	'37	'38	'39	'40	'41	'42	'43	'44	'32–'44	Total
251	317	238	239	247	219	220	249	213	2,840	3,004
14	23	1	17	23	18	23	102	55	362	405
10	7	9	10	15	6	10	9	6	111	115
76	57	52	79	85	96	52	80	53	813	942
1,055	1,047	1,235	—	—	—	—	—	—	6,772	8,729
101	136	136	138	185	167	170	223	219	1,974	2,251
353	304	246	—	—	—	—	—	—	1,825	2,243
100	60	55	19	17	—	34	—	—	512	610
19	31	36	—	—	—	—	—	—	190	207
9	14	4	—	—	—	—	—	—	50	62
2,441	1,878	2,289	1,843	2,399	2,019	1,614	1,124	689	23,427	24,019
8,970	7,835	4,105	—	5,018	5,975	7,164	9,055	7,502	86,018	145,453
322	524	466	406	930	1,237	3,054	3,941	3,194	16,721	20,460
313	470	374	375	360	—	667	—	—	3,688	4,017
52	72	59	95	123	104	121	144	88	1,074	1,147
130	82	58	25	24	—	68	—	—	633	797
1,432	1,404	1,409	1,329	1,332	—	2,139	—	—	13,256	16,320
7	8	2	22	10	12	10	6	2	115	135
113	78	11	—	—	—	—	—	—	237	271
363	387	393	—	—	—	—	—	—	1,623	1,729
2,199	1,944	1,544	1,470	1,523	1,512	1,323	1,469	1,255	19,264	20,483
617	550	511	555	552	—	620	—	—	4,852	5,503
106	41	33	—	—	—	—	—	—	614	1,010
3	2	2	3	1	—	2	—	—	15	15

(continued)

Appendix 3. (*continued*)

Crime*	1899	1900	'27	'28	'29	'32	'33	'34	'35
Prostitución clandestina	322	170	229	759	1,016	836	1,204	1,031	1,054
Rapto	10	8	71	132	125	94	143	185	157
Rebelión	—	—	—	—	8	21	—	3	—
Resistencia y desobediencia	—	—	—	—	183	53	—	—	—
Riña	1,551	1,520	—	—	5,170	1,908	2,446	2,589	2,280
Robos	9	8	—	—	376	455	412	—	391
Sedición	—	—	—	—	213	1,095	—	172	—
Suicidio	—	—	14	—	—	—	—	—	—
Testimonio falso	—	—	—	—	4	16	36	—	22
Turbación del orden público	—	—	—	—	177	43	—	6	9
Vagancia	2,496	1,816	—	—	2,488	712	1,450	952	789
Violación	—	—	53	522	125	94	75	108	150
Total	11,029	9,028	5,714	28,428	38,317	20,308	18,566	19,431	22,274

Source: Policía Nacional, *Memorias* 1899–1900, 1927–1944.
Notes: A dash (—) indicates that no data were available.
No data were available for 1930–1931.
The column of 1932–1944 subtotals is provided to show crimes recorded during the approximate years of Ubico's rule.
*English translations of crime categories

Abandono de hogar	Abandoning the home
Abandono de menor	Abandoning a child
Aborto	Abortion
Adulterio	Adultery
Agresión	Assault
Allanamiento	Home invasion
Amenaza	Threat
Amenaza y coacción	Threat and coercion
Asesinato	Murder
Atentado	Assault
Calumnia	Slander
Corrupción de menor	Corrupting a minor
Defraudación al Fisco en el ramo de licores y contrabando	Defrauding the Treasury of alcohol revenue
Ebriedad	Inebriation, drunkenness
Escándolo	Scandal
Estafa	Deceit
Estupro	Statutory rape

'36	'37	'38	'39	'40	'41	'42	'43	'44	'32–'44	Total
1,999	1,366	1,027	—	—	—	—	—	—	8,517	11,013
183	174	204	196	223	230	187	184	174	2,334	2,680
19	—	—	—	—	—	—	—	—	43	51
300	307	17	—	—	—	—	—	—	677	860
2,446	2,164	2,178	2,246	3,386	3,863	3,866	4,602	4,245	38,219	46,460
472	427	345	255	254	—	373	—	—	3,384	3,777
40	1	23	—	1	—	—	—	—	1,332	1,545
44	—	50	48	75	44	—	30	48	339	353
16	17	19	—	—	—	30	—	—	156	160
11	5	14	—	—	—	—	—	—	88	265
1,293	1,647	1,133	1,121	1,977	1,721	2,864	2,182	1,703	19,544	26,344
164	128	150	165	179	168	181	154	3	1,719	2,419
26,043	23,507	18,428	10,656	18,939	17,391	24,792	23,554	19,449	263,338	355,854

Golpe, heridas y lesiones	Assault, with injuries
Homicidio	Homicide
Hurto	Theft
Incendio	Arson
Infanticidio	Infanticide
Infracción a disposiciones de ornato	Infraction against forced—labor regulations
Infracción a disposiciones sanitarias	Infraction against sanitation regulations
Injuria y insulto	Offense and insult
Mozo fraudulento	Fraudulent or deceitful worker
Oposición a autoridad	Disobeying authority
Parricidio	Parricide
Prisión arbitraria	Arbitrary imprisonment
Prostitución clandestina	Clandestine prostitution
Rapto	Abduction
Rebelión	Rebellion
Resistencia y desobediencia	Resistance and disobedience
Riña	Fighting
Robo	Robbery
Sedición	Sedition
Suicidio	Suicide
Testimonio falso	False testimony
Turbación grave del orden público	Serious disturbance of public order
Vagancia	Vagrancy
Violación	Rape

Appendix 4. Selected crimes, Chimaltenango, 1900–1944

Crime*	1900	'01	'02	'03	'04	'05	'06	'07	'08	'09	'10	'11	'12	'13	'14	'15	'16	'17	'18
Abandono de hogar	0	0	0	1	0	0	0	0	0	0	0	0	0	0	1	0	0	3	0
Abandono de menor	0	1	0	0	0	0	0	1	0	0	0	0	0	0	0	0	0	0	0
Aborto	0	1	0	0	0	0	1	0	0	0	0	0	1	1	1	0	0	0	0
Adulterio	5	4	6	5	4	2	7	7	0	2	1	2	4	2	3	0	3	0	3
Agresión	1	3	2	14	4	3	6	1	7	7	7	2	5	4	3	1	2	1	0
Allanamiento	12	6	9	11	11	9	11	8	10	5	4	9	3	11	7	0	8	9	4
Amenaza	5	3	3	6	2	7	10	9	8	8	4	5	7	4	3	4	4	6	5
Asesinato	0	0	3	0	2	7	1	6	5	6	3	3	2	4	2	2	1	2	7
Atentado	3	6	4	6	7	4	5	2	3	5	1	4	2	3	0	2	2	3	3
Calumnia	1	4	5	1	0	1	2	0	1	0	0	2	1	2	1	0	1	1	3
Defraudación, licores	70	49	32	25	15	0	6	11	2	7	1	9	5	4	1	5	5	10	11
Ebriedad	—	—	—	—	—	—	—	—	—	—	—	—	—	—	—	—	—	—	—
Escándolo	—	—	—	1	—	—	—	—	—	—	—	—	—	—	—	—	—	—	—
Estafa	5	7	7	11	5	1	3	7	7	5	5	4	3	3	2	4	6	3	2
Estupro	2	0	2	1	2	1	5	2	4	2	3	4	2	2	3	4	2	6	2
Golpe, heridas	66	55	77	58	61	36	57	57	53	66	55	79	48	64	72	55	26	48	26
Homicidio	9	10	7	10	11	9	7	8	9	5	10	8	15	15	6	3	4	4	6
Hurto	36	37	42	39	45	58	23	28	25	18	23	33	31	25	22	33	18	34	19
Incendio	1	1	1	1	4	0	1	0	1	2	2	3	4	2	1	0	2	3	0
Infanticidio	1	1	0	0	1	0	0	1	0	1	0	1	1	0	0	1	0	1	0
Injuria y insulto	11	4	18	7	10	4	11	18	12	11	7	4	8	7	5	9	4	21	7
Oposición a autoridad	1	1	0	0	0	0	3	0	1	1	0	0	0	0	2	0	0	0	0
Parricidio	0	0	0	1	0	0	0	0	0	1	0	0	0	0	0	0	0	0	0
Prisión arbitraria	1	0	1	2	0	1	0	1	3	0	0	3	0	0	0	2	1	0	0

'19	'20–'23	'25	'26	'27	'28	'29	'32	'33	'34	'35	'36	'37	'38	'39	'40	'41	'42	'43	'44	'32–'44	Total
0	1	2	1	1	0	0	0	2	4	1	8	7	5	2	4	2	5	4	9	53	63
0	0	0	—	—	—	—	—	—	0	0	0	0	1	0	1	2	2	0	3	9	11
0	0	0	0	0	0	0	1	0	0	0	0	0	0	0	0	0	4	0	1	6	11
1	2	0	4	4	0	0	0	0	1	0	1	2	0	2	4	4	1	9	0	24	95
4	0	2	10	—	44	3	27	0	0	4	17	0	—	—	—	—	—	—	—	48	184
6	2	2	4	—	1	4	0	0	0	0	1	0	1	1	2	2	4	10	3	24	190
3	0	7	9	—	7	5	0	0	5	4	3	7	—	—	—	—	—	—	—	19	153
0	0	0	2	—	1	0	2	0	0	5	5	4	—	—	—	—	—	—	—	16	75
1	0	9	0	—	—	0	0	—	—	—	—	—	—	—	—	—	—	—	—	—	75
0	0	8	0	—	0	0	0	—	2	0	0	0	—	—	—	—	—	—	—	2	36
3	4	19	0	—	0	11	23	19	1	125	315	164	232	167	107	108	16	26	6	1,309	1,614
—	—	59	0	0	965	82	126	81	26	15	30	45	22	55	149	93	88	69	28	827	1,933
—	—	22	0	—	19	0	7	1	—	4	0	9	20	4	37	12	20	50	33	197	239
2	0	7	0	—	0	2	3	8	0	6	5	6	—	—	—	—	—	—	—	28	129
1	1	3	1	—	0	0	0	0	0	0	0	1	0	0	1	0	2	2	0	6	61
22	4	48	40	—	11	12	39	7	1	15	25	12	—	—	—	—	—	—	—	99	1,295
1	2	12	3	—	3	0	2	—	—	2	2	2	—	—	—	—	—	—	—	8	185
15	2	6	10	—	60	3	39	18	4	11	23	23	—	—	—	—	—	—	—	118	803
0	0	0	0	—	0	0	1	—	1	—	—	—	—	—	—	—	—	—	—	2	31
1	0	0	0	—	0	0	2	0	0	0	0	0	0	1	0	0	0	0	0	3	13
4	1	26	0	—	8	3	5	0	3	17	30	34	16	32	41	8	27	46	44	303	523
1	0	0	—	—	—	—	—	—	—	—	—	—	—	—	—	—	—	—	—	—	10
0	0	0	—	—	—	—	1	—	0	0	0	0	—	—	—	—	—	—	—	1	3
0	1	—	—	—	—	—	—	—	—	—	—	—	—	—	—	—	—	—	—	—	16

(continued)

Appendix 4. (*continued*)

Crime*	1900	'01	'02	'03	'04	'05	'06	'07	'08	'09	'10	'11	'12	'13	'14	'15	'16	'17	'18
Prostitución clandestina	—	—	—	—	—	—	—	—	—	—	—	—	—	—	—	—	—	—	—
Rapto	9	12	11	9	3	1	5	3	8	8	2	9	12	13	8	11	2	11	4
Riña	0	2	2	0	0	1	0	1	2	1	1	3	1	1	0	4	3	2	1
Robo	0	0	0	2	9	1	1	6	3	0	11	5	6	4	3	7	7	11	4
Suicidio	0	0	0	0	0	0	0	0	1	1	0	0	0	0	0	0	1	0	0
Testimonio falso	1	1	0	1	1	0	0	0	0	0	0	0	0	0	1	0	0	1	0
Vagancia	—	—	—	—	—	—	—	—	—	—	—	—	—	—	—	—	—	—	—
Violación	2	1	1	1	3	0	2	4	6	5	5	1	5	5	7	3	5	3	3
Total	242	209	233	213	200	146	167	181	171	167	145	193	166	176	154	150	107	183	110

Sources: Data for 1900–1923 are based on department court trials; the Chimaltenango crime index grouped data for 1920–1923. AGCA, *índice* 116, Chimaltenango department court, 1900–1925. Data for 1925–1944 are based on arrests recorded in Policía Nacional, *Memorias*. 1925–1944.

Note: A dash (—) indicates that no data were available.

No data were available for 1924 or 1930–1931.

The column of 1932–1944 subtotals is provided to show crimes recorded during the approximate years of Ubico's rule.

*English translations of crime categories

Abandono de hogar	Abandoning the home
Abandono de menor	Abandoning a child
Aborto	Abortion
Adulterio	Adultery
Agresión	Assault
Allanamiento	Home invasion
Amenaza	Threat
Amenaza y coacción	Threat and coercion
Asesinato	Murder
Atentado	Assault
Calumnia	Slander
Corrupción de menor	Corrupting a minor
Defraudación al Fisco en el ramo de licores y contrabando	Defrauding the Treasury of alcohol revenue
Ebriedad	Inebriation, drunkenness
Escándolo	Scandal
Estafa	Deceit
Estupro	Statutory rape
Golpe, heridas y lesiones	Assault, with injuries
Homicidio	Homicide
Hurto	Theft
Incendio	Arson
Infanticidio	Infanticide

'19	'20-'23	'25	'26	'27	'28	'29	'32	'33	'34	'35	'36	'37	'38	'39	'40	'41	'42	'43	'44	'32-'44	Total
—	—	7	0	—	1	2	5	8	0	2	14	11	—	—	—	—	—	—	—	40	50
3	2	3	0	—	0	0	7	—	3	2	3	3	4	—	4	0	2	1	2	31	180
0	0	7	44	—	160	32	48	59	16	23	20	26	16	38	47	40	68	71	96	568	836
0	0	8	4	—	2	5	29	10	4	9	0	9	0	0	0	0	0	0	0	61	160
0	0	0	0	—	0	0	0	0	0	0	0	0	0	0	0	0	0	0	0	—	3
0	0	0	—	—	0	—	0	0	—	0	3	0	—	—	—	—	—	—	—	3	9
—	—	19	0	—	15	13	35	8	4	6	17	18	6	9	127	45	198	88	62	623	670
4	—	5	0	—	9	0	4	—	2	4	3	2	2	6	6	5	3	0	2	39	119
72	22	281	132	5	1,306	177	406	221	77	255	525	385	325	317	530	321	440	376	289	4,467	9,775

Infracción a disposiciones de ornato	Infraction against forced-labor regulations
Infracción a disposiciones sanitarias	Infraction against sanitation regulations
Injuria y insulto	Offense and insult
Mozo fraudulento	Fraudulent or deceitful worker
Oposición a autoridad	Disobeying authority
Parricidio	Parricide
Prisión arbitraria	Arbitrary imprisonment
Prostitución clandestina	Clandestine prostitution
Rapto	Abduction
Rebelión	Rebellion
Resistencia y desobediencia	Resistance and disobedience
Riña	Fighting
Robo	Robbery
Sedición	Sedition
Suicidio	Suicide
Testimonio falso	False testimony
Turbación grave del orden público	Serious disturbance of public order
Vagancia	Vagrancy
Violación	Rape

Appendix 5. Sample of bootlegging cases, Chimaltenango, 1900–1925

Year	Number of cases	Defendant		Ruling
		Gender	Ethnicity	
1900	6	5F/M/?	2I/3L/2?	3CO/4NA
1901	3	3F	I/L/?	2CO/NA
1902	4	2F/M/?	2I/L/?	2CO/NA/ES
1903	1	M	I	NA
1907	4	3F/2M	3I/L/?	CO/4AB
1909	1	2M	2?	2CO
1912	1	M	I	AB
1916	2	4F	L/3?	CO/3NA
1917	1	F	?	CO
1918	1	F	L	CO
1921	2	2M	2L	CO/NR
Total	26	19F/10M/2?	10I/11L/10?	14CO/NR/10NA/5AB/ES

Source: AGCA, *índice* 116, Chimaltenango department court, 1900–1925.
Note: Some cases had multiple defendants and/or rulings.
Key: ? = unknown
Gender: F = female, M = male
Ethnicity: I = indígena, L = ladino
Ruling: AB = absolved, ES = escaped, CO = convicted, NA = not apprehended,
NR = no ruling

Appendix 6. Sample of economic-crime cases in municipal courts, 1925–1944

| | | Defendant | | | |
| | Number | | | | |
Town/year	of cases	Gender	Ethnicity	Defense	Ruling
Patzicía					
1935	1	F	I	CF	CO
1936	3	3F	3I	3?	3CO
1937	1	F	L	?	?
1941	1	F	L	CF	CO
1942	3	3F	1/2L	3R	3CO
1943	7	6F/3M	8I/L	5R/4?	7CO/AB/?
Subtotal	16	15F/3M	13I/5L	2CF/8R/8?	16CO/AB/2?
San Martín					
1925	5	32F/6M	36I/2L	25CF/13?	38CO
1933	1	F	I	R	?
1935	5	6F	5I/L	5CF/R	5CO/?
1944	3	2F/M	2I/L	3?	2CO/AB
Subtotal	14	41F/7M	44I/4L	30CF/2R/16?	45CO/AB/2?
Sololá					
1941	1	M	I	?	CO
Sample total	31	56F/11M	58I/9L	32CF/10R/25?	61CO/2AB/4?

Sources: AGCA, JP-C, 1925–1944; AMP, 1905–1944.
Note: Some cases had multiple defendants, defenses, and/or rulings.
Key: ? = unknown
Gender: F = female, M = male
Ethnicity: I = *indígena*, L = ladino
Defense: CF = confessed, R = refuted
Ruling: AB = absolved, CO = convicted

Appendix 7. Reproductive-crime cases, Chimaltenango, 1900–1925

| Crime/year | Number of cases | Defendant | | Defense | Ruling |
		Gender	Ethnicity		
Infanticide					
1900	1	F	L	R	CO
1904	1	M	I	R	CO
1907	1	F/M	2I	2ST	2AB
1909	1	2F	I/L	2R	2AB
1911	1	M	I	E	CO
1912	1	F	I	ST	CO
1914	1	2M	2I	2R	2AB
1915	1	M	L	R	AB
1917	1	M	I	R	AB
1919	1	2F	2L	2R	2CO
Subtotal	10	7F/7M	9I/5L	3ST/E/10R	6CO/8AB
Abortion					
1901	1	F	I	R	AB
1906	1	M	L	?	?
1912	1	M	I	R	NR
1913	1	F	I	R	AB
1914	1	?	?	?	?
Subtotal	5	2F/2M/?	3I/L/?	3R/2?	CO/2AB/2?
Total	15	9F/9M/?	12I/6L/?	3ST/E/13R/2?	7CO/10AB/2?

Source: AGCA, *índice* 116, Chimaltenango department court, 1900–1925.
Note: Some cases had multiple defendants, defenses, and/or rulings.
Key: ? = unknown
Gender: F = female, M = male
Ethnicity: I = indígena, L = ladino
Defense: CF = confessed, E = inebriated, R = refuted, ST = stillborn
Ruling: AB = absolved, CO = convicted, NR = no ruling

Appendix 8. Sample of domestic violence cases, 1900–1944

Court/year	Number of cases	Defendant			
		Gender	Ethnicity	Literacy	Profession
Chimaltenango[1]					
1901	1	M	?	?	?
1902	2	2M	2I	NL/?	J/?
1903	1	M	I	?	?
1907	1	M	I	?	?
1909	1	M	I	?	?
1914	1	M	I	?	?
1917	2	2M	2L	NL/?	A/J
1929	1	M	I	NL	J
Subtotal	10	10M	7I/2L/?	3NL/7?	3J/A/6?
Patzicía[2]					
1916	8	8M	6I/L/?	7NL/?	2J/C/A/4?
1928	3	3M	2I/L	3NL	J/A/?
1929	7	7M	5I/L/?	6NL/?	6J/A
1935	4	4M	3I/L	3NL/LT	3J/?
1936	4	4M	3I/L	4NL	3J/A
1941	1	M	I	NL	?
1942	4	4M	4I	4NL	4J
1943	6	6M	5I/?	4NL/LT/?	3J/A/2C
Subtotal	37	37M	29I/5L/3?	32NL/2LT/3?	22J/5A/3C/7?
San Martín[2]					
1925	1	M	I	NL	A
1926	10	F/9M	5I/L/4?	9NL/?	10?
1927	2	F/4M	5I	5NL	MO/4?
1931	6	6M	4I/2?	5NL/?	6?
1933	6	6M	5I/?	5NL/?	3J/3?
1935	6	6M	4I/L/?	5NL/LT	5J/?
Subtotal	31	2F/32M	24I/2L/8?	30NL/LT/3?	8J/MO/A/24?
Sample total	78	79M/2F	60I/9L/12?	65NL/3LT/13?	33J/7A/3C/MO/37?

Sources: AGCA, *índice* 116, Chimaltenango 1900–1925; AGCA, JP-C, 1925–1944; AMP, 1905–1944.
[1]Department court
[2]Municipal court
Note: Some cases had multiple defendants, defenses, and/or rulings.

| | Victim | | | |
Gender	Ethnicity	Literacy	Defense	Ruling
F	I	?	?	?
F/M	2I	2?	R/?	CO/?
F	I	NL	E	?
F	I	?	R	?
F	I	NL	FL	?
F	I	NL	R	NR
2F	2I	NL/?	2R	2NR
F	I	NL	R	NR
9F/M	10I	5NL/5?	6R/E/FL/2?	CO/4NR/5?
8F	7I/L	8?	R/2CF/5?	6CO/2?
3F	2I/L	3?	CF/E/?	3CO
7F	5I/L/?	7?	7CF	7CO
4F	3I/?	4?	4CF	4CO
4F	2I/L/?	4?	R/3?	4CO
F	?	?	CF	CO
5F	5I	5?	2R/CF/?	4CO
6F	6I	3NL/3?	3R/E/2?	5CO/?
38F	30I/4L/4?	3NL/35?	7R/16CF/2E/12?	34CO/3?
F	I	LT	CF	CO
10F	4I/5?	6NL/4?	10?	10?
2F	I/?	NL/?	5?	2CO/3?
6F	4I/2?	4NL/2?	6?	6?
6F	5I/?	NL/LT/4?	R/5?	CO/5?
6F	5I/?	2NL/4?	6CF	5CO/?
31F	20I/10?	14NL/2LT/15?	R/7CF/26?	9CO/25?
78F/M	60I/4L/15?	22NL/2LT/55?	14R/23CF/FL/3E/40?	44CO/4NR/33?

Key: ? = unknown
Gender: F = female, M = male
Ethnicity: I = indígena, L = ladino
Literacy: LT = literate, NL = not literate
Profession: A = agricultor, C = comerciante, J = jornalero, MO = molendera
Defense: CF = confessed, E = inebriated, FL = fled, R = refuted
Ruling: CO = convicted, NR = no ruling

Appendix 9. Sample of violence cases with female defendants, 1900–1944

Court/year	Number of cases	Gender	Ethnicity	Literacy	Profession
			Defendant		
Chimaltenango[1]					
1902	1	F	I	NL	T
1914	1	F	I	?	?
1919	1	F	I	NL	?
Subtotal	3	3F	3I	2NL/?	T/2?
Patzicía[2]					
1916	3	4F	2L/2?	4NL	4?
1928	1	F	?	NL	?
1929	3	3F	3I	3NL	MO/2?
1935	2	2F	2I	2NL	2?
1941	1	F	L	NL	?
1942	2	4F	3I/L	NL/LT/?	C/3?
Subtotal	12	15F	8I/4L/3?	13NL/ LT/?	MO/C/13?
San Martín[2]					
1926	3	4F	I/L/2?	2NL/2?	4?
1933	3	4F/2M	4I/2?	4NL/2?	6?
1935	2	2F	I/?	2NL	2?
1937	1	F	L	NL	?
Subtotal	9	11F/2M	6I/2L/5?	9NL/4?	13?
Sample total	24	29F/2M	17I/6L/8?	24NL/LT/6?	2MO/T/C/27?

Sources: AGCA, *índice* 116, Chimaltenango, 1900–1925; AGCA, JP-C 1925–1944; AMP, 1905–1944.
Notes: Some cases had multiple defendants, victims, and/or rulings.
[1]Department court
[2]Municipal court
[3]Since the Patzicía municipal judge twice (1929 and 1935) convicted the accuser/victim of assault because she fought back, there are two more convictions than perpetrators for these cases.
Key: ? = unknown
Gender: F = female, M = male
Ethnicity: I = *indígena*, L = ladino
Literacy: LT = literate, NL = not literate
Profession: C = *comerciante*, MO = *molendera*, T = *tortillera*
Defense: CF = confessed, R = refuted
Ruling: CO = convicted, NA = not apprehended, NR = no ruling

	Victim			
Gender	Ethnicity	Literacy	Defense	Ruling
F	I	?	CF	NR
F	I	NL	?	NA
F	I	NL	CF	NR
3F	3I	2NL/?	2CF/?	2NR/NA
4F	4I	4?	4?	2CO/2?
F	I	?	CF	CO
3F	3I	3?	3CF	4CO[3]
F/M	2I	NL/?	2CF	3CO
F	I	?	R	CO
F	I	?	4CF	4CO
11F/M	12I	NL/11?	10CF/R/4?	15CO/2?
3F	3L	3NL	4?	4?
3F	3I	3?	6?	6?
2F	2I	2?	2CF	2CO
F	L	LT	CF	CO
9F	5I/4L	3NL/LT/5?	3CF/10?	3CO/10?
23F/M	20I/4L	6NL/LT/17?	15CF/R/15?	18CO/2NR/NA/12?

Appendix 10. Sample of defamation cases, 1900–1943

| Court/year | Number of cases | Defendant | | | |
		Gender	Ethnicity	Literacy	Profession
Chimaltenango[1]					
1900	1	F	I	?	?
1901	1	F	L	LT	S
1902	1	F	I	NL	?
1907	1	2M	2L	2?	2?
1913	2	F/2M	2I/L	3NL	2J/?
1917	1	2F/M	3L	3?	3?
1940	1	F	L	?	?
Subtotal	8	7F/5M	4I/8L	4NL/LT/7?	S/2J/9?
Patzicía[2]					
1916	1	2F	2I	2?	2?
1923	1	F	L	?	?
1927	4	4F	2I/2L	3NL/?	4?
1928	7	4F/4M	3I/3L/2?	4NL/4?	4J/4?
1929	8	8F/1M	3I/6L	6NL/LT/2?	9?
1934	1	M	?	?	D
1935	2	2F	2I	2NL	MO/D
1936	1	F	L	NL	?
1937	1	2F	2L	2?	2?
1938	1	M	I	?	?
1941	3	2F/M	2I/L	2NL/LT	J/2?
1942	4	2F/2M	2I/L/?	3NL/?	J/3?
1943	11	6F/6M	6I/6L	7NL/2LT/3?	3J/2CH/2A/5?
Subtotal	45	34F/16M	23I/23L/4?	28NL/4LT/18?	9J/2D/2CH/2A/MO/34?
San Martín[2]					
1925	1	F	I	?	?
1926	3	3F/2M	3I/L/?	5?	5?
1927	1	F	L	?	?
1931	4	4F/2M	5I/?	6?	6?
1933	5	6F/2M	8I	8?	8?
1935	20	6F/14M	18I/L/?	19NL/?	11J/9?
1937	1	F/M	2L	2?	2?
Subtotal	35	22F/21M	35I/5L/3?	19NL/24?	11J/32?
Sample total	88	63F/42M	62I/36L/7?	51NL/5LT/49?	22J/S/2D/MO/2CH/2A/75?

Sources: AGCA, *índice* 116, Chimaltenango, 1900–1925; AGCA, JP-C 1925–1944; AMP, 1905–1944.
Notes: Some cases had multiple defendants, plaintiffs, and/or rulings.

Plaintiff					
Gender	Ethnicity	Literacy	Profession	Defense	Ruling
F	L	?	?	?	?
F	I	?	?	?	?
F	I	NL	?	R	AB
M	L	?	?	2?	2?
F/M	I/L	LT	A/?	3?	2AB/?
F	L	LT	?	3R	3?
M	L	?	T	?	RL
5F/3M	3I/5L	NL/3LT/4?	A/T/6?	4R/8?	3AB/RL/8?
F	L	?	?	2?	2?
M	L	?	?	?	?
3?/M	L/3?	LT/3?	3?/J	3CF/R	3CO/?
4F/3M	2I/5L	LT/6?	C/6?	2CF/2CM/2R/2?	8CO
6F/2M	I/6L/?	2NL/6?	8?	5CF/3R/?	9CO
F	?	?	AU	?	?
2F	2I	2NL	MO/D	2CF	2CO
M	?	?	AU	CF	CO
M	?	?	AU	2?	2?
M	I	?	AU	?	?
3F	2I/L	3?	3?	3CF	3CO
3F/?	3I/L	2NL/2?	4?	2CF/R/?	3CO/AB
7F/5M	7I/5L	4NL/8?	3J/9?	2CF/8R/2E	11C/AB
27F/15M/4?	18I/21L/7?	10NL/2LT/34?	4J/C/2D/MO/4AU/34?	20CF/2CM/15R/2E/10?	40CO/2AB/8?
F	I	NL	?	?	?
3F	I/2L	2NL/?	3?	5?	1CO/4?
F	L	NL	?	?	?
4F	2I/L/?	2NL/2?	4?	6?	6?
5F	5I	5NL	5?	8?	8?
5F/13M/2?	9I/7L/4?	2NL/18?	20?	18CF/2R	20CO
F	L	?	?	2?	2?
20F/13M/2?	18I/12L/5?	13NL/22?	35?	18CF/2R/23?	21CO/22?
52F/31M/6?	39I/38L/12?	24NL/5LT/60?	4J/A/T/C/MO/2D/AU/75?	38CF/21R/2CM/2E/41?	61CO/5AB/RL38?

(continued)

[1]Department court
[2]Municipal court
Key: ? = unknown
Gender: F = female, M = male
Ethnicity: I = indígena, L = ladino
Literacy: LT = literate, NL = not literate
Profession: A = *agricultor*, AU = authority, C = *comerciante*, CH = *chauffeur*, D = domestic servant, J = *jornalero*, MO = *molendera*, S = school director, T = tailor
Defense: CF = confessed, E = inebriated, R = refuted
Ruling: AB = absolved, CM = commuted, CO = convicted, RL = returned to lower court

Notes

Introduction

1. Archivo General de Centro América (hereafter AGCA), *índice* (index) 116, Chimaltenango 1914, *legajo* (*leg.*, dossier, bundle) 15d, *expediente* (*exp.*, proceeding) 19. Unless otherwise noted, all translations are mine.

2. Ibid.

3. Ibid. The peso was the official Guatemalan currency until 1925, when the José María Orellana government replaced it with the quetzal in an effort to halt currency devaluation. The peso continued to be used in the central highlands into the 1930s until the Jorge Ubico administration abolished it.

4. Comaroff, foreword, x.

5. Weber, *Economy and Society*; Gramsci, *Selections*.

6. Handy, "Chicken Thieves," 533, 555; Forster, *Time of Freedom*.

7. Merry, "Law as Fair," 177.

8. Christiansen, *Disobedience*.

9. Ixki'ch, 6/27/01, Comalapa. Unless otherwise indicated by a name in parentheses, I conducted all oral history interviews. All translations of oral history interviews are mine.

10. Black, *Behavior of Law*; Black, *Sociological Justice*.

11. Bliss, *Compromised Positions*; Stern, *Secret History*.

12. *Indio* is a derogatory term informed by non-indigenous Guatemalans' perceptions of *indígenas* as dirty, ignorant, lazy, and retrograde.

13. García Granados, *Evolución sociológica*, 25; Carey, "*Indigenismo* and Guatemalan History"; Grandin, *Blood of Guatemala*, 91, 97–98, 127–128, 141–142; C. Smith, "Race-Class-Gender Ideology," 725; Reeves, *Ladinos with Ladinos*, 156.

14. Gudmundson and Lindo-Fuentes, *Central America*; Sieder, "Customary Law," 100; McCreery, *Rural Guatemala*.

15. Reeves, *Ladinos with Ladinos*, 156; Carey, "Mayan Soldier-Citizens," 142–143, 151–152.

16. Wertheimer, "Gloria's Story," 392–393; Blum, "Public Welfare"; Blum, *Do-*

mestic Economies; Díaz, "Women"; Hünefeldt, *Liberalism in the Bedroom*; Dore, "One Step Forward."

17. Deutsch, "Gender and Sociopolitical Change"; Díaz, "Women"; Saladino García, "Función social"; Black, *Limits of Gender Domination*, 258.

18. Grandin, *Blood of Guatemala.*

19. Forster, *Time of Freedom*, 72.

20. Grandin, *Blood of Guatemala*; Reeves, *Ladinos with Ladinos.*

21. Foucault, *Discipline and Punish*, 26–27; Foucault, *Power/Knowledge*, 134–165; Wolf and Hansen, "Caudillo Politics."

22. For the most part I adhere to these conventions throughout the book when identifying women by their last names.

23. Stavig, *Amor y violencia*; Ericastilla Samayoa and Jiménez Chacón, "'A riesgo de perder'"; Few, *Women Who Live Evil Lives*; Komisaruk, "Rape Narratives"; Rodríguez Sáenz, "'Tiyita bea'"; Rodríguez Sáenz, *Hijas*; Rodríguez Sáenz, "Divorcio y violencia"; Palomo de Lewin, "Vida conyugal"; Lavrin, ed., *Sexuality and Marriage*; Seed, *To Love*; Stern, *Secret History*; Christiansen, *Disobedience*; Chambers, *From Subjects to Citizens*; Shumway, *Case of the Ugly Suitor*; Caulfield, Chambers, and Putnam, eds., *Honor.*

24. For the colonial era see, for example, Few, *Women Who Live Evil Lives*; Stern, *Peru's Indian Peoples*; Stern, *Secret History*; Schroeder, Wood, and Haskett, eds., *Indian Women*; and Taylor, *Drinking*. For the national era see Christiansen, *Disobedience*; Díaz, *Female Citizens*, 72–73, 167; Findlay, "Courtroom Tales"; Hünefeldt, *Liberalism in the Bedroom*; and O'Connor, *Gender.*

25. Guy, *Sex and Danger*; Lauderdale Graham, "Slavery's Impasse"; McCreery, "'This Life of Misery'"; K. Ruggiero, "Honor"; Besse, "Crimes of Passion."

26. Butler, *Psychic Life of Power*, 12–18.

27. J. W. Scott, "Gender"; J. W. Scott, *Gender*; A. Burton, "History Practice," 149. For a cogent critique of historians' tendency to approach patriarchy as a conclusion, see Gauderman, *Women's Lives.*

28. Restall, *Maya World*, 121–140. Schroeder, Wood, and Haskett, eds., *Indian Women*, especially Haskett, "Activist or Adulteress?"; Kellogg, "From Parallel and Equivalent"; Offutt, "Women's Voices from the Frontier"; and Sousa, "Women and Crime." Gosner and Kanter, eds., *Women, Power, and Resistance*, especially Few, "Women, Religion, and Power"; Kanter, "Native Female Land Tenure"; and Restall, "'He Wished It in Vain.'"

29. Kanter, "Native Female Land Tenure"; Chambers, *From Subjects to Citizens*; Christiansen, *Disobedience*; Caulfield, "Getting into Trouble," 163; O'Connor, *Gender*, xiv; Black, *Limits of Gender Domination.*

30. Dore, *Myths of Modernity*, 4–5; Dore and Molyneux, eds., *Hidden Histories*, especially Dore, "Property, Households, and Public Regulation"; Guy, "Parents before the Tribunals"; and Vaughn, "Modernizing Patriarchy."

31. Saladino García, "La función social"; Dore, "One Step Forward," 15; Hünefeldt, *Liberalism in the Bedroom*, 14; Díaz, "Women"; Aguirre and Salvatore, "Introduction," 23; Parker, "'Gentlemanly Responsibility,'" 112; Piccato, "Politics," 346.

32. República de Guatemala, *Código civil . . . 1877*, xii.

33. Ibid., for example, articles 151, 153, and 286.

34. Sieder, "'Paz,'" 300; Forster, *Time of Freedom*, 35–36; Gudmundson and Lindo-Fuentes, *Central America*, 118–120; Putnam, Chambers, and Caulfield, "Introduction," 7; Piccato, *City of Suspects*, 56–58.

35. Premo, *Children of the Father King*; Dore, *Myths of Modernity*, 60; Christiansen, *Disobedience*, 1–4; O'Connor, *Gender*, xiv–xv; Stern, *Secret History*, 253, 269, 323.

36. Díaz, *Female Citizens*, 72–73, 167; Findlay, "Courtroom Tales"; Christiansen, *Disobedience*.

37. AGCA, Jefatura Política Chimaltenango (henceforth JP-C) 1926, February 8, 1926.

38. Wagley, *Social and Religious Life*, 101. Fearful of this fate, Kaqchikel women advised each other to rub chilis on jail locks in the belief it would prevent their incarceration. Ixpril, 7/1/01, Poaquil.

39. Ixpril, 7/1/01, Poaquil.

40. Wisdom, *Chorti Indians*, 214.

41. Ix'achib'il, 8/1/05, Comalapa (Ixk'at).

42. Ixpop, 8/1/05, Comalapa (Ixk'at).

43. Foucault, *Discipline and Punish*, 9–10, 26, 59, 90, 108–109.

44. See Chambers, *From Subjects to Citizens*; de la Fuente, *Children of Facundo*; Guardino, *Peasants*; Mallon, *Peasant and Nation*; Walker, *Smoldering Ashes*.

45. For example, AGCA, Jefatura Política, Sacatepéquez (hereafter JP-S), 1928, cartas de Santiago Zamora municipality, February 11, May 12, June 9, 1928.

46. Reeves, *Ladinos with Ladinos*, 141–155; Grandin, *Blood of Guatemala*, 107–108; Carmack, *Rebels of Highland Guatemala*, 194–195, 204–205; Tax, *Penny Capitalism*, 10; La Farge and Byers, *Year Bearer's People*, 14–15, 23, 83; Rodas and Esquit, *Élite ladina*; Esquit, *Otros poderes*; Esquit, "Superación del indígena." The shift of power from indigenous to ladino municipalities was not irreversible, however; in at least one instance the national government disbanded a ladino municipality. Reeves, "From Household to Nation," 58.

47. Martínez Peláez, *Patria del criollo*, l; Grandin, *Blood of Guatemala*, 137; McCreery, *Rural Guatemala*, 311; Carey, *Our Elders*, 212–216; R. Adams, *Crucifixion by Power*, 176; Handy, *Gift of the Devil*, 99.

48. Wagley, *Economics of a Guatemalan Village*, 13; Gillin, *Culture of Security*, 73–74; Carmack, *Rebels of Highland Guatemala*, 194–195.

49. Ixtz'inik'an, 6/2/98, Tecpán.

50. La Farge and Byers, *Year Bearer's People*, 82; Carmack, *Rebels of Highland Guatemala*, 194–195; Grandin, *Blood of Guatemala*, 154; K. Warren, *Symbolism of Subordination*, 148–151; Handy, *Gift of the Devil*, 99; Little-Siebold, "Guatemalanist Ethnography."

51. Observing the system of indigenous *principales*, or leaders, in a Guatemalan community in the 1940s, John Gillin was convinced that "if the intendentes or Ubico had understood it, they would have considered it subversive." *Culture of Security*, 74.

52. Grandin, *Blood of Guatemala*, 157.

53. For example, *La Gaceta: Revista de Policía y Variedades* (henceforth *La Gaceta*), January 22, 1933.

54. Roseberry, "Hegemony."

55. Foucault, *Discipline and Punish*.

56. J. C. Scott, *Domination*; J. W. Scott, *Gender*; Wolf, *Peasant Wars*; Taylor, *Drinking*; R. Scott, *Slave Emancipation*; Mallon, *Defense of Community*; Mallon, *Peasant and Nation*; Stern, ed., *Resistance*.

57. Hobsbawm, "Peasants and Politics," 13 (quote); J. C. Scott, *Domination*; J. C. Scott, *Weapons of the Weak*; McCreery, "'This Life of Misery'"; K. Ruggiero, "Honor"; Besse, "Crimes of Passion"; Forster, "Violent and Violated."

58. G. Joseph, "On the Trail"; J. C. Scott, "Resistance," 452; Taylor, "Between Global Process and Local Knowledge," 142; Stern, "New Approaches," 10–11; Beezley, Martin, and French, eds., *Rituals of Rule*.

59. Gudmundson, "Firewater." See also Abu-Lughod, "Romance of Resistance."

60. Stern, *Secret History*, 301 (quote); K. Warren, *Indigenous Movements*, 191; R. Burton, *Afro-Creole*, 8.

61. Cited in Cruz-Malavé, "'What a Tangled Web!,'" 234.

62. Sahlins, "On the Anthropology of Modernity," 52.

63. Sahlins, "What Is Anthropological Enlightenment?" xvi.

64. Ibid., xvi.

65. Handy, *Gift of the Devil*; C. Smith, ed., *Guatemalan Indians*; McCreery, *Rural Guatemala*.

66. Foucault, *Power/Knowledge*, 1; Foucault, *Discipline and Punish*, 63, 65, 67; G. Joseph, "On the Trail," 21.

67. Foucault, *Discipline and Punish*, 104–105, 113, 116.

68. Carey, *Engendering Mayan History*, 177–206; Carey, *Our Elders*, 154–194; Carey, "Mayan Soldier-Citizens."

69. Rendon, "Gobierno de Manuel Estrada Cabrera"; Grieb, *Guatemalan Caudillo*; Little-Siebold, "Guatemala and the Dream," 123–124.

70. Corrigan, "State Formation," xvii, emphasis in the original.

71. Wells and Joseph, *Summer of Discontent*, 15; Gramsci, *Selections*, 195–196, 246–247.

72. Palacios, "Judges," 83–84, 100; Gotkowitz, "Trading Insults"; Caulfield, *In Defense of Honor*, 14.

73. Taylor, *Drinking*; Stavig, *Amor y violencia*; Stavig, *World of Tupac Amaru*; Van Young, *Other Rebellion*; Van Young, "Agustín Marroquín"; Vanderwood, *Disorder and Progress*; Stern, ed., *Resistance*; Katz, ed., *Riot*; S. Thompson, *We Alone Will Rule*; Contreras, *Una rebelión indígena*; Martínez Peláez, *Motines de indios*. For critiques of the focus on Latin American rebels see G. Joseph, "On the Trail"; Piccato, *City of Suspects*, 133.

74. Komisaruk, "Rape Narratives," 369, 371; Hames, "Maize-Beer," 353; Muir and Ruggiero, "Introduction"; Hunt, introduction, 14, 22; Darnton, *Great Cat Massacre*; Caulfield, Chambers, and Putnam, eds., *Honor*; Sigal, "Latin America," 1347; Wells and Joseph, *Summer of Discontent*, 13, 16–17.

75. AGCA, *índice* 116, Chimaltenango 1913, *leg.* 14a, *exp.* 16.

76. Aguirre and Salvatore, "Introduction," 22; Taylor, *Drinking*, 60, 73–74, 88; G. Joseph, "On the Trail," 15, 24; Piccato, *City of Suspects*, 6–8, 79; Walker, "Crime," 38; Wells and Joseph, *Summer of Discontent*, 14–15; Scardaville, "Alcohol Abuse," 645–646.

77. Matthew and Oudjik, conclusion, 317.

78. Taylor, *Drinking*, 77.

79. Davis, *Fiction in the Archives*; James, *Doña María's Story*.

80. As Kathryn Burns convincingly argues, notaries often created documents that more accurately reflected their interpretations than what litigants hoped to convey. "Notaries."

81. Watanabe, "With All the Means," 143; Larson, *Trials*, 53; Aguirre and Salvatore, "Introduction," 11; Taylor, *Drinking*, 92.

82. Court translations from Kaqchikel to Spanish were oral, and thus no record of them remains; however, interpreters likely would have translated the Kaqchikel word *k'a* as the Spanish word *pues*. In Kaqchikel and Spanish these words served phatic functions as placeholders that can be translated as "well" when they appear at the beginning of a phrase and "then," "okay?" or "y'know?" at the end of a phrase. At the end of a phrase, *k'a* and *pues* could also be translated as tag questions such as "don't I?" "aren't I?" or "isn't it?" I thank Judie Maxwell for helping me understand these linguistic subtleties.

83. Dirección General de Estadística (hereafter DGE), *Censo . . . 1893*; DGE, *Censo . . . 1921*. Unfortunately, Ubico altered data from the 1940 census, so its figures are unreliable. See C. Smith, "Beyond Dependency Theory," 613n24.

84. DGE, *Censo . . . 1893*; DGE, *Censo . . . 1921*.

85. Ibid.

86. Rodas and Esquit, *Élite ladina*; Carey, *Engendering Mayan History*, 129–158; Carey, "Democracy."

87. DGE, *Censo . . . 1893*; DGE, *Censo . . . 1921*.

88. A. Burton, *Archive Stories*; Trouillot, *Silencing the Past*; Carey, *Engendering Mayan History*.

89. For example, national authorities had denied that the National Police archive existed until officials from the Guatemalan government's human rights office discovered it while inspecting a rat-infested munitions depot in downtown Guatemala City on July 5, 2005. The Catholic Church's Curia archives in Guatemala City have been closed since 2001. Other challenges include misplaced or lost documents at the AGCA and municipal authorities who refused to grant archival access to researchers—foreign and domestic alike. Edgar Esquit, personal communication, August 2008, and Hector Concoha, personal communication, January 7, 2009. The disparate nature of Guatemalan archives challenged this study. Chimaltenango *juzgado de primera instancia* records cover most of the Estrada Cabrera regime but not the Ubico era. As such, municipal archives, particularly Patzicía's, which spanned the first half of the twentieth century, contain the threads that most closely tie this study together across time. Yet here too, limitations arose; the San Martín judicial record offered more documentation after 1925 than before it.

90. Wagley, *Economics of a Guatemalan Village*, 82. In contrast, John Gillin asserts that "Indians . . . recognize no classes among themselves"; *Culture of Security*, 62.

91. McBryde, *Sololá*. Similarly, Oliver La Farge II thanked Guatemalan government ministers and United Fruit Company employees in the foreword to his 1927 study of Jacaltenango, *Year Bearer's People*, ix.

92. Bunzel, *Chichicastenango*, 32.

93. Wagley, *Social and Religious Life*, 7. Other ethnographers of the period similarly warned against generalizing beyond the *municipio*. See McBryde, *Cultural and Historical Geography*, 88–91; Tax, "Municipios."

Chapter 1

1. Handy, "Chicken Thieves," 533, 555; Forster, *Time of Freedom*.
2. Kaji' Tz'ikin, 6/28/08, Sololá, Xajaxac; Wagley, *Social and Religious Life*, 8, 14, 80, 98; Wagley, *Economics of a Guatemalan Village*; Reina, *Law of the Saints*, 264–66; Wiebe, "Widening Paths"; Handy, "Chicken Thieves," 553–555; Gudmundson, "Firewater," 255; Sieder, "Customary Law"; Aguirre and Salvatore, "Introduction," 12; Taylor, *Drinking*, 60.
3. Wagley, *Social and Religious Life*, 80.
4. Gudmundson, "Firewater," 255; Mendelson, "Religion and World-View" (short version), 10–11; Mendelson, "Religion and World-View" (long version), 57, 87–89, 113; Wagley, *Social and Religious Life*, 8. As discussed earlier, in other areas of western Guatemala indigenous authorities retained control of local municipalities in the nineteenth and early twentieth centuries and thus would have presided over judicial proceedings involving indigenous litigants. See, for example, Reeves, *Ladinos with Ladinos*, 141–155; Grandin, *Blood of Guatemala*; Tax, *Penny Capitalism*, 10.
5. Sieder, "Customary Law," 114–115; Handy, "Chicken Thieves," 555.
6. Wells and Joseph, *Summer of Discontent*, 16; Taylor, *Drinking*, 76.
7. Bunzel, *Chichicastenango*, 31.
8. AGCA, JP-C 1935, Libro de Sentencias Económicas (hereafter LSE) abril 1935, April 16, 1935.
9. K. Warren, *Symbolism of Subordination*, 148–151.
10. J. C. Scott, *Domination*, 4.
11. AGCA, JP-C 1935, leg. 79, LSE febrero 1935, February 15, 1935.
12. J. C. Scott, *Domination*; McCreery, *Rural Guatemala*, 288, 291; Putnam, Chambers, and Caulfield, "Introduction," 9.
13. Watanabe, "With All the Means," 148.
14. Pratt, *Imperial Eyes*, 6–7.
15. Aguirre y Salvatore, "Introduction," 3–5; K. Ruggiero, "Passion," 231n7; Komisaruk, "Rape Narratives," 376; Martínez Peláez, *La Patria del Criollo*, 155, 265.
16. Woodward, *Central America*, 103, 108; Grandin, *Blood of Guatemala*, 101; Rodríguez, "Livingston Codes"; Luján Muñoz, "Derecho colonial"; Reeves, *Ladinos with Ladinos*, 1, 2, 45, 149, 173–174; Sieder, "Customary Law," 99; Woodward, *Rafael Carrera*, 53.
17. Sieder, "Customary Law," 99–100; Woodward, *Rafael Carrera*; McCreery, *Rural Guatemala*; Taracena Arriola, "Nación y república," 47.
18. Carmack, "State and Community," 119–120; Grandin, *Blood of Guatemala*, 103–104.
19. República de Guatemala, *Código civil . . . 1877*, 1.
20. República de Guatemala, *Código penal . . . 1889*, i.
21. Ibid., x.

22. AGCA, Correspondencia al Congreso caja número 41232, Carta al Honorable Asamblea Legislativa de San Antonio Aguas Calientes, May 10, 1886.

23. Ibid.

24. McCreery, *Rural Guatemala*, 222; Carey, *Our Elders*, 195–219; Sieder, "Customary Law," 100–101.

25. Rendon, "Gobierno de Manuel Estrada Cabrera," 19.

26. Ibid., 20, 35.

27. Archivo Municipal de Sololá (hereafter AMS), Libro de actas de sesiones municipales del 1–10–35 al 10–6-43 (henceforth Libro 1935–1943), January 23, 1937, and February 9, 1938; Carey, *Our Elders*, 211–212. Ironically, although Ubico projected a populist image with his motorcycle trips to even the most remote communities, the increased bureaucracy during his reign decreased *indígenas'* direct access to him in the capital. Grandin, *Blood of Guatemala*, 195–196.

28. Archivo Municipal de Patzicía (hereafter AMP), Ramo Civil II 1.2, carta de Anselmo y Josefa Mutzutz al jefe político, March 29, 1939; Sieder, "'Paz.'"

29. *La Gaceta*, November 10, 1934.

30. Ibid.

31. Guillén, "Prólogo," 25–27.

32. *La Gaceta*, November 10, 1934.

33. Wolfe, *Everyday Nation-State*.

34. Carey, *Engendering Mayan History*, 183–192; Esquit, "Superación del indígena."

35. Grandin, *Blood of Guatemala*, 185. Interestingly, in Grandin's examples men represented modernity and progress, while K'iche women in their indigenous dress represented tradition and stability. In contrast, Kaqchikel men often presented themselves in photographs as representing and reconciling both tradition and modernity.

36. *La Gaceta*, November 10, 1934.

37. Sahlins, "Anthropology of Modernity," 48; Sahlins, "What Is Anthropological Enlightenment?" vii, x; Sahlins, "Economics of Develop-Man."

38. Buffington, "Introduction," xvi–xvii; Stepan, *"Hour of Eugenics"*; Woodward, *Central America*, 151–175; Piccato, *City of Suspects*; Grandin, *Blood of Guatemala*; McCreery, *Rural Guatemala*; Vanderwood, *Power of God*; Díaz, *Female Citizens*, 176.

39. Gudmundson and Lindo-Fuentes, *Central America*; Reeves, *Ladinos with Ladinos*; Grandin, *Blood of Guatemala*, 167; Sullivan-González, *Piety*.

40. Grandin, *Blood of Guatemala*, 162–164; McCreery, *Rural Guatemala*; Piccato, *City of Suspects*; Little, "Visual Political Economy"; Caulfield, "Getting into Trouble," 166.

41. Dosal, *Power in Transition*, 43, 68–77.

42. Carey, "Empowered through Labor," 509–515; Carey, *Engendering Mayan History*, 92–96; Carmack, "State and Community," 123.

43. Policia Nacional, *Memoria* 1933, 81–82; Policia Nacional, *Memoria* 1937, 22; Carey, *Engendering Mayan History*, 93–94; Carey, "Empowered through Labor," 510; McCreery, "Wage Labor"; McCreery, *Rural Guatemala*, 161–193, 301–322; C. Smith, "Beyond Dependency Theory."

44. Chazkel, *Laws of Chance*, 7.

45. Cruz Salazar, "El ejercito," 96; Ericastilla and Jiménez, "Las clandestinistas," 21; Carmack, "State and Community," 122; Rendon, "Gobierno de Manuel Estrada Cabrera," 15–22; McCreery, *Rural Guatemala*, 179; Opie, "Adios Jim Crow," 141–143; Dosal, *Power in Transition*, 42–51.

46. Ixjo'q, 11/6/97, Comalapa.

47. Carmack, "State and Community," 122; Woodward, *Central America*, 166, 208; McCreery, *Rural Guatemala*, 290, 297; Handy, *Gift of the Devil*, 57; Dosal, *Power in Transition*, 42.

48. Junlajuj Ajpu', 8/2/98, Comalapa; K. Warren, *Symbolism of Subordination*, 149.

49. Junlajuj Imox, 9/15/98, Comalapa. *Ixto* is a pejorative term ladinos used to denigrate *indígenas*.

50. Gudmundson, "Firewater," 274; Dosal, *Power in Transition*, 42.

51. Arévalo Martínez, *Ecce Pericles!*; Wyld Ospina, *Autocrata*; Vidaurre, *Últimos treinta años*; Rendon, "Gobierno de Manuel Estrada Cabrera," 17–18, 34.

52. Esquit, *Otros poderes*, 350; Handy, "Chicken Thieves," 555.

53. Díaz Romeu, "Del régimen de Carlos Herrera," 38; Handy, *Gift of the Devil*; McCreery, *Rural Guatemala*; Woodward, *Central America*, 207–216; Dosal, *Power in Transition*, 42, 52–54.

54. Dosal, *Power in Transition*, 54; Díaz Romeu, "Del régimen de Carlos Herrera," 39.

55. Carey, *Our Elders*, 132–137, 183; Díaz Romeu, "Del régimen de Carlos Herrera," 39–40; Dosal, *Power in Transition*, 55, 58, 63–64; Handy, *Gift of the Devil*, 92.

56. Molyneux, "Twentieth-Century State Formations," 36–37.

57. Junlajuj Imox, 9/15/98, Comalapa; K. Warren, *Symbolism of Subordination*, 149; Carey, *Our Elders*, 195–219; Gudmundson, "Firewater," 276.

58. Ixjo'q, 11/6/97, Comalapa.

59. K. Warren, *Symbolism of Subordination*, 149; Sieder, "'Paz,'" 301; Metz, *Ch'orti'-Maya Survival*, 113.

60. Ixsimïl, 2/9/05, Comalapa (Ix'ey).

61. For example, *Diario de Centro América*, November 5 and 19, 1936.

62. Esquit, "Superación del indígena"; Grandin, *Blood of Guatemala*, 139–140; Grieb, "Gobierno de Jorge Ubico," 45; Carey, "Mayan Soldier-Citizens."

63. Carey, *Our Elders*, Chapter 7; Esquit, "Superación del indígena."

64. *La Gaceta*, July 19, 1935.

65. To refer to individual litigants or suspects (in the case of *La Gaceta*), I use the terms by which they identified themselves or were identified in the record. Although it is clear from the documents that *indígenas* understood themselves to be part of a larger group distinct from ladinos and Creoles, for the most part they tended to identify first with their places of residence. See also Wagley, *Social and Religious Life*, 7. To refer to the ethnic division within Guatemala, I use the terms *indígenas* and "Mayas" to denote indigenous people. Since there are twenty-two Maya languages in Guatemala, I use the term "Kaqchikel" to refer to the specific group that comprised the majority population in the departments of Chimaltenango, Sacatepéquez, and Sololá. Beginning in the 1970s and taking hold in the 1990s, the term "Maya" took on more specific and intentional cultural and political

connotations as described, for example, in K. Warren, *Indigenous Movements*, but I do not use it as such. As the judicial record reveals, Mayas in the early twentieth century were concerned about their rights, but references to rights tended to arise when individuals were advocating for themselves or small groups of people, not indigenous people or Mayas more broadly. Similarly, Edgar Esquit found that in the early twentieth century Kaqchikel elites advocated for Chimaltenango's indigenous people and their rights. "Superación del indígena."

66. Watanabe, "Liberalism"; Grandin, *Blood of Guatemala*, 84–85, 239, 265–266n9; Lutz, *Santiago de Guatemala*; Taracena Arriola, *Invención criolla*; Casaús Arzú, *Guatemala*, 119–126; Martínez Peláez, *La Patria del Criollo*, 155–156.

67. See Taracena Arriola, *Invención criolla*; Taracena Arriola et al., eds., *Etnicidad*; Hale, *Más que un indio*; Hale, "Mestizaje"; Casaús Arzú, *La metamorfosis*; Casaús Arzú, *Guatemala*; Menjívar, *Enduring Violence*.

68. Grandin, *Blood of Guatemala*; Gabbert, "Of Friends and Foes," 93, 96, 105, 107n10; Gabbert, *Becoming Maya*; Fallaw, "Bartolomé García Correa," 566.

69. Casaús Arzú, *Guatemala*; Casaús Arzú and García Giráldez, *Las redes intelectuales*.

70. AGCA, índice 116, Chimaltenango 1913, *leg.* 14a, *exp.* 16.

71. Bunzel, *Chichicastenango*, 90–91, 121, 139–142; Wagley, *Economics of a Guatemalan Village*, 15, 54, 76; Wagley, *Social and Religious Life*, 16–17; Desmond, "'Pido Justicia.'"

72. AGCA, índice 116, Chimaltenango 1913, *leg.* 14a, *exp.* 16.

73. Ibid.

74. Ibid.

75. Piccato, *City of Suspects*, 6.

76. AGCA, índice 116, Chimaltenango, *leg.* 19a, *exp.* 42.

77. Taracena Arriola, *Invención criolla*, 408.

78. *Diario de Centro América*, September 25, 1936.

79. AGCA, JP-C 1935, LSE 1935, April 8, 1935.

80. Piccato, *Tyranny of Opinion*, 15–16, 62, 98–99; Joseph and Nugent, eds., *Everyday Forms*; Forment, *Democracy in Latin America*; Dym, "Citizen of Which Republic?"; Benton, "'Laws of This Country'"; Sabato, *Ciudadanía política*, especially Sabato's introduction and Annino's essay "Ciudadanía versus gobernabilidad."

81. AGCA, JP-C 1935, LSE abril 1935, April 10, 1935.

82. Gillin, *Culture of Security*, 60. As Gramsci reminds us, more than just words devoid of content, language encompasses worldviews, epistemologies, and perceptions. *Prison Notebooks*.

83. AGCA, JP-C 1935, LSE abril, April 19, 1935.

84. AGCA, JP-C 1935, LSE abril, April 21, 1935. By 1939 municipal clerks were referring to Kaqchikel men with the title *don* in Sololá. AMS, Libro 1935–1943, March 15, 1939.

85. Carey, "Drunks and Dictators."

86. Policia Nacional, *Memoria* 1932, 6; Piccato, *City of Suspects*, 212; Caimiri, "Remembering Freedom," 391–392; Aguirre, *Criminals of Lima*.

87. Foucault, *Discipline and Punish*, 251–253.

88. G. Joseph, "On the Trail," 25; Piccato, *City of Suspects*, 2–3.

89. Stepan, *"Hour of Eugenics,"* 41.

90. Foucault, *Discipline and Punish*, 83.

91. Policia Nacional, *Memoria* 1933, 81.

92. Sullivan, *Unfinished Conversations*.

93. Policia Nacional, *Memoria* 1928, 42–43.

94. Bunzel, *Chichicastenango*, 68, 74.

95. Policia Nacional, *Memoria* 1932, 40–41.

96. For explorations of criminal sociology in Latin America and farther afield, see Baratta, *Criminología crítica*; del Olmo, *América Latina*; and Garland, "Of Crimes and Criminals."

97. Policia Nacional, *Memoria* 1932, 40–41.

98. Buffington, *"Jotos,"* 123; Piccato, *City of Suspects*, 3; Speckman Guerra, "'I Was a Man of Pleasure,'" 75.

99. Policia Nacional, *Memoria* 1937, 15.

100. Sarmiento, *Life in Argentina*.

101. Policia Nacional, *Memoria* 1938, 17.

102. Policia Nacional, *Memoria* 1940, 31.

103. Policia Nacional, *Memoria* 1929, 50–51.

Chapter 2

1. *Diario de Centro América*, December 8, 1932.

2. *Diario de Centro América*, December 13, 1932.

3. Wells and Joseph, *Summer of Discontent*, 15.

4. Sanders, *Contentious Republicans*, 15, 52–53; Kennedy, "Role of Beer"; Taylor, *Drinking*, 38, 53–54; Scardaville, "Alcohol Abuse," 646–647; Eber, *Women and Alcohol*, 7–8, 22, 33; Ericastilla and Jiménez, "Las clandestinistas"; Reeves, *Ladinos with Ladinos*, 106, 111–112, 116–124; Reeves, "From Household to Nation"; Gudmundson, "Firewater," 257–265; Schwartzkopf, "Maya Power"; McCreery, *Rural Guatemala*; Reiche, "Estudio sobre el patrón," 121; Bunzel, *Chichicastenango*, 255; Wolfe, *Everyday Nation-State*, 63; Hames, "Maize-Beer," 352; Colson and Scudder, *For Prayer and Profit*; Akyeampong, *Drink*, 101, 104, 109.

5. Reeves, "From Household to Nation," 62; Garrard-Burnett, "Conclusion," 162.

6. Reiche, "Estudio sobre el patrón," 110, 123.

7. AMP, Libro de Conocimientos Criminales (henceforth LCC), Juzgado Patzicía, 1935, *paq.* 27, May 14, 1937; AGCA, JP-C 1935, en la villa de San Martín, March 10, 1935.

8. Ericastilla y Jiménez, "Las clandestinistas," 21.

9. Reeves, *Ladinos with Ladinos*, 14, 103–135; Ericastilla y Jiménez, "Las clandestinistas," 14.

10. McCreery, *Rural Guatemala*, 87–88, 176–177; Reeves, *Ladinos with Ladinos*, 104, 116, 227n47; González Alzate, "History of Los Altos," 141–148; Bunzel, "Role of Alcoholism," 363, 386; Gudmundson, "Firewater," 254–255n30; Ingersoll, "War of the Mountain"; Schwartzkopf, "Maya Power"; Reeves, "From Household to Nation."

11. Pompejano, *Crisis de antiguo régimen*; Reeves, *Ladinos with Ladinos*, 133, 135; Woodward, *Rafael Carrera*, 436; Ingersoll, "War of the Mountain," 337;

Schwartzkopf, "Maya Power"; Schwartzkopf, "Consumption," 32–33; Burgess, *Justo Rufino Barrios*, 81; Clegern, *Origins of Liberal Dictatorship*, 112, 116; Reeves, "From Household to Nation," 59–61.

12. Ingersoll, "War of the Mountain," 337; Burgess, *Justo Rufino Barrios*, 75–78n4; Schwartzkopf, "Consumption," 33–34.

13. Reeves, *Ladinos with Ladinos*, 116, 122, 123; McCreery, *Rural Guatemala*; Gudmundson, "Firewater," 261–262; Ericastilla y Jiménez, "Las clandestinistas," 14–15.

14. McCreery, *Rural Guatemala*, 87–88, 176–177; Reeves, *Ladinos with Ladinos*, 104, 116, 227n47; Pompejano, *Crisis de antiguo régimen*, 16; González Alzate, "History of Los Altos," 141–148; Bunzel, "Role of Alcoholism," 363, 386; Gudmundson, "Firewater," 254–255n30; Ingersoll, "War of the Mountain"; Schwartzkopf, "Maya Power"; Schwartzkopf, "Consumption."

15. Rendon, "Gobierno de Manuel Estrada Cabrera," 15; McCreery, *Rural Guatemala*, 176–179; Opie, "Alcohol and Lowdown Culture."

16. Ericastilla y Jiménez, "Las clandestinistas," 21.

17. Garrard-Burnett, "Indians Are Drunks," 350–353. During the Ubico period, the quetzal was pegged to the U.S. dollar.

18. If the data for Chimaltenango are any indication, the campaign against moonshiners expanded during the Ubico dictatorship. Appendix 3. Based on a comparison with the first years of the Estrada Cabrera dictatorship, 1899 and 1900, national statistics also suggest this trend.

19. AMS, Libro 1935–1943, March 22, 1937.

20. *La Gaceta*, June 1, 1931.

21. *La Gaceta*, June 21, 1931.

22. Juárez Muñoz, *Indio guatemalteco*, 84–85.

23. AGCA, JP-C 1930, *leg.* 73, carta de Jefe Político de Chimaltenango al alcalde de San Martín, October 11, 1930.

24. AGCA, JP-C 1931, carta al Señor Alcalde Primero Municipal, last of October 1931.

25. *Diario de Centro América*, April 22, 1933.

26. Archivo Municipal de San Juan Comalapa (hereafter AMC), Municipalidad de San Juan Comalapa, Libro para actas de sesiones ordinaries y extraordinarias comenzado el 23 de julio de 1928 terminado 1 de enero de 1930 (hereafter Libro 1928–1930), April 19, 1929.

27. AGCA, JP-C 1926, carta de Jefe Político de Chimaltenango al alcalde de San Martín, September 10, 1926.

28. AGCA, JP-C 1926, carta de alcalde de San Martín al señores patentados para vender aguardiente, tabaco y cerveza, September 14, 1926.

29. *La Gaceta*, May 24, 1931; *La Gaceta*, June 7, 1931.

30. J. C. Scott, *Domination*.

31. AGCA, JP-S, carta de Barahona, May 14, 1924; *Diario de Centro América*, December 8 and 13, 1932, and February 24, March 27, July 29, and August 18, 1933; McCreery, *Rural Guatemala*, 384n79.

32. AGCA, *índice* 116, Chimaltenango 1902, *leg.* 3F, *exp.* 20; AGCA, *índice* 116, Chimaltenango 1902, *leg.* 3, *exp.* 37; AGCA, *índice* 116, Chimaltenango 1902, *leg.* 3F, *exp.* 35; Oxlajuj Ajpu', 1/19/98, Comalapa, Panabajal.

33. *Diario de Centro América*, March 15, 1933.

34. AGCA, *índice* 116, Chimaltenango 1911, *leg*. 12, *exp*. 3.

35. AGCA, *índice* 116, Chimaltenango 1902, *leg*. 3F, *exp*. 35.

36. In *La Gaceta*, February 5, 1933.

37. Ix'ey, 6/25/03, Comalapa.

38. McCreery, *Rural Guatemala*, 167.

39. Ixte', 8/5/05, Comalapa.

40. *La Gaceta*, June 1, 1941.

41. *Diario de Centro América*, January 26, 1933.

42. *La Gaceta*, February 5 and 19, 1933; Grandin, *Blood of Guatemala*, 177.

43. Ixsub'äl, 8/23/05, Comalapa (Ix'ey).

44. Bunzel, "Role of Alcoholism," 362; Lincoln, "Ethnographic Study of the Ixil."

45. Sontag, *On Photography*, 156; Tagg, "Evidence"; Griffiths, *Wondrous Difference*, especially Chapter 3.

46. Carey, *Engendering Mayan History*, 39; Schwartzkopf, "Consumption," 31.

47. Bunzel, *Chichicastenango*, 259.

48. Tax, "Changing Consumption," 157.

49. Wagley, *Economics of a Guatemalan Village*, 51–52.

50. Ibid.

51. Bunzel, "Role of Alcoholism," 362–363; Bunzel, *Chichicastenango*, 258, 259; Wagley, *Economics of a Guatemalan Village*, 74–77; McCreery, *Rural Guatemala*, 176, 293–294; Castellanos Cambranes, *Coffee and Peasants*, 110; Colby and van de Berghe, *Ixil Country*, 72–73; Stoll, *Between Two Armies*, 33; Eber, *Women and Alcohol*, 28–29; W. Adams, "Guatemala," 100–101.

52. Bunzel, "Role of Alcoholism," 363.

53. Burkitt, "Explorations in the Highlands," 59.

54. Garrard-Burnett, "Indians Are Drunks," 352–354.

55. Secretaría de Estado, Despacho de Gobernación y Justicia (SCJ), *Memorias . . . 1941*, 113.

56. Policia Nacional, *Memoria* 1940, 31, capitals in the original.

57. AGCA, JP-C 1927, *leg*. 70A, Lista de personas que solicitaron licencia para vender aguardiente durante el mes de febrero, February 16, 1927; DGE, *Censo . . . 1921*, 101.

58. *La Gaceta*, August 2, 1942.

59. Garrard-Burnett, "Indians Are Drunks," 354.

60. Reeves, *Ladinos with Ladinos*.

61. Guillén, "Prólogo," 22.

62. Ixsub'äl, 8/23/05, Comalapa (Ix'ey).

63. AGCA, *índice* 116, Chimaltenango 1907, *leg*. 8E, *exp*. 15; AGCA, *índice* 116, Chimaltenango 1921, *leg*. 21, *exp*. 20.

64. Policia Nacional, *Memoria* 1932, 12.

65. *La Gaceta*, July 19, 1935.

66. *La Gaceta*, March 19, 1933.

67. Ixte', 8/5/05, Comalapa.

68. Ix'eya', 8/10/05, Comalapa (Ix'ey).

69. Reiche, "Estudio sobre el patrón," 111.

70. *La Gaceta*, July 19, 1935.

71. AGCA, *índice* 116, Chimaltenango 1921, *leg.* 21, *exp.* 21.

72. Carey, "'Hard Working, Orderly Little Women.'"

73. Arrom, *Women of Mexico City*, 85 (quote); Rodríguez Saenz, "Civilizing Domestic Life," 87.

74. Ericastilla y Jiménez, "Las clandestinistas," 21; Chambers, "Private Crimes," 35.

75. AGCA, *índice* 116, Chimaltenango 1918, *leg.* 19, *exp.* 34.

76. AGCA, *índice* 116, Chimaltenango 1900, *leg.* 1G, *exp.* 75.

77. During the Estrada Cabrera regime, the typical punishment for making and selling *aguardiente* in Chimaltenango was three months in prison commutable by a fine of around 300 pesos.

78. Ericastilla y Jiménez, "Las clandestinistas," 21.

79. AGCA, *índice* 116, Chimaltenango 1902, *leg.* 3F, *exp.* 20.

80. *La Gaceta*, January 15, 1933.

81. AGCA, *índice* 116, Chimaltenango 1907, *leg.* 8B, *exp.* 22.

82. AGCA, *índice* 116, Chimaltenango 1916, *leg.* 17, *exp.* 18.

83. Milton, *Many Meanings of Poverty*, 47.

84. AGCA, *índice* 116, Chimaltenango 1901, *leg.* 2F, *exp.* 39.

85. Ixkotz'i'j, 8/6/05, Comalapa, Pamamus.

86. AGCA, *índice* 116, Chimaltenango 1907, *leg.* 8B, *exp.* 22.

87. Ibid.

88. Ibid.

89. AGCA, *índice* 116, Chimaltenango 1918, *leg.* 19, *exp.* 34.

90. AGCA, *índice* 116, Chimaltenango 1901, *leg.* 2F, *exp.* 40.

91. AGCA, *índice* 116, Chimaltenango 1909, *leg.* 10D, *exp.* 5.

92. AGCA, *índice* 116, Chimaltenango 1900, *leg.* 1A, *exp.* 32.

93. AGCA, *índice* 116, Chimaltenango 1918, *leg.* 19, *exp.* 34.

94. Carey, "Runaway Mothers."

95. AGCA, *índice* 116, Chimaltenango 1907, *leg.* 8C, *exp.* 10.

96. Schwartzkopf, "Consumption."

97. AGCA, *índice* 116, Chimaltenango 1902, *leg.* 3, *exp.* 37.

98. Ibid.

99. Ibid.

100. For a similar interpretation regarding nineteenth-century Quezaltenango see Reeves, "From Household to Nation."

101. AGCA, *índice* 116, Chimaltenango 1912, *leg.* 13C, *exp.* 30.

102. Schwartzkopf, "Consumption"; W. Adams, "Guatemala," 102; Bunzel, "Role of Alcoholism," 365–366, 384; Bunzel, *Chichicastenango*, 256, 259–260; La Farge, *Santa Eulalia*, 91–99, 161; Reina, *Law of the Saints*, 123, 126, 133, 138, 155, 161, 164, 176, 178; Reiche, "Estudio sobre el patrón," 114–120; Ericastilla y Jiménez, "Las clandestinistas," 16–17. Interestingly, Stoll in *Between Two Armies* and Bunzel in "Role of Alcoholism" observe that during Holy Week in Nebaj and Chichicastenango alcohol was consumed only moderately.

103. AGCA, *índice* 116, Chimaltenango 1907, *leg.* 8E, *exp.* 15.

104. Historian Lowell Gudmundson similarly argues that moonshine revenues were "central to Guatemala's process of state formation." "Firewater," 276.

105. Juárez Muñoz, *Indio guatemalteco*, 166.

106. Chazkel, *Laws of Chance*, 15 (quotes), 25, 47.
107. Reeves, "From Household to Nation," 53.
108. Reeves, *Ladinos with Ladinos*; Gudmundson, "Firewater."
109. *La Gaceta*, July 19, 1935.
110. J. C. Scott, *Domination*.
111. Foucault, *Discipline and Punish*, 89.

Chapter 3

1. AGCA, JP-C, 1935, *leg.* 79, LSE, febrero 1935, February 11. Although wholesaling of goods was not unusual in large trade centers such as Totonicapán and Quetzaltenango, perhaps municipal restrictions like this one in San Martín explain why many wholesale merchants preferred not to do their business in the smaller marketplaces but rather purchased their goods directly from producers in their homes. See McBryde, *Cultural and Historical Geography*, 82–83.
2. AGCA, JP-C, 1935, *leg.* 79, LSE, abril 1935, July 8, 1935.
3. In the 1930s the average wage for day laborers was ten cents a day. See Carey, *Our Elders*, 200, 215; Metz, *Ch'orti'-Maya Survival*, 204.
4. Watanabe and Fischer, "Introduction," 13, 25; Watanabe, "Culture History," 42, 60; La Farge and Byers, *Year Bearer's People*; Tax, *Penny Capitalism*.
5. Watanabe, "Culture History," 55.
6. Joseph and Nugent, *Everyday Forms*.
7. Dore and Molyneux, eds., *Hidden Histories*, especially Dore, "Property, Households and Public Regulation"; Guy, "Parents before the Tribunals"; and Vaughn, "Modernizing Patriarchy."
8. McCreery, "'This Life of Misery,'" 334; Carey, *Engendering Mayan History*, 43–52.
9. AGCA, JP-C 1925, *leg.* 68, Sentencias económicas en el ramo criminal (hereafter SERC), 1, 11, 129; AGCA, JP-C 1935, *leg.* 79, LSE, febrero 1935, February 11, 1935; *La Gaceta*, March 28 and May 16, 1943; Goldín, "Organizing the World"; McCreery, "'This Life of Misery,'" 334; Grandin, *Blood of Guatemala*, 91, 97–98, 127–128, 141–142; Carey, *Engendering Mayan History*, 153–154.
10. Eiss, *"Pueblo Mestizo."*
11. McBryde, *Cultural and Historical Geography*, 81–84.
12. C. Smith, "Beyond Dependency Theory," 605.
13. Ibid., 605–606.
14. Carmack, *Rebels of Highland Guatemala*, 28; Coe, *Maya*, 233; Tax, *Penny Capitalism*, 123–125; La Farge and Byers, *Year Bearer's People*, 59; McBryde, *Cultural and Historical Geography*, 83, 124–125, map 24; Tax and Hinshaw, "Maya of the Midwestern Highlands," 84; Huxley, *Beyond the Mexique Bay*, 64–65; Jones, *Guatemala*, 20, 34, 38, 45, 47–49, 54, 56–58; Sweatnam, "Women and Market," 327–328; Goldín, "Organizing the World"; Few, *Women Who Live Evil Lives*, 24.
15. McCreery, *Rural Guatemala*, 18–19, 323; Contreras, *Una rebelión indígena*; Patch, *Maya Revolt*.
16. McCreery, "State Power," 101; Woodward, *Rafael Carrera*; Grandin, *Blood of Guatemala*, 82–109; Handy, *Gift of the Devil*, 36–53. After declaring its independence from Spain in 1821 and Mexico in 1823, Guatemala declared its indepen-

dence from the dissolving Central American Federation in 1839 and proclaimed itself a republic in 1847.

17. Gudmundson and Lindo-Fuentes, *Central America*; Grandin, *Blood of Guatemala*, 111; McCreery, "State Power," 107; Carey, *Engendering Mayan History*, 63–68.

18. Polanyi, *Great Transformation*, 44–80; McCreery, *Rural Guatemala*, 327; Carey, "Empowered through Labor"; Grandin, *Blood of Guatemala*.

19. Sellers, *Market Revolution*, 5.

20. C. Smith, "Race-Class-Gender," 742.

21. Carey, *Our Elders*, 259–265; Grandin, *Blood of Guatemala*, 6, 140.

22. Little, "Visual Political Economy."

23. Carey, *Engendering Mayan History*, 157.

24. AMC, Libro 1928–1930, September 5, 7, 17–18, 25, and 28 and December 31, 1928; April 19, July 15, and November 16, 1929; AMC, Libro para actas de sesiones ordinaries y extraordinarias, comenzando 13 de febrero 1942 terminado al 21 de julio 1945 (hereafter Libro 1942–1945), August 13, 1942, 67.

25. República de Guatemala, *Recopilación de las leyes de la República de Guatemala*, decree no. 1996, 53: 71–75; McCreery, *Rural Guatemala*, 316–317; Carey, "Empowered through Labor."

26. *La Gaceta*, May 17, 1931, emphasis my own.

27. McCreery, "'This Life of Misery,'" 334; Buffington and Piccato, "Tales of Two Women," 417, 423.

28. AGCA, JP-C 1935, *leg.* 79, Informe de comisión encargada de formular el proyecto para la recaudación del impuesto de luz en la población, December 10, 1935.

29. *La Gaceta*, January 10, 1943. This celebration of indigenous merchants and porters stands in stark contrast to late nineteenth-century intellectuals and advocates of railroad development in Guatemala who argued that "tumplines were a particularly pernicious obstacle to efficient production" and that railroad development would obviate the need for indigenous porters and thus advance the nation. Grandin, *Blood of Guatemala*, 181.

30. Policia Nacional, *Memoria* 1929, 50–51.

31. AMS, Libro número 01, September 5, 6, and 26, 1941.

32. Indigenous influence in the department capital did not necessarily mean the city itself had an indigenous feel to it. McBryde describes it as adhering to "European features," with its library, theater, hotels, stores, and department-level administrative offices. He calculated that more than half the town's 2,600 people were ladinos. *Cultural and Historical Geography*, 85.

33. *La Gaceta*, July 25, 1943.

34. For example, AMP, *paq.* 237, Menor María Magdalena Figueroa, 1948.

35. Boddam-Whetham, *Across Central America*, 44; La Farge and Byers, *Year Bearer's People*, 59; Tax, *Penny Capitalism*, 125; McBryde, *Cultural and Historical Geography*, 83. McBryde notes that women's limited access to long-distance trade was not related to a lack of physical strength or endurance on their part. After observing that traders commonly carried loads of one hundred pounds, he added that "women seem to have arms as well muscled as men." *Cultural and Historical Geography*, 9.

36. Gudmundson, "Firewater," 264.

37. *La Gaceta*, November 1, 1942.

38. Goldín, "De plaza a mercado," 257.

39. AMC, Libro 1928–1930, April 19, 1929; AMC, Libro 1942–1945, January 11, 1944; Goldín, "De plaza a mercado," 246, 248, 257.

40. AMS, Libro 1935–1943, March 22, September 29, and October 25, 1937; February 9, March 3, and August 8, 1938; August 24, 1939; and June 1, 1943.

41. Goldín, "De plaza a mercado," 249.

42. Tax and Hinshaw, "Maya of the Midwestern Highlands," 85; La Farge and Byers, *Year Bearer's People*, 32; McBryde, *Cultural and Historical Geography*, 83; Goldín, "De plaza a mercado"; Grandin, *Blood of Guatemala*, 162; Edgar Esquit, personal communication.

43. Lauderdale Graham, *House and Street*, 50; Few, *Women Who Live Evil Lives*, 41.

44. For example, AMP, *paq.* 107, LSE 1943, August 18, 1943.

45. AMP, *paq.* 127, LSE, 1935; *paq.* 107, LSE, 1945–1947; AGCA, JP-C, carta del jefe político al alcaldes, November 20, 1930. AMC, Libro, 1928–1930, February 11, 1929; García Granados, *Evolución sociológica*, 71.

46. AGCA, JP-C 1930, *leg.* 73, Carta d jefe político al alcalde de San Martín, November 20, 1930; AMC, Libro 1928–1930, February 11, 1929; Carey, *Our Elders*, 125–127; Goldín, "De plaza a mercado," 244, 249–250, 257–258.

47. Guardia Civil, *Memoria* 1945, 25–32; *La Gaceta*, January 3 and 10, February 28, May 2, June 13, and July 25, 1943; AMP, *paq.* 127, LSE 1935; AMP, *paq.* 107, LSE, 1945–1947; Goldín, "De plaza a mercado," 251.

48. *La Gaceta*, September 19, 1943.

49. AGCA, JP-C 1935, *leg.* 79, LSE, abril 1935, September 2.

50. AGCA, JP-C 1944, *leg.* 88a, Emilia Ajquejay Bac contra Ramiro Rodriguez Alburez, October 1944.

51. Ibid.

52. AGCA, JP-C 1933, *leg.* 76, Monografía de San Martín, 1933.

53. AGCA, JP-C 1944, *leg.* 88a, Reportaje de Policía a Juez de Paz, June 9.

54. AGCA, JP-C 1944, *leg.* 88, Secretaría Municipal de San Martín, December 5, 1944.

55. AGCA, JP-C 1935, *leg.* 79, LSE, abril 1935, April 21.

56. Bunzel, *Chichicastenango*, 74; Goldín, "De plaza a mercado," 247–248, 259; McBryde, *Cultural and Historical Geography*, 124–125, map 24.

57. AGCA, JP-C 1944, *leg.* 88a, carta de señor juez de regidor de abastos, August 10, 1944.

58. Joseph, "On the Trail," 25.

59. AGCA, JP-C, 1925, *leg.* 68, SERC, 1.

60. B'eleje' Imox, 8/6/05, Comalapa.

61. Edgar Esquit, personal communication, August 22, 2005, Patzicía.

62. For further explorations about the ways oral histories and archival records shed light on market contestations, see Carey, "'Hard Working, Orderly Little Women,'" 597–600.

63. AGCA, JP-C, 1933, *leg.* 76, Monografía de San Martín 1933.

64. AGCA, JP-C, 1933, *leg.* 76, Manuel Elías v. Alcalde Primero Municipal.

65. Policia Nacional, *Memoria* 1937, 22.

66. AMP, *paq.* 107, LSE 1941, juzgado de Patzicía, February 20, 1943. An *arroba* is a Spanish weight of twenty-five pounds.

67. AMP, *paq.* 127, LSE 1935.

68. See, for example, Metz, *Ch'orti'-Maya Survival*, 204.

69. Policía Nacional, *Memoria* 1937, 22; AMS, Libro de actas, August 22, 1942; Tax, *Penny Capitalism*, 136–137. In some markets, Maya vendors did not haggle with other Mayas, only with ladinos and tourists. Bunzel, *Chichicastenango*, 75.

70. AGCA, JP-C 1933, *leg.* 76, Monografía de San Martín, 1933.

71. Policía Nacional, *Memoria* 1932, 32; 1933, 81–82; 1935, 35; 1936, 28; 1937, 22; and 1938, 19–20; Tax, *Penny Capitalism*, 136–137; McBryde, *Cultural and Historical Geography*, 84.

72. Ixq'anil, 8/5/05, Comalapa.

73. AMP, *paq.* 127, LSE 1935, juzgado de paz, January 15, 1935.

74. AMP, *paq.* 127, LSE 1935," *La Gaceta*, July 25, 1943.

75. Sahlins, "Anthropology of Modernity," 52.

76. Salvatore, *Wandering Paysanos*, 398.

77. J. C. Scott, *Weapons of the Weak*, 302 (quote); G. Joseph, "On the Trail."

78. Forster, *Time of Freedom*, 35.

79. AMP, *paq.* 107, LSE 1941, juzgado de Patzicía, May 2, 1942; AMP, *paq.* 107, LSE 1941, juzgado de Patzicía, September 26, 1942.

80. AGCA, JP-C 1925, *leg.* 68, SERC, 11.

81. AMP, *paq.* 107, LSE 1941, juzgado de paz, October 31, 1941.

82. McCreery, *Rural Guatemala*, 403n45.

83. Tax, *Penny Capitalism*, 137.

84. McBryde, *Sololá*, 124; Tax, *Penny Capitalism*, 138.

85. AGCA, JP-C 1925, *leg.* 68, no. 76, SERC, April 19, 1925.

86. Tax, *Penny Capitalism*, 137; McBryde, *Cultural and Historical Geography*, 84.

87. AMP, *paq.* 107, LSE 1943, September 11, 1943.

88. AMP, *paq.* 127, LSE 1935.

89. AMP, *paq.* 107, LSE 1943, October 15, 1943.

90. AGCA, JP-C, 1944, *leg.* 88a, solicitud de matrícula de las pesas de Isabel Camey Colon, April 3, 1944; Guillermina Escobar, April 15, 1944; and Clara P. de Valle, January 22, 1944.

91. Thompson, *Customs in Common*, 335.

92. AMP, *paq.* 107, LSE 1943, June 9.

93. AMP, *paq.* 107, LSE 1941, July 22, 1942.

94. Ibid.

95. At the same time, local officials were not averse to adhering to some indigenous methods if doing so served their interests. Since pitch pine was of great importance to Panajachel local officials, particularly messengers who used it to light their way at night, vendors there could pay their taxes in pitch-pine bundles as late as 1936. McBryde, *Cultural and Historical Geography*, 84.

96. AMP, *paq.* 107, LSE 1943, November 13, 1943.

97. Weismantel, *Cholas and Pishtacos*, 118.

98. AMP, *paq.* 107, LSE 1943, September 29, 1943.

99. La Farge and Byers, *Year Bearer's People*, 59; Sweatnam, "Women and Market," 327–328; Goldín, "Organizing the World."

100. Tax, *Penny Capitalism*, 123.

101. Ix'ajpu', 9/01, Patzún (Ixkawoq).

102. Perera, *Rites*, 145. See also Harms, "Imagining a Place."

103. Sweatnam, "Women and Market," 328.

104. McBryde, *Cultural and Historical Geography*, 82.

105. Larson, *Trials of Nation Making*, 15, 246; Watanabe and Fischer, "Introduction," 29.

106. Carey, "*'Oficios de su raza.'*"

107. Gudmundson, "Firewater," 258; Reeves, *Ladinos with Ladinos*.

108. AMP, *paq.* 107, LSE 1943, Timotea Miculax.

109. Dore, *Myths of Modernity*, 107.

110. Wagley, *Social and Religious Life*, 16.

111. Nandy, *Intimate Enemy*; Comaroff, *Body of Power*.

112. Mangan, *Trading Roles*.

Chapter 4

1. In an indication of how seldom these crimes were tried, the records show no one accused of abortion from 1914 to 1925 or of infanticide from 1919 to 1925.

2. AGCA, *índice* 116, Chimaltenango 1900–1925.

3. Caulfield, "Getting into Trouble," 155–156; K. Ruggiero, "Honor," 354; Bliss, *Compromised Positions*, 198n40.

4. República de Guatemala, *Código penal... 1889*, article 298, 62–63.

5. Sahlins, "Anthropology of Modernity," 52; Sahlins, "What Is Anthropological Enlightenment?" xvi.

6. After living in Chichicastenango in the 1930s, Bunzel concluded that "there is no infanticide." *Chichicastenango*, 99.

7. AGCA, *índice* 116, Chimaltenango 1907, *leg.* 7e, *exp.* 27.

8. AGCA, *índice* 116, Chimaltenango 1909, *leg.* 10c, *exp.* 13.

9. Forster, *Time of Freedom*, 68.

10. AGCA, JP-C 1937, Dominga Currichiche Cana por presunciones de abandono de hogar, December 23, 1937.

11. AGCA, *índice* 116, Chimaltenango 1901, *leg.* 2, *exp.* 27.

12. AGCA, *índice* 116, Chimaltenango 1913, *leg.* 14a, *exp.* 14.

13. Forster, "Violent and Violated," 69.

14. AGCA, *índice* 116, Chimaltenango 1914, *leg.* 15d, *exp.* 50.

15. Ibid.

16. AGCA, *índice* 116, Chimaltenango 1911, *leg.* 12f, *exp.* 25.

17. Ibid.

18. Ibid.

19. Ibid.

20. Ibid.

21. AGCA, *índice* 116, Chimaltenango 1904, *leg.* 5D, *exp.* 18.

22. Ibid.

23. República de Guatemala, *Código penal... 1889*, 61–63.

24. AGCA, *índice* 116, Chimaltenango 1904, *leg.* 5D, *exp.* 18.

25. República de Guatemala, *Código penal . . . 1889*, 61–63.

26. Ibid., 63; *Código penal . . . 1936*, 60; *Código penal . . . 1941*, 60.

27. Sloan, *Runaway Daughters*, 111.

28. Carey, "Runaway Mothers."

29. Forster, "Violent and Violated," 66.

30. AGCA, *índice* 116, Chimaltenango 1912, *leg.* 13e, *exp.* 6.

31. Ibid.

32. Ibid.

33. Wagley, *Social and Religious Life*, 11–17, 37–47; Bunzel, *Chichicastenango*, 117–121, 132–143.

34. Bunzel, *Chichicastenango*, 119.

35. AGCA, *índice* 116, Chimaltenango 1912, *leg.* 13e, *exp.* 6.

36. Ixsinka, Patzún, 7/18/03 (Ixkawoq).

37. AGCA, *índice* 116, Chimaltenango 1906, *leg.* 7c, *exp.* 23.

38. AGCA, *índice* 116, Chimaltenango 1908, *leg.* 9c, *exp.* 30.

39. AGCA, *índice* 116, Chimaltenango 1915, *leg.* 16c, *exp.* 39.

40. Ibid.

41. Ibid.

42. AGCA, *índice* 116, Chimaltenango 1917, *leg.* 18, *exp.* 13.

43. Ibid.

44. Ibid.

45. Ibid.

46. AGCA, *índice* 116, Chimaltenango 1912, *leg.* 13, *exp.* 18.

47. *La Gaceta*, June 14, 1942.

48. AGCA, *índice* 116, Chimaltenango 1912, *leg.* 13, *exp.* 18.

49. República de Guatemala, *Código penal . . . 1889*, article 298, 62–63.

50. AGCA, *índice* 116, Chimaltenango 1912, *leg.* 13, *exp.* 18. A real was worth one-eighth of a peso.

51. *La Gaceta*, October 12, 1941.

52. *La Gaceta*, June 14, 1942.

53. AGCA, *índice* 116, Chimaltenango 1904, leg. 5D, *exp.* 18.

54. Guy, "Mothers Alive and Dead," 166 (quote); *New York Times*, January 16, 1871. Peruvian officials considered women who committed any crime "unnatural." Chambers, *From Subjects to Citizens*, 207.

55. *La Gaceta*, March 16, 1941.

56. Ibid.

57. *La Gaceta*, March 29, 1931.

58. *La Gaceta*, June 7, 1931.

59. *La Gaceta*, June 21, 1931.

60. *La Gaceta*, February 23, 1941.

61. Butler, *Bodies that Matter*, 3.

62. McClintock, *Imperial Leather*, 72.

63. Buffington, "Subjectivity," 1653.

64. On homosexuality in Latin America, see Balderston and Guy, *Sex and Sexuality*; Sigal, *Infamous Desire*; Green, *Beyond Carnival*; Irwin, McCaughlin, and Rocío Nasser, eds., *Famous 41*; Gutmann, ed., *Changing Men and Masculinities*; Gutmann, *Meanings of Macho*.

65. *La Gaceta*, March 29, 1931.

66. *La Gaceta*, January 22, 1933.

67. *La Gaceta*, June 7, 1931.

68. *La Gaceta*, June 14, 1931.

69. Foucault, *Discipline and Punish*.

70. *La Gaceta*, May 24, 1931. Such reporting dismissed the possibility that some strangled babies died because umbilical cords became wrapped around their necks in the birth canals and no one skilled in delivery was present at their births.

71. Butler, *Bodies that Matter*, 3.

72. Windler, "Madame Durocher's Performance," 59–60; Sifuentes Jáuregui, "Gender without Limits," 49.

73. Windler, "Madame Durocher's Performance," 53–54, 59–61 (quote p. 60); Díaz, *Female Citizens*, 75; Masiello, "Gender," 221–226; Green, "Doctoring the National Body," 202.

74. Olcott, "Soldiers"; Cano, "Unconcealable Realities"; Vaughn, "Introduction," 23–26.

75. AGCA, *índice* 116, Chimaltenango 1911, *leg.* 12E, *exp.* 31.

76. Ritual cross-dressing by males and females was not uncommon in Maya communities, but doing so outside of ritual contexts upset their gender norms as well. Carey, "*Oficios de su raza*," 120–121. Even then, cross-dressing or effeminate men did not face the same sanctions as cross-dressing or masculine women. *La Gaceta*, January 11, 1931; Grandin, *Last Colonial Massacre*, Chapter 1, especially 33–34.

77. AGCA, *índice* 116, Chimaltenango 1911, *leg.* 12E, *exp.* 31.

78. Reeves, *Ladinos and Ladinos*; Carey, "*Oficios de su raza*"; Mallon, *Peasant and Nation*, 324.

79. *La Gaceta*, January 1, 1941.

80. Carey, *Engendering Mayan History*, 214–215.

81. *La Gaceta*, January 1, 1941.

82. AGCA, JP-C 1933, *leg.* 76, carta de Silverio Atz al juez de paz de San Martín, June 20, 1933.

83. Carey and Torres, "Precursors to Femicide."

84. Forster, "Violent and Violated," 66.

85. AGCA, *índice* 116, Chimaltenango 1914, *leg.* 15c, *exp.* 45.

86. K. Ruggiero, "Honor," 371.

87. Forster, "Violent and Violated," 56. Grandin similarly argues that during the Ubico period, men used abortion and infanticide laws to "discipline women." *Last Colonial Massacre*, 136. While that certainly happened, women used such laws to discipline men as well.

Chapter 5

1. *La Gaceta*, May 24, 1931.

2. AGCA, JP-C 1926, carta al Sr. Juez de San Martín de Tomasa Morejón, March 29, 1926.

3. AGCA, JP-C 1926, carta al sr. juez de San Martín de Alejandra Aguilar, April 26, 1926.

4. AGCA, JP-C 1926, carta al sr. juez de San Martín de Juana Ajbal de Díaz, May 11, 1926.

5. República de Guatemala, *Código penal . . . 1889*, 101, article 454; *Código penal . . . 1936*, 94, article 469.

6. Forster, "Violent and Violated," 72 (quote); Forster, *Time of Freedom*, 28.

7. Godoy-Paiz, "Women in Guatemala's Metropolitan Area," 42.

8. Poole, "Introduction," 8.

9. Menjívar, *Enduring Violence*, 7; Taussig, *Law in a Lawless Land*; Torres-Rivas, "Sobre el terror."

10. Forster, *Time of Freedom*, 64; Daly and Maher, eds., *Criminology at the Crossroads*; Chesney-Lind, "Girls."

11. Christiansen, *Disobedience*, 9, 65, 69.

12. Few, *Women Who Live Evil Lives*, 44; Socolow, "Women and Crime," 148–53; Kellogg, *Weaving the Past*, 75–76; Stern, *Secret History*, 110–111.

13. Bunzel, *Chichicastenango*, 28; Wagley, *Social and Religious Life*, 16, 21, 41; Reina, *Law of the Saints*, 265; Bunzel, *Chichicastenango*, 121, 126–129; Handy, "Chicken Thieves," 555.

14. La Farge, *Santa Eulalia*, 25.

15. Wagley, *Economics of a Guatemalan Village*, 15 (quote); Wagley, *Social and Religious Life*, 16–17.

16. Rodríguez Sáenz, "'Tiyita Bea'"; Kellogg, *Weaving the Past*, 160–161; Carey, *Engendering Mayan History*; Forster, *Time of Freedom*, 63; Wiebe, "Widening Paths."

17. Kaji' Tz'ikin, 6/24/08, Sololá, Xajaxac.

18. Carey, "Runaway Mothers"; Forster, "Violent and Violated." Unfortunately, culling domestic violence from aggregate national and department data is difficult because the crime was not recorded as such, another indication that authorities were not particularly concerned about it, but rather fell under the broader categories associated with assault and battery such as *agresión, bofetadas, lesiones*, and *injurias*. Appendices 3 and 4. Statistics pertaining to suspects' gender, ethnicity, and literacy were kept during the Ubico regime, in contrast to the sparse data collected during the Estrada Cabrera regime, but officials did not tabulate data pertaining to victims.

19. AMP, *paq.* 24, LSE 1906, July 30, 1916.

20. AGCA, JP-C 1935, *leg.* 79, LSE febrero 1935, Agustina Martín, February 19, 1935.

21. Foucault, *Discipline and Punish*, 11.

22. República de Guatemala, *Código penal . . . 1889*, 101, article 454; *Código penal . . . 1936*, 94, article 469.

23. Forster, "Violent and Violated," 58, 70.

24. *La Gaceta*, June 21, 1931.

25. Bunzel, *Chichicastenango*, 90–91.

26. Wagley, *Economics of a Guatemalan Village*, 76.

27. Bunzel, *Chichicastenango*, 28; Wagley, *Social and Religious Life*, 16–17. Sim-

ilarly, La Farge insisted, "Women . . . show no signs of being cowed or repressed." *Santa Eulalia*, 26. Although this myopia can be attributed partly to their methodologies and inability to speak indigenous languages, the personal and vulnerable nature of domestic violence undoubtedly discouraged locals from discussing it with foreign academics.

28. See, for example, Galtung, "Violence"; Galtung, "Cultural Violence"; Kent, "Children as Victims"; Torres-Rivas, "Sobre el terror"; Farmer, "On Suffering"; Farmer, "Anthropology of Structural Violence." For two fine studies that apply this framework to twentieth-century Guatemala, see Menjívar, *Enduring Violence*, and Forster, "Violent and Violated," especially 57–58.

29. McCreery, *Rural Guatemala*, 317.

30. Menjívar, *Enduring Violence*, 4–6; Forster, "Violent and Violated," 57–58.

31. Wagley, *Economics of a Guatemalan Village*, 15, 54, 76; Wagley, *Social and Religious Life*, 16–17; Bunzel, *Chichicastenango*, 90–91, 121, 139–142.

32. AGCA, JP-C 1926, carta al señor juez de paz de Benita Cajá, June 1, 1926.

33. Bunzel, *Chichicastenango*, 28 (quote), 117–121; Wagley, *Social and Religious Life*, 14–15.

34. Bunzel, *Chichicastenango*, 28.

35. AGCA, JP-C 1926, carta al señor juez de paz de Benita Cajá, June 1, 1926.

36. Bunzel, *Chichicastenango*, 30.

37. AGCA, JP-C 1926, carta al señor juez de paz de Benita Cajá, June 1, 1926.

38. Kellogg, *Weaving the Past*, 131; Putnam, Chambers, and Caulfield, "Introduction," 17; Stern, *Secret History*, 110–111; Alonso, "Rationalizing Patriarchy," 36–39.

39. Lancaster, *Life Is Hard*; Gutmann, *Meanings of Macho*; Irwin, *Mexican Masculinities*; Buffington, "Subjectivity," 1652–1654.

40. Butler, *Psychic Life of Power*, 136–137.

41. Buffington, "Subjectivity," 1654.

42. AGCA, *indice* 116, Chimaltenango, 1914, *leg.* 15b, *exp.* 7.

43. Piccato, *Tyranny of Opinion*, 15, emphasis in the original.

44. AGCA, JP-C 1931, petición al señor Juez de Paz de San Martín de Leoncia Bálan de Ruiz, February 2, 1931.

45. AGCA, JP-C 1933, petición a Señor Juez de Paz de San Martín de Victoria Sutuj, July 14, 1933.

46. Boyer, "Women."

47. Carey, "Runaway Mothers."

48. AGCA, JP-C 1933, petición a Señor Juez de Paz de San Martín de Victoria Sutuj, July 14, 1933.

49. K. Ruggiero, "Wives on 'Deposit'"; Delgado, "*Sin Temor de Dios*," 113–114.

50. AGCA, JP-C 1933, petición a Señor Juez de Paz de San Martín de Victoria Sutuj, July 14, 1933.

51. AGCA, JP-S 1932, carta al jefe político de Aguas Calientes, September 5, 1932; Forster, "Violent and Violated," 71; Mendelson, "Religion and World-View" (short version), 9; Mendelson, "Religion and World-View" (long version), 61–62; Bunzel, *Chichicastenango*, 25–27, 113–116; Wagley, *Social and Religious Life*, 37–40; Wagley, *Economics of a Guatemalan Village*, 14; La Farge, *Santa Eulalia*, 42–43; Tax, *Penny Capitalism*, 178–179; La Farge and Byers, *Year Bearer's People*, 87–88.

52. AGCA, JP-C 1933, petición a Señor Juez de Paz de San Martín de Victoria Sutuj, October 19, 1933.

53. AGCA, JP-C 1926, petición a Señor Juez de Paz de San Martín de Alejandra Aguilar, April 26, 1926.

54. Carmack, *Rebels of Highland Guatemala*, 194.

55. Castro Gutiérez, "Condición femenina," 8, 10, 13; Hünefeldt, *Liberalism in the Bedroom*, 70; Christiansen, *Disobedience*, 87, 183.

56. AGCA, JP-C 1933, petición a Señor Juez de Paz de San Martín de Víctor Cumatzil, October 19, 1933.

57. AGCA, JP-C 1933, petición a Señor Juez de Paz de San Martín de Julián Balan, June 27, 1933.

58. AGCA, *índice* 116, Chimaltenango 1917, *leg.* 18c, *exp.* 29.

59. AGCA, *índice* 116, Chimaltenango 1914, *leg.* 15b, *exp.* 7.

60. La Farge, *Santa Eulalia*, 25–26.

61. AGCA, *índice* 116, Chimaltenango 1902, *leg.* 3, *exp.* 20.

62. Tinsman, "Good Wives," 601–602.

63. AGCA, JP-C 1933, petición a Señor Juez de Paz de San Martín de Víctor Cumatzil, October 19, 1933.

64. Hydén, *Woman Battering*, ix.

65. In Reina, *Law of the Saints*, 265.

66. Wagley, *Social and Religious Life*, 16.

67. Carey, *Engendering Mayan History*.

68. O'Connor, *Gender*; Stern, *Secret History*.

69. Sen, *Idea of Justice*, 167.

70. Ibid., 167.

71. AMP, Juzgado Primero Municipal, June 4, 1929.

72. AMP, LSE 1935, March 12, 1936.

73. For a fuller discussion of rape in highland Guatemala, see Carey, "Forced and Forbidden Sex."

74. Forster, "Violent and Violated," 58; Forster, *Time of Freedom*, 68.

75. Carey, *Engendering Mayan History*, 108–118, 185–186.

76. AGCA, *índice* 116, Chimaltenango, 1911, *leg.* 12e, *exp.* 43.

77. AGCA, *índice* 116, Chimaltenango, 1900, *leg.* 1g, *exp.* 76.

78. AGCA, JP-S, carta al jefe político de San Lorenzo El Cubo, November 13, 1933.

79. Komisaruk, "Rape Narratives," 376; Piccato, *City of Suspects*, 126; Forster, *Time of Freedom*, 70; Hünefeldt, *Liberalism in the Bedroom*, 181; Christiansen, *Disobedience*, 52–53, 119; Bliss and Blum, "Dangerous Driving," 181.

80. AMP, *paq.* 24, February 24, 1923.

81. AMP, *paq.* 24, LSE 1906, October 8, 1916.

82. Carey, "'Oficios de su raza.'"

83. AMP, *paq.* 24, Libro de Sentencias (hereafter LS) 1929, June 13, 1929.

84. Butler, *Excitable Speech*, 163.

85. AGCA, JP-C 1926, carta al sr. juez de San Martín de Tomasa Morejón, March 29, 1926, emphasis my own.

86. Butler, *Psychic Life of Power*, 2, 12.

87. AGCA, *índice* 116, Chimaltenango 1901, *leg.* 2E, *exp.* 63.

88. Bliss, *Compromised Positions*; Guy, *Sex and Danger*; French and James, eds., *Gendered Worlds*; Olcott, Vaughn, and Cano, eds., *Sex in Revolution*; K. Ruggiero, "Honor."

89. AGCA, JP-C 1931, petición a Señor Juez de Paz de San Martín de Lorenza Elías de Tun, December 23, 1923.

90. Ibid.

91. AMP, *paq.* 107, LSE 1941, January 29, 1942.

92. See, for example, La Farge, *Santa Eulalia*, 25.

93. AMP, *paq.* 24, Ramo Civil II, carta a Señor Intendente Municipal y Juez de Paz de Manuela Umul de Can, February 24, 1936.

94. AGCA, JP-C 1927, petición a Señor Juez de Paz de San Martín de Julia Hernández de Camey, January 4, 1927.

95. AGCA, *índice* 116, Chimaltenango 1909, *leg.* 10c, *exp.* 16.

96. Forster, "Violent and Violated," 59.

97. Ibid., 70.

98. AMP, *paq.* 24, LS 1929, August 1, 1929.

99. AGCA, JP-C, 1925, *leg.* 68, *exp.* 72.

100. In Forster, *Time of Freedom*, 75.

101. AGCA, JP-C, 1925, *leg.* 68, *exp.* 72.

102. Ibid.

103. AGCA, JP-C 1931, *leg.* 74, Renuncias y Escritos del año 1931 petición al Juez de Paz de Luz Guerra de Luch.

104. AMP, *paq.* 107, LSE 1943, December 17, 1943.

105. AMP, *paq.* 24, LSE 1906, July 30, 1916.

106. AMP, *paq.* 24, LSE 1906, October 8, 1916.

107. Carey, "Runaway Mothers."

108. AGCA, JP-C 1926, Señor Juez de Paz de San Martín de Juana Ávila de Lool, March 20, 1926.

109. Bunzel, *Chichicastenango*, 28.

110. AGCA, JP-C 1926, Señor Juez de Paz de San Martín de Juana Ávila de Lool, March 20, 1926.

111. Wagley, *Economics of a Guatemalan Village*, 15.

112. Stern, *Secret History of Gender*, 110, 253, 301, 313–314; Alonso, "Rationalizing Patriarchy," 36–37, 40, 42, 43.

113. Stern, *Secret History of Gender*, 97.

114. AGCA, JP-C 1933, *leg.* 76, carta al Señor Juez de Paz de San Martín de Antonia Cumatzil de Balan, April 10, 1933.

115. AGCA, JP-C 1926, carta al Señor Juez de Paz de San Martín de Francisca Chiroy de Sutuj, December 6, 1926, underscore in original.

116. Ibid.

117. AGCA, *índice* 116, Chimaltenango 1914, *leg.* 15D, *exp.* 53.

118. For an exploration of why so few Maya women had access to schools, see Carey, *Engendering Mayan History*, 177–206.

119. Wagley, *Social and Religious Life*.

120. AMP, *paq.* 107, December 2, 1942.

121. Christiansen, *Disobedience*, 112, 156–157, 186; Chambers, *From Subjects to Citizens*, 207; Stern, *Secret History*, 15.

122. *La Gaceta*, March 12, 1933.

123. Speckman Guerra, "'I Was a Man of Pleasure,'" 75.

124. *La Gaceta*, June 21, 1931.

125. Ibid.

126. Piccato, *City of Suspects*, 77–102; Piccato, *Tyranny of Opinion*, 15, 217–218; Gutmann, *Meanings of Macho*, 61, 200, 210–211, 233–234, 237, 239, 244; Gutmann, ed., *Changing Men*; Piccato, "Girl Who Killed a Senator," 141; Lewis, *Children of Sánchez*, 38; Connell, *Masculinities*; Gilmore, *Manhood in the Making*; Alonso, "Rationalizing Patriarchy."

127. Forster, *Time of Freedom*, 36.

128. AGCA, *índice* 116, Chimaltenango 1902, *leg.* 3, *exp.* 20.

129. AMP, *paq.* 127, LSE 1935, January 14, 1935.

130. AMP, *paq.* 127, LSE 1935, January 17, 1935.

131. Carey, *Engendering Mayan History*, 77–79, 91–92, 97–99.

132. Guardia Civil, *La Revista de la Guardia Civil*, August 15, 1946.

133. Ibid.

134. Aguirre and Salvatore, "Introduction," 23.

135. Wagley, *Social and Religious Life*, 14–15; Wagley, *Economics of a Guatemalan Village*, 54, 67; Bunzel, *Chichicastenango*, 139–142.

136. Buffington, "Subjectivity," 1654.

137. Bolton and Bolton, *Conflictos en la familia andina*, 33–35; Sánchez Parga, *¿Por que golpearla?*, 40–41; Nash, *We Eat the Mines*, 77–78; Harvey, "'Hechos naturales'"; Harvey, "Domestic Violence," 75. McKee, "Men's Rights/Women's Wrongs," 176–179; Christiansen, *Disobedience*, 74.

138. J. C. Scott, *Weapons of the Weak*, 35.

139. *La Gaceta*, May 24, 1931.

140. Alonso, "Rationalizing Patriarchy," 39.

141. Merry, "Courts as Performance."

142. Hay, "Time."

143. Carey, *Engendering Mayan History*.

144. O'Connor, *Gender*.

Chapter 6

1. Piccato, *Tyranny of Opinion*, 158, 185–186, 261.

2. Sabean, *Power in the Blood*.

3. For exceptions see Wertheimer, "Gloria's Story"; Piccato, "Hidden Story," 437.

4. Johnson and Lipsett-Rivera, *Faces of Honor*; Caulfield, Chambers, and Putnam, eds., *Honor*; Piccato, *Tyranny of Opinion*; Chambers, *From Subjects to Citizens*.

5. Piccato, *Tyranny of Opinion*, 207–211; Christiansen, *Disobedience*, 54, 118.

6. Piccato, *Tyranny of Opinion*, 64, 126–127, 170–171, 187; Christiansen, *Disobedience*, 6, 52.

7. Mendelson, "Religion and World-View" (long version), 70; Chambers, *From Subjects to Citizens*, 161–188; Sloan, *Runaway Daughters*, 218n4; Christiansen, *Disobedience*, 3, 91–92.

8. For an argument that common folk shifted the emphasis of honor from status to virtue, see Chambers, *From Subjects to Citizens*, 4. In contrast, Christine Hünefeldt suggests that elite efforts to regulate society during the national era led to an expansion of honor's definition. *Liberalism in the Bedroom*.

9. Komisaruk, "Rape Narratives," 387.

10. AMP, *paq.* 24, LSE 1929, June 3, 1929.

11. *La Gaceta*, January 8, 1933.

12. Sloan, *Runaway Daughters*, 116–117; Hames, "Maize-Beer," 354–355.

13. Carey, *Our Elders*, 251; Carey, *Engendering Mayan History*, 151–155.

14. AGCA, *índice* 116, Chimaltenango 1900, *leg.* 1G, *exp.* 19.

15. AGCA, JP-C 1933, petición al Señor Juez de Paz de Pasenala Xajil, May 8, 1933.

16. Christiansen, *Disobedience*, 6.

17. *La Gaceta*, June 14, 1931, 642–643.

18. Taylor, *Drinking*, 88; Carmack, "State and Community," 122.

19. Lanzilli, *Código de honor*, 5–6.

20. AMP, *paq.* 24, LSE 1929, February 4, 1929.

21. AMP, *paq.* 24, LSE 1929, January 3, 1929. Unlike assault and battery litigation, litigants seldom cited inebriation as a factor in verbal abuse or insults. Of the eighty-eight cases I examined, only seven (8 percent) involved drunken offenders.

22. Johnson, "Dangerous Words," 145.

23. AMP, *paq.* 107, LSE 1945–1947, August 22, 1947.

24. AMP, *paq.* 24, July 1, 1929.

25. White, *Speaking Vampires*, 59.

26. AMP, *paq.* 24, LSE 1929, April 26, 1929.

27. AGCA, JP-C 1935 *leg.* 79, LSE febrero 1935, February 4, 1935.

28. While only ten of the litigants in the eighty municipal defamation cases identified themselves as being related (12.5 percent), often the notary did not betray the relationships of the parties.

29. Johnson, "Dangerous Words," 135; Twinam, *Public Lives*; Twinam, "Negotiation of Honor," 79; Chambers, *From Subject to Citizen*, 212.

30. Habermas, *Structural Transformation*; Habermas, "Further Reflections"; Maza, *Private Lives*; Landes, *Women and the Public Sphere*; M. Warren, *Letters of the Republic*; Sennet, *Fall of Public Man*.

31. Gayol, "'Honor Moderno,'" 497.

32. Pitt-Rivers, "Honour and Social Status," 21.

33. Enrique Ahrens, "El derecho concerniente a la dignidad y al honor," *La Gaceta*, March 16, 1941.

34. Sloan, *Runaway Daughters*.

35. Bunzel, *Chichicastenango*, 119; Wagley, *Social and Religious Life*, 41.

36. AGCA, *índice* 116, Chimaltenango 1919 *leg.* 20a, *exp.* 39.

37. Bunzel, *Chichicastenango*, 31, 119, 141; Wagley, *Social and Religious Life*, 16, 41.

38. AMP, *paq.* 107, LSE 1945–1947, May 24, 1947.

39. AGCA, JP-C 1935, *leg.* 79, LSE febrero 1935, February 16, 1935.

40. AMP, *paq.* 107, LSE 1943, September 29, 1943.

41. Ibid.

42. AGCA, JP-C 1926, petición al Señor Juez de Paz de Petronila Luis, January 22, 1926.

43. Bunzel, *Chichicastenango*, 119.

44. AGCA, JP-C 1926, petición al Señor Juez de Paz de Petronila Luis, January 22, 1926.

45. AGCA, JP-C 1931, Escritos del Año 1931, May 14, 1931; Boyer, "Honor among Plebeians"; Putnam, "Sex and Standing"; Fischer, "Slandering Citizens"; K. Ruggiero, "Honor," 367; Sloan, *Runaway Daughters*, 35–36, 115.

46. Gayol, "*Honor Moderno*," 496; Putnam, Chambers, and Caulfield, "Introduction," 16; Sloan, *Runaway Daughters*, 175; Christiansen, *Disobedience*, 78, 94, 101, 103; Chambers, *From Subjects to Citizens*, 101; Komisaruk, "Rape Narratives," 385, 387.

47. Piccato, *Tyranny of Opinion*, 215, 218.

48. AGCA, JP-C 1931, Escritos del Año 1931, May 29, 1931 (underlined in the original).

49. Tax, *Penny Capitalism*, 12.

50. AMP, *paq.* 107, LSE 1941, October 24, 1941.

51. AMP, *paq.* 24, February 6, 1928.

52. AMP, *paq.* 127, LSE 1935, October 14, 1935.

53. Sloan, *Runaway Daughters*, 181; Piccato, *Tyranny of Opinion*, 188–219.

54. Haines, "Sticks and Stones."

55. AMP, *paq.* 127, LSE 1935, November 24, 1935. He was sentenced to ten days in jail commutable by fifty cents a day.

56. AGCA, *índice* 116, Chimaltenango 1908, *leg.* 9c, *exp.* 57.

57. AGCA, JP-C 1931, Escritos del Año 1931, May 14, 1931.

58. Ibid.

59. Sloan, *Runaway Daughters*, 176; Putnam, "Sex and Standing"; Fischer, "Slandering Citizens"; Twinam, *Public Lives*, 41.

60. AGCA, *índice* 116, Chimaltenango 1911, *leg.* 12d, *exp.* 44; AGCA, *índice* 116, Chimaltenango, 1914, *leg.* 15, *exp.* 35; Mendelson, "Religion and World-View" (long version), 64, 370–397; Tax, *Penny Capitalism*, 12; Carey, "Forced and Forbidden Sex."

61. AGCA, JP-C 1927, *leg.* 70A, Escritos presentados por la personas a la Municipalidad de San Martín, 1927.

62. Ibid.

63. AMP, *paq.* 107, LSE 1941, October 14, 1941, Luisa Can contra Mercedes Choy. Rumors of male infidelity could adversely affect men's lives, too, see Mendelson, "Religion and World-View" (long version), 66.

64. AMP, *paq.* 107, LSE 1941, February 15, 1943.

65. Dore, "Holy Family," 109; Lauderdale Graham, *House and Street*, 77; Porter, "'And That It Is Custom,'" 127; Forster, *Time of Freedom*, 64.

66. AGCA, JP-C 1926, September 20, 1926.

67. AGCA, *índice* 116, Chimaltenango 1900, *leg.* 1e, *exp.* 37.

68. Ibid.

69. Weismantel, *Cholas and Pishtacos*, 116.

70. AGCA, *índice* 116, Chimaltenango 1900, *leg.* 1e, *exp.* 37.

71. Pitt-Rivers, *Fate of Shechem*, 18.

72. Piccato, *Tyranny of Opinion*, 217.

73. Rodríguez Sáenz, *Hijas*, 123–124 (quote); Piccato, *Tyranny of Opinion*, 218; Menjívar, *Enduring Violence*, 79–90.

74. Socolow, *Women of Colonial Latin America*, 148; Stern, *Secret History*, 15; Van Vleet, "Partial Theories"; Haviland, *Gossip*; Merry, "Rethinking Gossip and Scandal," 48. Menjívar argues that gossip is a form of violence. *Enduring Violence*, 79.

75. AGCA, JP-C 1931, *leg.* 74, Renuncias y Escritos del Año 1931, November 12, 1931. Christiansen, *Disobedience*, 78–79. In Argentina archival evidence revealed how men used gossip to further their own agendas; K. Ruggiero, "Honor," 367–368. Guatemalan judicial records reveal little about men's use of gossip.

76. AMP, *paq.* 127, LSE 1935, November 27, 1935.

77. AMP, *paq.* 45 II 1.1, July 22, 1940.

78. Ibid., emphasis in the original.

79. Ibid.

80. Parker, "'Gentlemanly Responsibility,'" 118–119, 125–126; Gayol, "'Honor Moderno,'" 492.

81. Piccato, *Tyranny of Opinion*, 214; Christiansen, *Disobedience*, 141.

82. Putnam, *Company They Kept*, 154.

83. AMP, *paq.* 107, LSE 1941, September 2, 1941.

84. Weismantel, *Cholas and Pishtacos*, 14–15; Seligmann, "Between Worlds of Exchange."

85. AMP, *paq.* 24, juzgado municipal, January 14, 1928.

86. Ix'ajpu', 9/01, Patzún (Ixkawoq).

87. C. Smith, "Race-Class-Gender Ideology," 742 (quote); Esquit, *Otros poderes*; Esquit, "Superación del indígena."

88. Forster, "Violent and Violated," 71.

89. AGCA, *índice* 116, Chimaltenango 1902, *leg.* 3, *exp.* 25.

90. Bunzel, *Chichicastenango*, 113.

91. AGCA, *índice* 116, Chimaltenango, 1914, *leg.* 15d, *exp.* 58.

92. AGCA, *índice* 116, Chimaltenango 1917, *leg.* 18, *exp.* 46.

93. Carey, *Our Elders*, 182–183.

94. Carey, "Mayan-Soldier Citizens," 142–143.

95. Ix'ajpu', 9/01, Patzún (Ixkawoq).

96. AGCA, *índice* 116, Chimaltenango 1902, *leg.* 3f, *exp.* 16.

97. AMP, *paq.* 107, LSE 1943, August 25, 1943.

98. Gillin, *Culture of Security*, 66.

99. For an exploration of the terms, particularly *m'os*, that Mayas used to disparage ladinos, see Carey, *Our Elders*, 251–252; Gillin, *Culture of Security*, 66.

100. AGCA, *índice* 116, Chimaltenango 1902, *leg.* 3, *exp.* 25.

101. AMP, *paq.* 24, LSE 1929, February 8, 1929.

102. K. Ruggiero, "Honor," 371; Putnam, *Company They Kept*; Caulfield, Chambers, and Putnam, *Honor*.

103. Findlay, "Courtroom Tales," 221n21; Christiansen, *Disobedience*; Buffington and Piccato, "Tales of Two Women," 397; Díaz, *Female Citizens*, 192–193.

104. In contrast, in nineteenth-century Nicaragua, municipalities eroded these differences by consolidating power. Dore, *Myths of Modernity*, 60.

105. AGCA, *índice* 116, Chimaltenango 1918, *leg.* 19. *exp.* 34.

106. AGCA, *índice* 116, Chimaltenango 1917, *leg.* 18, *exp.* 28.

107. Ibid.

108. Ibid.

109. AMP, *paq.* 107, LSE 1941, September 14, 1943, Señora María de la Cruz, maltratada de palabra por Juan de la Cruz Corona.

110. Ibid.

111. AMP, *paq.* 24, LS, June 17, 1929.

112. AMP, *paq.* 24, LS, June 19, 1929.

113. Putnam, Chambers, and Caulfield, "Introduction," 11 (quote); Chambers, "Private Crimes," 31.

114. Ixpril, 7/1/01, Poaquil; Bunzel, "Role of Alcoholism," 367; Bunzel, *Chichicastenango*, 257; Wagley, *Social and Religious Life*, 101. The police too understood that arrests and imprisonment dishonored suspects. See, for example, *La Gaceta*, March 19, 1933.

115. Beattie, *Tribute of Blood*, 76.

116. Gayol, "*Honor Moderno*,'" 498; Parker, "Law."

117. Ahrens, "El derecho," *La Gaceta*, March 16, 1941; Lanzilli, *Código de honor*; Parker, "Law," 338–339.

118. Sabean, *Power in the Blood*, 95.

119. Forster, *Time of Freedom*, 64.

120. Gayol, "*Honor Moderno*,'" 495; Piccato, *Tyranny of Opinion*; Christiansen, *Disobedience*: Chambers, *Subjects to Citizens*.

121. McCreery, *Rural Guatemala*, 280.

122. Carey, "Empowered through Labor."

123. Esquit, "Nationalist Contradictions"; Esquit, "Superación del indígena."

124. Sloan, *Runaway Daughters*, 176.

125. Piccato, *Tyranny of Opinion*, 158, 185–186.

Conclusion

1. AGCA, JP-C 1930, *leg.* 73, Jefe Político carta al alcalde de San Martín, November 20, 1930; AMC, Libro 1928–1930, February 11, 1929; Carey, *Our Elders*, 125–127; Goldín, "Plaza a mercado," 244, 249–250, 257–258; Carey, *Engendering Mayan History*, 44.

2. Handy, "Chicken Thieves," 533, 555; Forster, *Time of Freedom*; Asturias, *El señor presidente*.

3. Stuntz, *Collapse of American Criminal Justice*.

4. AGCA, JP-S 1931, Carta al Jefe Político de Sacatepéquez de Tomasa Pérez, February 24, 1931.

5. Aguirre and Salvatore, "Introduction," 1 (quote), 15–16; Poole, "Between Threat and Guarantee"; Black, *Limits of Gender Domination*, 88.

6. Christiansen, *Disobedience*, 40–49; O'Connor, *Gender*, xvi–xvii; Barragán, "'Spirit' of Bolivian Laws," 67–68.

7. See, for example, Grandin, *Last Colonial Massacre*, 136–137.

8. Reeves, *Ladinos with Ladinos*; Little-Siebold, "Guatemala and the Dream"; Aguirre and Salvatore, "Introduction," 16.

9. Sen, *Idea of Justice*, 20–21, 212–213.

10. Foucault, "Subject and Power."

11. Herzog, *Upholding Justice*.

12. Handy, "Chicken Thieves," 553; Christiansen, *Disobedience*, 157.

13. Roseberry, "Hegemony," 360–361.

14. See, for example, Scott, *Weapons of the Weak*, 309, 322–340; Gould and Lauria-Santiago, *To Rise in Darkness*.

15. Taylor, foreword, xi (quote); Reeves, *Ladinos with Ladinos*; Grandin, *Blood of Guatemala*.

16. Kaqchikel elites developed a sophisticated discourse of rights during the early twentieth century. See Esquit, "Superación del indígena."

17. Grandin, *Blood of Guatemala*, 140.

18. Poole, "Between Threat and Guarantee," 36, 38, 42.

19. Reeves, *Ladinos with Ladinos*; Grandin, *Blood of Guatemala*; Aguirre and Salvatore, "Introduction," 16.

20. Díaz, *Female Citizens*, 187, 208; Bliss and Blum, "Dangerous Driving," 59; Díaz, "Women," 57; Dore, "One Step Forward," 15; Blum, "Public Welfare"; Deutsch, "Gender and Sociopolitical Change"; Szuchman, *Order*, 225–235; Masiello, "Gender"; Balmori and Voss, *Notable Family Networks*; G. Ruggiero, "Re-Reading the Renaissance"; Muir and Ruggiero, eds., *Sex and Gender*; Handley, "Social Sites."

21. AMP, *paq.* 24, LS 1929, August 1, 1929.

22. Grandin, *Last Colonial Massacre*, 136.

23. Grandin, "It Was Heaven."

24. Carey, "Runaway Mothers."

25. Rodríguez Sáenz, *Hijas*, 137.

26. Carey, "Drunks and Dictators"; Fallaw, "Dry Law."

27. Butler, *Gender Trouble*, 145, 147.

28. Putnam, Chambers, and Caulfield, "Introduction," 11; Sloan, *Runaway Daughters*, 175; Findlay, "Courtroom Tales."

29. Caulfield, "Getting into Trouble," 163; Premo, *Children of the Father King*; Díaz, *Female Citizens*, 60; Black, *Limits of Gender Domination*, 2.

30. Carey, "Forced and Forbidden Sex."

31. Lavrin, *Women*, 5.

32. Stern, *Secret History*, 97 (quotes), 70–111.

33. Buffington, "Subjectivity," 1648; Klubock, "Writing the History," 509.

34. See, for example, Brown, "History of Women"; Engel, "Russia and the Soviet Union"; Twinam, "Estado de la cuestión."

35. Stern, *Secret History*, 70–75, 110, 313–314, 323; Díaz, *Female Citizens*, 217, 229–233.

36. O'Connor, *Gender*.

37. See, for example, Chambers, "Private Crimes," 35; Díaz, *Female Citizens*, 124–130, 240.

38. Knight, "Racism," 76 (quote); S. Smith, *Gender and the Mexican Revolution*, 69.

39. AGCA, *índice* 116, Chimaltenango 1911, 12f, *exp.* 25.

40. S. Joseph, "Gendering Citizenship"; Stolcke, "'Nature' of Nationality"; Phil-

ips, *Which Equalities Matter?*; Díaz, *Female Citizens*, 4–5, 7, 9–14, 19, 168–170, 192, 238.

41. Gould, *To Lead as Equals*, 6–7; Chambers, "Private Crimes," 35; R. Burton, *Afro-Creoles*; Guardino, *Peasants*; Salvatore, Aguirre, and Joseph, eds., *Crime and Punishment*; da Viotti Costa, *Crowns of Glory*.

42. Butler, *Excitable Speech*, 133.

43. Herzfeld, *Anthropology through the Looking Glass*, 146.

44. Ibid., 133.

Glossary

abuso mercantil. Commercial abuse.

acaparamiento. Stockpiling, hoarding.

Administración de Rentas. Treasury Administration.

agricultor. Landowning farmer.

aguardiente. Distilled sugar cane spirits or rum.

aguardiente clandestino. Moonshine or untaxed liquor sold by unlicensed individuals.

alcalde. Mayor and often justice of the peace; *alcalde primero,* first mayor; *alcalde segundo,* second mayor.

aldea. Village.

alguacil. Bailiff.

arroba. A Spanish weight of twenty-five pounds.

asistencia de empírico. Unlicensed physician's assistant.

bandido. Crook, thief.

buhonero. Long-distance or ambulatory merchant.

cabecera. Municipal center.

calumnia. Slander.

chicha. Fermented beverage made from some combination of corn, sugarcane, and fruit.

chorizo. Sausage.

clandestinismo. Moonshining.

cofrade. Member of a *cofradía,* or religious confraternity.

cofradía. Religious confraternity.

comandante. Commander.

compadre. Fictive kin connected by godparent relationship.

conciliación. Mediation, court meeting to reconcile disputes.

concubina. Female domestic partner.

contrabandista. Smuggler.

contratista. Labor broker.

curanderismo. Shamanism.

defraudación al Fisco en el ramo de licores. Defrauding the Treasury of alcohol revenue, a crime.

don. Honorific title, Mr.

doña. Honorific title, Mrs.

empírico. Unlicensed physician.

enganchador. Labor broker.

falta. Misdeed.

finca. Large landed estate.

finquero. Finca owner.

garrafón. Demijohn.

guardia. Militia, armed police force or soldiers.

güipil. Handwoven traditional Maya blouse.

impuesto de piso. Municipal tax on a vendor's space.

indígena. Indigenous person.

indio. Indian, often used as a pejorative.

injuria. Offense, verbal and/or physical abuse.

intendente. Intendant.

ixto. Derogatory term used to denigrate Mayas.

Jefatura Política. Governor's Office.

jefe político. Governor.

jornalero. Day or wage laborer.

juez de paz. Municipal justice of the peace.

juez de primera instancia. Department judge, literally judge of first jurisdiction.

juez del mercado. Market inspector and tax collector.

justicia. Justice.

juzgado de primera instancia. Department court, literally court of first jurisdiction.

ladrón. Thief.

madre desnaturalizada. Unnatural mother.

madre sin entrañas. Soulless mother.

mandamiento. Forced-labor draft.

maxtate. Loincloth wrap that *indígenas* used to wear, diaper.

milpa. Family cornfield.

Ministerio de Hacienda. Treasury Ministry.

molendera. Female corn grinder, often makes tortillas.

mo's. Derogatory Kaqchikel term for ladino.

municipalidad indígena. Indigenous municipality.

municipio. Municipality.

nativo. Native.

natural. Native.

oficios de su sexo y raza. Occupations appropriate to one's sex and race.

patria potestad. A father's legal control over his children and their property.

peso. Guatemalan official currency until 1925, used in the central highlands into the 1930s.

Policía de Hacienda. Treasury Police.

po't. Traditional indigenous, handwoven blouse.

potestad marital. A man's right over the person and property of his wife.

principal. Indigenous religious and political leader.

pues. Well, often serving a phatic function as a placeholder.

puta. Whore.

qawinäq. Literally "our people," Kaqchikel term for indigenous people.

quetzal. Guatemalan currency adopted in 1925 and later pegged to the U.S. dollar.

quintal. One hundred pounds.

real. ⅛ of a peso.

regidor. Councilman or alderman.

regidor de indígenas. Indigenous councilman.

reo. Criminal.

Resguardo de Hacienda. Treasury Police.

sapa. A gossip.

sin instrucción. Without formal education.

sinvergüenza. "Shameless" as adjective, "scoundrel" as noun.

soltera. Single woman.

susto. Fright.

tapa de panela. Brown-sugar cake or disk, often used to produce *aguardiente*.

texel. Member of a religious sisterhood.

tinaja. Large earthen jar.

tortillera. Female tortilla maker and vendor.

tribunal. Court.

üq. Traditional indigenous skirt.

Bibliography

The bibliography is organized into primary and secondary sources. Primary sources are grouped into three categories: archives, Guatemalan government documents, and oral histories. Secondary sources are the published works cited.

Primary Sources

Archives

Archivo General de Centro América (AGCA), Guatemala City

> Hemeroteca and Hemeroteca Nacional. Both these archives are housed in the AGCA building. The Hemeroteca Nacional has a collection of national newspapers, the most important of which for this study was *La Gaceta: Revista de Policía y Variedades* (1921–1943). The Hemeroteca-AGCA has government publications including the *Memorias de la Dirección General de la Policía Nacional.*
>
> *Índice* (index) 116, criminal Chimaltenango, 1900–1925. This index corresponds to the criminal records generated by the Juzgado de Primera Instancia de Chimaltenango. The documents to which the index refers are organized by year, *legajo* (*leg.*, dossier, bundle), and *expediente* (*exp.*, proceeding).
>
> Jefatura Política de Chimaltenango (JP-C). Chimaltenango department governor's records. These documents are catalogued by year, *legajo*, and *expediente*. Where appropriate and helpful, I further list a brief description of the document itself. The vast majority of these documents, if not all, pertain to San Martín Jilotepeque.
>
> Jefatura Política de Sacatepéquez (JP-S). Sacatepéquez department governor's records. These documents are arranged by *bulto* (bundle) and year. I also delineate them by date and heading.

Archivo Municipal de Patzicía (AMP). Thanks to the work of Edgar Esquit and others these archives are organized by *paquetes* (bundles) and indexed. The archive has been moved at least once since the index was completed, and consequently the *paquetes* are not in any particular order and a few have been lost. I identify each document by *paquete* (*paq.*) and a brief description.

Archivo Municipal de San Juan Comalapa (AMC). Municipal authorities insisted most of the records were destroyed during the 1970s and 1980s because of the civil war and 1976 earthquake; the archives to which I gained access were mainly records from municipal meetings.

Archivo Municipal de Sololá (AMS). Destroyed during earthquakes and the civil war, the capital's historical records have been reduced to documentation of municipal meetings and national identity cards.

Bancroft Library, University of California, Berkeley. In addition to published Guatemalan legislation, this library holds a number of Guatemalan government ministries' annual reports.

Boston Athenaeum, Boston. This private archive holds a collection of Eadweard Muybridge's late nineteenth-century Central America photographs.

Centro de Investigaciones Regionales de Mesoamérica (CIRMA), Antigua, Guatemala. CIRMA has an excellent photograph archive and significant newspaper collection.

Latin American Library, Tulane University, New Orleans. This collection includes Guatemalan legislation, annual reports from government ministries, national newspapers, and specialized periodicals such as *La Gaceta*.

Nettie Lee Benson Latin American Collection, University of Texas, Austin. In addition to some issues of *La Gaceta*, this library holds bound copies of Guatemalan civil and penal codes from the nineteenth and twentieth centuries.

Guatemalan Government Documents

Dirección General de Estadística (DGE). *Censo general de la República de Guatemala, levantado en 26 de febrero de 1893*. Guatemala: Tipografía y Encuadernación Nacional, 1894.

———. *Censo de la República de Guatemala 1921*. Guatemala City: Talleres Gutenburg, 1924.

———. *Quinto censo general de población levantado el 7 de abril de 1940*. Guatemala City, June 1942.

Guardia Civil. *Memoria de los trabajos realizados por la Guardia Civil de Guatemala durante el ano de 1945*. Guatemala: Tipografía Nacional, 1949.

———. *La Revista de la Guardia Civil*, August 15, 1946.

Policía Nacional. *Memoria de la Dirección General de la Policía Nacional, presentada al Ministro de Gobernación y Justicia*, 1899–1944. Guatemala City: Tipografía Nacional.

República de Guatemala. *Código civil de la República de Guatemala, 1877*. Guatemala City: Imprenta de El Progreso, 1877.

———. *Código civil de la República de Guatemala, 1927*. Guatemala City: Tipografía Nacional, 1927.

———. *Código civil de la República de Guatemala, 1933*. Guatemala City: Centro Editorial, 1933.

———. *Código civil de la República de Guatemala, 1937*. Guatemala City: Tipografía Nacional, 1937.

————. *Código penal: Incluyendo las reformas de que ha sido objeto hasta la fecha, 1945*. Guatemala City: December 1945.

————. *Código penal, ley de notario y otras leyes de importancia, 1936*. Guatemala City: Tipografía Nacional, 1936.

————. *Código penal de la República de Guatemala, 1889*. Guatemala City: Establecimiento Tipográfico La Unión, 1889.

————. *Código penal y de procedimientos penales de la República de Guatemala, 1941*. Guatemala City: Tipografía Nacional, 1941.

————. *Recopilación de las leyes de la República de Guatemala*, 1917–1937. 21 vols. Guatemala City: Tipografía Nacional.

Secretaría de Estado, Despacho de Gobernación y Justicia (SGJ). *Memorias de la Secretaría de Gobernación y Justicia 1940*. Guatemala City: Tipografía Nacional, 1941.

Oral Histories

Due to the continued political volatility of Guatemala and recurrent human rights abuses, I have preserved the anonymity of my informants for their safety. I have used pseudonyms that derive from the Maya calendar. Female informants can be recognized by the "Ix" prefix to their one-word names, while male names have two words. When research assistants performed the interviews, they are listed by their Maya names here and in parentheses in the endnotes. I conducted all other interviews. With one exception, the interviews were conducted in Kaqchikel. Since Ixjo'q is a bilingual Mam and Spanish speaker, I conducted the interview in Spanish.

Name	Date	Town/*aldea* (village)	Interviewer
B'eleje' Imox	6/5/03, 8/6/05	Comalapa	Author
Ix'achib'il	8/1/05	Comalapa	Ixk'at
Ix'aj	12/17/97, 2/9/98	Comalapa	Author
Ix'ajpu'	9/01	Patzún	Ixkawoq
Ix'ey	6/25/03	Comalapa	Author
Ix'eya'	8/10/05	Comalapa	Ix'ey
Ixjo'q	11/6/97	Comalapa	Author
Ixki'ch	6/27/01	Comalapa	Author
Ixkotz'i'j	8/6/05	Comalapa, Pamamus	Author
Ixpop	8/1/05	Comalapa	Ixk'at
Ixpril	7/1/01	Poaquil	Author
Ixq'anil	8/5/05	Comalapa	Author
Ixsimïl	2/9/05	Comalapa	Ix'ey
Ixsinka	7/18/03	Patzún	Ixkawoq
Ixsub'äl	8/23/05	Comalapa	Ix'ey
Ixte'	8/5/05	Comalapa	Author
Ixtz'inik'an	6/2/98	Tecpán	Author
Junlajuj Ajpu'	8/2/98	Comalapa	Author
Junlajuj Imox	9/15/98	Comalapa	Author
Kaji' Tz'ikin	6/24/08	Sololá, Xajaxac	Author
Oxlajuj Ajpu'	1/19/98	Comalapa, Panabajal	Author

Secondary Sources

Abu-Lughod, Lila. "The Romance of Resistance: Tracing the Transformations of Power through Bedouin Women." *American Ethnologist* 17, no. 1 (1990): 41–55.

Adams, Richard Newbold. *Crucifixion by Power: Essays on Guatemalan National Social Structure, 1944–1966.* Austin: University of Texas Press, 1970.

Adams, Walter Randolph. "Guatemala." In *International Handbook on Alcohol and Culture,* edited by Dwight B. Heath, 99–109. Westport, CT: Greenwood Press, 1995.

Aguirre, Carlos. *The Criminals of Lima and Their Worlds: The Prison Experience, 1850–1935.* Durham, NC: Duke University Press, 2005.

Aguirre, Carlos, and Ricardo D. Salvatore. "Introduction: Writing the History of Law, Crime, and Punishment in Latin America." In *Crime and Punishment in Latin America,* edited by Ricardo D. Salvatore, Carlos Aguirre, and Gilbert Joseph, 1–32. Durham, NC: Duke University Press, 2001.

Akyeampong, Emmanuel. *Drink, Power, and Cultural Change: A Social History of Alcohol in Ghana, c. 1800 to Recent Times.* Oxford, England: James Currey, 1996.

Alonso, Anna María. "Rationalizing Patriarchy: Gender, Domestic Violence, and Law in Mexico." *Identities* 2, nos. 1–2 (1997): 29–47.

Annino, Antonio. "Ciudadanía versus gobernabilidad republicana en México. Los orígenes de un dilema." In *Ciudadanía política y formación de las naciones: Perspectivas históricas de América Latina,* edited by Hilda Sabato, 62–93. Mexico City: Colegio de México, Fideicomiso Historia de las Américas, Fondo de Cultura Económica, 1999.

Arévalo Martínez, Rafael. *Ecce Pericles! La tiranía de Manuel Estrada Cabrera en Guatemala.* 3rd ed. San José, Costa Rica: Editorial Universitaria Centroamericana, 1971.

Asturias, Miguel Angel. *El señor presidente.* Buenos Aires: Editorial Losada, 1948.

Balderston, Daniel, and Donna J. Guy, eds. *Sex and Sexuality in Latin America.* New York: New York University Press, 1997.

Balmori, Diana A., and Stuart Voss. *Notable Family Networks in Latin America.* Chicago: University of Chicago Press, 1984.

Baratta, Alessandro. *Criminología crítica y crítica del derecho penal.* Mexico City: Siglo Veintiuno, 1991.

Barragán, Rossana. "The 'Spirit' of Bolivian Laws: Citizenship, Patriarchy, and Infamy." In *Honor, Status, and Law in Modern Latin America,* edited by Sueann Caulfield, Sarah C. Chambers, and Lara Putnam, 66–86. Durham, NC: Duke University Press, 2005.

Beattie, Peter. *The Tribute of Blood: Army, Race, and Nation in Brazil, 1864–1945.* Durham, NC: Duke University Press, 2001.

Beezley, William H., Cheryl E. Martin, and William E. French, eds. *Rituals of Rule, Rituals of Resistance: Public Celebrations and Popular Culture in Mexico.* Wilmington, DE: Scholarly Resources, 1994.

Benton, Laura. "'The Laws of This Country': Foreigners and the Legal Construction of Sovereignty in Uruguay, 1830–1875." *Law and History Review* 19, no. 3 (2001): 479–511.

Besse, Susan K. "Crimes of Passion: The Campaign against Wife-Killing in Brazil, 1910–1940." *Journal of Social History* 22, no. 4 (1989): 653–666.

Black, Chad. *The Limits of Gender Domination: Women, the Law, and Political Crisis in Quito, 1765–1830*. Albuquerque: University of New Mexico Press, 2011.
Black, Donald. *The Behavior of Law*. New York: Academic Press, 1976.
———. *Sociological Justice*. Oxford, England: Oxford University Press, 1989.
Bliss, Katherine. *Compromised Positions: Prostitution, Public Health, and Gender Politics in Revolutionary Mexico City*. University Park: Pennsylvania State University Press, 2001.
Bliss, Katherine, and Ann Blum. "Dangerous Driving: Adolescence, Sex, and the Gendered Experience of Public Space in Early Twentieth-Century Mexico City." In *Gender, Sexuality, and Power in Latin America Since Independence*, edited by William E. French and Katherine Elaine Bliss, 163–186. Lanham, MD: Rowman and Littlefield, 2007.
Blum, Ann S. *Domestic Economies: Family, Work, and Welfare in Mexico City, 1884–1943*. Lincoln: University of Nebraska Press, 2009.
———. "Public Welfare and Child Circulation, Mexico City, 1877–1925." *Journal of Family History* 23, no. 3 (1998): 240–271.
Boddam-Whetham, J. W. *Across Central America*. London: Hurst, 1877.
Bolton, Ralph, and Charlene Bolton. *Conflictos en la familia andina*. Translated by Jorge A. Flores Ochoa and Yemira D. Nájar Vizcarra. Cuzco: Centro de Estudios Andinos, 1975.
Boyer, Richard. "Honor among Plebeians: *Mala Sangre* and Social Reputation." In *The Faces of Honor: Sex, Shame, and Violence in Colonial Latin America*, edited by Lyman L. Johnson and Sonya Lipsett-Rivera, 152–178. Albuquerque: University of New Mexico Press, 1998.
———. "Women, *La Mala Vida*, and the Politics of Marriage." In *Sexuality and Marriage in Colonial Latin America*, edited by Asunción Lavrin, 252–286. Lincoln: University of Nebraska Press, 1989.
Bronfman, Alejandra. "Mismeasured Women: Gender and Social Science on the Eve of Female Suffrage in Cuba." In *Gender, Sexuality, and Power in Latin America since Independence*, edited by William E. French and Katherine Elaine Bliss, 71–86. Lanham, MD: Rowman and Littlefield, 2007.
Brown, Kathleen. "The History of Women in the United States to 1865." In *Women's History in Global Perspective*, vol. 2, edited by Bonnie G. Smith, 238–279. Urbana: University of Illinois Press, 2005.
Buffington, Robert M. "Introduction: Conceptualizing Criminality in Latin America." In *Reconstructing Criminality in Latin America*, edited by Carlos A. Aguirre and Robert Buffington, xi–xix. Wilmington, DE: Scholarly Resources, 2000.
———. "*Los Jotos*: Contested Visions of Homosexuality in Modern Mexico." In *Sex and Sexuality in Latin America*, edited by Daniel Balderston and Donna J. Guy, 118–132. New York: New York University Press, 1997.
———. "Subjectivity, Agency, and the New Latin American History of Gender and Sexuality." *History Compass* 5, no. 5 (2007): 1640–1660.
Buffington, Robert, and Pablo Piccato. "Tales of Two Women: The Narrative Construal of Porfirian Reality." *The Americas* 55, no. 3 (January 1999): 391–424.
Bunzel, Ruth. *Chichicastenango: A Guatemalan Village*. Seattle: University of Washington Press, 1967. Originally published 1952.
———. "The Role of Alcoholism in Two Central American Cultures." *Psychiatry*, no. 3 (1940): 361–387.

Burgess, Paul. *Justo Rufino Barrios: A Biography*. Philadelphia: Dorrance, 1926.

Burkitt, Robert. "Explorations in the Highlands of Western Guatemala," *Museum Journal* 21, no. 1 (1930): 41–72.

Burns, Kathryn. "Notaries, Truth, and Consequences." *American Historical Review* 110, no. 2 (April 2005): 350–379.

Burton, Antoinette, ed. *Archive Stories: Facts, Fictions, and the Writing of History*. Durham, NC: Duke University Press, 2005.

———. "History Practice: Finding Women in the Archive: Introduction." *Journal of Women's History* 20, no. 1 (Spring 2008): 149–150.

Burton, Richard D.E. *Afro-Creole: Power, Opposition, and Play in the Caribbean*. Ithaca, NY: Cornell University Press, 1997.

Butler, Judith. *Bodies that Matter: On the Discursive Limits of Sex*. New York: Routledge, 1993.

———. *Excitable Speech*. New York: Routledge, 1997.

———. *Gender Trouble: Feminism and the Subversion of Identity*. New York: Routledge, 1990.

———. *The Psychic Life of Power: Theories in Subjection*. Stanford, CA: Stanford University Press, 1997.

Caimiri, Lila M. "Remembering Freedom: Life as Seen from the Prison Cell." In *Crime and Punishment in Latin America*, edited by Ricardo D. Salvatore, Carlos Aguirre, and Gilbert M. Joseph, 391–414. Durham, NC: Duke University Press, 2001.

Cano, Gabriela. "Unconcealable Realities of Desire: Amelio Robles's (Transgender) Masculinity in the Mexican Revolution." In *Sex in Revolution: Gender, Politics, and Power in Modern Mexico*, edited by Jocelyn Olcott, Mary Kay Vaughn, and Gabriela Cano, 35–56. Durham, NC: Duke University Press, 2006.

Carey, David Jr. "A Democracy Born in Violence: Maya Perceptions of the 1944 Patzicía Massacre and the 1954 Coup." In *After the Coup: An Ethnographic Reframing of Guatemala 1954*, edited by Timothy J. Smith and Abigail E. Adams, 73–98. Champaign: University of Illinois Press, 2010.

———. "Drunks and Dictators: Inebriation's Gendered, Ethnic, and Class Components in Guatemala, 1898–1944." Unpublished manuscript.

———. "Empowered through Labor and Buttressing Their Communities: Mayan Women and Coastal Migration, 1875–1965." *Hispanic American Historical Review* 86, no. 3 (August 2006): 501–534.

———. *Engendering Mayan History: Kaqchikel Women as Conduits and Agents of the Past, 1875–1970*. New York: Routledge, 2006.

———. "Forced and Forbidden Sex: Rape and Sexual Freedom in Early Twentieth-Century Guatemala." *The Americas* 69, no. 3 (January 2013): 357–389.

———. "'Hard Working, Orderly Little Women': Mayan Vendors and Marketplace Struggles in Early-Twentieth-Century Guatemala." *Ethnohistory* 55, no. 4 (Fall 2008): 579–607.

———. "*Indigenismo* and Guatemalan History in the Twentieth Century." *Revista Interamericana de Bibliografía* 48, no. 2 (1998): 379–408.

———. "Mayan Soldier-Citizens: Ethnic Pride in the Guatemalan Military, 1925–1945." In *Military Struggle and Identity Formation in Latin America: Race, Nation, and Community 1850–1950*, edited by Nicola Foote and René D. Harder Horst, 136–156. Gainesville: University Press of Florida, 2010.

———. "'*Oficios de Su Raza y Sexo*' (Occupations Appropriate to Her Race and Sex): Mayan Women and Expanding Gender Identities in Early Twentieth-Century Guatemala." *Journal of Women's History* 20, no. 1 (Spring 2008): 114–148.

———. *Our Elders Teach Us: Maya-Kaqchikel Historical Perspectives. Xkib'ij kan qate' qatata'.* Tuscaloosa: University of Alabama Press, 2001.

———. "Runaway Mothers and Daughters: Crimes of Abandonment in Twentieth-Century Guatemala." *Journal of Family History,* forthcoming 2013.

Carey, David Jr., and M. Gabriela Torres. "Precursors to Femicide: Guatemalan Women in a Vortex of Violence." *Latin American Research Review* 45, no. 3 (2010): 142–164.

Carmack, Robert M. *Rebels of Highland Guatemala: The Quiche-Mayas of Momostenango.* Norman: University of Oklahoma Press, 1995.

———. "State and Community in Nineteenth-Century Guatemala: The Momostenango Case." In *Guatemalan Indians and the State, 1540–1988,* edited by Carol Smith, 116–136. Austin: University of Texas Press, 1990.

Casaús Arzú, Marta Elena. *Guatemala: Linaje y racismo.* Guatemala City: Facultad Latinoamericana de Ciencias Sociales, 1995.

———. *La metamorfosis del racismo en Guatemala/Uk' Exwachiziik Ri Kaxlan Na'Ooj Pa Iximuleev.* Guatemala City: Editorial Cholsamaj, 1998.

Casaús Arzú, Marta Elena, and Teresa García Giráldez. *Las redes intelectuales centroamericanas: un siglo de imaginarios nacionales (1820–1920).* Guatemala City: F y G Editores, 2009.

Castellanos Cambranes, Julio. *Coffee and Peasants: The Origins of the Modern Plantation Economy in Guatemala, 1853–1897.* South Woodstock, VT: CIRMA/Plumsock Mesoamerican Studies, 1991.

Castro Gutiérrez, Felipe. "Condición femenina y violencia conyugal entre los Purepechas durante la época colonial." *Mexican Studies/Estudios Mexicanos* 14, no. 1 (1998): 5–21.

Caulfield, Sueann. "Getting into Trouble: Dishonest Women, Modern Girls, and Women-Men in the Conceptual Language of Vida Policial, 1925–1927." *Signs: Journal of Women in Culture and Society* 19, no. 11 (Autumn 1993): 146–176.

———. *In Defense of Honor: Sexual Morality, Modernity, and Nation in Early Twentieth-Century Brazil.* Durham, NC: Duke University Press, 2000.

Caulfield, Sueann, Sarah C. Chambers, and Lara Putnam, eds. *Honor, Status, and Law in Modern Latin America.* Durham, NC: Duke University Press, 2005.

Chambers, Sarah C. *From Subjects to Citizens: Honor, Gender, and Politics in Arequipa, Peru, 1780–1854.* University Park: Pennsylvania State University Press, 1999.

———. "Private Crimes, Public Order: Honor, Gender, and the Law in Early Republican Peru." In *Honor, Status, and Law in Modern Latin America,* edited by Sueann Caulfield, Sarah C. Chambers, and Lara Putnam, 27–49. Durham, NC: Duke University Press, 2005.

Chazkel, Amy. *Laws of Chance: Brazil's Clandestine Public Lottery and the Making of Urban Public Life.* Durham, NC: Duke University Press, 2011.

Chesney-Lind, Meda. "Girls, Delinquency, and Juvenile Justice: Toward a Feminist Theory of Young Women's Crime." In *The Criminal Justice System and Women,* edited by Barbara Raffel Price and Natalie J. Sokoloff, 71–88. New York: McGraw-Hill, 1995.

Christiansen, Tanja. *Disobedience, Slander, Seduction, and Assault: Women and Men in Cajamarca, Peru, 1862–1900.* Austin: University of Texas Press, 2004.

Clegern, Wayne M. *Origins of Liberal Dictatorship in Central America: Guatemala, 1865–1873.* Niwot: University Press of Colorado, 1994.

Coe, Michael. *The Maya.* New York: Thames and Hudson, 1999.

Colby, Benjamin, and Pierre L. van de Berghe. *Ixil Country: A Plural Society in Highland Guatemala.* Berkeley: University of California Press, 1969.

Colson, Elizabeth, and Thayer Scudder. *For Prayer and Profit: The Ritual, Economic, and Social Importance of Beer in Gwembe District, Zambia, 1950–1982.* Stanford, CA: Stanford University Press, 1988.

Comaroff, Jean. *Body of Power, Spirit of Resistance: The Culture and History of a South African People.* Chicago: University of Chicago Press, 1985.

Comaroff, John L. Foreword to *Contested States: Law, Hegemony, and Resistance.* Edited by Mindie Lazarus-Black and Susan F. Hirsh, ix–xiii. New York: Routledge, 1994.

Connell, R. W. *Masculinities.* Berkeley: University of California Press, 1995.

Contreras, J. Daniel. *Una rebelión indígena en el partido de Totonicapán en 1820: El indio y la Independencia.* Guatemala City: Imprenta Universitaria de la Universidad de San Carlos, 1968.

Corrigan, Philip. "State Formation." In *Everyday Forms of State Formation: Revolution and Integration of Rule in Modern Mexico,* edited by Gilbert M. Joseph and Daniel Nugent, xvii–xix. Durham, NC: Duke University Press, 1994.

Cruz-Malavé, Arnaldo. "'What a Tangled Web!' Masculinity, Abjection, and the Foundations of Puerto Rican Literature in the United States." In *Sex and Sexuality in Latin America,* edited by Daniel Balderston and Donna J. Guy, 234–249. New York: New York University Press, 1997.

Cruz Salazar, José Luiz. "El ejercito como una fuerza política." *Estudios Sociales: Revista de Ciencias Sociales* (April 1972): 74–98.

Daly, Kathleen, and Lisa Maher, eds. *Criminology at the Crossroads: Feminist Readings in Crime and Justice.* New York: Oxford University Press, 1998.

Darnton, Robert. *The Great Cat Massacre and Other Episodes from French Cultural History.* New York: Vintage Books, 1984.

da Viotti Costa, Emília. *Crowns of Glory, Tears of Blood.* New York: Oxford University Press, 1994.

Davis, Natalie Zemon. *Fiction in the Archives: Pardon Tales and Their Tellers in Sixteenth-Century France.* Stanford, CA: Stanford University Press, 1987.

de la Fuente, Ariel. *Children of Facundo: Caudillo and Gaucho Insurgency during the Argentine State-Formation Process (La Rioja, 1853–1870).* Durham, NC: Duke University Press, 2000.

Delgado, Jessica. "*Sin Temor de Dios*: Women and Ecclesiastical Justice in Eighteenth-Century Toluca." *Colonial Latin American Research Review* 18, no. 1 (April 2009): 99–121.

del Olmo, Rosa. *América Latina y su criminología.* Mexico City: Siglo Veintiuno, 1981.

Desmond, Lucas. "*Pido Justicia*': Women and Land in Rural Guatemala." *Student Journal of Latin American Studies* 1, no. 1 (2009): 10–25.

Deutsch, Sandra McGee. "Gender and Sociopolitical Change in Twentieth-

Century Latin America." *Hispanic American Historical Review* 71, no. 2 (1991): 259–306.

Díaz, Arlene. *Female Citizens, Patriarchs, and the Law in Venezuela, 1786–1904.* Lincoln: University of Nebraska Press, 2004.

———. "Women, Order, and Progress in Guzman Blanco's Venezuela, 1870–1888." In *Crime and Punishment in Latin America*, edited by Ricardo D. Salvatore, Carlos Aguirre, and Gilbert M. Joseph, 56–82. Durham, NC: Duke University Press, 2001.

Díaz Romeu, Guillermo. "Del régimen de Carlos Herrera a la elección de Jorge Ubico." In *Historia general de Guatemala*. Vol. 5: *Época contemporánea: 1898–1944*, edited by Jorge Luján Muñoz and J. Daniel Contreras R., 37–42. Guatemala City: Asociación de Amigos del País, Fundación para la Cultura y el Desarrollo, 1996.

Dore, Elizabeth. "The Holy Family: Imagined Households in Latin American History." In *Gender Politics in Latin America: Debates in Theory and Practice*, edited by Elizabeth Dore, 101–117. New York: Monthly Review Press, 1997.

———. *Myths of Modernity: Peonage and Patriarchy in Nicaragua*. Durham, NC: Duke University Press, 2006.

———. "One Step Forward, Two Steps Back: Gender and the State in the Long Nineteenth Century." In *Hidden Histories of Gender and the State in Latin America*, edited by Elizabeth Dore and Maxine Molyneux, 3–32. Durham, NC: Duke University Press, 2000.

———. "Property, Households, and Public Regulation of Domestic Life: Diormo, Nicaragua, 1840–1900." In *Hidden Histories of Gender and the State in Latin America*, edited by Elizabeth Dore and Maxine Molyneux, 194–214. Durham, NC: Duke University Press, 2000.

Dore, Elizabeth, and Maxine Molyneux, eds. *Hidden Histories of Gender and the State in Latin America*. Durham, NC: Duke University Press, 2000.

Dosal, Paul J. *Power in Transition: The Rise of Guatemala's Industrial Oligarchy, 1871–1994*. Westport, CT: Praeger, 1995.

Dym, Jordana. "Citizen of Which Republic?: Foreigners and the Construction of National Citizenship in Central America, 1823–1845." *The Americas* 64, no. 4 (2008): 477–510.

Eber, Christine. *Women and Alcohol in a Highland Maya Town: Water of Hope, Water of Sorrow*. Austin: University of Texas Press, 2000.

Eiss, Paul K. "*El Pueblo Mestizo*: Modernity, Tradition, and Statecraft in Yucatán, 1870–1907." *Ethnohistory* 55, no. 4 (Fall 2008): 525–552.

Engel, Barbara. "Russia and the Soviet Union." In *Women's History in Global Perspective*, vol. 3, edited by Bonnie G. Smith, 145–179. Urbana: University of Illinois Press, 2005.

Ericastilla, Ana Carla, and Liseth Jiménez. "Las clandestinistas de aguardiente en Guatemala a fines del siglo XIX." In *Mujeres, género e historia en América Central durante los siglos XVIII, XIX, Y XX*, edited by Eugenia Rodríguez Sáenz, 13–24. Mexico City: UNIFEM Oficina Regional de México, Centroamérica, Cuba y República Dominicana; South Woodstock, VT: Plumsock Mesoamerican Studies, 2002.

Ericastilla Samayoa, Ana Carla, and Liseth Jiménez Chacón. "'A riesgo de perder el honor': Transgresiones sexuales de las mujeres en Quetzaltenango Guatemala, siglo XIX." *Diálogos: Revista Electrónica de Historia* 5, no. 1 (April 2004). *http://historia.fcs.ucr.ac.cr/dialogos.htm* (Accessed November 15, 2009).

Esquit, Edgar. "Nationalist Contradictions: Pan-Mayanism, Representations of the Past, and the Reproduction of Inequalities in Guatemala." In *Decolonizing Native Histories: Collaboration, Knowledge, and Language in the Americas*, edited by Florencia E. Mallon, 196–218. Durham, NC: Duke University Press, 2012.

———. *Otros poderes, nuevos desafíos: Relaciones interétnicas en Tecpán y su entorno departamental (1871–1935)*. Guatemala City: Magna Terra Editores, 2002.

———. "La superación del indígena: La política de la modernización entre las elites indígenas de Comalapa, siglo XX." PhD diss., El Colegio de Michoacán, Mexico, 2008.

Fallaw, Ben. "Bartolomé García Correa and the Politics of Maya Identity in Postrevolutionary Yucatán, 1911–1933." *Ethnohistory* 55, no. 4 (Fall 2008): 553–578.

———. "Dry Law, Wet Politics: Drinking and Prohibition in Post-Revolutionary Yucatán, 1915–1935." *Latin American Research Review* 37, no. 2 (2001): 37–64.

———. "Rethinking Mayan Resistance: Changing Relations between Federal Teachers and Mayan Communities in Eastern Yucatan, 1929–1935." *Journal of Latin American Anthropology* 9, no. 1 (2004): 151–178.

Farmer, Paul. "An Anthropology of Structural Violence." *Current Anthropology* 45, no. 3 (2004): 305–325.

———. "On Suffering and Structural Violence: A View from Below." *Daedalus* 125, no. 1 (Winter 1996): 261–283.

Few, Martha. "Women, Religion, and Power: Gender and Resistance in Daily Life in Late Seventeenth-Century Guatemala." *Women, Power, and Resistance in Colonial Mesoamerica*, special issue, edited by Kevin Gosner and Deborah E. Kanter, *Ethnohistory* 42, no. 4 (Autumn 1995): 627–637.

———. *Women Who Live Evil Lives: Gender, Religion, and the Politics of Power in Colonial Guatemala*. Austin: University of Texas Press, 2002.

Findlay, Eileen J. "Courtroom Tales of Sex and Honor: *Rapto* and Rape in Late Nineteenth-Century Puerto Rico." In *Honor, Status and Law in Modern Latin America*, edited by Sueann Caulfield, Sarah C. Chambers, and Lara Putnam, 201–222. Durham, NC: Duke University Press, 2005.

Fischer, Brodwyn. "Slandering Citizens: Insults, Class, and Social Legitimacy in Rio de Janeiro's Criminal Courts." In *Honor, Status, and Law in Modern Latin America*, edited by Sueann Caulfield, Sarah C. Chambers, and Lara Putnam, 176–200. Durham, NC: Duke University Press, 2005.

Forment, Carlos A. *Democracy in Latin America, 1760–1900*. Chicago: University of Chicago Press, 2003.

Forster, Cindy. *The Time of Freedom: Campesino Workers in Guatemala's October Revolution*. Pittsburgh: University of Pittsburgh Press, 2001.

———. "Violent and Violated Women: Justice and Gender in Rural Guatemala, 1936–1956." *Journal of Women's History* 11, no. 3 (1999): 68–72.

Foucault, Michel. *Discipline and Punish: The Birth of the Prison*. 2nd ed. New York: Vintage Books, 1995.

———. *Power/Knowledge: Selected Interviews and Other Writings, 1972–1977*. Edited by Colin Gordon. New York: Harvester Press, 1980.

———. "The Subject and Power." *Critical Inquiry* 8, no. 4 (1982): 777–795.

French, John D., and Daniel James, eds. *The Gendered Worlds of Latin American Women Workers: From Household and Factory to Union Hall and Ballot Box*. Durham, NC: Duke University Press, 1998.

Gabbert, Wolfgang. *Becoming Maya: Ethnicity and Social Inequality in Yucatán Since 1500*. Tucson: University of Arizona Press, 2004.

———. "Of Friends and Foes: The Caste War and Ethnicity in Yucatan." *Journal of Latin American Anthropology* 9, no. 1 (2004): 90–118.

Galtung, Johan. "Cultural Violence." *Journal of Peace Research* 27, no. 3 (1990): 291–305.

———. "Violence, Peace, and Peace Research." *Journal of Peace Research* 6, no. 3 (1969): 167–191.

García Granados, Jorge. *Evolución sociológica de Guatemala/Ensayo sobre el gobierno del Dr. Mariano Gálvez*. Guatemala City: Sánchez & de guise, 1927.

Garland, David. "Of Crimes and Criminals: The Development of Criminology in Britain." In *The Oxford Handbook of Criminology*, edited by Mike Maguire, Rod Morgan, and Robert Reiner, 17–68. New York: Clarendon Press, 1994.

Garrard-Burnett, Virginia. "Conclusion: Community Drunkenness and Control in Guatemala." In *Distilling the Influence of Alcohol: Aguardiente in Guatemalan History*, edited by David Carey Jr., 157–179. Gainesville: University Press of Florida, 2012.

———. "Indians Are Drunks, Drunks Are Indians: Alcohol and *Indigenismo* in Guatemala, 1890–1940." *Bulletin of Latin American Research* 19, no. 3 (July 2000): 341–356.

Gauderman, Kimberly. *Women's Lives in Colonial Quito: Gender, Law, and the Economy in Spanish America*. Austin: University of Texas Press, 2003.

Gayol, Sandra. "'*Honor Moderno*': The Significance of Honor in Fin-de-Siècle Argentina." *Hispanic American Historical Review* 84, no. 3 (2004): 475–498.

Gillin, John. *The Culture of Security in San Carlos: A Study of a Guatemalan Community of Indians and Ladinos*. Publication no. 16. New Orleans: Middle American Research Institute, Tulane University of Louisiana, 1951.

Gilmore, David. *Manhood in the Making: Cultural Concepts of Masculinity*. New Haven, CT: Yale University Press, 1990.

Godoy-Paiz, Paula. "Women in Guatemala's Metropolitan Area: Violence, Law, and Social Justice." *Studies in Social Justice* 2 no. 1 (2008): 27–47.

Goldín, Liliana. "De plaza a mercado: La expresión de dos sistemas conceptuales en la organización de los mercados del occidente de Guatemala." *Anales de Antropología* 24 (1987): 243–261.

———. "Organizing the World through the Market: A Symbolic Analysis of Markets and Exchange in the Western Highlands of Guatemala." PhD diss., State University of New York, 1985.

González Alzate, Jorge. "History of Los Altos, Guatemala: A Study of Regional Conflict and National Integration, 1750–1885." PhD diss., Tulane University, 1994.

Gosner, Kevin, and Deborah E. Kanter, eds. *Women, Power, and Resistance in Colonial Mesoamerica*. Special issue of *Ethnohistory* 42, no. 4 (Autumn 1995).

Gotkowitz, Laura. "Trading Insults: Honor, Violence, and the Gendered Culture of Commerce in Cochabamba, Bolivia, 1870s–1950s." In *Honor, Status, and Law in Modern Latin America*, edited by Sueann Caulfield, Sarah C. Chambers, and Lara Putnam, 131–154. Durham, NC: Duke University Press, 2005.

Gould, Jeffrey L. *To Lead as Equals: Rural Protests and Political Consciousness in Chinandega, Nicaragua, 1912–1979*. Chapel Hill: University of North Carolina Press, 1990.

Gould, Jeffrey L., and Aldo A. Lauria-Santiago. *To Rise in Darkness: Revolution, Repression, and Memory in El Salvador, 1920–1932*. Durham, NC: Duke University Press, 2008.

Gramsci, Antonio. *Selections from the Prison Notebooks of Antonio Gramsci*. Edited and translated by Quintin Hoare and Geoffrey Nowell Smith. London: Lawrence and Wishart, 1971.

Grandin, Greg. *The Blood of Guatemala: A History of Race and Nation*. Durham, NC: Duke University Press, 2000.

———. "It Was Heaven that They Burned." *The Nation*, September 8, 2010.

———. *The Last Colonial Massacre: Latin America in the Cold War*. Chicago: Chicago University Press, 2004.

Green, James N. *Beyond Carnival: Homosexuality in Twentieth-Century Brazil*. Chicago: University of Chicago Press, 2001.

———. "Doctoring the National Body: Gender, Race, Eugenics, and the 'Invert' in Urban Brazil, ca. 1920–1945." In *Gender, Sexuality, and Power in Latin America since Independence*, edited by William French and Kathleen Bliss, 187–211. New York: Rowman and Littlefield, 2007.

Grieb, Kenneth. "El gobierno de Jorge Ubico." In *Historia general de Guatemala*. Vol. 5: *Época contemporánea: 1898–1944*, edited by Jorge Luján Muñoz and J. Daniel Contreras R., 43–60. Guatemala City: Asociación de Amigos del País, Fundación para la Cultura y el Desarrollo, 1996.

———. *Guatemalan Caudillo: The Regime of Jorge Ubico, Guatemala 1931–1944*. Athens: Ohio University Press, 1979.

Griffiths, Alison. *Wondrous Difference: Cinema, Anthropology, and Turn-of-the-Century Visual Culture*. New York: Columbia University Press, 2002.

Guardino, Peter F. *Peasants, Politics, and the Formation of Mexico's National State: Guerrero, 1800–1857*. Stanford, CA: Stanford University Press, 1996.

Gudmundson, Lowell. "Firewater, Desire, and the Militiamen's Christmas Eve in San Gerónimo, Baja Verapaz, 1892." *Hispanic American Historical Review* 84, no. 2 (2004): 239–276.

Gudmundson, Lowell, and Héctor Lindo-Fuentes. *Central America, 1821–1871: Liberalism before Liberal Reform*. Tuscaloosa: University of Alabama Press, 1995.

Guillén, Flavio. "Prólogo, o casi, casi . . ." In *El indio guatemalteco: Ensayo de sociología nacionalista*, by J. Fernando Juárez Muñoz, 5–27. Guatemala City: Tipografía Latina, 1931.

Gutmann, Matthew, ed. *Changing Men and Masculinities in Latin America*. Durham, NC: Duke University Press, 2003.

———. *The Meanings of Macho: Being a Man in Mexico City*. Berkeley: University of California Press, 1996.

Guy, Donna J. "Mothers Alive and Dead: Multiple Concepts of Mothering in Buenos Aires." In *Sex and Sexuality in Latin America*, edited by Daniel Balderston and Donna J. Guy, 155–173. New York: New York University Press, 1997.

———. "Parents before the Tribunals: The Legal Construction of Patriarchy in Argentina." In *Hidden Histories of Gender and the State in Latin America*, edited by Elizabeth Dore and Maxine Molyneux, 172–193. Durham, NC: Duke University Press, 2000.

———. *Sex and Danger in Buenos Aires: Prostitution, Family, and Nation in Argentina.* Lincoln, NE: University of Nebraska Press, 1991.

Habermas, Jürgen. "Further Reflections on the Public Sphere." In *Habermas and the Public Sphere*, edited by Craig Calhoun, 421–461. Cambridge, MA: MIT Press, 1997.

———. *The Structural Transformation of the Public Sphere: An Inquiry into a Category of Bourgeois Society.* Cambridge, MA: MIT Press, 1991.

Haines, Shaun. "Sticks and Stones May Break My Bones: Honor and the Court System in Early Twentieth Century Guatemala." Paper presented at Thinking Matters Conference, University of Southern Maine, Portland, April 20, 2007.

Hale, Charles R. *Más que un indio/More than an Indian: Racial Ambivalence and Neoliberal Multiculturalism in Guatemala.* Santa Fe, NM: School of American Research, 2006.

———. "Mestizaje, Hybridity, and the Cultural Politics of Difference in post-Revolutionary Central America." *Journal of Latin American Anthropology* 2, no. 1 (1996): 34–61.

Hames, Gina. "Maize-Beer, Gossip, and Slander: Female Tavern Proprietors and Urban, Ethnic Cultural Elaboration in Bolivia, 1870–1930." *Journal of Social History* 37, no. 2 (Winter 2003): 351–364.

Handley, Sarah. "Social Sites of Political Practice in France: Lawsuits, Civil Rights, and the Separation of Powers in Domestic and State Government, 1500–1800." *American Historical Review* 102, no. 1 (1997): 27–52.

Handy, Jim. "Chicken Thieves, Witches, and Judges: Vigilante Justice and Customary Law in Guatemala." *Journal of Latin American Studies* 36 (2004): 533–561.

———. *Gift of the Devil: A History of Guatemala.* Boston: South End, 1984.

Harms, Patricia R. "Imagining a Place for Themselves: The Political and Social Roles of Guatemalan Women, 1871–1954." PhD diss., Arizona State University, 2007.

Harmworth's Atlas of the World and Pictorial Gazetteer. London: Educational Book Co., 1922.

Harvey, Penelope. "Domestic Violence in the Peruvian Andes." In *Sex and Violence: Issues in Representation and Experience*, edited by Penelope Harvey and Peter Gow, 66–89. London: Routledge, 1994.

———. "Los 'hechos naturales' de parentesco y género en un context andino." In *Gente de carne y hueso: Las tramas de parentesco en los Andes*, vol. 2, edited by Denise Y. Arnold, 69–82. La Paz, Bolivia: ILCA, 1998.

Haskett, Robert. "Activist or Adulteress? The Life and Struggle of Doña Josefa María of Tepoztlan." In *Indian Women of Early Mexico*, edited by Susan Schroeder, Stephanie Wood, and Robert Haskett, 145–163. Norman: University of Oklahoma Press, 1997.

Haviland, John Beard. *Gossip, Reputation, and Knowledge in Zinacatan.* Chicago: University of Chicago Press, 1977.

Hay, Douglas. "Time, Inequality, and Law's Violence." In *Law's Violence,* edited by Austin Sarat and Thomas R. Kearns, 141–173. Ann Arbor: University of Michigan Press, 1992.

Herzfeld, Michael. *Anthropology through the Looking Glass: Critical Ethnography in the Margins of Europe.* Cambridge, England: Cambridge University Press, 1987.

Herzog, Tamar. *Upholding Justice: Society, State, and the Penal System in Quito (1650–1750).* Ann Arbor: University of Michigan Press, 2004.

Hobsbawm, Eric. "Peasants and Politics." *Journal of Peasant Studies* 1, no. 1 (1973): 3–22.

Hünefeldt, Christine. *Liberalism in the Bedroom: Quarreling Spouses in Nineteenth-Century Lima.* University Park: Pennsylvania State University Press, 2000.

Hunt, Lynn. Introduction to *The New Cultural History,* edited by Lynn Hunt, 14–22. Berkeley: University of California Press, 1989.

Huxley, Aldous. *Beyond the Mexique Bay.* New York: Harper and Brothers, 1934.

Hydén, Margareta. *Woman Battering as a Marital Act: The Construction of a Violent Marriage.* Oslo: Scandinavian University Press, 1994.

Ingersoll, Hazel. "The War of the Mountain: A Study of Reactionary Peasant Insurgency in Guatemala, 1837–1873." PhD diss., University of Maryland, 1972.

Irwin, Robert McKee. *Mexican Masculinities.* Minneapolis: University of Minnesota Press, 2003.

Irwin, Robert McKee, Edward J. McCaughlin, and Michelle Rocío Nasser, eds. *The Famous 41: Sexuality and Social Control in Mexico, 1901.* New York: Palgrave, 2003.

James, Daniel. *Doña María's Story: Life, History, Memory, and Political Identity.* Durham, NC: Duke University Press, 2000.

Johnson, Lyman. "Dangerous Words, Provocative Gestures, and Violent Acts: The Disputed Hierarchies of Plebeian Life in Colonial Buenos Aires." In *The Faces of Honor: Sex, Shame, and Violence in Colonial Latin America,* edited by Lyman L. Johnson and Sonya Lipsett-Rivera, 127–151. Albuquerque: University of New Mexico Press, 1998.

———, ed. *The Problem of Order in Changing Societies: Essays in Crime and Policing in Argentina and Uruguay, 1750–1919.* Albuquerque: University of New Mexico Press, 1990.

Johnson, Lyman L., and Sonya Lipsett-Rivera, eds. *The Faces of Honor: Sex, Shame and Violence in Colonial Latin America.* Albuquerque: University of New Mexico Press, 1998.

Jones, Chester Lloyd. *Guatemala: Past and Present.* Minneapolis: University of Minnesota Press, 1940.

Joseph, Gilbert M. "On the Trail of Latin American Bandits: A Reexamination of Peasant Resistance." *Latin American Research Review* 25, no. 3 (1990): 7–53.

———. Preface to *Crime and Punishment in Latin America,* edited by Ricardo D. Salvatore, Carlos Aguirre, and Gilbert M. Joseph, ix–xxi. Durham, NC: Duke University Press, 2001.

Joseph, Gilbert M., and Daniel Nugent, eds. *Everyday Forms of State Formation:*

Revolution and the Negotiation of Rule in Modern Mexico. Durham, NC: Duke University Press, 1994.

Joseph, Suad. "Gendering Citizenship in the Middle East." In *Gender and Citizenship in the Middle East*, edited by Suad Joseph, 3–30. Syracuse, NY: Syracuse University Press, 2000.

Juárez Muñoz, J. Fernando. *El indio guatemalteco: Ensayo de sociología nacionalista.* Guatemala City: Tipografía Latina, 1931.

Kanter, Deborah. "Native Female Land Tenure and Its Decline in Mexico, 1750–1900." *Women, Power, and Resistance in Colonial Mesoamerica*, special issue, edited by Kevin Gosner and Deborah E. Kanter, *Ethnohistory* 42, no. 4 (Autumn 1995): 607–616.

Katz, Friedrich, ed. *Riot, Rebellion, and Revolution: Rural Social Conflict in Mexico.* Princeton, NJ: Princeton University Press, 1988.

Kellogg, Susan. "From Parallel and Equivalent to Separate but Unequal: Tenochca Mexica Women, 1500–1700." In *Indian Women of Early Mexico*, edited by Susan Schroeder, Stephanie Wood, and Robert Haskett, 123–143. Norman: University of Oklahoma Press, 1997.

———. *Weaving the Past: A History of Latin America's Indigenous Women from the Prehispanic Period to the Present.* New York: Oxford University Press, 2005.

Kennedy, John. "The Role of Beer in Tarahumara Culture." *American Anthropologist* 60 (1978): 620–640.

Kent, George. "Children as Victims of Structural Violence." *Societies without Borders* 1 (2006): 53–67.

Klubock, Thomas Miller. "Writing the History of Women in Twentieth-Century Chile." *Hispanic American Historical Review* 81, nos. 3–4 (2001): 493–518.

Knight, Alan. "Racism, Revolution, and *Indigenismo*: Mexico, 1910–1940." In *The Idea of Race in Latin America*, edited by Richard Graham, 71–113. Austin: University of Texas Press, 1990.

Komisaruk, Catherine. "Rape Narratives, Rape Silences: Sexual Violence and Judicial Testimony in Colonial Guatemala." *Biography* 31, no. 3 (Summer 2008): 369–396.

Kuznesof, Elizabeth. "Sexual Politics, Race, and Bastard Bearing in Nineteenth-Century Brazil: A Question of Culture or Power?" *Journal of Family History* 16, no. 3 (1991): 241–260.

La Farge, Oliver II. *Santa Eulalia: The Religion of a Cuchumatán Indian Town.* Chicago: University of Chicago Press, 1947.

La Farge, Oliver II, and Douglas Byers. *The Year Bearer's People.* New Orleans: Tulane University, 1931.

Lancaster, Roger. *Life Is Hard: Machismo, Danger, and the Intimacy of Power in Nicaragua.* Berkeley: University of California Press, 1992.

Landes, Joan B. *Women and the Public Sphere in the Age of the French Revolution.* Ithaca, NY: Cornell University Press, 1988.

Lanzilli, Pietro. *Código de honor para América Latina.* Guatemala City: Tipografía Nacional, 1898.

Larson, Brooke. *Trials of Nation Making: Liberalism, Race, and Ethnicity in the Andes, 1810–1910.* Cambridge, England: Cambridge University Press, 2004.

Lauderdale Graham, Sandra. *House and Street: The Domestic World of Servants and Masters in Nineteenth-Century Rio de Janeiro*. Cambridge, England: Cambridge University Press, 1988.

———. "Making the Public Private: A Brazilian Perspective." *Journal of Women's History* 15, no. 1 (2003): 28–42.

———. "Slavery's Impasse: Slave Prostitutes, Small-Time Mistresses, and the Brazilian Law of 1871." *Comparative Studies in Society and History* 33 (1991): 669–694.

Lavrin, Asunción, ed. *Sexuality and Marriage in Colonial Latin America*. Lincoln: University of Nebraska Press, 1989.

———. *Women, Feminism, and Social Change in Argentina, Chile, and Uruguay, 1890–1940*. Lincoln: University of Nebraska Press, 1995.

Lewis, Oscar. *The Children of Sánchez: Autobiography of a Mexican Family*. New York: Vintage, 1961.

Lincoln, Jackson Steward. "An Ethnographic Study of the Ixil Indians of the Guatemalan Highlands." Microfilm Collection of Manuscripts on Middle American Cultural Anthropology, University of Chicago, no. 1, 1945.

Little, Walter E. "A Visual Political Economy of Maya Representations in Guatemala, 1931–1944." *Ethnohistory* 55, no. 4 (Fall 2008): 633–663.

Little-Siebold, Todd. "Guatemala and the Dream of a Nation: National Policy and Regional Practice in the Liberal Era, 1871–1945 (Chiquimula, San Marcos)." PhD diss., Tulane University, 1995.

———. "Guatemalanist Ethnography and the State: Reading the Ethnographic Archive." Paper presented at the Latin American Studies Association Conference, March 15–18, San Juan, Puerto Rico.

———. "'Where Have All the Spaniards Gone?' Independent Identities: Ethnicities, Class and the Emergent National State." *Journal of Latin American Anthropology* 6, no. 2 (2001): 106–133.

Luján Muñoz, Jorge. "Del derecho colonial al derecho nacional: El caso de Guatemala." *Jahrbuch für Geschichte Lateinameikas* 38 (2001): 85–107.

Lutz, Christopher H. *Santiago de Guatemala, 1541–1773*. Norman: University of Oklahoma Press, 1994.

Mallon, Florencia. *The Defense of Community in Peru's Central Highlands: Peasant Struggle and Capitalist Transition, 1860–1940*. Princeton, NJ: Princeton University Press, 1983.

———. *Peasant and Nation: The Making of Postcolonial Mexico and Peru*. Berkeley: University of California Press, 1995.

Mangan, Jane. *Trading Roles: Gender, Ethnicity, and the Urban Economy in Colonial Potosí*. Durham, NC: Duke University Press, 2005.

Martínez Peláez, Severo. *Motines de indios: La violencia colonial en Centroamérica y Chiapas*. Puebla, Mexico: Centro de Investigaciones Históricas y Sociales, 1985.

———. *La Patria del Criollo: An Interpretation of Colonial Guatemala*. Edited by W. George Lovell and Christopher Lutz. Translated by Susan M. Neve and W. George Lovell. Durham, NC: Duke University Press, 2009.

Masiello, Francine. "Gender, Dress, and Market: The Commerce of Citizenship in Latin America." In *Sex and Sexuality in Latin America*, edited by Daniel Balderston and Donna J. Guy, 219–233. New York: New York University Press, 1997.

Matthew, Laura, and Michel R. Oudjik. Conclusion. *Indigenous Allies in the Conquest of Mesoamerica*, edited by Laura Matthew and Michel R. Oudjik, 317. Norman: University of Oklahoma Press, 2007.

Maza, Sarah. *Private Lives and Public Affairs: The Causes Célèbres of Prerevolutionary France*. Berkeley: University of California Press, 1993.

McBryde, Felix Webster. *Cultural and Historical Geography of Southwest Guatemala*. Publication no. 4. Washington, DC: Smithsonian Institution, Institute of Social Anthropology, 1945.

———. *Sololá: A Guatemalan Town and Cakchiquel Market-Center*. New Orleans: Department of Middle American Research, Tulane University, 1933.

McClintock, Anne. *Imperial Leather: Race, Gender, and Sexuality in the Colonial Conquest*. New York: Routledge, 1995.

———. "No Longer in a Future Heaven: Gender, Race, and Nationalism." In *Dangerous Liaisons: Gender, Nation, and Postcolonial Perspectives*, edited by Anne McClintock, Aamir Mufti, and Ella Shohat, 89–112. Minneapolis: University of Minnesota Press, 1997.

McCreery, David. *Rural Guatemala 1760–1940*. Stanford, CA: Stanford University Press, 1994.

———. "State Power, Indigenous Communities, and Land in Nineteenth-Century Guatemala, 1820–1920." In *Guatemalan Indians and the State: 1540–1988*, edited by Carol Smith, 96–115. Austin: University of Texas Press, 1990.

———. "'This Life of Misery and Shame': Female Prostitution in Guatemala City." *Journal of Latin American Studies* 18, no. 2 (November 1, 1986): 333–353.

———. "Wage Labor, Free Labor, and Vagrancy Laws: The Transition to Capitalism in Guatemala, 1920–1945." In *Coffee, Society, and Power in Latin America*, edited by William Roseberry, Lowell Gudmundson, and Mario Samper Kutschabach, 206–231. Baltimore, MD: Johns Hopkins University Press, 1995.

McKee, Lauris. "Men's Rights/Women's Wrongs: Domestic Violence in Ecuador." In *To Have and to Hit: Cultural Perspectives on Wife Beating*, edited by Dorothy Ayers Counts, Judith K. Brown, and Jacquelyn C. Campbell. Urbana: University of Illinois Press, 1999.

Mendelson, E. Michael, "Religion and World-View in Santiago, Atitlán." PhD diss. (long version), University of Chicago, 1956.

———. "Religion and World-View in Santiago, Atitlán." PhD diss. (short version), University of Chicago, 1956.

Menjívar, Cecilia. *Enduring Violence: Ladina Women's Lives in Guatemala*. Berkeley: University of California Press, 2011.

Merry, Sally Engle. "Courts as Performance: Domestic Violence Hearings in Hawai'i Family Court." In *Contested States: Law, Hegemony, and Resistance*, edited by Mindie Lazarus-Black and Susan F. Hirsh, 35–58. New York: Routledge, 1994.

———. "Law as Fair, Law as Help: The Texture of Legitimacy in American Society." In *New Directions in the Study of Justice, Law, and Social Control*, prepared by School of Justice Studies, Arizona State University, 167–187. New York: Plenum Press, 1990.

———. "Rethinking Gossip and Scandal." In *Reputation: Studies in the Voluntary*

Elicitation of Good Conduct, edited by Daniel B. Klein, 47–74. Ann Arbor: University of Michigan Press, 1997.

Metz, Brent E. *Ch'orti'-Maya Survival in Eastern Guatemala: Indigeneity in Transition*. Albuquerque: University of New Mexico Press, 2006.

Milton, Cynthia E. *The Many Meanings of Poverty: Colonialism, Social Compacts, and Assistance in Eighteenth-Century Ecuador*. Stanford, CA: Stanford University Press, 2007.

Molyneux, Maxine. "Twentieth-Century State Formations in Latin America." In *Hidden Histories of Gender and the State in Latin America*, edited by Elizabeth Dore and Maxine Molyneux, 33–81. Durham, NC: Duke University Press, 2000.

Muir, Edward, and Guido Ruggiero. "Introduction: The Crime of History." In *History from Crime*, edited by Edward Muir and Guido Ruggiero. Translated by Corrada Biazzo Curry, Margaret A. Gallucci, and Mary M. Gallucci. Baltimore, MD: Johns Hopkins University Press, 1994.

———, eds. *Sex and Gender in Historical Perspective*. Translated by Margaret A. Gallucci. Baltimore, MD: Johns Hopkins University Press, 1991.

Nandy, Ashis. *The Intimate Enemy: Loss and Recovery of the Self under Colonialism*. Delhi, India: Oxford University Press, 1983.

Nash, June. *We Eat the Mines and the Mines Eat Us: Dependency and Exploitation in Bolivian Tin Mines*. New York: Columbia University Press, 1979.

O'Connor, Erin. *Gender, Indian, Nation: The Contradictions of Making Ecuador, 1830–1925*. Tucson: University of Arizona Press, 2007.

Offutt, Leslie S. "Women's Voices from the Frontier: San Esteban de Nueva Tlaxcala in the Late Eighteenth Century." In *Indian Women of Early Mexico*, edited by Susan Schroeder, Stephanie Wood, and Robert Haskett, 273–289. Norman, University of Oklahoma Press, 1997.

Olcott, Jocelyn. "Soldiers, Suffragists, and Sex Radicals: Women, Gender, and the Mexican Revolution." Paper presented at Bates College, Lewiston, ME, March 9, 2011.

Olcott, Jocelyn, Mary Kay Vaughn, and Gabriela Cano, eds. *Sex in Revolution: Gender, Politics, and Power in Modern Mexico*. Durham, NC: Duke University Press, 2006.

Opie, Frederick Douglass. "Adios Jim Crow: Afro–North American Workers and the Guatemalan Railroad Workers' League, 1884–1921." PhD diss., Syracuse University, 1999.

———. "Alcohol and Lowdown Culture in Caribbean Guatemala and Honduras, 1898–1920." In *Distilling the Influence of Alcohol: Aguardiente in Guatemalan History*, edited by David Carey Jr., 96–119. Gainesville: University Press of Florida, 2012.

Palacios, Juan Manuel R. "Judges, Lawyers, and Farmers: Uses of Justice and Circulation of Law in Rural Buenos Aires, 1900–1940." In *Crime and Punishment in Latin America*, edited by Ricardo D. Salvatore, Carlos Aguirre, and Gilbert M. Joseph, 83–100. Durham, NC: Duke University Press, 2001.

Palomo de Lewin, Beatriz. "Vida conyugal de las mujeres en Guatemala (1800–1950)." *Mujeres, género e historia en América Central durante los siglos XVIII, XIX y XX*, edited by Eugenia Rodríguez Sáenz, 25–34. Mexico City: UNIFEM Oficina Regional de México, Centroamérica, Cuba y República Dominicana; South Woodstock, VT: Plumsock Mesoamerican Studies, 2002.

Parker, David. "'Gentlemanly Responsibility' and 'Insults of a Woman': Dueling and the Unwritten Rules of Public Life in Uruguay, 1860–1920." In *Gender, Sexuality, and Power in Latin America since Independence*, edited by William French and Kathleen Bliss, 109–132. Lanham, MD: Rowman and Littlefield, 2007.

———. "Law, Honor, and Impunity in Spanish America: The Debate Over Dueling, 1870–1920." *Law and History Review* 19, no. 2 (Summer 2001): 311–341.

Patch, Robert. *Maya Revolt and Revolution in the Eighteenth Century.* Armonk, NY: M. E. Sharpe, 2002.

Perera, Víctor. *Rites: A Guatemalan Boyhood.* San Francisco, CA: Mercury House, 1994.

Philips, Anne. *Which Equalities Matter?* Cambridge, England/Malden, MA: Polity/Blackwell, 1999.

Piccato, Pablo. *City of Suspects: Crime in Mexico City, 1900–1931.* Durham, NC: Duke University Press, 2001.

———. "The Girl Who Killed a Senator: Femininity and the Public Sphere in Postrevolutionary Mexico." In *True Stories of Crime in Modern Mexico*, edited by Robert Buffington and Pablo Piccato, 128–153. Albuquerque: University of New Mexico Press, 2009.

———. "The Hidden Story—Violence and Law in Guatemala." *Law and History Review* 24, no. 2 (2006): 433–439.

———. "Politics and the Technology of Honor: Dueling in Turn-of-the-Century Mexico." *Journal of Social History* 33, no. 2 (1999): 331–354.

———. *The Tyranny of Opinion: Honor in the Construction of the Mexican Public Sphere.* Durham, NC: Duke University Press, 2010.

Pitt-Rivers, Julian A. *The Fate of Shechem, or the Politics of Sex: Essays in the Anthropology of the Mediterranean.* Cambridge, England: Cambridge University Press, 1977.

———. "Honour and Social Status." In *Honour and Shame: The Values of Mediterranean Society*, edited by Jean Peristiany, 19–77. London: Weidenfeld and Nicolson, 1966.

Polanyi, Karl. *The Great Transformation: The Political and Economic Origins of Our Time.* 2nd edition. Boston: Beacon Press, 2001.

Pompejano, Daniele. *La crisis de antiguo régimen en Guatemala (1839–1871).* Guatemala City: Editorial Universitaria, Universidad de San Carlos de Guatemala, 1997.

Poole, Deborah. "Between Threat and Guarantee: Justice and Community in the Margins of the Peruvian State." In *Anthropology in the Margins of the State*, edited by Veena Das and Deborah Poole, 35–65. Santa Fe, NM/Oxford, England: School of American Research/James Currey, 2004.

———. "Introduction: Anthropological Perspectives on Violence and Culture—A View from the Peruvian High Provinces." In *Unruly Order: Violence, Power, and Cultural Identity in the High Provinces of Southern Peru*, edited by Deborah Poole, 1–30. Boulder, CO: Westview, 1994.

Porter, Susie S. "'And That It Is Custom Makes It Law': Class Conflict and Gender

Ideology in the Public Sphere, Mexico City, 1880–1910." *Social Science History* 24, no. 1 (Spring 2000): 111–140.

Pratt, Mary Louise. *Imperial Eyes: Travel Writing and Transculturation.* New York: Routledge, 1992.

Premo, Bianca. *Children of the Father King: Youth, Authority, and Legal Minority in Colonial Lima.* Chapel Hill: University of North Carolina Press, 2005.

Putnam, Lara. *The Company They Kept: Migrants and the Politics of Gender in Caribbean Costa Rica, 1870–1960.* Chapel Hill: University of North Carolina Press, 2002.

———. "Sex and Standing in the Street of Port Limón, Costa Rica, 1890–1910." In *Honor, Status, and Law in Modern Latin America*, edited by Sueann Caulfield, Sarah C. Chambers, and Lara Putnam. Durham NC: Duke University Press, 2005.

Putnam, Lara, Sarah C. Chambers, and Sueann Caulfield. "Introduction: Transformations in Honor, Status, and Law over the Long Nineteenth Century." In *Honor, Status, and Law in Modern Latin America*, edited by Sueann Caulfield, Sarah C. Chambers, and Lara Putnam. Durham, NC: Duke University Press, 2005.

Reeves, René. "From Household to Nation: The Economic and Political Impact of Women and Alcohol in Nineteenth-Century Guatemala." In *Distilling the Influence of Alcohol: Aguardiente in Guatemalan History*, edited by David Carey Jr., 42–70. Gainesville: University Press of Florida, 2012.

———. *Ladinos with Ladinos, Indians with Indians: Land, Labor, and Regional Ethnic Conflict in the Making of Guatemala.* Stanford, CA: Stanford University Press, 2006.

Reiche, Carlos Enrique. "Estudio sobre el patrón de embriaguez en la región rural Altaverapacense." *Guatemala indígena* 5 (1970): 103–127.

Reina, Ruben. *The Law of the Saints: A Pokomam Pueblo and Its Community Culture.* New York: Bobbs-Merrill, 1966.

Rendon, Catherine. "El gobierno de Manuel Estrada Cabrera." In *Historia general de Guatemala*. Vol. 5: *Época contemporánea: 1898–1944*, edited by Jorge Luján Muñoz and J. Daniel Contreras R., 15–36. Guatemala City: Asociación de Amigos del País, Fundación para la Cultura y el Desarrollo, 1996.

Restall, Matthew. "'He Wished It in Vain': Subordination and Resistance among Maya Women in Post-Conquest Yucatan." *Women, Power, and Resistance in Colonial Mesoamerica*, special issue, edited by Kevin Gosner and Deborah E. Kanter, *Ethnohistory* 42, no. 4 (Autumn 1995): 577–594.

———. *Maya World: Yucatec Culture and Society, 1550–1850.* Stanford, CA: Stanford University Press, 1997.

Rodas, Isabel, and Edgar Esquit. *Élite ladina—vanguardia indígena de la tolerancia a la violencia, Patzicía 1944.* Guatemala City: CAUDAL, 1997.

Rodríguez, Mario. "The Livingston Codes in the Guatemalan Crisis of 1837–1838." In *Applied Enlightenment: Nineteenth-Century Liberalism, 1830–1839*, edited by Mario Rodríguez, Ralph Lee Woodward Jr., Miriam Williford, and William J. Griffith, 1–32. New Orleans: Middle American Research Institute Tulane University, 1972. Originally published 1955.

Rodríguez Sáenz, Eugenia. "Civilizing Domestic Life in the Central Valley of

Costa Rica, 1750–1850." In *Hidden Histories of Gender and the State in Latin America*, edited by Elizabeth Dore and Maxine Molyneux, 85–107. Durham, NC: Duke University Press, 2000.

———. "Divorcio y violencia de pareja en Costa Rica (1800–1950)." In *Mujeres, género e historia en América Central durante los siglos XVIII, XIX y XX*, edited by Eugenia Rodríguez Sáenz, 35–51. Mexico City: UNIFEM Oficina Regional de México, Centroamérica, Cuba y República Dominicana; South Woodstock, VT: Plumsock Mesoamerican Studies, 2002.

———. *Hijas, novias y esposas: Familia, matrimonio y violencia doméstica en el Valle Central de Costa Rica (1750–1850)*. San José, Costa Rica: Editorial Universidad Nacional Heredia, 2000.

———. "'Tiyita bea lo que me han hecho.' Estupro e incesto en Costa Rica (1800–1850)." In *El paso del cometa: Estado, políticas sociales y culturales populares en Costa Rica, 1800–1950*, edited by Iván Molina and Steven Palmer, 19–45. San José, Costa Rica: Editorial Porvenir, 1994.

Roseberry, William. "Hegemony and the Language of Contention." In *Everyday Forms of State Formation: Revolution and Integration of Rule in Modern Mexico*, edited by Gilbert M. Joseph and Daniel Nugent, 355–366. Durham, NC: Duke University Press, 1994.

Ruggiero, Guido. "Re-reading the Renaissance: Civic Morality and the World of Marriage, Love, and Sex." In *Sexuality and Gender in Early Modern Europe: Institutions, Texts, Images*, edited by James Turner. Cambridge, England: Cambridge University Press, 1997.

Ruggiero, Kristin. "Honor, Maternity, and the Disciplining of Women: Infanticide in Late Nineteenth-Century Buenos Aires." *Hispanic American Historical Review* 72, no. 3 (1992): 353–373.

———. "Passion, Perversity, and the Pace of Justice in Argentina at the Turn of the Last Century." In *Crime and Punishment in Latin America*, edited by Ricardo D. Salvatore, Carlos Aguirre, and Gilbert M. Joseph, 211–232. Durham, NC: Duke University Press, 2001.

———. "Wives on 'Deposit': Internment and the Preservation of Husbands' Honor in Late Nineteenth-Century Buenos Aires." *Journal of Family History* 17, no. 3 (1992): 253–270.

Sabato, Hilda, ed. *Ciudadanía política y formación de las naciones: Perspectivas históricas de América Latina*. Mexico City: El Colegio de Mexico: Fideicomiso Historia de las Américas, 1999.

———. Introduction to *Ciudadanía política y formación de las naciones: Perspectivas históricas de América Latina*, edited by Hilda Sabato, 11–29.

Sabean, David Warren. *Power in the Blood: Popular Culture and Village Discourse in Early Modern Germany*. Cambridge: Cambridge University Press, 1984.

Sahlins, Marshall. "The Economics of Develop-man in the Pacific." *Res 21* (1992): 12–25.

———. "On the Anthropology of Modernity, or, Some Triumphs of Culture over Despondency Theory." In *Culture and Sustainable Development in the Pacific*, edited by Anthony Hooper, 45–61. Canberra, Australia: Asia Pacific Press, 2000.

———. "What Is Anthropological Enlightenment?: Some Lessons of the Twentieth Century." *Annual Review of Anthropology* 28 (1999): i–xxiii.

Saladino García, Alberto. "La función social de las mujeres entre los liberales latinoamericanos." *Siglo XIX* (Mexico City) 1, no. 2 (1986): 175–187.

Salvatore, Ricardo D. *Wandering Paysanos: State Order and Subaltern Experience in Buenos Aires during the Rosas Era.* Durham, NC: Duke University Press, 2003.

Salvatore, Ricardo D., Carlos Aguirre, and Gilbert M. Joseph, eds. *Crime and Punishment in Latin America.* Durham, NC: Duke University Press, 2001.

Sánchez Parga, José. *¿Por que golpearla? Ética, estética y ritual en los Andes: Estudios y analisis.* Quito: Centro Andino de Acción Popular, 1990.

Sanders, James E. *Contentious Republicans: Popular Politics, Race, and Class in Nineteenth-Century Colombia.* Durham, NC: Duke University Press, 2004.

Sarmiento, Domingo F. *Life in Argentina in the Days of the Tyrants; or Civilization and Barbarism.* New York: Hafner Press, 1868.

Scardaville, Michael. "Alcohol Abuse and Tavern Reform in Late Colonial Mexico City." *Hispanic American Historical Review* 60 (1980): 643–671.

———. "(Hapsburg) Law and (Bourbon) Order: State Authority, Popular Unrest, and the Criminal Justice System in Bourbon Mexico City." *The Americas* 50, no. 4 (April 1994): 501–525.

Schroeder, Susan, Stephanie Wood, and Robert Haskett, eds. *Indian Women of Early Mexico.* Norman, University of Oklahoma Press, 1997.

Schwartz, Norman B. "Drinking Patterns, Drunks, and Maturity in a Petén Town (Guatemala)." *Sociologus* 28, no. 1 (1978): 35–53.

Schwartzkopf, Stacey. "Consumption, Custom, and Control: Aguardiente in Nineteenth-Century Maya Guatemala." In *Distilling the Influence of Alcohol: Aguardiente in Guatemalan History,* edited by David Carey Jr., 17–41. Gainesville: University Press of Florida, 2012.

———. "Maya Power and State Culture: Indigenous Politics and State Formation in Nineteenth-Century Guatemala." PhD diss., Tulane University, 2008.

Scott, James C. *Domination and the Arts of Resistance: Hidden Transcripts.* New Haven, CT: Yale University Press, 1990.

———. "Resistance without Protest and without Organization: Peasant Opposition to the Islamic *Zacat* and the Christian Tithe." *Comparative Studies in Society and History,* no. 293 (1987): 417–452.

———. *Weapons of the Weak: Everyday Forms of Peasant Resistance.* New Haven, CT: Yale University Press, 1985.

Scott, Joan Wallach. "Gender: A Useful Category of Historical Analysis." *American Historical Review* 91, no. 5 (December 1986).

———. *Gender and the Politics of History.* New York: Columbia University Press, 1988.

Scott, Rebecca. *Slave Emancipation in Cuba: Transition to Free Labor, 1860–1899.* Princeton, NJ: Princeton University Press, 1985.

Seed, Patricia. *To Love, Honor, and Obey in Colonial Mexico: Conflicts over Marriage Choice, 1574–1821.* Stanford, CA: Stanford University Press, 1988.

Seligmann, Linda J. "Between Worlds of Exchange: Ethnicity among Peruvian Market Women." *Cultural Anthropology* 8, no. 2 (1993): 187–213.

Sellers, Charles. *The Market Revolution: Jacksonian America, 1815–1846.* Oxford, England: Oxford University Press, 1991.

Sen, Amartya. *The Idea of Justice.* Cambridge, MA: Belknap Press of Harvard University Press, 2009.

Sennet, Richard. *The Fall of Public Man*. New York: Knopf, 1977.

Shumway, Jeffrey. *The Case of the Ugly Suitor and Other Histories of Love, Gender, and Nation in Buenos Aires, 1776–1870*. Lincoln: University of Nebraska Press, 2005.

Sieder, Rachel. "Customary Law and Local Power in Guatemala." In *Guatemala After the Peace Accords*, edited by Rachel Sieder, 97–115. London: Institute of Latin American Studies, 1998.

———. "'Paz, progreso, justicia y honradez': Law and Citizenship in Alta Verapaz during the Regime of Jorge Ubico." *Bulletin of Latin American Research* 19 (2000): 283–302.

Sifuentes Jáuregui, Ben. "Gender without Limits: Transvestism and Subjectivity in *El lugar sin límites*." In *Sex and Sexuality in Latin America*, edited by Daniel Balderston and Donna J. Guy, 44–61. New York: New York University Press, 1997.

Sigal, Pete, ed. *Infamous Desire: Male Homosexuality in Colonial Latin America*. Chicago: University of Chicago Press, 2003.

———. "Latin America and the Challenge of Globalizing the History of Sexuality." *American Historical Review* 114, no. 5 (2009): 1340–1353.

Sloan, Kathryn. *Runaway Daughters: Seduction, Elopement, and Honor in Nineteenth-Century Mexico*. Albuquerque: University of New Mexico Press, 2009.

Smith, Carol. "Beyond Dependency Theory: National and Regional Patterns of Underdevelopment in Guatemala." *American Ethnologist* 5, no. 3 (1978): 574–617.

———, ed. *Guatemalan Indians and the State, 1540–1988*. Austin: University of Texas Press, 1990.

———. "Race-Class-Gender Ideology in Guatemala: Modern and Anti-Modern Forms." *Comparative Studies in Society and History* 37 (1995): 723–749.

Smith, Stephanie. *Gender and the Mexican Revolution: Yucatán Women and the Realities of Patriarchy*. Chapel Hill: University of North Carolina Press, 2009.

Socolow, Susan Migden. "Women and Crime: Buenos Aires, 1757–1797." *Journal of Latin American Studies* 12, no. 1 (1980): 39–54.

———. *The Women of Colonial Latin America*. Cambridge: Cambridge University Press, 2000.

Sontag, Susan. *On Photography*. New York: Farrar, Straus, and Giroux, 1973.

Sousa, Lisa Mary. "Women and Crime in Colonial Oaxaca: Evidence of Complementary Gender Roles in Mixtec and Zapotec Societies." In *Indian Women of Early Mexico*, edited by Susan Schroeder, Stephanie Wood, and Robert Haskett, 199–214. Norman, University of Oklahoma Press, 1997.

Speckman Guerra, Elisa. "'I Was a Man of Pleasure, I Can't Deny It': Histories of José de Jesús Negrete, a.k.a. 'The Tiger of Santa Julia.'" In *True Stories of Crime in Modern Mexico*, edited by Robert Buffington and Pablo Piccato, 57–105. Albuquerque: University of New Mexico Press, 2009.

Stavig, Ward. *Amor y violencia sexual: Valores indígenas en la sociedad colonial*. Lima, 1995.

———. *The World of Tupac Amaru: Conflict, Community, and Identity in Colonial Peru*. Lincoln: University of Nebraska Press, 1999.

Stepan, Nancy. *"The Hour of Eugenics": Race, Gender, and Nation in Latin America*. Ithaca, NY: Cornell University Press, 1991.

Stern, Steve J. "New Approaches to the Study of Peasant Rebellion and Consciousness: Implications of the Andean Experience." In *Resistance, Rebellion, and Con-*

sciousness in the Andean Peasant World, 18th to 20th Centuries, edited by Steve J. Stern, 3–25. Madison: University of Wisconsin Press, 1987.

———. *Peru's Indian Peoples and the Challenge of the Spanish Conquest: Huamanga to 1640*. Madison: University of Wisconsin Press, 1982.

———, ed. *Resistance, Rebellion, and Consciousness in the Andean Peasant World*. Madison: University of Wisconsin Press, 1987.

———. *The Secret History of Gender: Women, Men, and Power in Late Colonial Mexico*. Chapel Hill: University of North Carolina Press, 1995.

Stolcke, Verena. "The 'Nature' of Nationality." In *Citizenship and Exclusion*, edited by Veit Bader, 61–80. New York: St. Martin's Press, 1997.

Stoll, David. *Between Two Armies: In the Ixil Towns of Guatemala*. New York: Columbia University Press, 1993.

Stuntz, William J. *The Collapse of American Criminal Justice*. Cambridge, MA: Belknap Press of Harvard University Press, 2011.

Sullivan, Paul. *Unfinished Conversations: Mayas and Foreigners between Two Wars*. New York: Alfred A. Knopf, 1989.

Sullivan-González, Douglass. *Piety, Power, and Politics: Religion and Nation Formation in Guatemala, 1821–1871*. Pittsburgh, PA: University of Pittsburgh Press, 1998.

Sweatnam, John. "Women and Market: A Problem in the Assessment of Sexual Inequality." *Ethnology* 27, no. 4 (1988): 327–338.

Szuchman, Mark. *Order, Family, and Community in Buenos Aires, 1810–1860*. Stanford, CA: Stanford University Press, 1988.

Tagg, John. "Evidence, Truth, and Order: A Means of Surveillance." In *Visual Culture: The Reader*, edited by Jessica Evans and Stuart Hall, 244–273. Thousand Oaks, CA: Sage, 1999.

Taracena Arriola, Arturo. *Invención criolla, sueño ladino, pesadilla indígena: Los altos de Guatemala: De región a Estado, 1740–1850*. San José, Costa Rica/Antigua, Guatemala: Editorial Porvenir/CIRMA, 1997.

———. "Nación y república en Centroamérica (1821–65)." In *Identidades nacionales y estado moderno en Centroamérica*, edited by Arturo Taracena Arriola and Jean Piel. San José, Costa Rica: Editorial de la Universidad de Costa Rica, 1995.

Taracena Arriola, Arturo, Gisela Gellert, Enrique Gordillo Castillo, Tania Sagastume Paiz, and Knut Walter, eds. *Etnicidad, estado y nación en Guatemala, 1808–1944*. Antigua, Guatemala: Nawal Wuj/Centro de Investigaciones Regionales de Mesoamérica, 2002.

Taussig, Michael. *Law in a Lawless Land: Diary of a Limpieza in Colombia*. Chicago: University of Chicago Press, 2005.

Tax, Sol. "Changing Consumption in Indian Guatemala." *Economic Development and Cultural Change* 5, no. 2 (1957): 147–158.

———. "The Municipios of the Midwestern Highlands of Guatemala." *American Anthropologist* 39, no. 3 (1937): 423–444.

———. *Penny Capitalism: A Guatemalan Indian Economy*. Chicago: University of Chicago Press, 1963. Originally published 1953.

Tax, Sol, and Robert Hinshaw. "The Maya of the Midwestern Highlands." In *Handbook of Middle American Indians*. Vol. 7, *Ethnology*, edited by Evon Z. Vogt, 69–100. Austin: University of Texas Press, 1969.

Taylor, William. "Between Global Process and Local Knowledge: An Inquiry into Early Latin American Social History, 1500–1900." In *Reliving the Past: The Worlds of Social History*, edited by Oliver Zunz, 115–190. Chapel Hill: University of North Carolina Press, 1985.

———. *Drinking, Homicide, and Rebellion in Colonial Mexican Villages.* Stanford, CA: Stanford University Press, 1979.

———. Foreword to *Distilling the Influence of Alcohol: Aguardiente in Guatemalan History*, edited by David Carey Jr., ix–xi. Gainesville: University Press of Florida, 2012.

Thompson, E. P. *Customs in Common: Studies in Traditional Popular Culture.* New York: New Press, 1991.

Thompson, Sinclair. *We Alone Will Rule: Native Andean Politics in the Age of Insurgency.* Madison: University of Wisconsin Press, 2002.

Tinsman, Heidi. "Good Wives and Unfaithful Men: Gender Negotiations and Sexual Conflicts in the Chilean Agrarian Reform, 1964–1973." *Hispanic American Historical Review* 81, nos. 3–4 (2001): 587–619.

Torres-Rivas, Edelberto. "Sobre el terror y la violencia política en América Latina." In *Violencia en una sociedad en transición*, edited by Programa de las Naciones Unidas para el Desarrollo, El Salvador, 46–59. San Salvador: Programa de Naciones Unidas para el Desarrollo, United Nations, 1998.

Trouillot, Michel-Rolph. *Silencing the Past: Power and Production of History.* Boston: Beacon Press, 1995.

Twinam, Ann. "El estado de la cuestión—La historia de la familia, la historia de genero-pasado, presente y futuro." In *Familia y organización social en Europa y América, siglos XV–XX*, edited by Francisco Chacón Jiménez, Juan Hernández Franco, Francisco García González, 329–342. Murcia, Spain: Ediciones de la Universidad de Murcia, 2007.

———. "The Negotiation of Honor: Elites, Sexuality, and Illegitimacy in Eighteenth-Century Spanish America." In *The Faces of Honor: Sex, Shame, and Violence in Colonial Latin America*, edited by Lyman L. Johnson and Sonya Lipsett-Rivera, 68–102. Albuquerque: University of New Mexico Press, 1998.

———. *Public Lives, Private Secrets: Gender, Honor, Sexuality, and Illegitimacy in Colonial Spanish America.* Stanford, CA: Stanford University Press, 1999.

Vanderwood, Paul. *Disorder and Progress: Bandits, Police, and Mexican Development.* Wilmington, DE: Scholarly Resources, 1992.

———. *The Power of God against the Guns of the Government: Religious Upheaval in Mexico at the Turn of the Nineteenth Century.* Stanford, CA: Stanford University Press, 1998.

Van Vleet, Krista. "Partial Theories: On Gossip, Envy, and Ethnography in the Andes." *Ethnography* 4, no. 4 (2003): 491–519.

Van Young, Eric. "Agustín Marroquín: The Sociopath as Rebel." In *The Human Tradition in Latin America: The Nineteenth Century*, edited by Judith Ewell and William Beezley, 17–38. New York: Scholarly Resources, 1989.

———. *The Other Rebellion: Popular Violence, Ideology, and the Mexican Struggle for Independence, 1810–1821.* Stanford, CA: Stanford University Press, 2001.

Vaughn, Mary Kay. "Introduction: Pancho Villa, the Daughters of Mary, and the Modern Woman: Gender in the Long Mexican Revolution." In *Sex in Revo-*

lution: Gender, Politics, and Power in Modern Mexico, edited by Jocelyn Olcott, Mary Kay Vaughn, and Gabriela Cano, 21–32. Durham, NC: Duke University Press, 2006.

———. "Modernizing Patriarchy: State Policies, Rural Households, and Women in Mexico, 1930–1940." In *Hidden Histories of Gender and the State in Latin America*, edited by Elizabeth Dore and Maxine Molyneux, 194–214. Durham, NC: Duke University Press, 2000.

Vidaurre, Adrián. *Los últimos treinta años de la vida política de Guatemala: Memorias.* Havana: Imp. Sainz, Arca, 1921.

Wagley, Charles. *Economics of a Guatemalan Village.* No. 58. Menasha, WI: American Anthropological Association, 1941.

———. *The Social and Religious Life of a Guatemalan Village.* No. 71. Menasha, WI: American Anthropological Association, 1949.

Walker, Charles F. "Crime in the Time of Great Fear: Indians and the State in the Peruvian Southern Andes, 1780–1820." In *Crime and Punishment in Latin America*, edited by Ricardo D. Salvatore, Carlos Aguirre, and Gilbert M. Joseph, 35–55. Durham, NC: Duke University Press, 2001.

———. *Smoldering Ashes: Cuzco and the Creation of Republican Peru, 1780–1840.* Durham, NC: Duke University Press, 1999.

Warren, Kay B. *Indigenous Movements and Their Critics: Pan-Mayan Activism in Guatemala.* Princeton, NJ: Princeton University Press, 1998.

———. *The Symbolism of Subordination: Indian Identity in a Guatemalan Town.* Austin: University of Texas Press, 1992.

Warren, Michael. *The Letters of the Republic: Publication and the Public Sphere in Eighteenth-Century America.* Cambridge, MA: Harvard University Press, 1990.

Watanabe, John M. "Culture History in National Contexts: Nineteenth-Century Maya under Mexican and Guatemalan Rule." In *Pluralizing Ethnography: Comparison and Representation in Maya Cultures, Histories, and Identities*, edited by John M. Watanabe and Edward F. Fischer, 35–65. Santa Fe, NM/Oxford, England: School of Advanced Research Press/James Currey, 2004.

———. "Liberalism after Liberal Reforms: A View from the Peasant Periphery." Paper presented at the 29th International Congress of the Latin American Studies Association, Toronto, October 8, 2010.

———. "With All the Means that Prudence Would Suggest: 'Procedural Culture' and the Writing of Cultural Histories of Power about Nineteenth-Century Mesoamerica." *Journal of Latin American Anthropology* 6, no. 2 (2001): 134–175.

Watanabe, John M., and Edward Fischer. "Introduction: Emergent Anthropologies and Pluricultural Ethnography in Two Postcolonial Nations." In *Pluralizing Ethnography: Comparison and Representation in Maya Cultures, Histories, and Identities*, edited by John M. Watanabe and Edward F. Fischer, 3–33. Santa Fe, NM/Oxford, England: School of Advanced Research Press/James Currey, 2004.

Weber, Max. *Economy and Society.* Edited by G. Roth and C. Wittich. New York: Bedminster Press, 1968.

Weismantel, Mary. *Cholas and Pishtacos: Stories of Race and Sex in the Andes.* Chicago: University of Chicago Press, 2001.

Wells, Allen, and Gilbert Joseph. *Summer of Discontent, Seasons of Upheaval: Elite*

Politics and Rural Insurgency in Yucatan, 1876–1915. Stanford, CA: Stanford University Press, 1996.

Wertheimer, John W. "Gloria's Story: Adulterous Concubinage and the Law in Twentieth-Century Guatemala." *Law and History Review*, 24, no. 2 (2006), 375–421.

White, Louise. *Speaking Vampires: Rumor and History in Colonial Africa.* Berkeley: University of California Press, 2000.

Wiebe, Adrienne. "Widening Paths: The Lives of Three Generations of Maya-Mam Women," PhD diss., University of Alberta, 2002.

Windler, Erica M. "Madame Durocher's Performance: Cross-Dressing, Midwifery, and Authority in Nineteenth-Century Rio de Janeiro, Brazil." In *Gender, Sexuality and Power in Latin America since Independence*, edited by William E. French and Katherine Elaine Bliss, 52–70. Lanham, MD: Rowman and Littlefield, 2007.

Wisdom, Charles. *The Chorti Indians of Guatemala.* Chicago: University of Chicago Press, 1940.

Wolf, Eric. *Peasant Wars of the Twentieth Century.* New York: Harper and Row, 1969.

Wolf, Eric, and Edward C. Hansen. "Caudillo Politics: A Structural Analysis." *Comparative Studies in Society and History* 9, no. 2 (1967): 168–179.

Wolfe, Justin. *The Everyday Nation-State: Community and Ethnicity in Nineteenth-Century Nicaragua.* Lincoln: University of Nebraska Press, 2007.

Woodward, Ralph Lee Jr. *Central America: A Nation Divided.* 3rd ed. New York: Oxford University Press, 1999.

———. *Rafael Carrera and the Emergence of the Republic of Guatemala, 1821–1871.* Athens: University of Georgia Press, 1993.

Wortman, Miles. *Government and Society in Central America, 1680–1840.* New York: Columbia University Press, 1982.

Wyld Ospina, Carlos. *El autocrata: Ensayo politico-social.* Guatemala City: Tipografía Sanchez & de Guise, 1929.

Index

class, 194; and courts, 8, 27, 234; and crime, 25, 92, 113, 117, 136–146, 182, 186, 237; and empowerment, 6, 25, 78, 234; and ethnicity, 194, 230, 236; and extenuating circumstances, 119, 128; and gynecological exams (state-sanctioned), 1, 128, 147, 148, 151, 170, 235; and honor, 204–210, 218; and illiteracy, 16, 78, 177, 182; as market vendors, 94, 96, 99, 111–114, 117; as mothers, 83, 136–146, 173, 179, 180–181; and oppression, 154; and patriarchy, 164, 186, 232–236; as perpetrators of violence, 181–190; and reproductive crimes, 118–128, 134–136, 136–146, 150; single, 207, 209, 219; use of courts by, 9, 27, 34, 181, 230; as victims of violence, 8, 153–190; as weak, 78, 117

Wyld Ospina, Carlos, 49

Yepocapa, 125, 170
Yucatecan, 92

Zacapa, 73
Zaragoza, 21